PN 3451 JOS

THE WORLD AND THE BOOK

THE WORLD AND THE BOOK

A Study of Modern Fiction

Gabriel Josipovici

Third Edition

First edition 1971
Second edition 1979
Third edition 1994

Published by
THE MACMILLAN PRESS LTD
Houndmills, Basingstoke, Hampshire RG21 2XS
and London
Companies and representatives
throughout the world

ISBN 0–333–60901–8 hardcover
ISBN 0–333–60902–6 paperback

A catalogue record for this book is available
from the British Library.

Printed in Hong Kong

'Then came the revelation. Marini saw the rose as Adam might have seen it in the Garden of Eden, and he understood that it existed in its eternity, and not in his words, and that we can refer to or evoke, but never express, and that the high and splendid volumes which, in the shadows of his chamber gave out a golden glow, were not (as his vanity had dreamt) a mirror of the world, but one more object added to the world. This revelation came to Marini on the day of his death. It is possible that Homer and Dante experienced it too.'

Jorge Luis Borges

For

PETER MAXWELL DAVIES

Acknowledgements

Some of the material in this book has already appeared in *Adam International Review*, *The Critical Quarterly*, *European Judaism* and *French Literature and Its Background*, edited by John Cruikshank, and published by the Oxford University Press. I should like to thank the editors and publishers for permission to reprint.

Contents

Note on the Translations

I have given all extensive quotations from foreign languages in translation. Where the style of the original seemed particularly relevant to my argument I have given the original in the body of the text and have relegated the translation to a footnote. This is the procedure I have normally followed when quoting poetry.

All the translations are my own unless otherwise stated, with the exception of the quotations from Rabelais and Proust. For Rabelais I have used the Urquhart/Motteux translation, followed by the title of the book and the number of the chapter in which it occurs. Since all the chapters are extremely short the reader can find the passage either in the original or in another translation with little difficulty. In the case of Proust I have used the Scott-Moncrieff translation, though growing more and more aware of its inadequacy as I went along. Scott-Moncrieff used the old NRF edition of Proust, rightly castigated by Beckett, but its shortcomings have by and large been made good by the three-volume Pléiade edition of 1955. This includes, especially in the later portions of the book, a number of passages left out of the earlier edition. Scott-Moncrieff died before he could complete his task, and the work was finished by Stephen Hudson. An entirely new translation of this has at last come out, by Andreas Mayor, based on the Pléiade edition, and it is to be hoped that Mr Mayor will now tackle the whole work. The situation as it stands at present, though, is obviously extremely confusing. Where I have to quote a passage which is in the Pléiade edition but neither in Scott-Moncrieff nor in Mayor (which is not, that is, in *Le Temps Retrouvé*), I have translated it myself. After each quotation I give first the volume and page number of the English translation, or the page number preceded by *TR* for *Time Regained*; and then the volume and page number of the Pléiade edition.

Preface to the Third Edition (1993)

The first hint of what was eventually to be *The World and the Book* came to me in my third year as an undergraduate at Oxford, after an excited reading of Norman Brown's *Life against Death* and Northrop Frye's *Anatomy of Criticism*. However, like much else in my intellectual life, its seeds had probably been sown by reading *A la Recherche* three years earlier. Proust's extraordinary discussion of Giotto's Virtues and Vices in Padua in the context of the pregnancy of the serving-maid at Combray, and his wonderful evocations of the medieval churches of Normandy and St Mark's in Venice struck a chord in me, for I too had begun to respond to medieval art and to feel that something profound had been lost in the Renaissance which the modern writers I cherished were, in obscure ways, trying to rediscover. But it was only years later, when I had been reading Dante for some time and devouring the works of Beckett, Robbe-Grillet and Claude Simon, that the shape and thrust of my project began to grow clear to me. Finally, when I hit upon the title, I knew I had my book: I would come at my subject of the nature of modern fiction by way of the break-up of the medieval world picture (at the centre of which lay the notion of the world conceived as the book of God), and try to show how, for a handful of particularly perceptive writers – Chaucer, Rabelais, Hawthorne, Proust – the sense of the loss of that picture would lead to the elaboration of strategies both for articulating the nature of that loss and for coping with it.

For these writers, it seemed to me, the making of viable fiction went hand in hand with the laying bare of false values and false notions of art. Critique and invention went together, and the targets were essentially the same: that single vision which tried to pretend that world and book were still one, either by ignoring the changed circumstances in which books were now made or by having too exalted a notion of what the artist could do. But this single vision, which passes either for common sense or for poetic inspiration, is so difficult to criticise precisely because it affects the very tools of criticism: language and all the forms of discourse, from the philosophical treatise to the novel.

In the sixties, when I wrote the book, it seemed more important to uncover the hidden assumptions behind the Lockean philosophical traditions and the genre of the traditional novel than its opposite, though in the penultimate chapter I did explore the ways in which even so perceptive a reader as Roland Barthes could let himself be so carried away by his own rhetoric that in the end he proposed a view of art which was only the mirror image of what he was attacking. Proust, whom he invoked to back his claims was, I suggested there, a dangerous ally, for if the young Marcel does at first think that there is no gap between the word and what it signifies, he is soon to learn the bitter lesson that this is not the case.

In 1979, when the book was reissued with a new preface, the target had changed: a tide of intellectual opinion was building up in both France and England and in the States which saw the strengths of the Barthian position – that books are only books, made up only of words – and quite failed to see its weaknesses. Of course this did not in the least affect the attitudes of most readers (and reviewers) of fiction, who happily went on talking about the contents of novels as if the novel were merely a form of journalism, providing insights into African famines or the activities of the Mafia, homelessness in Britain or the dangerous power exerted by the media barons. In fact a split was opening up between the academy, where the ideas of Barthes, Foucault, Lévi-Strauss and Lacan were rapidly gaining ground, and the general public.

Since then the split has deepened so much that it has become a chasm. Novels still go on being reviewed (and, it must be said, most of them still go on being written) as if they were a form of journalism, while the academy has come to be dominated by the 'movements' known as Deconstruction, Feminism and the New Historicism, which all, in their different ways, seek to show that all artefacts are constructs, put together less by the ostensible author than by impersonal forces of which he is hardly aware, forces which are themselves allied in covert ways to the dominant powers in the culture and which seek always to control and repress. The fervour of much of the new criticism derives from its authors' belief that they are unmasking prejudice – the prejudice of writers previously regarded with awe and respect, and the prejudice of the readers and critics who so regarded them.

What is interesting from my point of view is that, just as the old discussions of fiction foundered on the unspoken assumption that novels mirrored the world, so the new ones founder on the assumption that *suspicion* is the only attitude for the reader or critic to take to his material. What I tried to argue in *The World and the Book*, on the other hand, and what I still believe today, is that what the greatest writers – Chaucer, Rabelais and Proust for example – all have in common is *both* a profound suspicion of books *and* an equally profound delight in the act of writing. Books tend to falsify our relation to the world not through what they say but through their implicit assertion that the world is like a book; at the same time only books – I am talking about fiction here, whether written in verse or prose – can both unmask this and give us back the sense of our own multifold possibilities and of the multifold nature of the world. Of course the two, the suspicion and the trust, go hand in hand, and must do if the world is not to collapse into either cynicism or sentimentality. Even in Proust there is no guarantee that Marcel, at the end, has reached a position from which he will be able to begin. Even – I now think – canto 33 of Dante's *Paradiso* holds back from suggesting that *now* Dante – and the reader – has reached his goal. For both authors are only too aware that true beginnings, like ultimate goals, though they are what we long for, are only mirages thrown up by our desires. And yet enough has been done in the preceding hundreds of pages, in both Dante and Proust, to give both protagonist and reader the sense of what self-fulfilment, of what meaningful activity, might entail. The possibility of such activity had not been lacking before, it had simply been dormant, until woken into life by the artistic skill and imaginative vision of the author.

For these writers – and for the others I examine here – the notion that nothing can ever make sense, that all human activities are inherently corrupt, and that the task of the writer and critic is only to unravel that senselessness and corruption – that would have seemed to them not merely cynical but fatally blinkered. These are, in the end, moral writers, but ethics and aesthetics are seen by them as absolutely inseperable. Marcel is a better person than Swann not because he writes and Swann fails to do so, but because he is morally suppler than Swann, more intelligent, more prepared to remain in a state of partial confusion and uncertainty. In fact, it is *because* of his suppleness, intelligence, etc. that Marcel can write and Swann cannot. The writing is an index of moral responsiveness, of imaginative empathy. And the same is true even of Beckett: the narrative speaks of despair, boredom, hopelessness – but the books enact vigour, wit, openness and curiosity.

By contrast Foucault, Derrida, de Man and the other luminaries of the intellectual life of the eighties, like their postmodernist counterparts, the writers of magical realism, for all their talk of playfulness and openness, are Puritans at heart, convinced that they alone are right, proud of their intransigence and convinced of their moral reactitude, whose task, as they see it, is to unmask power and authority wherever it may be found and to speak up for the downtrodden, the underprivileged and all those to whom history has denied a voice. These are admirable sentiments, with which all right-thinking people would readily concur, but they do not make for good criticism or good art. For all their talk of letting conflicting voices speak out and of dialogic form, there is a remorseless singleness about their tone and a refusal to turn their questions upon themselves, which makes them ultimately wearisome and unconvincing.

Of course other, subtler voices have been heard in the past decade. The writings in Russian of Mikhail Bakhtin and in German of Walter Benjamin have slowly been making their way into English and it has become almost *de rigueur* to bring their names into any critical discussion. Yet it has to be said that for all Bakhtin's width of reference, his is a rather crude version of Rabelais and his key notion if dialogue too vague and all-embracing to be really helpful, while, compared to two of his great heroes, Kafka and Proust, Benjamin's touch seems often unsure and his humourlessness a grave disadvantage.

The eighties, though, have also seen an upsurge in interest in the *literary* qualities of the Bible and of Homer and the Greek tragedians. Students of those ancient texts have come to see that it is the strangeness and otherness, as well as the startling modernity of those works that needs to be understood, and that such understanding can allow us to bring into focus areas of feeling and expression which had not been lost but simply forgotten. Away from the dreary polemics about the canon and political correctness genuine advances have occurred and large areas of the past brought into touch with the present.

Our response to the really genuine writing of today depends on our openness to the past. That was an old theme of Eliot's, and it is no less true today than it was in 1919 or 1971. That is why, somewhat to my surprise, I find that, looking back at *The World and the Book* after twenty years, I do not feel that its time has been and gone but on the contrary that the positions it took up and the causes it espoused, even if they were not always argued with the finesse I would have liked, are as timely as ever. The implications of the title, which the rest of the book seeks to draw out, will, I am coming to see, perhaps never be exhausted.

Gabriel Josipovici
March 1993

Preface to the Second Edition

When I wrote this book, in the sixties, English culture was in a state of turmoil. Nevertheless one still had the sense of a powerful official culture, conservative in outlook and as solidly based as ever on the traditional English virtues of pragmatism and common sense. In France things were a little different. Although French culture had its own brand of chauvinism and insularity and French intellectuals were often enmeshed in arid private quarrels, the best critics seemed to operate within a wider frame of reference than their English counterparts, and seemed aware of the implications of the artistic and cultural revolution of the late nineteenth and early twentieth century in ways English critics rarely were. Thus, although my quarry in this book was not quite the same as theirs, I found myself championing the work of Blanchot, Barthes, Genette and Ricardou, and making frequent use of their many insights into the workings of art and of modern art in particular.

Today it looks as if the battle against English insularity has finally been won. The names of Lévi-Strauss, Jakobson, Foucault and Lacan are now common currency in British universities and are invoked by scholars, critics and reviewers in much the same way as the names of Leavis and Empson were ten or fifteen years ago. Members of the general public as well as students suddenly seem eager to know all about structuralism and semiotics, and publishers are hurrying to satisfy them by commissioning introductions to the subjects and surveys of the field.

I wonder, though, whether this advance is not largely illusory. A whole cultural climate cannot be altered overnight, if it ever can. And the very spate of introductions and surveys is a sad reminder of this fact. For only those with a deeply ingrained belief in the triviality of ideas would imagine that these subjects can be easily summarised, packaged and passed on. The truth of the matter is that there are no entities called 'structuralism' or 'semiotics' or 'the *nouveau roman*', whose basic elements can be abstracted in this way and then reproduced in easily digestible form, like baby food; there are only a number of thinkers and writers, of greater or lesser sensitivity and intelligence, struggling to make sense of those perennial mysteries, language, literature and the modes of classification.

What has in fact happened is that the many *problems* raised by the late nineteenth- and early twentieth-century crisis have been surreptitiously converted into so many *fields of study*. This was perhaps inevitable, but to treat these problems as fields, as areas which merely need mapping out, is of course to avoid their really disturbing implications, to rob them of precisely that which characterises them, their critical cutting edge.

If this is correct then what we are at present witnessing is a classic example of the *trahison des clercs*. Cultural critics in England seem to have lost confidence in the subtlety and range of the native tradition but failed to come to terms with the continental one. Instead they have been bemused by the worst aspects of contemporary French culture, those which spring from the desire for global solutions and final answers – a perennial temptation to French intellectuals.

It was precisely with these aspects of French culture that I felt it necessary to take issue in my original Preface and elsewhere in this book. That is why I began the book with Proust, a novelist, and not with a theoretician like Barthes or Ricardou. For Proust, like Eliot and Virginia Woolf, was not out to prove a theory or build a system. He was struggling to tell the truth as he saw it, and if this involved a radical rethinking of the forms of narrative, then that would have to be accepted. At the same time he recognised the precarious nature of the endeavour and its cost in human and artistic terms. It is this tension between the sense of achievement and the recognition of inevitable failure, between the sense of triumph and the discovery of the cost of triumph, that is central to his achievement, as to that of the other great modern writers.

Such a tension disappears in glib or solemn talk about 'the text writing itself' or 'the generative grammar of narrative systems'. It also disappears when such works are labelled 'experimental' and put away on a special shelf, as they too often are by English critics. Proust, Virginia Woolf, Golding, Robbe-Grillet – these are no more 'experimental' than Jane Austen, George Eliot, Arnold Bennett or H. G. Wells. Every writer inevitably experiments in his study, if by that we mean that he rewrites, re-organises, finds that he can't say just what he means straight off. The only difference is perhaps that a Proust or a Virginia Woolf is a little less easily satisfied than a Bennett or a Wells, goes on trying to get it right for a little while longer. Why this should be so, and what 'getting it right' might mean are, I suppose, the central questions to which this book addresses itself. I don't believe that there are simple or single answers, or that critical 'developments' in the last seven years have made the questions themselves any less pressing.

Gabriel Josipovici
1.i.78

Preface to the First Edition

'We must constantly remember that earlier, at the time of the
Impressionists or of Cézanne, modern painting was something
you never saw. Or else, when people did open their eyes to it,
it caused a scandal . . . Today, provided it doesn't look like
anything that could really be called painting, everything is
modern . . . and as soon as it appears it's a work of genius,
and all the rest doesn't even exist. As though people had
suddenly become so perceptive that they know all about it as
soon as it has even begun to take shape. Whereas in reality
they see precisely as they always did or even worse. Because
now they see in exactly the same way but they imagine they've
learnt to see properly.'

Picasso (1966)

There are far too many books in the world for any author to feel
entirely happy about adding to their number; nor can any attempt
at justification in the guise of a preface really relieve him of the
burden of guilt. Nevertheless, a few words may be necessary to
explain the scope and intention of what follows.

The last decade has seen a torrent of books on modern authors
and at least a steady stream on the phenomenon of modernism
and its importance for an understanding of avant-garde art today.
Never have scholarship and criticism trodden so close on the heels
of the creative artist, and this phenomenon itself calls for some
explanation, though it will not receive it here. I am concerned
rather with the curious fact that though many of these books are
sensitive and intelligent they seem, strangely enough, rather to
perpetuate than to dispel the fog of confusion and misunderstanding that surrounds the subject. Gone are the happy days (as
they say) when the majority of the public rejected modernism
out of hand and only a few brave voices were raised in its defence.
At least then the situation was clear. Now we have a situation
where everyone writes and speaks as though they understood what
modernism was about but where in fact most of the old prejudices
still prevail – as Picasso notes. The position is further confused
by the fact that traditionalists frequently take the line of attacking avant-garde art for failing to follow in the great modernist

tradition while on the other hand the excuse that they are simply following this tradition is used by many a contemporary artist to bolster up shoddy third-rate work or to defend so-called 'experiments' that would have seemed tired and hackneyed to Rabelais and Sterne.

In such a climate one might argue that it would be better to forget about theory and 'isms', and look only at individual authors with our minds free of prejudice. Unfortunately our minds are never free of prejudice, even when it masquerades (as is most often the case) as plain common sense. As Stravinsky and Picasso have demonstrated over and over again, we implicitly judge new art in terms of the norms of the arts with which we are already familiar. Moreover, one of the peculiarities of modern art is that its meaning rests to a far larger extent than most previous art on the kinds of relations it tacitly establishes with the tradition. To understand any single work or author, then, we really need to know how he understands his own relation to tradition. Yet to try and do this is to involve ourselves in the sort of confusion outlined above. Is there any way out of this dilemma?

There is an extremely interesting difference between the response to modernism in the Anglo-Saxon countries and in France. In England and America the books and articles tend to be scholarly and detached, in France they are passionate and partisan. Both help to perpetuate the confusions, though for different reasons. In England, and even more in America, modernism appears to be firmly established. Joyce, Pound and Eliot are now regarded as classics of our literature: they are on the syllabuses of our schools and universities, the standard biographies are being written, theses form a swelling river of exegesis. But in a sense this is just the trouble. Few people seem to feel that the issues raised by these writers really *matter* any more. Like Fulke Greville, Gay or Landor, they are the classics of our literature, and, as far as most readers and critics – and, alas, writers – are concerned, they are well and truly dead. Indeed, their too easy assimilation into the curriculum suggests that they have not really been understood. Because their work is seen simply as one more stage in the inevitable march of literature, from 1800 to 1850, from 1850 to 1900, from 1900 to 1950, and from 1950 to the present day, the *radical* nature of their art and of what it sought to express has been blurred. Consequently the critics, faced with genuine developments of modernism, such as the work of Robbe-Grillet or Claude Simon, seem unable to cope with it. Not that they dismiss it out of hand. As I have said, the days of such overt philistinism are over, and we are presented with something more insidious. Both Robbe-Grillet and Simon have been highly praised in newspaper reviews and in scholarly journals and books, but this sympathy is often based on a misunderstanding of what they are up to. They are accepted, so to speak, but made to conform in the process to the norms of art of a Tolstoy or a George Eliot. Perhaps they do. We shall have to see.

In France the situation is rather different. The division into rival camps is much more clear-cut. There are those who are indiscriminately *for* and those who are indiscriminately *against*, which leads to the absurd position, noted by Christine Brooke-Rose, of critics defending mediocre authors simply because they are 'on their side' in this battle of the books. The English, at least, can congratulate themselves on the fact that their cautious pragmatism saves them from such absurdities. It doesn't save them from much else. For the French admirers of modernism, who are themselves more often writers than either academics or reviewers, do seem to have a real grasp of what is at issue. To begin with they have correctly intuited that the battle is to be fought over the nature of prose fiction rather than of poetry, whereas the influence of Pound and Eliot in England has always led to the unexpressed assumption that modernism is primarily an affair of the *diction* of poetry. But of course it is prose fiction and painting which raise the real questions about the nature of modernism, because it is here that the Renaissance norms of verisimilitude, against which the moderns were reacting, play the largest role. It is not by chance that the recent theoretical debates over avant-garde literature in France have centred on the Nouveau Roman rather than on any new poetry. But the Nouveau Roman itself is seen as the heir to a long artistic tradition. The Nouvelle Critique in France discerns an unbroken line that runs from Mallarmé to Pinget via Proust, Valéry, Roussel, Blanchot, Queneau and Beckett. Even Sartre, who has devoted so much effort to trying to break with this tradition, can only be understood in its context. There is the recognition here that something decisive happened in the fifty or so years before the First World War, that things

can never again be what they were before that, and that we have
barely begun to understand or draw the full consequences from
that decisive event, whatever it might be.

Unfortunately, while Robbe-Grillet, Barthes and Ricardou
write with more insight and understanding about the problems
of the modern novel than do any Anglo-Saxon critics, their essays
also tend to perpetuate a number of misunderstandings. One
could say that where the Anglo-Saxon critics assimilate modernism
too easily to the whole Western tradition, the French critics, by
the narrowness of their taste, give the impression that only the
writers in the tradition from Mallarmé to themselves, plus a tiny
handful of assorted foreigners, such as Borges, Poe and (of all
people) H. P. Lovecraft, have any claim to consideration at all.
The break with the past is here too radical. Moreover, there is
something stifling and parochial about the French intellectual
scene which has frequently been noticed: Butor writes about
Boulez, Leiris about Butor, Barthes about Leiris, and everyone
refers respectfully to Lévi-Strauss and Lacan. There is a great
deal of exchange between anthropology, philosophy, literary
theory, music theory, art theory, psychoanalytic theory and
Marxist theory, but the exchange is all between friends and disciples and no one seems to notice the fact that elsewhere their
conclusions are by no means taken for granted. As far as literature is concerned this has had the unfortunate result of separating
the Nouveau Roman from the Western literary tradition and
giving outsiders the impression that it is a phenomenon that must
be treated on its own, with perhaps a few esoteric references to
Mallarmé and Roussel. Many of the writers of the Nouveau
Roman have stressed that they do not belong to any 'school' and
that they have little in common except perhaps an enterprising
and intelligent publisher; but they are themselves, in their role
as critics, largely to blame for the way in which they have been
lumped together.

The narrowness of taste evinced by the Nouvelle Critique goes
hand in hand with a certain selectivity in those aspects of
modernism that are emphasised and a certain jargon that is
deployed in talking about it. The interest of Boulez in Webern
and Debussy is exactly parallel to the interest of Butor and Robbe-
Grillet in Mallarmé and Roussel. But modernism is the post-cubist
Picasso as well as Braque and Mondrian, Stravinsky as well as

Webern, Joyce as well as Mallarmé. To recognise this is to see that the Nouveau Roman has developed only some of the implications of modernism, and that writers like Nabokov, Bellow, Heller and Muriel Spark have developed others. These last would, I am sure, be horrified to find themselves placed in the same category as writers who have too often been considered coldly intellectual and concerned only with abstract structural problems, but that is only one more example of the pernicious division into rival blocks which characterises the current literary scene, a division which does no good to either side.

Yet it is not a division that one can simply wish away. It is part of a difficult problem of method (discussed in Chapters 11 and 12), which we come up against in other fields than literature – in the antagonism between English and Continental philosophy or anthropology, for example. Put very crudely, the problem is that if we talk about modernism in its own terms we seem to remain incomprehensible to those who don't share a prior understanding with us, while if we talk about it in other terms, extraneous to it, we seem to miss the point completely. In other words, the split between the Anglo-Saxon and the French approaches only mirrors a much more fundamental problem, which is there at the heart not just of modernism but of Romanticism as well (I deal with their interrelations in Chapter 7). Once again, then, is there any way out of this dilemma?

Interestingly enough, it is modernism itself which can give us a clue as to how we may set about our task. Though it has become conventional in some quarters to view modernism as the response to social and economic factors, such an interpretation seems incapable of accounting for many of the characteristics of the movement. Primarily modernism was a calling into question of the norms and values not just of the nineteenth century, but of Western art and culture since the Renaissance. What all the moderns have in common – perhaps the only thing they have in common – is an insistence on the fact that what previous generations had taken for *the world* was only *the world seen through the spectacles of habit*. That similar discoveries were being made in the realms of science and philosophy seems significant, but not vitally so. Modern art has in no way been influenced by Einstein or Heisenberg or Wittgenstein. Most artists are too busy with their own problems to have the energy or the inclination to master alien modes of thought, even if these things could be mastered without the proper training, which is highly dubious. All that we can safely say is that the discovery that the world is not 'given' but depends on the kinds of assumptions we bring to its study seems to have occurred in the fields of art, science and philosophy at about the same time, giving rise to an exploration not of new fields but of the *foundations* of mathematics, of logic, of art. In art it led to a twofold exploration: into the nature of the medium of art itself and into a reappraisal of the entire Western tradition. Nor, it must be emphasised, was this double exploration left to the theorists, while the artists got on with their work. On the contrary, there is no better way of defining the achievement of Picasso, Stravinsky or Eliot than to say that it is an exploration both of the medium in which they are working and of the traditional exploitations of that medium. The relation of the individual talent to tradition is at the root not just of Eliot's art, but of modernism in general.

If modern art, then, is anti-representational, the best way to understand it is to grasp the premises on which representation rests, as Gombrich correctly intuited. If the modern novel is to some extent an anti-novel, then the best way of coming to grips with it is to understand the premises of the traditional novel. To study the modern novel, as most Anglo-Saxon critics have done, in the very terms of the traditional novel, is to condemn oneself to superficiality from the start. But so strong is the pull of the Renaissance norms and of their embodiment in the 'realistic' novel of the eighteenth and nineteenth centuries that it seems at first sight difficult to know in what other terms such a discussion could be conducted. Yet the clues, if we would see them, are staring us in the face.

The norms of the traditional novel, as Hulme pointed out again and again, are no more 'given' than is perspective: they emerge in the sixteenth and seventeenth centuries. So that if we could get back behind those centuries we might be able to see not only out of what they sprang, but also what other possibilities were open at the time. Eliot's love of Dante is well known, and the predilection of many modern artists for the art of the Middle Ages has frequently been noted. But it has usually been dismissed as the hankering after some lost mythic unity of the age of faith. I believe that this is a misreading of the situation, and that an understanding of the nature of medieval art and of Renaissance attitudes towards it will help us to understand the modernist revolution. To see modern fiction neither in the perspective of the nineteenth-century 'realist' novel, nor in that of Romantic and symbolist poetic theory, but in that of the art of Dante and Langland has a number of advantages. The new perspective allows us to see the 'realist' novel as a specific product of the seventeenth century and, in more general terms, of the Renaissance, and thus removes the notion of its necessary and ineluctable growth through some form of Darwinian evolution. Further, it throws into a new prominence a number of authors who seem to stand outside the tradition of 'realist' fiction and yet apparently belong to no other; who seem firmly rooted in their own time yet have curious affinities with many modern writers: I am thinking of Rabelais, Cervantes, Swift and Sterne. It is fashionable for scholars writing on these authors to make passing references to their similarity to Joyce or Beckett or Robbe-Grillet, but this is more of a sop to a youthful audience than a critical argument, just as the parallel backward glance on the part of critics dealing with the modern writers is usually nothing but a bid to boost the value of their wares in the eyes of the traditionally minded. But what exactly is the relation of this tradition of Humanist wit to the anti-novel of today? What are the implications of finding burlesques of and attacks on the traditional novel in these works when most of them were written *well before the traditional novel had got under way*? Once we take Eliot at his word and re-examine literary history in the light of modernism we have to acknowledge that the old ways of accounting for those works of fiction which do not conform to the norms of the 'realist' novel are totally inadequate. On the other hand, as Eliot saw, the play between tradition and the individual talent is a two-way process: by using the insights of modernism to guide us through tradition and of tradition to put modernism in perspective, we may come to a closer understanding of both.

   To take as our point of vantage Dante and the art of the Middle Ages will doubtless go against the ingrained cultural Darwinism of many readers, and I can only say that it is meant to. Though the moderns unanimously rejected the implication that the norms of the Renaissance corresponded with the necessary structure of reality, few readers or critics have followed them, however much

they may claim to admire modern art. And this is hardly surprising since these norms have such strong roots in human psychology.
For we must understand that the great modern revolutionaries
did not say: 'Don't look at the world the way people have been
doing for the last four centuries, it's wrong'; but: 'Don't look at
the world the way people have been doing for the last four centuries, it's *lazy*'. Habit and laziness, not faulty vision, is what they
were trying to fight, and it is this which the present book is also
trying to expose. As a result it finds itself primarily concerned
with ways of *reading*. For the Renaissance norms affect not only
the creation of art but also its reception. It is our view of what a
book *ought* to be, of what a novel *ought* to do, which comes
between us and the understanding of much modern fiction. Thus
behind every chapter in this book lies the impulse to make us read
certain books as they themselves ask to be read. For that reason I
begin with a form of demonstration, a 'reading' of *A la Recherche
du temps perdu*. Since Proust's novel is itself the most thorough
exploration of the ways of false and correct reading known to me,
it will act both as a model and as an introduction to the major
themes of the ensuing chapters. In these I move between further
detailed readings of single works or authors, and what one might
call reorientative sketches, where I use the wide perspective to
rephrase certain questions of literary history and to place certain
facts in what may perhaps be a new light. As my interest is in
the reading of modern fiction I nowhere aim to be comprehensive
in these chapters but rather to stimulate thought along what
might be unfamiliar lines in order to break the deadlock between
the moderns and their opponents. Although, after the chapter on
Proust, the order followed is chronological, and although I do
occasionally refer from one to another, the chapters are self-
contained and I see them more as overlapping explorations of
the subject than as part of a continuous argument. In other
words, though the book radiates out in the direction of the
history of fiction and in that of the theory of fiction, it is not
meant primarily as a contribution either to literary history or to
aesthetics.

In my choice of examples too I have not tried to deal with
either 'the best' or 'the most typical'. Three factors have influenced my choice. First, love and admiration for a work or
author and the desire to understand more clearly what it was

that made me feel that way. Indeed, the whole book is written in the spirit of St Augustine's comment on his study of the Trinity (and in the awareness that if my subject is not so exalted as his it is perhaps of an equally baffling complexity): 'Therefore I have undertaken this work . . . not for the sake of speaking with authority about what I know but rather to know these subjects by speaking of them with reverence.' Secondly, I have not dealt with any writer who, though close to my heart like Kafka or Claude Simon, has already been commented upon so well that I would not be able to add anything of real interest.[1] And, finally, just because it is the obviously experimental writer like Beckett or Robbe-Grillet who springs to mind when one talks about 'the new novel', I have deliberately concentrated on writers like Nabokov, Golding and Bellow, who do not flaunt their newness quite so obviously; though a study of their work should better help us to appreciate the real nature of the achievement of a Beckett, a Robbe-Grillet, a Pinget, by allowing us to see that they belong not to a unique category of literature, which requires of us unprecedented efforts of the imagination and a heroic concentration, but rather that they reveal just one facet of what for want of a better term we must continue to call the flowering of modernism.

The only other book I know which approaches its subject from a perspective somewhat similar to mine, Marthe Robert's *L'Ancien et le Nouveau*, deals exclusively with *Don Quixote* and Kafka's *The Castle*. Though I do not agree with all its conclusions or emphases, its appearance a few years ago confirmed me in my hunches and gave me the confidence to press on with what at times seemed an absurdly overambitious task. My understanding of the Middle Ages owes a great deal to the brilliant studies of C. S. Singleton on Dante, and to V. A. Kolve's *The Play Called Corpus Christi*. Throughout I have benefited from the studies of the nature of fiction by Butor and by Ricardou, and of the nature of art and perception by Gombrich.

This book has been living with me for ten years and the record

---

[1] For Kafka, see Marthe Robert's two books, *Kafka* (Paris, 1960), and *L'Ancien et le Nouveau* (Paris, 1963). For Claude Simon, see Jean Ricardou, 'Un Ordre dans le débâcle', in his *Problèmes du nouveau roman* (Paris, 1967).

of those to whom I owe a personal debt is the record of my friend-
ships in these years. (No doubt few of those from whom I have
learnt would feel that I had not distorted beyond recognition
what they meant.) I began to have an inkling of its possible shape
and scope in conversations long ago with Robert Henderson,
Gordon Crosse, Rachel Trickett and Del Kolve. More recently
I have benefited from the combined scholarship and intellectual
passion of Tony Nuttall, Stephen Medcalf and Gāmini Salgādo,
as well as from the thoughtfulness of Peter France. Ian Gregor
helped me to see much in Proust and in Golding which I might
otherwise have missed, Bernard Harrison guided me through the
abrupt turns of Wittgenstein's thought, and John Mepham's
acute mind and genuine concern for the truth saved me from
many an error. Much of the final unity of the book, such as it is, is
due to the painstaking efforts of George Craig, who read the whole
manuscript through and made innumerable wise suggestions.
Without his encouragement and that of P. N. Furbank this book
might never have been finished. My greatest debt is to my mother,
who listened patiently and prodded gently, while the dedication
acknowledges a debt to the composer and friend who has been a
source of inspiration in all my work.

I   Proust: A Voice in Search of Itself

Eight words emerge from the silence, hang for a moment in the air, then die away: 'Longtemps, je me suis couché de bonne heure.' Perhaps they settle in some corner of the reader's mind, to be reactivated later by an allusion, a suggestion, but other sounds, other words, fill in the silence, and to all intents and purposes they disappear. Yet the black print holds them prisoner, thirty-five letters on the white page. Or does it? Since they make up not the statement of a logical proposition but the utterance of an individual person it is not enough to check the words in the dictionary; we have to ask, not: What do these words mean? but: What do these words when spoken by that person mean? And why does he break the silence to utter *them* and not another set of words? Who *is* he, this 'I' who goes or went to bed so early? Marcel, we say, reading on, and, perhaps, Marcel Proust, if we are a certain kind of reader. But is that really an answer? What is the relation between the name 'Marcel' and the voice that speaks, between the name and its owner?

That is not only our problem as readers of *A la Recherche du temps perdu*; it is first and foremost Marcel's own. The three thousand three hundred pages which follow provide the most subtle, tenacious and profound exploration of the problem ever undertaken, as the 'I' of that opening sentence unfolds in search of his identity. Let us follow him in that strange quest.

Appropriately enough, the novel opens in the no-man's-land between sleep and waking, when the self first becomes conscious of itself:

> When I awoke at midnight, not knowing where I was, I could not be sure at first who I was; I had only the most rudimentary sense of existence, such as may lurk and flicker in the depths of an animal's consciousness; I was more destitute of human qualities than the cave-dweller; but then the memory, not yet

of the place in which I was, but of various other places where
I had lived, and might now very possibly be, would come like
a rope let down from heaven to draw me up out of the abyss
of not-being, from which I could never have escaped by myself:
in a flash I would traverse and surmount centuries of civilisation, and out of a half-visualised succession of oil-lamps,
followed by shirts with turned-down collars, would put together
by degrees the component parts of my ego. (1 4; 1 5–6)

There are thus four stages in the journey from sleep to waking
life. First there is sleep itself, a purely negative experience of non-
being, 'néant'; then comes the sheer animal sensation of pure
being; only after this do images and memory begin to return,
still dependent on the body, on the physical disposition of the
limbs, a memory which takes no account of strict chronology but
indiscriminately jumbles impressions from the whole of the
sleeper's past life, any one of which *might* correspond to the
present reality; and finally, after this, full consciousness returns,
bringing with it the recognition of which room he has in fact been
sleeping in, what has happened the day before, and what he has
to do that day. His 'moi' has been recomposed and he can now
get up.

Sometimes, when we arrive in a new town, or move into a new
room, we experience an analogous sensation to that of waking up,
but spread out over a longer period of time. The strangeness, the
newness of everything around us, makes it difficult for us to get
our bearings, but eventually we always triumph over these circumstances, just as eventually we are always able to get up and
go about our daily tasks. What makes it possible for us to do this
is not consciousness itself, but habit, which goes hand in hand
with consciousness:

Custom [*L'habitude*]! that skilful but unhurrying manager
who begins by torturing the mind for weeks on end with her
provisional arrangements; whom the mind, for all that, is
fortunate in discovering, for without the help of custom [*sans
l'habitude*] it would never contrive, by its own efforts, to make
any room seem habitable. (1 8; 1 8)

But here we begin to discern a curious quality of habit: it makes
the room habitable by effectively sealing us off from it, by reduc-

ing it from this unique room to a room I know and therefore take for granted, cease to see. Habit allows us to go about our business in the world, but only by reducing everything we encounter to the most general terms, so that it is no longer reality but a cliché of the mind which we take for reality. Thus it is only when Marcel hears his grandmother's voice over the telephone, divorced from the rest of her person, which he has always taken for granted, that he feels that he is hearing it for the first time for what it really is: the voice of an old lady close to death. Again, it is only because he surprises her in the house before she has had time to prepare herself for the encounter with him, to put on a face to meet the faces that we meet, that he realises that he has in front of him a crazy old woman and not some abstraction of habit called his grandmother.

Habit then has two aspects. On the one hand it renders the room habitable and makes it possible for us to go about our daily tasks; but it does this at the cost of reducing every particular to a generality. We tame the world around us by slotting everything in it to some prior generalised notion that we have of things; so that to live in the world of habit is to live shut up in a private world, incapable of noticing what goes on around us, since every-thing that happens is immediately neutralised by being assimilated to what we already know. But is it even really we who know? Habit deadens our response to the world by deadening our aware-ness of ourselves. The individual himself becomes a ghost who is given consistency only by the way other people think of him; and as this differs according to the social status, political views and private desires of other people, we become phantoms with as many different selves as there are people who know us. The 'moi' that Marcel so elaborately recomposes as sleep gives way to consciousness seems only to exist by reason of the space it occupies:

So, as the self lives unceasingly by thinking a quantity of things, is in fact only the thought of these things, when, by chance, instead of having things in front of it, it suddenly thinks of itself, it finds only an empty box, something it does not know, and to which it adds, in order to give it some particle of reality, the memory of a face seen in the mirror. This odd smile, these uneven moustaches, it is this which will disappear from the face of the earth. (– ; III 466)

Is the self then made up of nothing but stray thoughts on the one hand and a strange face seen in a mirror on the other? Most people keep their minds turned firmly away from such dizzying perspectives, but for Marcel to find an answer to these questions is more than a matter of curiosity, it is a driving need. For if the world of habit is the true one then we are indeed nothing and less than nothing, we have no self at all. But, obscurely, he feels that this is not the case, that we live in time as well as in space, and that therefore each one of us is a unique individual because each one of us has a unique past which reflects upon his present. The very fact that he is aware of the gap between the random thoughts and the stranger's face suggests that there has been a time when the gap was not there. Once again sleeping and waking provide a paradigm case, but now the progressive stages of waking can be read not as the recovery of the self but, on the contrary, as the loss of the self:

> Then, from the black tempest through which we seem to have passed (but we do not even say *we*), we emerge prostrate, without a thought, a *we* that is void of content. What hammer-blow has the person or thing that is lying there received to make it unconscious of anything, stupefied until the moment when memory, flooding back, restores to it consciousness or personality? . . . We may of course insist that there is but one time, for the futile reason that it is by looking at the clock that we have discovered to have been merely a quarter of an hour what we had supposed a day. But at the moment when we make this discovery we are a man awake, plunged in the time of waking men, we have deserted the other time. Perhaps indeed more than another time: another life. (VIII 175-7; II 981-3)

Instead of a gulf, a 'néant' from which the self is rescued, is not sleep perhaps the true home of the self, like that sea from which mankind first emerged at the dawn of time, 'notre milieu vital ou il faille replonger notre sang pour retrouver nos forces'? But if that is so, how can waking man re-enter that other life *and yet remain awake enough to know it*? If to wake up means to leave that world are we not faced with an insurmountable contradiction?

*

Just as the first thought on waking up is the consciousness of separation which is also the consciousness of self, so there is in each individual life a moment when the self becomes conscious of itself as unique, and this too is the result of loss, separation. Thus Marcel's first memory, behind which he cannot go, is of his mother's kiss withheld. The kiss, which he compares to the host at mass, is the tangible symbol of communion with the world; it reflects a universe in which there is no distinction between the self and other people or between the self and the world of nature. It is because his mother withholds her kiss (because Swann has come to dinner), that Marcel is forced to recognise that his desires and those of other people do not always coincide; that other people, even those who are closest to us, have thoughts and desires which we can never discover. This is his earliest memory, to which, on waking up, he always returns, not out of morbidity or for any pathological reason, but because this awareness of separation is nothing other than the self's first awareness of itself. The kiss withheld is simply the earliest demonstration of the law that our only consciousness of unity, of a fullness of being, comes when we no longer possess it; for, possessing it, we are not conscious of it: the only paradise is paradise lost.

How then to regain the lost paradise? The force of habit is bent upon making us forget the loss by making us forget ourselves; but for Marcel the smooth surface of everyday existence ruled over by the Goddess of Habit is too frequently torn apart by intimations of another life, another and more meaningful state of being, for him ever to be completely at his ease in it. The story of his childhood and youth is the story of these intimations and of how he responds to them. But before we examine these there is one more example of the consciousness of loss which we ought to consider.

The imagination of childhood is entirely subjective, projecting its reveries upon the world as the magic lantern projects the story of Gilbert le Mauvais over the walls of Marcel's room at Combray. Implicit in it is the belief that simply to know the name of a person is to know that person, and that, by possessing the former, we automatically possess the latter:

Words present to us little pictures of things, lucid and normal, like the pictures that are hung on the walls of schoolrooms to give children an illustration of what is meant by a carpenter's bench, a bird, an ant-hill; things chosen as typical of everything else of the same sort. But names present to us – of persons and of towns which they accustom us to regard as individual, as unique, like persons – a confused picture, which draws from the names, from the brightness or darkness of their sound, the colour in which it is uniformly painted. . . . (II 235; I 387–8)

Thus the name of Parme seems to Marcel to be 'compact, lisse, mauve et doux', and he imagines the houses in the town as having similar characteristics; Florence he imagines 'semblable à une corolle, parce qu'elle s'appelait la cité des lys'; and as for Mme de Guermantes, descendant of that Geneviève de Brabant whose image the magic lantern projected onto the walls of his room, 'je me la representais avec les couleurs d'une tapisserie ou d'un vitrail, d'une autre manière que le reste des personnes vivantes'. But the imagination cannot survive the confrontation with reality. Just as Marcel became aware of himself as a distinct being at the same time as he became aware of the impossible distance between himself and other people, so here he becomes aware of other people when he recognises how little they have in common with what his imagination has made of the name they bear. Like Troilus, forced to acknowledge Cressida's faithlessness by the evidence of his eyes, Marcel watches Mme de Guermantes in church and tries in vain to reconcile the name with the person in front of him:

'It is, it must be Mme de Guermantes, and no one else!' were the words underlying the attentive and astonished expression with which I was gazing upon this image, which, naturally enough, bore no resemblance to those that had so often, under the same title of 'Mme de Guermantes', appeared to me in dreams, since this one had not been, like the others, formed arbitrarily by myself, but had sprung into sight for the first time, only a moment ago, here in church. . . . (I 240–1; I 175)

And yet the name goes on casting a glow over the person, even after Marcel has got to know Oriane and found her to be as shallow, vain and frivolous as the rest of her sex. It is as though, however often he learnt the lesson that the name is no less arbitrary, no less of a label, than any word we use, it still retains something of its old power. For most of us habit so dulls the senses that we accept the fact that a name is merely a label, helpful for identifying people and no more; so that we live among people whose appearance and even whose place and function in life are simply the projection of our own imagination helped on by a few hints from reality. But if, like Marcel, we feel that there must be a relation between a person's name and himself, that he must have an essence which we can, if we only make a sufficient effort, grasp and understand, then the gap between what must be and what appears to be will force us to recognise that we live among people who alter every day, appearing under different guises nearly every time we see them. It is because Marcel is so much more concerned with who and what people *really* are that he is so much more aware than most of us that they are not any one thing. He has spent so long imagining what a *cocotte* must look like that the shock of seeing Odette de Crecy and finding her to be just like any other woman he has ever seen is almost physical. And how to describe Swann? Is he 'striking' as Odette first thinks, or is he 'ludicrous' as the little clan later find him to be? Or Saint-Loup, who first appears to Marcel as a haughty and disdainful aristocrat; then as a warm and loyal friend; an ardent republican; the jealous lover of an actress; a cruel husband, using his mistresses as a cover for his homosexual practices; and finally a hero and patriot, killed fighting for his country. None of these characters seems to have anything to do with any of the others; they are like photographic stills, each quickly obliterated by the next one, which in turn yields to the one after that. Nothing connects them except the name, Saint-Loup, which we read beneath each of the photos. But this peculiar fact does not strike Marcel because of his indifference to his friend, because of any failure to see the real Saint-Loup beneath all these disguises. On the contrary, it is just because Marcel is so aware of the people around him that he is aware of the gap between the arbitrariness and, so to speak, the conservativeness of the imagination, and the facts of reality. It is for this reason that the world he describes so minutely seems to have no more centre to it than an onion, to be nothing but a series of surfaces unrelated to any essence. The imagination, he comes to realise, is not at all opposed to habit and to the intellect; that is merely a vulgar romantic distinction. In reality habit and intellect merely cloak the purely subjective and solipsistic nature of the imagination.

Marcel's fascination with the aristocracy can now be understood, for it is only among the old families of France that the
name still seems to stand for something real, still seems to be more
than a mere label. Marcel takes peculiar pleasure in finding himself in the same room as people whose names are also the names
of places not because he is a snob but because only here does the
name seem to adhere to the thing. (Similarly, his interest in
etymologies reveals the desire to trace a place-name back to its
origin and see how it sprang from the physical nature of the place,
thus once again rooting the word in actuality.) Marcel's need to
believe that the name reflects the person is a metaphysical need,
for if such a thing is possible then by grasping the name, by turning it over in our minds and on our tongues, feeling the weight
and colour of the syllables, we may come to know the person, to
bridge the gap between ourselves and the world. But this, as
Marcel is to discover, can never occur, and to imagine that it can
is an illusion, one which is shattered for the first time by the kiss
withheld, and which is doomed to be shattered again and again
every time he gets to know a person or a place. The name
'Guermantes' is, in fact, the only stable thing about that volatile
family, and all the more deceptive for that, since the more we
insist on an identity between the name and the object, the more
bitter will our disillusion be. By a final marvellous irony it is none
other than the ludicrous Mme Verdurin who comes to bear that
sacred name when, at the close of the book, she marries the now
senile Prince.

But there are moments when a reverse process takes place and
it is not the illusion of our imaginations that is brought home to
us, but the illusion of what we normally take for reality. For just
as habit makes us look at something without really seeing it, so it
makes us remember something without really remembering it. We
recall what happened, but we do not recall what we felt at the
time; we look at our past as though it was the past of someone
else. And, in a sense, it is. Because the body is like a vase we tend
to think that what it has experienced or thought is permanently
present in it, but this is not the case. We die daily and our new
self knows nothing of the old. And yet the old selves inhabit our
body, they leave their trace, 'les jambes et les bras sont pleins de
souvenirs engourdis', and these memories may accidentally be
revived. So, when Marcel bends down to undo the buttons of his

boots he suddenly feels the presence of his grandmother flooding through his limbs. It is his body that relives the moment when she had first helped him off with his boots, so many years before that his mind had forgotten the incident. And now Marcel realises that his grandmother, who had been dead for so long, had never been dead to him at all because he had never felt her as alive. So that, paradoxically, it is only when he becomes conscious of her presence, conscious of her as a living person rather than as an abstraction called his grandmother, that he becomes aware of her death:

> And as Habit weakens every impression, what a person recalls to us most vividly is precisely what we had forgotten, because it was of no importance, and had therefore left in full possession of its strength. That is why the better part of our memory exists outside ourself, in a blatter of rain, in the smell of an unaired room or of the first crackling brushwood fire in a cold grate: wherever, in short, we happen upon what our mind, having no use for it, had rejected, the last treasure that the past has in store, the richest, that which when all our flow of tears seems to have dried at the source can make us weep again. Outside ourself, did I say; rather within ourself, but hidden from our eyes in an oblivion more or less prolonged. It is thanks to this oblivion alone that we can from time to time recover the creature that we were. . . . In the broad daylight of our ordinary memory the images of the past turn gradually pale and fade out of sight, nothing remains of them, we shall never find them again. (III 308; I 643)

Ordinary memory is the memory of habit, of the intellect, which smooths out the specific in favour of a generalised view of the past. It is always those senses which are the furthest removed from the intellect (smell, taste, touch) which reawaken our past selves. Thus it is only when Marcel *tastes* the madeleine, not when he sees it, that the whole of Combray floods into his mind and senses, Combray not as he had consciously remembered it, but Combray as it *felt* when he lived in it. And he explains this by saying that he had probably seen plenty of madeleines between that time and this, so that they too had taken on the familiar, generalised look of habit. Taste and smell, however, because they cannot be conceptualised, remain uncorrupted.

The madeleine episode occupies a key position in the structure of the novel, since without it there would have been no Combray, no two 'sides', and therefore no book, for the book flows out of the episode as memory is reactivated by the taste. But if this involuntary memory is the most striking reminder that the life of habit and of the intellect is not the only life we have, it is far from being the sole reminder. Marcel himself, at the end of the novel, distinguishes between 'memories' and 'impressions', and the opening volumes provide many examples of the way in which the external world – a hawthorn bush, the reflection of the sun in water, certain trees – seem suddenly to strike at our imagination, causing us the same thrill of pleasure, the same wrenching of habit, as does the influx of involuntary memory.

Particularly interesting is a scene which takes place on one of Marcel's walks towards Méséglise, when he suddenly sees the sun reflected in the water, and his heart leaps up in his body with joy:

> And, seeing upon the water, where it reflected the wall, a pallid smile responding to the smiling sky, I cried aloud in my enthusiasm, brandishing my furled umbrella: 'Damn, damn, damn, damn!' But at the same time I felt that I was in duty bound not to content myself with these unilluminating words, but to endeavour to see more clearly into the sources of my enjoyment.
>
> And it was at that moment, too – thanks to a peasant who went past, apparently in a bad enough humour already, but more so when he nearly received my umbrella in his face, and who replied without any cordiality to my 'Fine day, what! good to be out walking!' – that I learned that identical emotions do not spring up in the hearts of all men simultaneously, by a pre-established order. (I 213; I 155)

Here, as with involuntary memory, the joy felt by Marcel seems to be dependent on his making sense of his experience. Instead of responding with simple inarticulate cries of pleasure, he should have tried to see clearly 'dans mon ravissement'. But the different reactions of Marcel and of the peasant to the same scene show that it is not enough to react by saying that it is a beautiful day – such words are too general, no more expressive of what he really feels than the inarticulate 'damn' ('zut'). In a sense Marcel is as much outside his own sudden sensation of joy as is the peasant, and he will remain outside it unless he can translate it into something more meaningful than either 'zut' or 'beau temps'.

But, however hard he tries, Marcel never seems to be able to make sense of his experiences in the face of nature, and consequently they always slip away and disappear, leaving nothing more behind than the memory of an encounter, never the actual sensation of it. Even when he succeeds in putting down on paper what he has felt on seeing the three spires on the ride to Martinville, he fails to convey why it is that he reacts as he does, while in the other two major instances, that of the hawthorn bush and that of the three trees at Hudismenil, the pleasure of perception is accompanied by a keen sense of frustration: 'Le sentiment qu'elles éveillaient en moi restait obscur et vague, cherchant à se dégager, à venir adhérer à leurs fleurs', he remarks about the first; while of his last glimpse of the trees he says: 'dans leur gesticulation naive et passionée, je reconnaissais le regret impuissant d'un être aimé qui a perdu l'usage de la parole, sent qu'il ne pourra nous dire ce qu'il veut, et que nous ne savons pas deviner'. These natural objects seem to be gesturing towards us, but it is in vain that we try to interpret their gestures. Marcel knows that if only he could understand what they were trying to say, if only he could somehow 'hold' these trees, that hawthorn bush, in his consciousness, 'hold' them as they appeared to him in that first breathtaking moment, he would possess a secret more precious than any other, for it would be nothing less than the secret of life itself. But the longer he goes on looking at them the more inscrutable they become, and the more certain he grows that the feeling will fade, that habit and its deadening effect will replace it, and that he will then see the scene as little as had the peasant.

It is thus not surprising that the frustrated longing before a landscape or a natural object should be followed by the desire for a person who will embody that landscape or object, but who at least will be humanly possessable:

But if this desire that a woman should appear added for me something more exalting than the charms of nature, they in their turn enlarged what I might, in the woman's charm, have found too much restricted. It seemed to me that the beauty of the trees was hers also, and that, as for the spirit of those horizons, of the village of Roussainville, of the books which I was reading that year, it was her kiss which would make me master of them all [*son baiser me la livrerait*]. . . . The passing figure which my desire evoked seemed to be not any one example of the general type of 'woman', but a necessary and natural product of the soil. (1214–15; 1156–7).

Here, already, we see what Marcel is later to call the pathological aspect of love, the reason why all love is an aberration, since it is always in search of something other than the beloved. The desire for a woman is the desire for a possessable incarnation of the landscape, and is thus the direct outcome of Marcel's failure to 'grasp' it by himself.

But *is* a woman easier to possess than a landscape? Physically, no doubt, she is, but since it is not just her body which is desirable, mere physical possession is hardly sufficient: 'Je savais que je ne possederais pas cette jeune cycliste, si je ne possedais aussi ce qu'il y avait dans ses yeux. Et c'était par consequent toute sa vie qui m'inspirait.' The transfer from the landscape to the woman has been made because the woman seemed easier to possess; but what we possess when we possess a woman is precisely that which is dispensable, unimportant. There is thus an ineradicable contradiction set up in the very heart of love.

A woman's name, as we have seen, cannot yield up her essence, so that desire for her only makes her inaccessibility more obvious. No less than natural objects, women emit signs which we strive to interpret, though never with any guarantee of success.[1] Marcel's first encounter with Gilberte sets the pattern for all his later relationships with women. He has lingered behind his family on one of their walks through Swann's property, and Gilberte seems to have done the same with hers, for suddenly the two children come face to face across an alley bordered by flowers. He fixes her with a look which, he says, would have liked to 'toucher, capturer, emmener le corps qu'il regarde et l'âme avec lui'; then his

---

[1] See the excellent monograph by G. Deleuze, *Marcel Proust et les signes* (Paris, 1964). This, Butor's long essay, 'Les Œuvres d'art imaginaires chez Proust', *Répertoire*, 1 (Paris, 1960), and the two essays by Genette referred to on p. 271 are the only really illuminating studies I know of an author who makes good criticism so difficult by forestalling it all and embodying it in the novel itself. (For the same reason there are few really bad works among the many thousands devoted to Proust.)

look changes to one of beseechment, begging her mutely to acknowledge his presence. She in turn glances round to make sure
no one is watching, then

> she allowed her eyes to wander, over the space that lay between
> us, in my direction, without any particular expression, without
> appearing to have seen me, but with an intensity, a half-hidden
> smile which I was unable to interpret, according to the
> instruction which I had received in the ways of good breeding,
> save as a mark of infinite disgust; and her hand, at the same
> time, sketched in the air an indelicate gesture, for which,
> when it was addressed in public to a person whom one did not
> know, the little dictionary of manners which I carried in my
> mind, supplied only one meaning, namely, a deliberate insult.
> (1 193; 1 141)

And then she is called on, leaving him with nothing but her name
and a series of gestures which he has to interpret as best he can
according to the code he thinks he should use. At it happens, we
learn at the end of the novel, he interprets wrongly.

Who is Gilberte? Who is Albertine? What is the relation between the name and the woman who bears it? The metamorphoses through which they pass are even more dizzying than those
of Swann or Saint-Loup simply because Marcel is more aware of
them, more tormented at the discrepancy between their old and
their new selves, between what he had taken them to be and what
he now sees they are. But whenever Marcel imagines that he has
understood them, he ceases to love them, which means that he
ceases to see them. Understanding here, as with the room in which
he wakes up, is simply another word for the reassertion of habit;
love, like sleep, is the temporary setting aside of the deadening
grip of habit. The syndrome of habit, as it relates to love, is easy
to trace and impossible to avoid: since what has drawn the lover
in the first place is the 'otherness' of the beloved, for her to lose
this is equivalent to losing his love, but to maintain it is to cause
him unbearable anguish in the knowledge that there is a portion
of her life that he doesn't know. Thus when Marcel has finally
made up his mind to break with Albertine, since he is beginning
to find her a bore and an imposition, she reveals to him her friendship with Mlle Vinteuil, with all its lesbian implications, and so
sets the whole complex cycle of desire and frustration in motion

once again. And, in a parallel peripety later in the novel, it is just when he finally decides to let her go and himself travel to Venice, where he may forget her as he forgot Gilberte, by an effort of the will – it is just at this moment that he learns of her escape, and all the old love and anguish flood back into his body, no less powerfully and spontaneously than had his childhood in Combray on tasting the madeleine. The conscious mind can never forestall the senses; we can never *imagine* what true joy and suffering will be like, since it is a condition of such sensations that they come to us *from the outside*: they are what we cannot imagine.

The desire to possess the beloved is thus bound to be frustrated. Marcel may keep Albertine a prisoner in his house, but then she either bores him because, as a prisoner, she has ceased to embody the freedom of the sea which was what he longed to possess in her, or he realises that even as a prisoner she retains her liberty and escapes him, however much he may caress her body: 'Je sentais que je touchais seulement l'enveloppe close d'un être qui par l'interieur accédait a l'infini.' Even the kiss, which had seemed to the child Marcel to be the sign of a total communion, and which, a little later, he thought would yield up the essence of Roussainville, is now seen to be nothing but a mockery, a final affirmation of the fact that the union of two bodies is never the union of two souls.

Yet women, unlike trees, can talk, and so, we would think, make it possible for the lover to know them in their essence, as they really are, rather than as the changing creatures they appear to the senses. But that is to forget the lesson of the encounter with the peasant on the road to Méseglise, and Marcel's recognition there that words are incapable of conveying private sensations. Because he kisses her, Albertine imagines that Marcel loves her, but he, less prone to thinking in clichés, recognises that her saying she loves him does not necessarily mean that she does so. And because Marcel is so desperate to find out the truth about her he is rewarded with nothing but lies. But what is truth? In normal social intercourse we do not demand of people that they justify their actions and testify to the truth of what they say. Marcel is well aware of this when he goes out into society – the words of Mme Verdurin, of Norpois, of Charlus, are, no less than their gestures, codes to be interpreted according to certain rules rather than the direct utterances of the truth. But when it comes to a

woman one loves it becomes vitally important to determine the
truth of what she is saying. And how is one to decide what code
she is using? How is one to discover the rules of the conventions?

The fact of the matter is that Albertine is not concealing anything from Marcel; rather, he is trying to discover in her something she does not know she has. When he probes and questions
her she answers the first thing that comes into her head, or else
she answers what she thinks he wants to hear, and this is not
strictly a lie since she is not conscious of a truth which is other
than what she utters. The past is not something fixed and stable
which we can call up at any time; actions do not have fixed
meanings which we can simply pass on to someone else. Prodded
by Marcel, Albertine's memory wanders over her own past, in-
venting, remembering, unconsciously mingling memory and
desire. Marcel's anguish lies not so much in the revelation of suspected relationships as in never being able to know for certain
whether or not she is telling the truth. That is why it is only when
she is asleep that he feels he does to some extent possess her
entirely:

> By shutting her eyes, by losing consciousness, Albertine had
> stripped off, one after another, the different human characters
> with which she had deceived me ever since the day when I
> had first made her acquaintance. She was animated now only
> by the unconscious life of vegetation, of trees, a life more
> different from my own, more alien, and yet one that belonged
> more to me. (IX 85; III 70)

The more 'other' the beloved becomes, the further she gets from
the social image we have of her, the more she appears to be – in
some mysterious way – oneself. Eve rose out of Adam's rib; so
Marcel may be in love with Albertine because she incarnates the
sea, but the sea itself is only an incarnation of something else, of
that which is totally other only because it was once totally himself:

> In any case, just because we are furiously pursuing a dream in
> a succession of individuals, our loves for people cannot fail to
> be more or less of an aberration. (TR 187; III 839)

But what is it then that we desire? When Marcel first catches sight
of Gilberte he mutely pleads with her to acknowledge his presence,

and later muses over an encounter with Albertine: 'Si elle m'avait vu, qu'avais-je pu lui représenter? Du sein de quel univers me distinguait-elle?' What Marcel ultimately longs for is to possess that look from another universe, *without it ceasing to be other*. This is why homosexual love is seen as being so much more primitive, so much less distorted by society, than heterosexual love; for here at least there is the frank acknowledgement that the sexual partner is both other and oneself. If love is only the effort of the self to incarnate desire so as to possess itself, then there is no difference *in kind* between Charlus asking to be beaten more viciously in Jupien's male brothel as the German planes swoop down over war-time Paris (the horrific scene that forms the nadir of the novel), and Marcel's own efforts to possess the women he loves. Indeed, in his very first encounter with Gilberte, across the alley of flowers, he had noted that: 'Je l'aimais, je regrettais de ne pas avoir eue le temps et l'inspiration de l'offenser, de lui faire mal, et de la forcer à se souvenir de moi.' The later scene is simply more blatant, less disguised and distorted by social and moral codes. For the real form of cruelty is not sadism but indifference.

Unlike the society of the Faubourg St Germain, that of the invert does not merely appear to be, but really is, closer to the primitive roots of man, made up as it is of the original hermaphrodites, men and women who are both man and woman. But every kind of love, even this, which looks for satisfaction from the object, is doomed to failure. Like the three trees at Hudismenil, the women in Marcel's life, like the men in Charlus's, beckon mutely and disappear. Soon the soothing hand of habit softens the pain of loss, and the self that loved joins the myriads of other dead selves in the recesses of the body, only to be briefly resurrected by a chance encounter, an unexpected word, a smell, a taste.

The failure of love seems to presage the failure of Marcel's quest, a quest all the more bewildering in that Marcel has only fitfully understood his goal. In relation to Names and to love it was an attempt to incarnate a dream at the same time as to understand the world; in relation to the flashes of involuntary memory or of the encounters with nature and with women it was the attempt to possess that other world which momentarily revealed itself beneath the smooth surface of habit and clock time. At the end

of the novel he seems to be as far from achieving one of these aims
as the other. But the effect is not one of total failure, for in the
meanwhile he has come to understand the nature of art and
learnt how to apply its lessons to himself.

Among the many desires felt by the young Marcel is the desire
to write. But this is subject to a double frustration: on the one
hand he feels himself to be inadequate, lacking in the powers of
description which seem to be a prerequisite of the novelist and of
the powers of invention which would suggest a subject about
which to write. On the other hand his experience with the peasant
and other encounters have made him aware of the fact that words
are mere labels, generalisers, and thus unable to convey anything
except the tired life of habit, the progression of instants devoid
of any meaning. Art then seems pointless, all surface and no
meaning, the simple reduplication of the pointlessness of life. Yet
just as there had been moments when life did not seem entirely
meaningless, so there are moments when art too seems both
necessary and true. Not the art of words, but, in the first place,
music:

> This music seemed to me to be something truer than all the
> books that I knew. Sometimes I thought that this was due to
> the fact that what we feel in life, not being felt in the form of
> ideas, its literary (that is to say an intellectual) translation in
> giving an account of it, explains it, analyses it, but does not
> recompose it as does music, in which the sounds seem to assume
> the inflexion of the thing itself, to reproduce that interior and
> extreme point of our sensation which is the part that gives us
> that peculiar exhilaration which we recapture from time to
> time and which when we say: 'What a fine day! What glorious
> sunshine!' we do not in the least communicate to our neigh-
> bour, in whom the same sun and the same weather arouse
> wholly different vibrations. (x 232–2; III 374–5)

In music there is no distinction between form and content, word
and meaning, for the sound is the meaning, both abstract and
concrete at the same time. But this is not the only difference.
The real distinctiveness of music lies in the fact that it is both
passing sound and a kind of eternal architecture, as Swann had so
strongly felt the first time he was struck by the 'petite phrase' of
the Vinteuil sonata. 'At first,' we are told, 'he had appreciated

only the material quality of the sounds', constantly disappearing and constantly being replaced by new ones. But as he went on listening the music began gradually to spread itself before him as a definite shape, a pattern both fixed in his mind and changing as he began to understand it:

> He was able to picture to himself its extent, its symmetrical arrangement, its notation, the strength of its expression; he had before him that definite object which was no longer pure music, but rather design, architecture, thought, and which allowed the actual music to be recalled. This time he had distinguished, quite clearly, a phrase which emerged for a few moments from the waves of sound. It had at once held out to him an invitation to partake of intimate pleasures, of whose existence, before hearing it, he had never dreamed, into which he felt that nothing but this phrase could initiate him; and he had been filled with love for it, as with a new and strange desire. (1 289; 1 209–10)

But if the composer can reveal to himself and to others that 'pointe interieur et extrême des sensations' which is the sole source of joy, what is the artist whose tools are merely poor words to do? Is he condemned forever to a sterile imitation of the arbitrary and meaningless surface of life?

The answer to these questions is to be given in the climactic series of revelations which introduce the coda of the novel. The law of being, as Marcel had experienced it, said that we only understand that which we no longer feel; that we only desire that which we can never know. But he now discovers the real law of the lost paradise, which is that it is not till something has been lost that it can truly be found. Involuntary memory does not just call up a moment of the past; it holds together something that is common at the same time to the past and to the present, and which is thus more essential than either. Living through an experience, we cannot grasp it with our consciousness, and when we do we no longer live through it. But with involuntary memory the experience is present at the same time to both the sense and the consciousness:

> But let a noise or a scent, once heard or once smelt, be heard or smelt again in the present and at the same time in the past,

real without being actual, ideal without being abstract, and
immediately the permanent and habitually concealed essence
of things is liberated and our true self which seemed – had
perhaps for long years seemed – to be dead but was not altogether dead, is awakened and reanimated as it receives the
celestial nourishment that is brought to it. A minute freed from
the order of time has re-created in us, to feel it, the man freed
from the order of time. And one can understand that this man
should have confidence in his joy, even if the simple taste of a
madeleine does not seem logically to contain within it the
reasons for this joy, one can understand that the word 'death'
should have no meaning for him; situated outside time, why
should he fear the future? (*TR* 231; III 872–3)

This explains why Marcel could never think of a subject about
which to write. For truth does not rest in the object – the person,
the tree, the incident, the anecdote. That is always arbitrary – arbitrary if Marcel were to sit down and invent them, and arbitrary
too if Marcel were to sit down and record the incidents which
have made up his life. For here at this point is where life and art
come together, and where Marcel's understanding of the laws of
one lead to an understanding of the laws of the other. For the
incidents which make up Marcel's own life are no less a matter of
chance than those which make up a novel by Balzac. Had he
never known Swann, for instance, he would never have gone to
Balbec; had he not gone to Balbec he would never have met
Saint-Loup and Charlus and Albertine. In short, his whole life
would have followed quite a different path, been filled with quite
other incidents and people. And what if Mlle de Stermaria *had*
turned up when he had waited for her, or he *had* met the
chambermaid of Mme Putbus? Thousands of unfilled lives lie
waiting all about us, and to become aware of them is to become
aware of how little we have fulfilled the infinite potential with
which we were born.

Now we can understand the true cause of the anguish felt by
Marcel that evening at Combray when his mother withheld her
kiss. For not only did that reveal that other people are inaccessible, their innermost selves forever hidden from us, but it also
showed that our own realisation that we are ourselves and not
another implies that for everything that happens to us there are

an infinite number of possible things that *might* have happened. To recognise that we are individual, unique, is also to recognise that we are committed, in this our body, to just one life out of the limitless possibilities, a life whose incidents will be determined more by chance than by our own will or desires. This explains not only Marcel's early anguish, but also his later dissatisfaction with 'realist' art, intellectual conversation, and friendship. All these merely yield the possible, they reveal a world which could have been quite otherwise, a world ruled entirely by chance and, what is more, a world quite unaware of this fact, a world which takes its 'given' and necessary quality for granted.

But is it possible to escape this subjection to the arbitrary, as music had seemed to suggest one might? What would a being devoid of individuating traits really be like? The answer to that is that he would be like the self asleep or in the first stages of waking, feeling only 'dans sa simplicité première le sentiment de l'existence comme il peut frémir au fond d'un animal'. Sleep is not only a 'néant', negation, it is also the plenitude of time, for 'un homme qui dort tient en cercle autour de lui le fil des heures, l'ordre des années et des mondes'. But sleep itself is only this because it is the state where the human body comes into its own, more animal than human, more vegetable than animal. And even when memories do begin to return to the sleeper who is waking up, these are still dictated by the actual position of his limbs:

> My body, still too heavy with sleep to move, would make an effort to construe the form which its tiredness took as an orientation of its various members, so as to induce from that where the wall lay and the furniture stood, to piece together and to give a name to the house in which it must be living. Its memory, the composite memory of its ribs, knees, and shoulder-blades offered it a whole series of rooms in which it had at one time or another slept. . . . (1 5 ; 1 6)

In sleep, as in childhood, the self *is* the world. And our discovery that the world is other than the self, that our bodies exist *in* the world, occupying only a tiny point in space, leads to the formulation of our unconscious determination to return to that state of total potential. It had long since dawned on Marcel that there was a pattern of repetition and compulsion in the kinds of woman

he fell in love with as well as in the actual shape of each affair, a
pattern of which he seems to be the victim till he comes to understand its nature and its cause. All our actions, he now sees, are the
result of the displacement of that primal unsatisfied desire to
return to that state of absolute potential. But if this is the case
then what we can learn from the play of involuntary memory is
that the incidents of our life may be arbitrary, but not the laws
which govern these incidents:

> Already the consequences came flooding into my mind: first,
> whether I considered reminiscences of the kind evoked by the
> noise of the spoon or the taste of the madeleine, or those truths
> written with the aid of shapes for whose meaning I searched in
> my brain, where – church steeples or wild grass growing in a
> wall – they composed a magical scrawl, complex and elabor-
> ately flourished, their essential character was that I was not
> free to choose them, that such as they were they were given to
> me. And I realised that this must be the mark of their authen-
> ticity [*la griffe de leur authenticité*]. I had not gone in search
> of the two uneven paving-stones of the courtyard upon which
> I had stumbled. But it was precisely the fortuitous and
> inevitable fashion in which this and the other sensations had
> been encountered that proved the trueness of the past which
> they brought back to life. . . . (*TR* 239–40; III 879)

What Marcel has been looking for all his life is not to be found
outside himself, in a name, a place, a woman. But it is not to be
found inside him either, in his psyche or his imagination. It is not
a 'thing' at all, but only the recognition that 'le livre au caracteres
figurés, non tracés par nous, est notre seul livre'.

The role of art in life, and hence the role of Marcel's as yet
unwritten novel, is now apparent. Since all of our adult life is
subject to the displacement of desire, all that we encounter is
symbolic. The literal does not exist: trees turn into women and
women into words, and all, without exception, have to be interpreted. There are no essences only analogies. But if this is the case
then words do not suffer from a unique disadvantage; they are
only dangerous in that they appear to secrete meanings which can
be dragged from them. But as Marcel had learnt to discern in
each person he met the pattern which underlay their speech
habits, and was thus able to 'read off' or interpret what they said

by relating the content of their utterance to the laws which generated them, so he now discovers the true function of an art whose medium is language.

Such an art must reveal and make sensible the *laws* which govern existence, those formal laws which remain constant no matter how much chance and coincidence there may be in a man's choice of friends and love-objects, places to live in and works of art to admire. The object, the subject-matter of art (the anecdote), will thus cease to have any particular importance; what will matter will be the relation of the elements one to the other. In this way the discovery of the authenticity of his involuntary memory leads to the discovery of what will constitute an authentic novel, as well as helping to explain why it was that Marcel found himself unable to write so long as he thought he had to find a 'subject' about which to write. Any subject will do, just as any life will do; we cannot exist in the state of childhood for ever, and our task as adults is to try to discover the laws of the displacement of desire. For, once discovered and experienced, these laws free us from the tyranny of the trivial and meaningless flow of moments and events, from the implicitly 'given' quality of our lives.

We can now see too the double significance of Swann's role in the book as in Marcel's life. For if it is because of Swann that Marcel's existence follows the chance path it does, it is also true that Swann's affair with Odette, far from being a mere digression, plays a crucial role in revealing to Marcel that his own lifelong search is not the result of his particular physiology (persistent ill-health) or psychology (say, mother-fixation), but is rather a universal factor, prior to any individual, common to all mankind. Without Swann Marcel would have thought himself unique and uniquely damned to perpetual frustration. As it is the example of Swann sets up a series which will, necessarily, include the reader.

But before Marcel can sit down and write, or rather translate (since all authentic writing is not invention of new subjects but the translation of particularities into laws), the book of himself, one final revelation still awaits him. That is the discovery that the man who is 'affranchi de l'ordre du temps' does not, as he at first supposed, live in a kind of eternity. The final law that has to be learnt is that freedom from time rests on the ability to understand time, to grasp it with the senses and the consciousness as he had grasped the essence of Combray in tasting the madeleine. Marcel's final understanding does not come from his stepping out of time into some Platonic realm of timeless Ideas. It comes from his experiencing the law under which time operates. For though the body – his own or any man's – does not know the meaning of clock time and lives in an apparently timeless world, it still moves steadily from birth through maturity to death. Habit fools us with the simple contrast between clock time and eternity; it tries to hide from us the fact that the body grows and flowers and decays, this body, my body, the only one I possess. This is the last and hardest lesson, for it involves the recognition that the world is other than our body, that there will be a time when we will be no more and yet the world will go on. It is the understanding of this that makes art more meaningful than sleep, makes of the adult Marcel someone whose experience is even richer than that of the child. Once Marcel has learnt his lesson, discerning the passage of time on the faces of all those he had known so well in the past as they assemble for one last time at the Princess de Guermantes', he finally realises that the moment has come for him to begin the novel which will allow him to bring together, at long last, the name Marcel and the self that bears that name. But he will have to hurry. As the Curé had said so long before to old Tante Léonie about the steeple of Saint-Hilaire, from which one could see the pattern of the town as one never could while down on the ground, 'il fait un de ces courants d'air une fois arrivé là-haut! Certaines personnes affirment y avoir ressenti le froid de la mort.' To experience the laws of time is to be both asleep and totally conscious of one's sleeping self, it is to recognise that one's life *could* have been otherwise, but that *this* is how it had to be. It is not possible to grasp this paradox unless one has already, to some extent, passed over into death.

Marcel's novel is an attempt to make conscious to himself the whole of his body, to resurrect all the dead selves, to open the door to all the selves that were never born, and to catch the very movement of time as the body progresses towards its final disintegration. What he has never been able to capture in the flashes of involuntary memory, in the joyful perception of sunlight reflected in water, in the name of Florence or Mme de Guermantes, in Gilberte or Albertine, he finally captures in words.

But it is words in action, words both seeking and revealing the laws which underlie our lives, words which, finally, reveal the fact that they too are only symbols, inadequate substitutes for a desire which only the creation of this particular artifact will appease. It is up to the reader to let the words echo in his mind, from that opening sentence to the closing one, as they echo in the mind of the man who sits in his cork-lined room, night after night and day after day, writing himself into total consciousness of himself, sacrificing everything to this end, yet in reality sacrificing what he knows to be of no importance, since it is only in the act of writing that the lost unity will be restored, the lost paradise regained. But, if the reader perseveres in this, a strange pheno-menon will occur, for since this is a novel which goes in search of and uncovers the laws not just of Marcel's life, but of that of every human being, one can say of it as Proust does:

> Every reader is, while he is reading, the reader of his own self. The writer's work is merely a kind of optical instrument, which he offers to the reader to enable him to discern what, without this book, he would perhaps never have perceived for himself. (*TR* 283; III 911)

Then, as Vinteuil's music led Marcel to the final consciousness of his own body and of the world beyond it, so Proust's book will lead the willing reader.

2 The World as a Book

'Within its depths I saw ingathered, bound by love in one
volume, the scattered leaves of all the universe.'

Dante

Nearly every social group possesses a myth of its own origins and
of the origins of the world. What is peculiar to the Judaeo-
Christian culture is that its central myths are not those of the
creation of the world by God but of God's intervention in the
affairs of man. Exodus and Incarnation, rather than Genesis, are
the decisive events. And these, described in what is known as *the*
Book, reveal to us a God who not only creates but also talks,
listens and replies to the words of men, a God not only of origins
but one who is ever-present and always actively engaged in the
moulding of history to his own ends.

The Middle Ages reinforced this view of the relations between
God and Man by the application of a whole series of analogies
which sprang from the firm belief, attested in Scripture, that
when God created man, it was in his own image. A fourteenth-
century writer expresses the mystery in this way:

> The heavenly father created all men in his own image. His
> image is his Son . . . who was before all creation. It is in refer-
> ence to this eternal image that we have all been created. It is
> to be found essentially and personally in all men; each one
> possesses it whole and entire and undivided, and all together
> have no more than one. In this way we are all one, intimately
> united in our eternal image, which is the image of God and in
> all of us the source of our life and of our creation.[1]

This image was blurred or, say some writers, shattered into fragments by the Fall. The Incarnation, however, restored to man

---

[1] Quoted in Henri de Lubac, *Catholicism*, trans. L. C. Sheppard (London,
1958) 5. As well as containing abundant quotations from the Fathers and
from medieval writers in the body of the text, this book includes an
excellent short anthology of writings concerning the views of the early
Church on God, Man and the Church. The quotations in the following
paragraphs, except for those from Irenaeus, all come from chapters I to IV.

the possibility of regaining the lost image. We all fell with Adam, but with Christ, the second Adam, there is a chance for each of us to undo the effects of the Fall, to put off the old man and put on the new.

Such an attitude takes it for granted that there is an analogy between man and God. Not only is man made in God's image; in some sense, God is *in* man. 'By the sacrifice of Christ the first man was saved, that man who is in us all', says the Pseudo-Chrysostom, and St Paul frequently stresses the fact that Christ is within each man as well as a historical being who was born, lived, died and rose again: 'But when it pleased God, who separated me from my mother's womb, and called me by his grace, to reveal his Son in me, that I might preach him among the heathens . . .' (Galatians 1:15). The Incarnation can bring salvation to the individual Christian because Christ, putting on human nature, died as all men have had to die since the Fall, and then *undid* the effects of the Fall by his Resurrection. So, as each man had been born to death as a result of the Fall, each man can now be born to life everlasting as a result of the Incarnation:

> For as by disobedience of the one man who was originally moulded from virgin soil, the many were made sinners, and forfeited life; so was it necessary that, by the obedience of one man, who was originally born from a virgin, many should be justified and receive salvation. Thus, then, was the Word of God made man. . . . God recapitulated in Himself the ancient formation of man, that He might kill sin, deprive death of its power, and vivify man. . . .[1]

Individual salvation does not, however, automatically follow from the Incarnation, as the blurring or shattering of the image of God followed from the Fall; the Incarnation has only given man back the *possibility* of salvation, not the certainty. The 'new man' is only to be found 'in Christ', but Christ can only be found in the Church which is his body. Thus Origen speaks of the Church as the 'real and perfect body of Christ', in direct comparison with that physical body which was crucified and rose again, while St

---

[1] Irenaeus, *Against Heresies*, trans. Roberts and Rambaut (The Ante-Nicene Christian Library, Edinburgh, 1868) III 18.

Gregory of Nyssa quite simply says: 'He who beholds the Church really beholds Christ.' The Christian enters and renews his ties with the Church by means of the sacraments, which are thus the means to salvation. Chief among them is of course the Eucharist, instituted by Christ himself when he broke the bread and poured the wine, asking his disciples to 'do this in remembrance of me' – the Greek word *anamnesis* implying here much more the notion of re-enactment than of simple remembrance, Proust's involuntary rather than voluntary memory.[1] The Eucharist is thus the chief means of achieving salvation, and medieval authors naturally spent much time and ingenuity discoursing on its properties. St Cyril of Alexandria, for instance, writes:

> To merge us all in unity with God and among ourselves, although we have each a distinct personality, the Only Son devised a wonderful means: through one only body, his own, he sanctifies his faithful in mystic communion, making them one body with him and among themselves. Within Christ no division can arise. All united to the single Christ through his own body, all receiving him, the one and indivisible, into our own bodies, we are the members of this one body and he is thus, for us, the bond of unity.[2]

Just as Christ, the second Adam, came down to redeem the world from the effects of the Fall of the first Adam, so each Christian, by partaking of the eucharist, re-anacts Christ's redeeming action. There is thus added to the analogy between God and man an analogy between a historical act and an ever-renewed movement of the individual soul.

Since the Renaissance we have tended to feel that a man has most completely fulfilled himself when he has been able most sharply to distinguish himself from other men in the development of what is peculiar to himself. The Christians of the Middle Ages felt, on the contrary, that a man most completely fulfilled his human potential as he shed what was peculiar to himself and let the image of God, in which he had been made, shine through. But it would be a mistake to think that here we simply have two

[1] See Dom Gregory Dix, *The Shape of the Liturgy* (London, 1945) 243 ff., and Chapter 5 below.
[2] Lubac, op. cit. 39–40.

different views of human character. It is rather that the Middle
Ages understood the Renaissance view quite well, but judged it
in the light of their own view. The Renaissance view they saw
as the *denial* of man's *true* nature, but a denial that had been
endemic to man since the Fall. To hold on to one's individualising
traits, to strive even to accentuate them, was simply to repeat the
sin of pride committed first by Lucifer and then by Adam. It
is to believe that it is possible to live without the recognition of
the fact that the world is not subject to my will; in other words,
without a recognition of God. But to think in this way, they
argued, is to deny something of oneself, since man has been made
in God's image. In other words, the medieval view *accounts for*
the Renaissance view, since it places it within a larger context,
while the Renaissance view simply takes itself for granted.

Nor must we imagine that the re-enacting of Christ's own
action in the eucharist forces man to conform to a given pattern
and thus robs him of his freedom. This kind of strait-jacketing of
the personality would only occur if the notion of analogy between
God and man did not exist and Christ was seen only as someone
whose actions were to be *imitated* rather than re-enacted. But the
notion of analogy, with its implication that there is a Christ, as
well as an Adam in every man, makes sense of what would otherwise be a contradiction: that only by 'putting on' Christ can man
become fully himself.

In order to help man see where his salvation lies God has written two books. The first of these is the Book of Scripture, which
reveals to those who read it aright the working of God in man's
history. For the Jews the Old Testament was the history of their
people; for the Gnostics the Bible as a whole was a series of fables
hiding a mystical truth. For the Christians it was both history and
revelation – the revelation of God's dealings with man. The
events of the Old Testament were seen as foreshadowing or pre-
figuring the events of the New, which gave them their substance
and meaning. Thus the sacrifice of Isaac foreshadowed the sacrifice of Christ, the twelve tribes of Israel the twelve apostles, the
forty years in the desert the forty days of Christ's own sojourn in
the wilderness, and so on and so forth. In doing this these events
did not lose their historicity, they did not cease to be regarded
as having actually occurred. That was precisely the point which
the early Church Fathers stressed: the fact that these events had

occurred *and* that they foreshadowed other events which were to take place at a later time in history showed that every occurrence is a part of God's design, that every temporal event is filled with extratemporal significance. The Scriptures were proof that every man's life had meaning and that history, however arbitrary it might seem to mortal men, was really the fufilment of God's design.[1]

The notion that God works through history was reinforced by the notion that God is the author of a second book, the Book of Nature. Hugh of St Victor, writing in the twelfth century, put it like this:

> For this whole visible world is a book written by the finger of God, that is, created by divine power; and individual creatures are as figures therein not devised by human will but instituted by divine authority to show forth the wisdom of the invisible things of God. But just as some illiterate man who sees an open book looks at the figures but does not recognise the letters: just so the foolish natural man who does not perceive the things of God sees outwardly in these visible creatures the appearances but does not inwardly understand the reason. But he who is spiritual and can judge all things, while he considers outwardly the beauty of the work inwardly conceives how marvellous is the wisdom of the Creator.[2]

As God works through history, so he works through the world around us. Hugh has in mind the text of St Paul which is so fundamental to an understanding of medieval thought and art: 'For the invisible things of him from the creation of the world are clearly seen, being understood by the things that are made ...' (Romans 1:20). Just as God can be seen in his analogue, man, so he can be seen in both history and nature.

Never has there been such faith in the phenomenal. What guarantees this faith is the Incarnation, for it is the eruption into time of the eternal, into space of the infinite; it is the justification

[1] For this notion of history, see Auerbach's classic essay, 'Figura', trans. Ralph Mannheim, in *Scenes from the Drama of European Literature* (Meridian Books, New York, 1959); Jean Daniélou, *From Shadows to Reality*, trans. Dom Wulstan Hibberd (London, 1960); W. J. Burghardt, 'Early Christian Exegesis', *Theological Studies*, XI (1950) 78–116.

[2] Quoted in C. S. Singleton, *Commedia: Elements of Structure* (Harvard, 1965) 25.

of man's belief that he is made in God's image; it is proof that everywhere behind the natural order lies the Creator of that order, and that there is therefore an assured correspondence between meaning and appearance. The 'foolish natural' man will never be able to see this, but 'he who is spiritual' will recognise it without difficulty. It is not that he will 'read' such meanings into history or nature, but that if he learns to read correctly he will be able to spot these things where another would have missed them. Thus the task of the medieval artist and of the medieval preacher coincide: both will strive primarily not to inculcate moral lessons but to teach men to see by the accurate depiction of reality. Never have the pleasurable and the didactic been more closely identified.

Christianity is unique among the major religions in that it depends entirely on the historical fact of the Incarnation. It is this that gives meaning to the history of mankind on this earth. But the idea of the universe as itself meaningful, because an object created by a rational being, is not necessarily a Christian one. In the West the idea goes back a long way – at least as far as Plato's *Timaeus*, which, by a strange quirk of fate, was the only one of Plato's works directly known to the Middle Ages.

The *Timaeus* deals with the origin and structure of the universe, and it develops an analogy between the structure of the universe and the ideal forms that reside in the mind of the Creator:

> Let us therefore state the reason why the framer of this universe of change framed it at all. He was good, and what is good has no particle of envy in it; being therefore without envy he wished all things to be as like himself as possible. . . . God therefore, wishing that all things should be good, and so far as possible nothing be imperfect, and finding the visible universe in a state not of rest but of inharmonious and disorderly motion, reduced it to order from disorder, as he judged that order was in every way better.[1]

The primary elements of which the world is to be composed are thought of as building materials, waiting to be put together by the builder's hand. He does this by fixing the quantities in the

[1] *Timaeus*, trans. H. D. P. Lee (Penguin, Harmondsworth, 1969) 42.

perfect geometrical proportions of squares and cubes (1:2:4:8 and
1:3:9:27). These are the same proportions as those that go to the
making up of the world soul. According to this composition,

> the world's body, consisting of neither less nor more than four
> primary bodies, whose quantities are limited and linked in the
> most perfect proportion, is in unity and concord with itself and
> hence will not suffer dissolution from any internal disharmony
> of its parts. The bond is simply geometrical proportion.[1]

It is because Plato conceives of the universe in terms of mathe-
matical proportion in this way that he can find an analogy between it and the rational soul. When Plato was filtered through
to the Middle Ages by the great popularisers of late antiquity,
Boëthius, Macrobius and St Augustine, the Platonic concept of
numbers was extended until numbers and their relationships
were seen to lie behind moral as well as physical phenomena.[2]
Thus Macrobius sees the soul as being, 'as wise men have not
hesitated to proclaim . . . a number moving itself', and he says
of the number 8 that 'since it is the product of equal even numbers [2 × 2 × 2] and may be divided equally . . . it deserves to
receive the name Justice'. St Augustine, whose treatise *De musica*
was one of the most influential books of the Middle Ages, defined
music as the 'science of good modulation', and explained that
men and beasts can all listen to music with some degree of pleasure, but only those who know the *science* of music can discern
its laws and apply them in musical creation. These laws, as we
would expect, are entirely a matter of geometrical proportion, of
ratios and relationships. In this way the Pythagorean basis of
Plato's own cosmology is brought out into the open and adjusted
to Christian ends. Symbolic relations are seen to exist between
the structure of the universe and the perceptible world, and
number and music can reveal these. The number 6, for instance,
is a perfect number because 'it is completed in its own parts, for
it has these three: sixth, third, and half; nor is any other part in
it which can be called an aliquot part. For its sixth part is one,
its third two, and its half three. . . . And Holy Scripture com-

---

[1] F. M. Cornford, *Plato's Cosmology* (London, 1937) 51–2.
[2] See R. M. Jordan, *Chaucer and the Shape of Creation* (Harvard, 1967)
ch. 2 *passim*. The following quotations are taken from this chapter. I take
issue with Jordan's view of Chaucer in my next chapter

mends to us the perfection of this number, especially in this, that God finished his works in six days, and on the sixth day man was made in the image of God.'

The universe, then, is a structure of relations, created by God and perceivable by man in his mind's eye. It is non-organic, quantitative, something that is made by an artificer rather than planted by a gardener. But if this is so then it is possible for the artifacts of man to be made according to the same principles, thus providing not an imitation of a fragment of the visible universe, but a model or analogue of the universe itself. Because the universe is seen in terms not of essences but of structures it is possible for the human craftsman to imitate the *shape* of reality itself. Thus, as we have seen, since the world is conceived in terms of musical ratios it is natural for composers to write music that will mirror the world. Walter de Odington, an English theorist of the late thirteenth century, writes, for instance:

> Now with the older composers of organa the long had two beats, as in verse: but later on it is associated with the idea of perfection, so that it has three beats – after the likeness of the most blessed Trinity, who is the summit of perfection – and a long of this kind is called perfect. But the long which has only two beats is called imperfect.[1]

And Robert Jordan notes that:

> Sacred music, particularly motets, developed very subtle techniques of proportional imitation in rhythmic structure and contrapuntal imitation in melodic structure, and always favoured the perfect ratios, namely the consonant intervals of octave and fifth, at important cadential points.[2]

Similarly, as Otto von Simson has shown, the Gothic cathedral is conceived and constructed as the visible embodiment of divine order:

> With but a single basic dimension given, the Gothic architect developed all other magnitudes of his ground plan and elevation

[1] Quoted in Dom Anselm Hughes (ed.), *Early Medieval Music* (London, 1954) 401. A number of other fascinating examples are given by Manfred Bukofzer in a brilliant article, 'Speculative Thinking in Mediaeval Music', *Speculum*, xvii (142) 165–80.

[2] Op. cit., 59.

by strictly geometrical means, using as modules certain regular polygons, above all the square.

Matthew Roriczer, the builder of the cathedral at Regensburg,

> teaches 'how to take the elevation from the ground plan' by means of a single square. From this figure Roriczer derives all proportions of his edifice, in this case a pinnacle, inasmuch as its dimensions are related to one another as are the sides of a sequence of squares, the areas of which diminish (or increase) in geometrical progression. Proportions thus obtained the master considers to be 'according to true measure'.[1]

Von Simson explains the dual symbolism of the cathedral as it presented itself, for instance, to Abbot Suger, the founder of St Denis, or to the builders of Chartres Cathedral:

> Adam's fall on earth had obscured the theological order of the cosmos, its origin and end in what in Augustinian terms is the 'unison' with God. That order, however, is still manifest in the harmony of the heavenly spheres. Hence . . . the seemingly dual symbolism of the cathedral, which is at once a 'model' of the cosmos and an image of the Celestial City. If the architect designed his sanctuary according to the laws of harmonious proportion, he did not only imitate the order of the visible world, but conveyed an intimation, inasmuch as that is possible to man, of the perfection of the world to come.[2]

It is easy now to understand not only the anonymity of medieval art (even when we know the artist such knowledge seems strangely irrelevant), but also its reliance on tradition and convention. For if man's fall has obscured the theological order of the cosmos, how is the artist, who is only human, to discern that order, that perfection? Clearly it is not by relying on himself, his own inspiration, but rather by mastering the 'laws of harmonious proportion'. That there are such laws is attested by Scripture and by the event celebrated therein, the Incarnation of God. Thus the medieval artist, by shedding his own idiosyncrasies, can come to use his material in such a way as to reveal the laws which govern the

[1] Otto von Simson, *The Gothic Cathedral* (Harper Torchbooks, New York, 1964) 14–16.
[2] Ibid. 36–7.

universe. Art is thus seen as a quantitative, non-organic activity, the deployment of ready-made blocks rather than the cultivation of the plant of private vision. As St Thomas put it:

> The perfection of art does not consist in the artist but in the work which is accomplished. . . . Art concerns things that are made. . . . Therefore it is not requested that the artist operate according to the good, but that his work is well made.[1]

No one exemplifies this attitude better than Dante, and it may be useful to pause here for a moment and examine in a little more detail what Dante has to say about his art and how this is reflected in his actual practice. In an important passage in the *Convivio* he writes:

> Men call that thing beautiful the parts whereof duly corres-pond, because from their harmony pleasure results. Wherefore we think a man beautiful when his members duly correspond to each other; and we call singing beautiful when the voices correspond mutually according to the requirements of the art. (I 5)

In the *De vulgari eloquentia*, which is, among other things, a book of rules for those who 'write poetry by chance', he speaks with contempt of all those who 'lacking skill and science, trusting only to their talent, pretend to speak of high matters and use the high style', and there defines poetry in a way typical of his age as 'a work of inventiveness made by means of music and rhetoric'. As Montano points out,[2] the key words of the *De vulgari eloquentia* – *fastigiosus, subtilis, pexus, grandiosus, superbus* – accurately reflect his high regard for sheer technical competence and his contempt for all those who imagine that they can simply rely on their native wit and chance inspiration.

In the *Commedia* itself Dante never sees himself as an inventor

---

[1] Quoted in Rocco Montano, 'Dante's Aesthetic and Gothic Art', in *A Dante Symposium*, ed. de Sua and Rizzo (Chapel Hill, 1965) 11–33. Montano's conclusion, that Dante's workmanlike attitude to creation makes of him a secular poet closer in spirit to the Renaissance than to the Middle Ages, is one I obviously totally disagree with.

[2] Ibid. 32.

but always as a scribe, a copyist: 'quella materia ond'io son fatto scriba' he comments, and we see everywhere his concern to describe as accurately as possible what he sees, to intrude as little as possible between the reader and the vision. As he enters the ninth circle of Hell he calls on the Muses to help him convey the sight before him:

> Ma quelle Donne aiutino il mio verso,
> ch'aiutaro Anfion a chiuder Tebe,
> si che dal fatto il dir non sia diverso.
> (*Inferno*, XXXII 10–12)[1]

He needs the help of the Muses because he recognises the almost insuperable difficulty of putting into words the terrible sights before him. Again and again he stresses the difficulty of his task, and we feel the strain and effort of the duty he owes to God and to his reader, the duty to be absolutely accurate. But is such accuracy ever possible for fallen man? Is not his nature going to intrude and obstruct him at every turn? How can he presume to describe the entire shape and structure of the universe? If we turn from Dante's views on art to the fiction of the *Commedia* we will see that, like Proust's great novel, its theme is a journey towards salvation which is at the same time a journey towards the possibility of articulating such a theme.

The narrator-protagonist of the *Commedia* is Dante himself, but he is also any man who sets out in search of salvation in this life. The journey to salvation involves a descent to the centre of the earth, which is also the bottom of Hell, and then an arduous climb up Mount Purgatory to the limits of the sublunary realm. Each stage of this ascent is marked by the shedding of another deadly sin by the protagonist. At the top of the Mountain lies the Garden of Eden where Beatrice will come in glory to carry him to Heaven. Between Dante and the Garden there flows a river – Lethe, the classical river of forgetfulness. Beyond this point Virgil cannot go, and as they emerge from the flames which have cleansed Dante of the last of the deadly sins, Virgil, who has guided him all the way, turns to Dante and says:

---

[1] 'But may those Ladies help my verse, who helped Amphion to wall round Thebes; so that the fact may not differ from my words.'

> Non aspettar mio dir più, nè mio cenno.
> Libero, dritto e sano è tuo arbitrio,
> el fallo fora non fare a suo senno:
> per ch'io te sopra te corono e mitrio.
>
> *(Purgatorio*, XXVII 139–42)[1]

Cleansed of human imperfection, Dante is ready to enter the Garden where, so long before, Adam had been tempted and had fallen, thus blurring, seemingly forever, the image of God in which he had been created. The arduous journey travelled by Dante has thus been a quite literal *un-doing* of the harm done by the Fall, and a recovery of the image of God within him. And, as a sign that this is synonymous with the recovery of his own true and distinctive personality rather than a suppression of that personality, Dante is now for the first time in the poem addressed by name. It is Beatrice who speaks, rebuking him for weeping at the disappearance of his guide:

> Dante perchè Virgilio se ne vada,
> no pianger anco, no pianger ancora. . . .
>
> *(Purgatorio*, XXX 55–6)[2]

The structure of the poem is here, as everywhere, threefold. Virgil and Beatrice and the protagonist are first and foremost characters in Dante's narrative, in his fiction. The first happens to be a figure of whose historical existence we have ample proof, while scholars are still arguing about the existence of the 'real' Beatrice, but in Dante's poem their status is exactly the same. The first level then, is the literal level of the fiction. But it is also necessary, since the protagonist is not just Dante, but an 'I' who becomes any reader of the poem, to see that the literal journey is an analogue to the spiritual journey undergone by the reader, and here Virgil represents something like Reason and Beatrice something like Grace. But let us be clear about this. Since it is a question of reading the poem rather than experiencing life, the reader perceives the literal narrative as imagination and the inner or

---

[1] 'Do not expect my word or my sign any more. Now is your will free, upright and whole, and it would be a fault not to act as it prompts you: therefore I do crown and mitre you over yourself.'

[2] 'Dante, do not weep yet because Virgil goes away; do not weep yet.'

spiritual narrative as experience. At this point the poem reminds us that it starts on Good Friday and ends on Easter Sunday, and that Dante's descent into Hell and his ascent to Heaven exactly parallel Christ's Passion and Resurrection. So that, just as the Christian who partakes of the eucharist re-enacts in himself Christ's redemptive action, so the reader of the poem re-enacts Dante's journey, which is itself an analogue to the eucharistic action. Our earlier comparison of the eucharistic *anamnesis* with Proust's involuntary memory here finds its justification, for the task of art in both Dante and Proust is to render meaningful and communicable the intersection of the timeless with time in a specific action.

But there is a third focus in which Dante's poem has to be considered. We are here asked to remember that Virgil was the poet of Augustan Rome, man's most successful attempt to impose a secular peace on earth, as though to prepare it for the Divine Order that was about to manifest itself. The river Lethe, which Virgil cannot cross, is here seen as the dividing line of history, marking the point beyond which the purely natural cannot go. For the figural view of Scriptural history is only one instance of the working of God in human history, his creation of a pattern which will allow men to understand the plan he has for their salvation; there is a pattern in secular history as well.

There are thus three different areas of experience in the poem, analogous and co-inhering. The literal narrative reveals both the spiritual and the historical one. Without it the others would not exist in the poem, for it is this that gives them body – that incarnates them.[1] And we must guard against imagining that it is we who 'put' or 'read' these meanings into the poem. Rather it is the poem which draws them out and reveals them to the reader. As C. S. Singleton puts it: 'Dante's poem means to be an imitation of reality, mirroring the true nature of the real world wherein there are actual relationships between orders of existence.'[2] In other words, Dante's allegory signifies what it does, not because *Dante* means it to, but because *God* does. Here the contrast with Proust is absolute. For Dante history, if rightly apprehended, yields a pattern which points to God's work; Proust, on the other hand, has to create the historical dimension *within his own work*

[1] See Chapter 5 for a more detailed discussion of this point.
[2] *Journey to Beatrice* (Harvard, 1967) 95.

– the pattern he uncovers is the pattern of his life, not of the life of mankind. Dante simply asks the reader to look, to look hard, and he will then see in history and in the world around him evidence of the working of God and of the divine pattern of the universe. In this way the reader will be transformed from a 'foolish natural man' to one who is 'spiritual'. Dante does not teach, any more than Proust does. He simply asks the reader to *look*. But the reader who looks in the right way will come to see what he is and will thus be ready to start out on the path to salvation, which is nothing else but the path towards the recovery of what he really is.

But this path is none other than the one travelled by the poet himself. He too begins as a foolish natural man, lost in the wilderness of the world. He too has to discover that the recovery of the self depends on the acknowledgement that in God's will is our peace. Lost in the dark wood, he flounders amid the reflections of his private terrors in a state which differs from that of the sinners in Hell only by the fact that for them the choice of where they are and how they exist has been made for all eternity. But as Dante, guided by Virgil and then by Beatrice, moves ever upward in his journey, he comes to see more clearly not only what kind of thing he is himself, but, simultaneously, what kind of thing the universe is. His journey, which brings more and more of the universe into sight as he climbs towards the outermost ring of Heaven, the Empyrean where God exists, is thus not just the record of the spiritual education of a man, but also of the visual education of a poet.[1] The sinners in hell, prisoners of their own ego, could never write about Hell since they experience everything merely as extensions of themselves. It is typical that Paolo and Francesca read the story of Lancelot in purely sentimental fashion: they make no distinction between the characters in a romance and people they know, and see in the book only the cause of their present distress. It is only the poet, who has gone to Hell and climbed out again, who can really see it and describe it for us. Should the souls in Hell attempt to turn their experience into art they would be like those poets castigated by Dante in the *De vulgari eloquentia*, who, 'lacking skill and science, trusting only to their talent, pretend to speak of high matters and use the

[1] See Aldo Bernardo, 'Dante's Divine Comedy: the View from God's Eye', in *A Dante Symposium*, ed. de Sua and Rizzo, 45–58.

high style'. Indeed, it is for just this reliance on the self that they are in Hell, and we can see that it is not too great a step from Francesca's lovely lyric outburst to the meaningless cries of the giant Nimrod, 'for every language is to him, as to others his, which no one understands': the simple articulation of one's subjective feelings soon degenerates into animal screams and yelps.

The true poet, on the other hand, is he who can free himself from the chance whims of a private language and write a poem not from his own but from God's own point of view, so that Dante's journey describes not just the spiritual education of a man, but that of a poet. What this means is beautifully caught by Wallace Stevens in a late poem, 'Angel Surrounded by Paysans', when he tells how the angel of reality appeared silently in a room full of people, saying:

> I have neither ashen wing nor wear of ore
> And live without a tepid aureole,
>
> Or stars that follow me, not to attend,
> But, of my being and its knowing, part.
>
> I am one of you and being one of you
> Is being and knowing what I am and know.
>
> Yet I am the necessary angel of earth,
> Since, in my sight, you see the earth again,
>
> Cleansed of its stiff and stubborn, man-locked set,
> And, in my hearing, you hear its tragic drone
>
> Rise liquidly in liquid lingerings,
> Like watery words awash.

There is no better description of Dante's art. His poem, which tells the story of his journey from the darkness and confusion of the thick wood in the middle of the world to the very position that God occupies in the universe, could have been written only from that ultimate position; so that, like Proust's novel, it describes the journey to the point at which such a work can be undertaken, the ultimate vision being nothing else than a total understanding of the nature of the way.[1] Thus written, it cleanses us of our stiff and stubborn man-locked set, which Proust calls Habit, and gives us back the world of reality – and ourselves.

The *Commedia* is thus not only one of the greatest examples of medieval art, it also provides that art with a rationale. We can now see more clearly why it has to be an anonymous art and why the artist must learn the skills and techniques of handling the elements given him by tradition and convention. The artist is a scribe, a copyist, his whole skill devoted to freeing other men as well as himself from the privacy of their subjective natures. But this is no easy thing to do, as Dante shows us; no less than Proust he recognises that it requires a lifetime's unremitting effort. Where Gothic cathedral or religious motet is dumb to tell us about itself, literature is able to reveal both the process and the result. For it is part of Dante's argument that the submitting of the self to the disciplines of art, to the requirements of a public language and the demands of reality is one way of submitting to the will of God, in whose will is our peace. The process of the fiction and the argument of the poem thus mirror and reflect each other. But let us note this: If the poem *tells* of the education of the narrator, it *provides* an education for the reader. What the fiction tells, and what the poem is, form an analogy, and the reader living imaginatively through the fiction of a descent into Hell and a journey up to Paradise, lives through the reality of the shedding of his man-locked set and the discovery of the universe and of himself as they really are. In the letter to Can Grande Dante defined the aim of his poem as being 'to remove those living in this life from a state of misery and to lead them to a state of happiness', and one can see how the poem accomplishes this task not in the telling but in the doing. No less than Proust, Dante can claim that

In reality, every reader is, while he is reading, the reader of his

[1] In both Dante and Proust we falsify the response if we look at the work either from a purely spatial or from a purely temporal viewpoint. To take the final vision as the true one and then forget the way that led there is like seeing Jouy only from the top of Saint-Hilaire, whereas the Curé had specifically said: 'To get it all quite perfect you would have to be in both places at once: up here on the top of Saint-Hilaire and down there at Jouy-le-Vicomte.' See my discussion of Chaucer's *Troilus* in the next chapter, and the more general discussion of critical viewpoint in Chapters 11 and 12.

own self. The writer's work is merely a kind of optical instrument which he offers to the reader to enable him to discern what, without this book, he would perhaps never have perceived in himself.

But in saying this one is only saying that Dante is at one with the theory and practice of his age.[1]

The medieval Church can be said to have reached its high-water mark in 1264, when it showed a conscious awareness of its own nature by instituting the feast of Corpus Christi. Although it was not to be decisively challenged until the early sixteenth century, and although its greatest monuments were to be the product of the next hundred and fifty years, it would not be too arbitrary to trace the process of its decline from this point. Like all decisive changes this one went unnoticed for a long time, but slowly the premises upon which the medieval analogical synthesis had rested disappeared, to be replaced by others which could not carry such a system. Since it is from these new premises that the Renaissance launched its attacks on the Middle Ages, it is important that we understand the nature of the change.

The Church had always been aware of the possible misunderstanding of its true nature. It could fight formulated heresy with formulated dogma, with crusades, or, more desperately, with the Inquisition. More difficult to deal with, however, was that mechanisation of Christianity which had to some extent been a problem ever since the mass conversions of the fourth century. It is easy to see how a religion which rests upon the doctrine of the Incarnation is open to such mechanisation. It is a small though crucial step from the belief that there can be no salvation except through the sacraments of the Church to the belief that merely to partake of the sacraments is to ensure salvation. The enormous increase in mechanical aids to salvation in the later Middle Ages has many causes: the Black Death, which decimated Europe and reinforced the feeling that evil was not simply a denial of good but a positive force in the world; the economic conditions which resulted from the breakdown of the feudal system and the growth of towns; the abuses within the Church itself. Historians are still

[1] See, for example, V. A. Kolve's study of how a popular form like the drama strove for and achieved the same effect: *The Play Called Corpus Christi* (Stanford, 1967).

debating the causes; the results are indisputable. Pardons, relics, indulgencies, could all be bought for money, and all were thought capable of conferring spiritual benefits on their possessors. We hear of a parrot which, being carried away by a kite, uttered the invocation dear to its mistress, 'Sancte Thoma, adjuva me', and was miraculously restored. A merchant of Groningen, having purloined what purported to be an arm of John the Baptist, grew richer and richer so long as he kept it in his house, but was reduced to beggary as soon as his secret was discovered and the relic taken away from him.[1] Men invoked saints against the toothache as well as the plague; it was thought to be enough to have looked at an image or statue of St Christopher to be sure of escaping accidental death.

In reaction to this widespread mechanisation of religion a new wave of piety set in during the fourteenth century. This was the movement known as the Devotio Moderna which sprang up around the figure of Gerard Groote in the Netherlands, and led to the foundation of the Brethren of the Common Life. The most famous product of the Brethren was the *Imitation of Christ*, the most popular book of the later Middle Ages, written around 1418 and usually attributed to Thomas à Kempis. In it one can see very clearly the characteristics of the whole movement: a great emphasis on personal piety and on the *inner* life and a consequent lack of interest in the Church or the sacraments. The author's concentration on the inner life is so intense that he tends to regard all visible symbols and formal acts as entirely without value unless accompanied by strong internal feelings. Even when, as in the last book, he does consider the sacrament of the Eucharist, it is as food for the spirit rather than as the means of salvation: it arouses in us a psychological understanding of Christ's passion rather than affording us the means of re-enacting it.

The notion of human character taken for granted by *The Imitation of Christ* is clearly very different from that of the medieval Church, outlined above. What it stresses is not the mystery of the Incarnation but the moral goodness of Christ the man; not his Passion and Resurrection, but his parables and teachings. The medieval Church did not talk about an *imitation* of Christ. Man, since he was made in God's image, was, essen-

[1] See P. Sabatier, *Life of St. Francis of Assisi*, trans. L. S. Houghton (London, 1894) 33 ff.

tially, already like Christ, though because of the Fall, he required
Christ's Incarnation to give him back the possibility of realising
what he essentially was. The only kind of imitation envisaged by
the Church is the mystical imitation of Christ's *action*, not of his
person. *The Imitation of Christ*, on the other hand, seems to take
it for granted that man is essentially unlike Christ and that only
through a studied conformity of the spirit will he find any salvation. Where the medieval Church saw man as a being in the
process of realising himself, the *Imitation* is not interested in what
he is but only in what he ought to be. The stress on *imitation*
thus implies a loss of faith in the phenomenal world and a loss of
belief in the idea that man is made in God's image. By advocating
the imitation of Christ in this way the author implicitly dismisses
the idea that there is something in man which is not only like
Christ, but *is* Christ. As a result freedom and morality, outer and
inner are set up in opposition to one another. It is the first symptom of a far-reaching change.

It was at about the same time as the appearance of *The
Imitation of Christ* in the Netherlands that the artists of the great
towns of Italy were themselves beginning to show an interest in
the notion of artistic imitation. This was partly the result of the
changing situation of the artist within this society, so well described by Anthony Blunt:

> The artist was no longer a purveyor of goods which everyone
> needed and which could be ordered like any other material
> goods, but an individual facing a public. . . . In this spirit of
> competition he began to carry out works other than those
> directly commissioned. We are here at the beginning of those
> modern ideas which make of the artist a creator who works for
> himself alone.[1]

What this change meant in practice is shown by a letter sent to
Vasari by one of his patrons:

> My wish to have a notable work by your hand is as much for
> your fame as for my pleasure, because I would like to show it
> to certain persons who know you better as a speedy than as an
> excellent painter. . . . Whether you do it fast or slowly I leave
> to you, because I believe one can be both speedy and good

[1] *Artistic Theory in Italy, 1450–1600* (Oxford, 1962) 56.

when carried away by passion. . . . As to invention [of subject-matter], that too I leave to you.[1]

The contrast between the way of working implied here and that of the medieval artist is striking and absolute. As an example of the latter we may take Émile Mâle's discussion of a French illuminated manuscript of the thirteenth century. This manuscript, he says,

> contains a collection of the gospels for all the Sundays of the year, and numerous miniatures accompany the text. The book opens with the gospels for Christmas-time, which relate the stories surrounding the childhood of Jesus. Faithful to his text the artist illustrates in turn the Flight into Egypt, the Circumcision and the Adoration of the Magi. The gospels which refer to the public life follow, and here the artist shows the Baptism, the Marriage at Cana, the Temptation and the Transfiguration. Then suddenly he stops, and half the book is left without illustrations, until the work is begun again in Holy Week with the Passion, the Resurrection and the Appearances of Christ as subjects for the pictures. It is evident that the artist has used pounced tracings of older drawings whose number was strictly determined. Where tradition offered him no model it did not occur to him to invent, he did but what others before him had done and no more.[2]

The medieval artist is a scribe; an artist like Vasari, free to choose his own subject and to treat it as he wishes, has become an *inventor*.

As we would expect, the views of the artists themselves reflect this new situation. Leonardo, for instance, insists on the artist's following his own inner image, and compares the inventive faculty to the power of God in creating the world:

> That divine power, which lies in the knowledge of the painter, transforms the mind of the painter into the likeness of the divine mind, for with a free hand he can produce different

---

[1] Quoted by E. H. Gombrich in 'Icones Symbolicae: The Visual Image in Neo-Platonic Thought', *Journal of the Warburg and Courtauld Institutes*, XI (1948) 171, n. 1 (my translation).

[2] *The Gothic Image*, trans. Dora Nussey (Fontana, London, 1961) 178.

beings, animals, plants, fruits, landscapes, open fields, abysses, terrifying and fearful places.[1]

Leonardo, however, never encourages the artist to give free play to his imagination; what he invents must always be an exact imitation of nature: 'That painting is most to be praised which agrees most exactly with the things imitated', he says.

It is interesting to note that it is no longer, as with Dante or the anonymous illustrator mentioned by Mâle, an *action* that has to be imitated, but a thing. And it is clear that the greater the freedom of the artist to invent, the more he will need to refer himself to external objects. But verisimilitude can never be the sole criterion, for however accurately the artist has imitated the objects of nature the question will still remain as to why he should choose *this* subject to imitate rather than that, or why he should select *this* detail rather than that (since he cannot reproduce all the details). Once an artist feels free to paint what he likes he also raises the question of the truth and meaning of what he paints. Although at first it looks as if verisimilitude, the exact imitation of nature, would answer this question, it soon becomes clear that another criterion is needed to justify the choice of subject-matter and the kind of treatment it receives. This does not seem to worry the painters, who stress more and more strongly the self-authenticating power of the artist's imagination,[2] but it does worry such writers as Chaucer, Rabelais and Cervantes, who again and again raise the question of why one man's inner image should necessarily be considered either true or meaningful. Although these issues will be dealt with at length in the next few chapters, it may be helpful to give here a brief example of what is involved, since this will by contrast bring home to us the real nature of medieval art. In a famous scene of Rabelais's *Pantagruel* the hero visits the sepulchre of his ancestor, Geoffroy 'à la grand dent'. There he sees a portrait of Geoffroy.

which made him somewhat afraid, looking upon the picture, whose lively draughts did set him forth in the representation of a man in an extreme fury, drawing his great *Malchus* faulchion

---

[1] Quoted in Blunt, op. cit. 37.
[2] See E. Panofsky, *Idea* (Leipzig and Berlin, 1924); and Blunt, op. cit. *passim*.

half way out of his scabbard; when the reason hereof was demanded, the Chanons of the said place told him, that there was no other cause of it, but that *Pictoribus atque Poetis*, etc., that is to say, that Painters and Poets have liberty to paint and devise what they list after their own fancie: but he was not satisfied with their answer, and said, He is not thus painted without a cause; and I suspect that at his death there was some wrong done him, whereof he requireth his Kinred to take revenge. . . . (*Pantagruel*, v)

The monks make use of the well-known Renaissance dictum *Pictoribus atque poetis*, which they take to mean that the artist is free to invent whatever he pleases. That may be so, says Pantagruel, but what does the picture *mean*? For it must mean *something*. And, once it is raised, the question clearly demands an answer. Pantagruel sees the answer in terms of the content of the picture: it must, he says, represent Geoffroy, like the elder Hamlet, asking from beyond the grave for vengeance on those who have wronged him. Other answers may be given in terms of the author's intention or his psychology, but what is clear is that (*a*) no set of signs is meaningless, and (*b*) its meaning cannot be found with any certainty simply by scrutinising it.

If we look again at Singleton's statement about Dante's mode of imitation we will begin to understand the difference between Dante's world and that of Rabelais. 'Dante's poem', he says, 'means to be an imitation of reality, mirroring the true nature of the real world.' Dante's poem is meaningful, that is, because it describes – and mimes – an action and a universe that is itself considered to be meaningful. It imitates not nature but reality. What this reality is, however, cannot, obviously, be derived *from* the universe itself. It is only because the universe is itself seen as a book, written by God, that the books of men can imitate it. Once the universe ceases to be seen in this way then the criteria both for understanding it and for understanding the 'real' meaning of books or pictures seem to disappear.[1] The problem can be ignored, but only at the artist's peril. The new freedom of the artist, far from conferring greater value on art, seems to go hand in hand with the relegation of art to the realm of the superfluous.

[1] This is the problem Wittgenstein tackles in the *Tractatus*. See below, Chapter 12.

If art means whatever the artist wants it to mean then one could also say that it means nothing at all. Many voices are going to be raised in the following centuries, suggesting something of the sort. With the disappearance of the medieval notion of analogy inner meaning and outer form no longer seem to reinforce one another, and as the world, instead of manifesting the 'invisible things of God', becomes an enigma without a key, there is the danger that art will be relegated to the status of a mere commodity, a luxury.

In order to understand Pantagruel's position a little more clearly it is necessary to turn to two men who were to influence the sixteenth century perhaps more than any others: Luther and Erasmus. Both, interestingly enough, were pupils of the Brethren of the Common Life, and this serves to emphasise the point made earlier that even the bitterest antagonists of the period start from the same basic premises: the late medieval pietistic view of human character, with its strong stress on the opposition between internal worth and external observance.

Although the Reformation is usually regarded as having begun in 1517, when Luther nailed the ninety-five theses to the door of the church at Wittenberg, the really decisive break seems to have come in 1519, when Luther debated with his Catholic opponents at Leipzig, and in 1520, when he put forward his views in *The Appeal to the German Nobility*. At Leipzig he denied the authority of the Pope and the Councils, and in the *Appeal* he claimed that Scripture outranks even the Pope in determining what is right and what is wrong: the truth is what my conscience is compelled to believe on reading Scripture, not what the Pope and Councils say. This at first sight would seem to replace one authority – the Church – with another – the Bible. But in fact it raises a fundamental question about authority, and one which could not be resolved in the terms proposed by Luther. As the Catholics were quick to point out, the individual conscience is extremely unreliable, and the fact that people have differed about the interpretation of passages of Scripture shows that there is no way of telling what the correct interpretation is without the guidance of the Church. For how is one to tell a perverse interpretation from a sound one without recourse to some external authority? The Reformers, however, retaliated by asking why it should be taken for granted that the Church would always be right and the individual conscience wrong. By what authority did the Church arrogate to itself this authority? If all men are fallible except the Pope, ran one extremist argument, then only the Pope can know who is Pope, and there is no reason for accepting the judgement of the present occupant of the pontifical chair.[1]

The Catholic position is in fact open to the same reductionist argument as the Protestant one. Luther's questioning of the criterion of authority seems to have raised an unanswerable problem. For no text, whether it is the Book of God or the portrait of Pantagruel's ancestor, is self-explicating. If it means something then that meaning was put into it by someone, but by itself it is dumb to tell what that meaning is. All we can do is to make more or less well-informed inferences and reach a high degree of probability; absolute certainty is inaccessible.[2] So long as there was a community of belief in the Church as to the 'real body of Christ' the problem of the criterion did not arise in any acute form. Irenaeus, in the second century, had formulated the position clearly enough:

A sound mind, and one which does not expose its possessor to danger, and is devoted to piety and the love of truth, will eagerly meditate upon those things which God has placed within the power of mankind, and has subjected to our knowledge, and will make advancement in [acquaintance with] them, rendering the knowledge of them easy to him by means of daily study. These things are such as fall [plainly] under our observation, and are clearly and unambiguously in express terms set forth in the sacred Scriptures. And therefore the parables ought not to be adapted to ambiguous expressions. For, if this be not done, both he who explains them will do so without danger, and the parables will receive a like interpretation from all, and the body of truth remains entire, with a harmonious adaptation of its members, and without any collision [of its several parts]. But to apply expressions which are not

[1] For an extended discussion of the debate and an excellent account of the nature of the issues raised by it, see R. H. Popkin, *The History of Scepticism from Erasmus to Descartes* (Assen, 1960). I am indebted to him for much of the material in this paragraph.

[2] See E. D. Hirsch Jr, *Validity in Interpretation* (Yale, 1967), for an excellent discussion of the philosophical issues.

clear or evident to interpretations of the parables, such as every one discovers for himself as inclination leads him [is absurd]. For in this way no one will possess the rule of truth; but in accordance with the number of persons who explain the parables will be found the various systems of truth, in mutual opposition to each other, and setting forth antagonistic doctrines, like the questions current among the Gentile philosophers.[1]

Irenaeus is well aware of the fact that confusion is only to be avoided if Christians realise that the act of faith required of them is one which gives the Scriptures a different status from the writings of the ancient philosophers. It depends for its interpretation on the common-sense application of the 'rule of truth', which is the Christian's creed. He takes it for granted that all Christians will agree about this rule, and he reserves his attack for those heretics who deny the Incarnation of Christ or the uniqueness of God. It does not occur to him that the rule may itself be in need of interpretation. But this is just the question that is raised in the sixteenth century. With the growing opposition between faith and works, experience and authority, inner feeling and outer observance it is only a matter of time before someone forces the issue out into the open. For when inner and outer are contrasted in this way, any institution claiming to be directly in touch with the divine and arrogating to itself authority for this reason will inevitably be regarded as either hypocritical and fraudulent or simply superstitious. Philosophically the problem of the criterion cannot be solved in terms of either the Catholics, with their insistence on the need to accept external authority, or the Protestants, with their claims for the primacy of an internal authority. It requires the medieval analogical notions of man and nature to resolve it, and that view, it now becomes clear, rests only on faith. Luther's 1520 pamphlet is a clear indication that such faith could never again be taken for granted.[2]

[1] Irenaeus, op. cit. II 27. On the meaning of the 'rule of truth' and its implications for Christianity, see C. N. Cochrane, *Christianity and Classical Culture* (New York, 1957).

[2] Another factor to be taken into consideration is the effect of scholarly editions and vernacular translations of the Bible, which began to appear at about this time. By revealing the discrepancies between the Vulgate and the Septuagint, for instance, these undermined people's faith in an exegesis

In reaction to the extremists of either side there arose in the sixteenth century an attitude that Popkin has aptly called 'mitigated scepticism'. The chief exponent of this point of view was Erasmus, who had, of course, formed his opinions well before Luther's break with Rome, but who came to be seen by many of the more intelligent men of the time as offering one possible solution to the issues raised by Luther. Erasmus argued that since we cannot in this life know with any certainty what the ultimate truth is, the most sensible course is to accept the traditional solutions offered by the Church, though without committing ourselves to a belief in them. Erasmus regarded extremists of either side with distaste because he felt that what they really desired was to be released from the painful daily responsibility of exercising their human faculties in a free choice of the will. What he felt to be important was a simple Christian piety, such as the Brethren of the Common Life had advocated, tinged with a healthy scepticism about all absolute solutions. Such an attitude was to lie behind much that was best in sixteenth-and seventeenth-century culture, but it is easy to see how it could degenerate into a nerveless deism, as it did in the eighteenth century. For the Christ of Erasmus is not really very different from Socrates (as he himself admitted): a good man whom we ought to imitate in order to lead the good life. All notion of the Incarnation as the appearance of the second Adam come to redeem us from the sin of the first has disappeared. As Luther rightly pointed out, Erasmus's position is really a secular one – he can very well do without God.[1] The natural and the divine have quite parted company, and Truth can now be defined only in negative terms: it is that which is *not*

---

based solely on the Vulgate. If the words the Fathers and the Schoolmen had spent so much time analysing and discussing were not even the true words of God but a mistranslation by St Jerome, then all the more reason for doubting their pronouncements. The Bible, people began to realise, is not just God's word, but God's word in the form of a *book*, and thus subject to all the vicissitudes of corruption and decay that language and books are heir to. On the effects of Biblical translation, see W. Schwarz, *Principles and Problems of Biblical Translation* (Cambridge, 1955).

[1] Erasmus's *De libero arbitrio* (1524) and Luther's reply, *De servo arbitrio* (1525) have been newly translated and edited together as *Erasmus–Luther: Discourse on Free Will*, trans. E. F. Winter (New York, 1961). Something of their relevance to the present day can be gauged by the fact that Thomas Mann has built *Dr. Faustus* round just this debate.

what the extremists take as truth. However hard we look at the world around us it will not yield its secrets; it will only throw back our own distorted reflections.

In the twelfth century Hugh of St Victor had been able to talk about the visible world as a 'book written by the finger of God', and of men as 'instituted by divine authority to show forth the wisdom of the invisible things of God'. On this optimistic faith the whole of medieval art and thought had rested. But events were so to shake this faith that by the end of the sixteenth century Montaigne could write: 'We no longer know what things are really like, for nothing comes to us except falsified and altered by our senses. . . . The uncertainty of our senses renders uncertain all that they produce.' In such a world the discovery of truth is the prerogative of the scientist who measures rather than of the artist who sees. Whether, when it has been found, this truth is of any value, is a question that will occasionally be asked in the following centuries. The great majority of thinkers and artists of the time, however, prefer to ignore it, and turn with tremendous gusto to the attack of their immediate predecessors. In the course of this attack the last vestiges of the medieval analogical system are destroyed, and a new world emerges – our world.

It would, however, be falling into the old trap of viewing the history of human culture in terms of Darwinian evolution to imagine that the old world simply passed away while a new one quietly took its place. It will be a useful corrective to this tendency to examine the work of two writers, one of whom is commonly seen as a 'typical' medieval artist, and the other as a no less typical Renaissance artist, and see how they reacted to the changing situation. They have little in common with Dante or with each other except for an extreme honesty in the face of their art and an absolute determination to be as truthful as it is possible to be. Perhaps, though, it is just this honesty and this determination which distinguishes the major from the minor artist.

3   Chaucer: The Teller and the Tale

'Rather I feel that I have done nothing but wish to speak: if
I have spoken, I have not said what I wished to say.'

St Augustine

I. EXPERIENCE AND AUTHORITY

Although they differ completely in tone and method, Dante's
Commedia and Langland's *Piers Plowman* share a common
design. Both poems open with the hero-narrator's sudden awareness of being lost and his asking a figure of authority (Virgil, Holy
Church) who appears before him what it is he needs to do to find
salvation. Both poems then provide an answer to this question
not in terms of logic or metaphysical argument, though there is
plenty of both in the poems, but in terms of experience. The hero
undergoes a number of experiences which lead him eventually to
see that the universe and his own life make sense. In Dante such
understanding is finally established at the end of the literal
journey, when the poet finds himself, in his present body, standing
next to God and able to look at him and see the entire universe
'bound by love in one volume'. At this point his own experience
and what his many guides have taught him come together and
he grasps at last the full meaning of La Pia's words, 'In His will
is our peace.' In Langland too the public and the private, his
own history and that of the world, come together when he wakes
up on Easter Sunday to hear the bells ringing for 'God's resurrection'. Here, for the first time in the entire poem, the dream vision
and the waking reality coincide, significantly enough in the one
event which stands outside human time and yet gives meaning to
all human history: the Passion and the Resurrection, eternally
re-enacted in the sacrament.

It is as if both journeys had been undertaken to cleanse man of
the stiff and stubborn man-locked set, the private vision of the
foolish natural man which led only to the dark wood of chaos and
confusion, and to give him back himself by revealing to him the
reality of the world and the meaning of God's plan. But this is

not simply a matter of listening to what people have to say to you. Virgil and Beatrice and St Bernard have much to say to Dante, but they are important to him primarily for what they are and for where they lead him, rather than for what they teach. Similarly, in passus xii of *Piers Plowman* Imagination warns the dreamer that 'learning and intelligence are both worthy of praise', for 'without the use of learning, bread could not be changed into the Body of Christ, which is a source of healing to the righteous', and without intelligence, which 'springs from men's observations of many things – of birds and beasts, and of experiments both true and false', man could not come to the Truth.[1] So long as the dreamer tries to resolve his problems through purely intellectual means he keeps coming up against dead ends; it is only with the appearance of Piers Plowman at the climax of the poem that the dreamer finds understanding and, with it, the possibility of salvation. As the passage quoted from Hugh of St Victor in the previous chapter suggests, then, if man learns to read the universe aright he will find that his experience reinforces what the Church has taught. For the world is a book and all the parts fit and yield forth God's meaning. Dante and Langland thus both construct their poems so as to elicit from the hero (and hence from the reader) the exclamation: 'Now I see how it is!' Seeing the world as if for the first time, they acknowledge it to be meaningful. Their previous despair is now recognised as a *failure to see*. Other books than the Bible are also guides to truth: the works of Virgil, Ovid, Seneca can also help man to see God's purpose, but again this is only if we learn to read them aright. They are, in fact, not so much books, that is, objects, as transparent windows on reality; correctly used, as Dante uses Virgil, they can guide us to the truth.[2]

The contrast with Chaucer is absolute and startling. There is a

[1] B text, xii, ll. 72 ff. Because the language of the original is rather difficult here I have used Goodridge's Penguin translation (Harmondsworth, 1959).

[2] Dante seems to distinguish between 'volume' and 'libro'. The former term is applied to Virgil and to the two 'books' of God, the Bible and the universe, while the latter is used to refer to such things as the 'book' of Lancelot, which led Paolo and Francesca astray. Similarly 'autore' is reserved for the author of a 'volume': the poets of antiquity he meets in *Inferno*, iv are men of 'grande autorita', and God in *Paradiso*, xxvi is three times called 'verace autore'.

passage in *The House of Fame* which is worth bearing in mind
as we explore Chaucer's vast and varied output. The Eagle, so
reminiscent of Beatrice, has seized the dreamer despite his pro-
testations that he is no Enoch or Ganymede, and borne him up
into the sky towards the Palace of Rumour. Like many guides the
Eagle is an inveterate talker and a tremendous bore, and he
delivers a running commentary on all they see and are about to
see. Eventually, however, his monologue comes to an end and
the dreamer-poet is able to take stock of the situation:

> Tho gan y loken under me
> And beheld the ayerissh bestes,
> Cloudes, mystes, and tempestes,
> Snowes, hayles, reynes, wyndes,
> And th' engendrynge in hir kyndes,
> All the wey thrugh which I cam.
> 'O God!' quod y, 'that made Adam,
> Moche ys thy myght and thy noblesse!'
> And thoo thoughte y upon Boece,
> That writ 'a thought may flee so hye
> Wyth fetheres of Philosophye . . .'
>
> And than thoughte y on Marcian,
> And eke on Anteclaudian,
> That sooth was her descripsion
> Of alle the hevenes region,
> As fer as that y sey the preve;
> Therfore y kan hem now beleve.
>   With that this egle gan to crye,
> 'Lat be,' quod he, 'thy fantasye!
> Wilt thou lere of sterres aught?'
> 'Nay, certeynly,' quod y, 'ryght naught.'
> 'And why?' 'For y am now to old.'
> 'Elles I wolde the have told,'
> Quod he, 'the sterres names, lo,
> And al the hevenes sygnes therto,
> And which they ben.' 'No fors,' quod y.
> 'Yis, pardee!' quod he; 'wostow why?
> For when thou redest poetrie,
> How goddes gonne stellifye   [turn into a constellation]
> Bridd, fissh, best, or him or here,

As the Raven, or eyther Bere,
Or Arionis harpe fyn,
Castor, Pollux, or Delphyn,
Or Athalantes daughtres sevene,
How alle these arn set in hevene;
For though thou have hem ofte on honde,
Yet nostow not wher that they stonde.'
'No fors,' quod y, 'hyt is no nede.
I leve as wel, so God me spede,
Hem that write of this matere,
As though I knew her places here;
And eke they shynen here so bryghte,
Hit shulde shenden al my syghte,
To loke on hem.' 'That may well be,'
Quod he.   (*HF* 964–1018)[1]

This is an extraordinary passage. It is not enough to say that it is a parody of Dante. It is partly that, but this is no explanation. The dreamer-poet, asked by the eagle to look at the stars he and other poets have so often written about, refuses – their brightness hurts his eyes, he says, and, besides, he is too old for any fresh experience! But of course the feeling we get is that he has not had *any* experience in his life; what he has written about has only come from books. And, as the eagle tells him in an earlier passage, his continuous poring over old books has made him 'mased', unable to respond to the world around him.

Why does the poet present himself in this way? The *persona* of the bookish dreamer of no experience is one that we meet with again and again in these early dream vision poems, and that undergoes only slight modifications in the depiction of the narrator of *Troilus* and of *The Canterbury Tales*. Instead of making experience reinforce what old books say Chaucer seems to be at pains to pull the two apart. The perpetual concern with dreams is just another aspect of this problem, since the question whether dreams are prophetic or not is really the question of how far God impinges on this world and how far we can tell what kinds of relation exist between this world and God's providence. In Dante and Langland, we saw, there was an answer to these

[1] All quotations are from *The Poetical Works of Geoffrey Chaucer*, ed. F. N. Robinson (London, 1937).

questions, an answer that had to be sought for, but which was connected with the public facts of the Incarnation and the sacraments of the Church. But Chaucer's poems make no mention of this. Instead they merely raise the question and leave us more puzzled than before. The prologue to the *Legend of Good Women* provides a good example of the method:

> A thousand sythes have I herd men telle
> That there is joye in hevene and peyne in helle,
> And I accorde wel that it be so;
> But natheless, this wot I wel also,
> That there ne is non that dwelleth in this contre,
> That eyther hath in helle or hevene ybe,
> Ne may of it non other weyes witen,
> But as he hath herd seyd or founde it writen;
> For by assay there may no man it preve.   [test, experience]
> But Goddes forbode, but men shulde leve
> Wel more thyng than men han seyn with ye!
> Men shal nat wenen every thyng a lye,
> For that he say it nat of yore ago.
> God wot, a thyng is nevere the lesse so,
> Thow every wyght ne may it nat yse.
> Bernard the monk ne say nat al, parde!
>   Thanne mote we to bokes that we fynde,
> Thourgh whiche that olde thynges ben in mynde,
> And to the doctryne of these olde wyse,
> Yeven credence, in every skylful wyse,
> And trowen on these olde approved storyes,
> Of holynesse, of regnes, of victoryes,
> Of love, of hate, of othere sondry thynges,
> Of whiche I may nat make rehersynges.
> And if that olde bokes were awaye,
> Yloren were of remembrance the keye.
> Wel oughte us thanne on olde bokes leve,
> There as there is non other assay by preve.
> And as for me, though that my wit be lite,
> On bokes for to rede I me delyte,
> And in myn herte have hem in reverence,
> And to hem yeve swich lust and swich credence. . . .

$$(LGW \text{ G } 1\text{--}32)$$

I think it would be wrong to read this passage entirely straight, as one of Chaucer's best critics has done.[1] The dreamer-narrator may be advocating the reliance on the authority of books – since they are all we have to rely on – but we know by now that he has a particular stake in such a recommendation. As Nietzsche remarked: beware of philosophers who recommend the philosophic life as the answer to all life's problems. In fact, the weight of the passage is evenly balanced on the incisive irony of the phrase: 'Bernard the monk ne say nat al, parde!' Taken at its face value this means: 'Surely men ought to believe more than simply what they see; after all, even Bernard[2] did not see everything he described and surely you don't doubt him?' But of course the passage can be taken in a diametrically opposite sense: 'Since no one has ever been to heaven and hell and returned to tell us about it, everyone is in the same position with regard to what these places are really like, so why should we believe what anyone tells us about it, whether it's Bernard or anyone else?' The effect is similar to the one we find in the Nun's Priest's Tale, where the narrator explains:

> This storie is also trewe, I undertake,
> As is the book of Launcelot de Lake,
> That wommen holde in ful greet reverence. (*CT* VII 3211–13)

My story is as true as that of Lancelot – but perhaps the story of Lancelot is no truer than my story. Instead of moving from (apparent) confusion to (real) clarity, as with Dante and Langland, these early poems of Chaucer's set up a rigid opposition of experience and authority from the start and never progress towards their reconciliation. They remain for the most part unfinished or badly flawed, as though the poet had been defeated by the contradiction between the two.

But it is not only these early poems that circle compulsively round the problem. Few, if any, of the *Canterbury Tales* do not address themselves to the conflicts it raises, and since there Chaucer is in greater control of his material it may be as well to pause a little and see just what he does with it.

Many of the characters in *The Canterbury Tales*, either the

---

[1] R. O. Payne, *The Key of Remembrance* (Yale, 1963) 94–6.
[2] There is some doubt as to who is meant here. See Robinson's note.

pilgrims themselves or the characters within the pilgrims' tales, raise the question of the relation of experience to authority. They do this either by insisting on their simple down-to-earth reliance on experience and thus making us suspect any reference to authority, or by piling up references to authorities and impressing us with the way their own views tally with those of the great men of the past. Occasionally, as with the Wife of Bath, they miraculously manage to combine the two. A good example of the first approach is the Franklin, who begs the pilgrims to

> Have me excused of my rude speeche.
> I lerned nevere rethorik, certeyn;
> Thyng that I speke, it moot be bare and pleyn.
> I sleep nevere on the Mount of Pernaso,
> Ne lerned Marcus Tullius Scithero.
> Colours ne knowe I none, withouten drede,
> But swiche colours as growen in the mede,
> Or elles swiche as men dye or peynte.
> Colours of rethoryk been to me queynte;
> My spirit feeleth noght of swich mateere.   (*CT* v 718–27)

But this we of course know to be itself a figure of rhetoric, cunningly deployed. The implication that because he isn't going to dress up his tale in high-flown rhetoric it will be honest and truthful is one that we will see dramatically challenged in the Pardoner's Tale, but the Franklin's words are sufficient to warn us that he is not as simple as he seems.

More interesting than this *ingénu* approach is the converse, the citing of authority to back up one's private prejudices, or the reliance on authority which reveals to the reader an unwillingness to learn from experience. There is, for example, the carpenter John, in the Miller's Tale, who

> knew nat Catoun, for his wit was rude,
> That bad man sholde wedde his simylitude. (*CT* i 3227–8)

and all of whose troubles come from an unnatural doting on his young wife. This leads him to accept the false astrology of the clerk Nicholas, with his assurances that the stars foretell a second flood. Although Nicholas tempts him with the notion that after the flood.

thanne shul we be lordes al oure lyf
Of al the world, as Noe and his wyf. . . . (*CT* I 3581–2)

he is not, like most of the other characters in Chaucer, really
interested in power, lordship. Nonetheless, his willingness to
accept unquestioningly the false authority of Nicholas is the
direct result of his failure to listen to the proper authority of Cato,
and he reaps the consequences of this neglect. With January in
the Merchant's Tale the technique grows clearer. He too has not
heard of Cato's advice and so marries a young wife, but this time
there is a friend at hand to remind him of the wise man's words:

Avyseth yow – ye been a man of age –
How that ye entren into mariage,
And namely with a yong wyf and a fair.
By him that made water, erthe and air,
The youngeste man that is in al this route,
Is bisy ynough to bryngen it aboute
To han his wyf allone. Trusteth me,
Ye shul nat plesen hire fully yeres thre,
This is to seyn, to doon hire ful plesaunce. (*CT* IV 1555–63)

But this of course is just what January does *not* want to hear:

'Wel,' quod this Januarie, 'and hastow sayd?
Straw for thy Senek, and for thy proverbes!
I counte nat a panyer ful of herbes
Of scole-termes. Wyser men than thow,
As thou hast herd, assenteden right now
To my purpos. . . . (*CT* IV 1566–71)

And January is not altogether wrong. For the puzzling thing
seems to be that the authorities contradict one another; however
many are produced on one side of an argument, an equal number seem capable of being produced on the other side. And nothing, as we saw in the case of Scripture in the previous chapter,
can tell us how we are to arbitrate between the rival authorities.
They fill the pages of Chaucer's tales, these classical and patristic
writers, they tumble over each other in a riot of profusion; but,
unlike the Virgil and St Bernard of Dante and the Holy Church
of Langland, they only add to the confusion. It is no longer a
matter of a fleshly as opposed to a spiritual reading: all reading

seems to be equally fleshly and equally spiritual, depending on the point of view.

What, for instance, are we to make of the debate between Chauntecleer and Pertelote in the Nun's Priest's Tale? The arguments between them are already familiar to us from Chaucer's early dream poems: what is the significance of dreams? Are they warnings sent from God or are they purely physiological in provenance, the mere result of overeating? Pertelote is in no doubt:

'Have ye no mannes herte, and han a berd?
Allas! and konne ye been agast of swevenys? [dreams]
Nothyng, God woot, but vanitee in sweven is.
Swevenes engendren of replecciouns,
And ofte of fumes and of complecciouns,
Whan humours been to habundant in a wight.
Certes this dreem, which ye han met tonyght,
Cometh of the greete superfluytee
Of youre rede colera, pardee. . . .

Lo Catoun, which that was so wys a man,
Seyde he nat thus, "Ne do no fors of dremes?"
Now sire,' quod she, 'whan we flee fro the bemes,
For Goddes love, as taak som laxatyf. . . .' (*CT* VII 2920–43)

But Chauntecleer will not have his dream dealt with in this reductive way:

'Madame,' quod he, 'graunt mercy of youre loore.
But nathelees, as touchyng daun Catoun,
That hath of wysdom swich a greet renoun,
Though that he bad no dremes for to drede,
By God, men may in olde bookes rede
Of many a man moore of auctorite
Than evere Caton was, so moot I thee,   [so may I thrive]
That al the revers seyn of this sentence,
And han wel founden by experience
That dremes been significaciouns
As wel of joye as of tribulaciouns
That folk enduren in this lif present. . . .

Dame Pertelote, I sey yow trewely,
Macrobeus, that writ the avisioun

In Affrike of the worthy Cipioun,
Affermeth dremes, and seith that they been
Warnynge of thynges that men after seen.
And forthermoore, I pray yow looketh wel
In the olde testament, of Daniel. . . . (*CT* vii 2970–3128)

and he goes on to cite Joseph, Croesus, Andromache, and many more biblical and classical figures whose dreams *were* prophetic. Our confidence in him is, however, slightly lessened, when he reveals the private and instinctive bias of his learning by translating 'mulier est hominis confusio' as 'woman is man's joy and all his bliss.' Here, surely, we are back with a figure not at all unlike the aged January, whose use of authorities is conditioned by his need to back up his own private desires. In the event, however, Chauntecleer turns out to have been right after all. His dream is prophetic, and his fears turn out to have been justified, since a little later a fox does in fact get hold of him. But it would I think, be wrong to read the story in this way as a *justification* of prophetic dreams. The effect of the tale on the reader, as I shall try to show later, is to make him laugh at the discrepancy between the importance of the subject (are dreams prophetic? does God really speak directly to us in this way?) and the barnyard incident that illustrates this. Is it *this* story that will allow us to adjudicate between all the learned authorities? It may be as true as the story of Lancelot, but, as we have seen, perhaps Lancelot's story is no more than this, the trivial tale of a farmyard cock. As the Nun's Priest says, in discussing the tremendous issues of free-will and predestination:

I wol nat han to do of swich mateere;
My tale is of a cok, as ye may heere. (*CT* vii 3251–2)

But this too, as I shall try to show later in this chapter, is only a partial view of the situation.

With the Wife of Bath we are on less slippery ground. Her prologue furnishes us with the *locus classicus* of Chaucer's exploration of the way in which private whim can transform authority' into a mere excuse for following one's own interests. She begins by insisting on her *experience* as the source of any wisdom she might now possess:

> Experience, though noon auctoritee
> Were in this world, is right ynogh for me
> To speke of wo that is in mariage;
> For, lordynges, sith I twelve yeer was of age,
> Thonked be God that is eterne on lyve,
> Housbondes at chirche dore I have had fyve. . . . (*CT* III 1–6)

And yet, as if to demonstrate the psychological fact that we always need to align our experience in some way with that of the rest of mankind if we are to make sense of it, she launches after this opening straight into a lengthy defence of her own character, citing the Old Testament, the Gospels and St Jerome, among others, in defence of her practice. D. W. Robertson Jr has shown in great (and not always convincing) detail how this citing of authority, while intended to provide evidence of the rightness of her actions, would, in fact, have damned her in the eyes of her audience.[1] Here, for example, is the way she treats the authority of Solomon:

> Lo, heere the wise kyng, daun Salomon;
> I trowe he hadde wyves mo than oon.
> As wolde God it were leveful unto me
> To be refresshed half so ofte as he!
> Which yifte of God hadde he for alle his wyvys!
> No man hath swich that in this world alyve is. . . .
>
> (*CT* III 35–40)

Robertson comments:

> The 'yifte of God' (cf. 1 Cor. 7.7) Solomon had is readily discernible in 3 Kings 11 : 'And king Solomon loved many strange women. . . . And he had seven hundred wives as queens, and three hundred concubines; and the women turned away his heart. And when he was now old, his heart was turned away by women to follow strange gods: and his heart was not perfect with the Lord his God. . . .' In fact, the foolishness of Solomon in his old age was proverbial. As Proserpyna observes in the Merchant's Tale,
>
> > He was a lecchour and an ydolastre,
> > And in his elde he verray God forsook.

Five husbands of which she has 'pyked out the beste/Bothe of

[1] *A Preface to Chaucer* (Princeton, 1963) 317 ff.

here nether purs and of her cheste' have been sufficient to bring
the wife to a similar position.[1]

The climax of the Wife's prologue beautifully mimes the misreading of authorities involved here. Her fifth husband, it will be
recalled, used to read to her continuously out of old authors who
dwelt on the evils of women, starting with Eve and moving
steadily (and at considerable length) down to the present, so that

> whan I saugh he wolde nevere fyne
> To reden on this cursed book al nyght,
> Al sodeynly thre leves have I plyght
> Out of his book, right as he radde, and eke
> I with my fest so took hym on the cheke
> That in oure fyr he fil bakward adoun.
> And he up stirte as dooth a wood leoun,
> And with his fest he smoot me on the heed. . . .(*CT* III 788–95)

After all the citing of learned authorities, after the endless flood
of *words* poured out by the Wife of Bath, experience bursts with
extraordinary violence into the situation.[2] It is as though the
literal and 'non-spiritual' nature of the Wife's interpretation of
Scripture had found its true outlet as she leaps forward and tears
the leaves out of the old book. And suddenly, with this action,
the book is there before us as an *object*, its power dependent
entirely on its remaining intact. In a flash we are made aware of
the fact that language is only literal when we think of it in purely
physical terms – marks on paper – and that otherwise all language is spiritual in that it is in need of *interpretation*. And we see
too that not only do the authorities bafflingly range themselves on
both sides of any question, but that these 'authorities' speak to
us only as marks on paper, never as people. But if *this* is authority,

[1] Ibid. 323–4.
[2] The tale which the pilgrim Chaucer tells of Melibee forms an interesting contrast to the Wife's prologue. In this tale a cruel incident – the
deliberate maiming of a man's wife and daughter – is drained of all
emotional flavour (it is described in five lines) and made the excuse for an
elaborate exercise in rhetorical argumentation (nine hundred lines). The
result is that when the evildoers are pardoned at the end we are only
confirmed in our feeling that the outrage never really took place at all.
Its function in the tale is rather like that of those baths that are perpetually in the process of being filled by hot and cold taps in elementary
algebra problems: the fact that the water might well overflow does not
make us worry about the contents of the house.

this book coming apart in my hands, how on earth can I trust it to guide me through my life? Yet without authorities to guide us, what sense are we going to make of the world and of ourselves? The climax of the Wife of Bath's prologue shows us that it is useless aligning experience against authority or authority against experience: neither speaks to us directly, both need interpreting, but where are we going to find a criterion for interpreting either?

Troilus and Criseyde, Chaucer's longest and most ambitious poem is, among other things, an exploration of just this theme. Troilus himself has much in common with Don Quixote. Like him he was once a relatively sane man, though one carrying within him the seeds of his folly. Very soon, as we watch him, he falls prey to an obsession which is, like Don Quixote's, nothing less than the absolute belief that he must carry out *literally* all the *conventions* of the chivalric code. Chaucer does not stress the absurdity of this enterprise as much as Cervantes does, with the result that for a long time readers have dismissed Troilus's extravagance as belonging *to* the courtly code, and have thought that to recognise this is to account for it. I would like to argue that Chaucer differs most crucially from his source, Boccaccio, just because the code *is* questioned, both within the dramatic terms of the poem and implicitly by the narrator of the story. Let's see how this works.

Troilus, who had always scorned love, is smitten by Cupid's dart at the start of the poem and finds himself wildly in love with Criseyde. Like a good follower of the courtly code he pines away and, alone in his chamber, throws himself on his bed and laments in the rhetorical terms required of every unhappy lover. The lament ends with these words:

> But now help, God, and ye, swete, for whom
> I pleyne, ikaught, ye, nevere wight so faste!
> O mercy, dere herte, and help me from
> The deth, for I, while that my lyf may laste,
> More than myself wol love yow to my laste.
> And with som frendly lok gladeth me, swete,
> Though nevere more thing ye me byheete. (*TC* 1 533–9)

The narrator now picks up the tale, apparently quite neutrally: he is simply giving us the facts of the situation as he got them from the 'author' he purports to be following, a certain Lollius:

Thise wordes, and ful many an other to,
He spak, and called evere in his compleynte,
Hire name, for to tellen hire his wo,
Till neigh that he in salte teres dreynte.
Al was for nought; she herde nat his pleynte. . . . (*TC* 1540–9)

'Al was for nought; she herde nat his pleynte.' The apparent
innocence of this phrase may easily cause us to overlook it. But if
we read with our ears attuned to Chaucer it will be apparent that
this elicits an extremely complex response from us. For it dawns
on us that there is a perfectly good reason why she didn't hear
his plaint, and this is that she wasn't in the room with Troilus at
the time! The remark of the narrator makes us see two things
simultaneously: that Troilus, like a good follower of the code, is
going through all the motions of a conventional 'plaint'; and that
he is taking the convention *literally*. The historian-narrator's
apparent endorsement of Troilus's attitude is no different in kind
from the pilgrim Chaucer's 'and I seyde his opinioun was good'
in the general prologue of *The Canterbury Tales*. In both places
the remark serves to draw the reader from his position *inside* the
main character and to place his words in the context of ordinary
life. But in such a context, where the remark is assented to as
objective truth, we are forced to recognise it as subjective fantasy.
What has happened is that the narrator has *dramatised* our initial
response and thus made us see how false it is.

It is necessary to pause for a moment and examine what this
means, since this relation of a reader to a text and the way it is
controlled by the author is one we will be meeting again and
again in the chapters that follow. As we read Boccaccio's poem
on which Chaucer's is based, we identify with the hero and so, we
feel, does the author. Boccaccio tells this story because it
'expresses' his own anguish in love, as he himself says in the
poem; the poem becomes a personal lyric, expressive of 'himself'.
Reading it we enter into the mind of his hero and act out his
adventures in our imagination. This tendency to go, as it were,
'through' the words on the page to the 'picture of reality' which
they conjure up, is one that seems to be inherent in human beings;
it is on this factor that the traditional novel is built.[1] And what
else is this tendency except a 'taking literally' of what is presented

[1] See Chapter 5 below.

to the imagination? What we have are words which conjure up a world in our imagination, but the fact that this is only in our imagination is constantly being disguised by the persuasive power of the imagination itself.

If this is the case then a curious realignment must take place in our view of Chaucer. We now see Troilus, in common with the other literalists of the imagination, as a reflection of the reader's own position. For the reader too accepts the courtly code as though it were reality itself; the power of his imagination converts a conventional system, which is devoted to codifying the triumph of the imagination of the troubadour and his lady over the realities of feudalism, into actuality. We can thus say that the relation of Troilus to the actual world around him is the same as the instinctive relation of the reader to the story. And in Boccaccio's poem nothing occurs which will disturb the reader. In Chaucer on the other hand the effect of the narrator's apparently innocent remark quoted above is not just to make us aware of the double standard Troilus is enmeshed in, but of the double standard the reader himself is unconsciously applying. The effect is to remind us not just that Troilus is perhaps being beguiled by his imagination, but that *we are as well*. We can now see, too, that it is possible to substitute for the dichotomy: authority/experience that of: imagination/reality, and see Chaucer's interest in false exegetes as one aspect of his interest in Truth.

All this may seem to be a great deal to derive from one or two apparently innocent remarks on the part of the apparently neutral narrator, and I certainly don't wish to suggest that all readers of the poem always identify wholly with Troilus. Clearly they don't. He is presented too ironically for that. But I think it is important to see the extent to which we do identify with him, and the implications of our ceasing to do so. Moreover, Chaucer has other means at his disposal than the tone of the narrator to bring home to us the differences between imagination and reality. The chief of these is Pandarus. In the central scene of the poem Pandarus has finally manœuvred Troilus and Criseyde into the same room. It is night, Criseyde is in bed and all the household are asleep. Pandarus pulls Troilus into the room and he realises that all his desires are about to be fulfilled. He rushes forward and kneels at Criseyde's bedside, but then the enormity of the situation bursts on him and he falls into a sudden swoon:

Therwith the sorwe so his herte shette,
That from his eyen fil ther nought a tere,
And every spirit his vigour in knette,
So they astoned or oppressed were.
The felyng of his sorwe, or of his fere,
Or of aught elles, fled was out of towne;
And down he fel al sodeynnly a-swowne.

This was no litel sorwe for to se;
But al was hust, and Pandare up as faste,
'O nece, pes, or we be lost!' quod he,
'Beth naught agast!' but certeyn, at the laste,
For this or that, he into bed hym caste,
And seyde, 'O thef, is this a mannes herte?'
And of he rente al to his bare sherte. . . . (*TC* III 1086–99)

This scene does not exist in Boccaccio. But even if it did we would accept Troilus's swoon without a thought, because the whole poem is written from *within* Troilus's scale of values. But in Chaucer the effect is quite different. The hero swoons as the courtly code tells him to, but the presence of Pandarus and his immediate action of rushing up, pulling off Troilus's shirt, and hoisting him into bed with Criseyde, gives us the sensation of the actual *weight* of the man. We are no longer inside him but, on the contrary, made suddenly aware in a way he does not seem to be himself, of what it means to swoon in the actual world where the sleeping servants may awake at any minute and absolute secrecy is essential.

It has often been remarked that Pandarus stage-manages the whole intrigue. Chaucer stresses his activity, his continous rushing about in order to accomplish that most difficult action, the bringing of the two lovers together. By himself Troilus is helpless, obviously incapable of even thinking of the practicalities of the situation. In most romances this would not matter, since the imagination of the author and reader would combine to turn his subjective desires into reality, even if, as in *Romeo and Juliet*, that reality is to be a tragic one. But in this poem the problems are forced upon us. Pandarus makes us aware of the *effort* involved in bringing the two of them together in the purely physical sense of being within touching distance of each other. By his presence in that central scene, too, he keeps us from entering too completely into Troilus's idealised world, he makes us aware of what the love of Troilus and Criseyde means not just to them, but in actuality.

We would, however, be grossly mistaken if we imagined that Chaucer intended to satirise Troilus for his idealism and wished us to sympathise with Pandarus. Robert Jordan, in one of the best recent studies of Chaucer, to which I have already had occasion to refer, argues that:

> According to Boëthius, and the rationalistic heritage he represents, understanding is attained by withdrawal from the matter addressed. . . . This movement is represented on many levels in *Troilus*. For example, Pandarus' superiority over Troilus is signified by his ability to distinguish between 'game and ernest' (III 253–6), while Troilus can see only the painful 'ernest'. . . .[1]

I will have more to say about the importance of the terms 'game' and 'ernest' later in this chapter. Here I only want to take issue with Jordan on his main thesis, namely that Pandarus is superior to Troilus because he can 'stand back' from the action and Troilus can't. It is certainly true that Pandarus is less involved in the action than Troilus. It is also true that in a poet like Dante the ability to stand back is a sign of greater understanding. But is this really true of Pandarus? Like Sancho Panza, Pandarus's main mode of speech is the proverb, and this means that, like him, he sees all men and women in *general* terms. He can thus say to Troilus, when Criseyde has left, that it is absurd for him to weep for her since there are so many other women left in the world. The trouble with this is that it is *too* general. Proverbs, because they apply to most situations, really apply to none. Pandarus quite fails to understand the particularity of Criseyde, her uniqueness for Troilus. We feel, in fact, that if Troilus stands too close to events to understand their 'real' nature, Pandarus stands too far from them.[2]

*

---

[1] *Chaucer and the Shape of Creation*, 109.
[2] In the early *Parliament of Foules* the goose and lower animals take a Pandarus-like stand while the Eagles respond exactly like Troilus, and again we feel that both are over-rigid in their attitudes.

If Troilus stands for a blind idealism then Pandarus stands for an equally blind 'realism'. The comparison here is not with *Don Quixote* so much as with *Othello*. Like Troilus, Othello is an idealist, a great lover and a great wielder of rhetoric; like Pandarus, Iago thinks of himself as a hard-headed realist, but his realism consists in seeing all human beings in generalised terms; both speak in proverbs and both stage-manage the action. The only difference between them – and of course in terms of the story it is a crucial one – is that Iago hates Othello whereas Pandarus is rather fond of Troilus.

But does this parallel with Shakespeare not confuse rather than clarify? Have I not been arguing that Dante only fully understands the meaning of his life when he is able to look down on the world from God's own point of view and see it as a book written by the Creator? And is this not a replacing of his subjectivity by a new objectivity? There are two points to be made here. First of all, as we have seen, what happens at the climax of the *Commedia* is a fusion of two modes, the subjective and the objective, the linear and the spatial, rather than the simple replacement of one by the other. That is why it is only then that Dante fully understands La Pia's words: 'In His will is our peace.' The second point, linked to this one, is that both Dante and Boëthius had an implicit faith in the meaningfulness and reasonableness of the universe. The pilgrim-poet does not simply accept, but *understands* God's divine plan. The universe is revealed to him as a book, full of a meaning which he can now grasp. Pandarus, on the other hand, understands nothing. He merely applies a set of abstract laws because he knows they *work*. And when these laws fail to take into account the subjectivity of Troilus's love and hence his refusal to submit to them, he is helpless to do anything about it.

In the central scene of *Troilus*, then, we also find ourselves stepping out of a subjective world, but here the subjective and the objective are divided between two different people, each of whom lacks what the other has. Both Troilus and Pandarus are frozen into their set attitudes and beliefs. There is something stiff about them, an inability to accommodate themselves to all the facts. It comes as no surprise, I think, when Troilus, at his death, swings suddenly round to Pandarus's own point of view. This happens when, translated to the eighth sphere, he looks down on the world

of men below him and laughs at human folly. It is a laughter
which shows as little understanding of what his love once meant
to him as Pandarus ever had, a parody of the Boëthian ideal.[1]

What was Chaucer trying to do in this poem? Clearly he is
asking the reader to bring together the points of view of Troilus
and of Pandarus. Though each of them remains shut up in himself, the unrecognised clash between them forces the *reader* into
a recognition both of the power of the imagination and of its
necessary limits.[2] And this is the real and decisive difference
between Chaucer and Boccaccio. It is not just that Chaucer
extends the range of the story; it is that Chaucer is vitally concerned, as Boccaccio is not, with establishing the poem's relation
to the *truth*. It will be recalled that when Dante met Bonaggiunta
of Lucca on the slopes of Purgatory and they discoursed of poetry
it was this honesty to the truth of things that struck the older
poet as being the distinguishing mark of the *dolce stil nuovo*:

> 'O frate, issa veggio,' disse, 'il nodo
>   che il Notaro, e Guittone e me ritenne
>   di qua dal dolce stil nuovo ch'i'odo.
>
> Io veggio ben come le vostre penne
>   di retro al dittator sen vanno strette,
>   che delle nostre certo non avenne.' (*Purgatorio*, xxiv 55–60)[3]

Bonaggiunta is too generous to the other members of Dante's
circle. If we turn to Dante's first book, the *Vita Nuova*, we will
be able to gauge a little more precisely the way in which his pen

---

[1] There is a similar rather hysterical reversal near the end of *Sir Gawain
and the Green Knight*. But that poem encompasses it in the comprehen-
siveness of the court's laughter on Gawain's return, while Chaucer leaves
us once more with a broken poem. See J. A. Burrow, *A Reading of Sir
Gawain and the Green Knight* (London, 1965).

[2] The role of Criseyde in the poem is interesting. If Troilus and Pandarus embody two kinds of 'set' which men bring with them to make sense
of the world, then Criseyde, 'sliding of corage', as Chaucer calls her,
surely embodies the undifferentiated flux itself – she goes with the tide and
does not try to make sense of the world, content only not to be engulfed by
it.

[3] 'O brother,' said he, 'now I see the knot which kept back the Notary
and Guittone and me, short of the sweet new style that I hear. Truly I
see how your pens follow close after him who dictates, which certainly
befell not with ours.'

followed close after 'him who dictates', and how this following close distinguishes him not just from Bonaggiunta, but from Cavalcanti and Boccaccio – and unites him with Chaucer.

The *Vita Nuova* is made up of poems written in Dante's youth which describe his first meeting with Beatrice and the flowering of his love for her, notwithstanding her early death. The poems are linked together by a prose commentary which sets the scene for each poem, explains how it came to be written, how it was received, whether Beatrice took any notice of it, and so on. But its function in the book is far more important than this might suggest; as Singleton has shown, its role is nothing less than crucial.[1] To understand why let us take a famous sonnet as an example:

Tanto gentile e tanto onesta pare
  La donna mia, quand'ella altrui saluta,
  Ch'ogni lingua divien tremando muta,
  E gli occhi non ardiscon di guardare.

Ella sen va, sentendosi laudare,
  Benignamente d'umiltà vestuta;
  E par che sia una cosa venuta
  Di cielo in terra a miracol mostrare.

Mostrasi si piacente a chi la mira,
  Che dà per gli occhi una dolcezza al core,
  Che intender non la può chi non la prova.

E par che della sua labbia si muova
  Uno spirto soave e pien d'amore,
  Che va dicendo all'anima: sospira. (*VN* xxvi)[2]

It is easy to analyse this poem in order to discover some of the methods by which it achieves its effects, but its peculiar power

---

[1] *An Essay on the Vita Nuova* (Harvard, 1948).
[2] 'So gentle and so modest seems my lady when she salutes others that every tongue grows tremblingly dumb and eyes dare not look on her. She goes her way, hearing her praises, benignly clothed in humility, and seems to be a thing come from heaven to earth to show forth a miracle. She shows herself so pleasing to whoever gazes on her that through his eyes she gives a sweetness to his heart such that he who does not experience it cannot understand it. And it seems that from her lips there moves a spirit gentle and filled with love, which goes, saying to the soul: sigh'

stems above all from the assurance with which it speaks, from
that feeling Eliot rightly saw as characteristic of Dante, his way
of making word and meaning one, so that the mind sinks straight
into the heart of the subject, unaware of the language as a separate entity, unaware of any effort or sense of strain, as if this was
the only and obvious way of saying what had to be said. The
skill and effort required to achieve this have been well analysed
by Auerbach, whose comparison with poems on similar themes
by Guinizelli and Cavalcanti demonstrates the possible pitfalls
avoided by Dante.[1] But in his analysis Auerbach forgets one vital
factor: the seemingly innocuous prose text in which the poem is
embedded. This runs, in part:

> This most gentle lady of whom the preceding words were
> spoken came to such favour among folk, that when she passed
> by the way people ran to behold her, wherefore wondrous joy
> possessed me thereat. And when she was near to any one,
> modesty so great possessed his heart that he dared not lift his
> eyes nor respond to her salutations; and of this many even
> from experience could bear witness for me, to him who should
> not believe it. She, crowned and clad in humility went her way,
> showing no pride at what she saw and heard. Said many after
> she had passed: This is no woman, rather is she one of the
> fairest angels of heaven. And others said: This is a marvel and
> blessed be the Lord who knoweth how to work so wondrously![2]

The effect of this, as Singleton has pointed out, is to add a new
dimension to the poem. It can no longer be seen as the effusion
of the poet's love but as the objective truth. What might have
been taken as hyperbole must now be taken as fact. We may not
believe the poet, but he is insistent that the miraculous nature of
Beatrice is not simply his own biased view of her but rather the
view of everyone who came in contact with her. Indeed, the
book is devoted to showing how Dante came to *see* the miraculous nature of Beatrice, rather than how he came to *invest* her
with it. The difference is crucial, and one that we have already
come across. Here the effect is achieved by giving the poems and
the prose commentaries each a different status within the one

[1] *Dante: Poet of the Secular World*, trans. Ralph Mannheim (Chicago,
1961) ch. ii.
[2] I have used the Temple Classics translation by Thomas Okey.

book. For the poems are acknowledged to have been written by Dante in his youth and now transcribed in this book; but the linking prose passages are not a transcription of anything previously *written*, but of *events that took place*. Or, as Singleton puts it, they *are* written, but by God rather than Dante. Thus when Dante finds that Beatrice is always associated with the number nine and deduces from this that this expresses her miraculous nature (the square of the Trinity), we must take care not to dismiss this as the poet's 'reading' of the number nine into the events of her life. On the contrary, he insists that they are there, put into her life by God, so to speak, to signify something to those who will learn how to read in a spiritual instead of a foolish natural way. Of course we have no evidence one way or the other, since Beatrice lives for us only in Dante's lines; but the fact is that Dante accommodates our incredulity by the construction of his book. By stressing the fact that the poems are *his* work he makes us accept the narrative as the work of *God*. No less than in the *Commedia* his task here is the difficult one of *scribe* rather than the easy one of *inventor*.

For all we know too, the poems of Dante's older contemporaries, Guido Guinizelli and Guido Cavalcanti, may also have been transcripts of reality rather than hyperbolic praise of their ladies. But the fact is we don't know. The question seems to have troubled these poets as little as it troubled Boccaccio. But it did trouble Dante. He could not rest till he had made manifest the truth of his assertions, the honesty of his transcriptions. This honesty, which is his distinctive quality, is the product not just of artistry but of existential commitment: his own life alters as he comes to understand the meaning of Beatrice, and he wants the reader to understand that *his* life may alter as well.

A similar honesty, we can now see, pervades the work of Chaucer. But it is an honesty that works in a way diametrically opposite to Dante's. Where Dante is concerned to stress the truth of his vision, Chaucer is concerned to stress the private and subjective nature of *Troilus's*. Instead of affirming the truth of Troilus's vision he makes us see that all visions are subjective and dependent on the presuppositions we bring to them. He holds the poem up before us and says: 'The Truth is: not this.'[1] Where

---

[1] Compare Wittgenstein's comment in the 1914-16 *Notebooks*: 'Think of the representation of *negative* facts by means of models. E.g.: two rail-

Dante tries to break down our prejudices and the misreadings to which we are naturally inclined by showing us his own progress from our position to the truth, Chaucer presents us with mirrors of our natural reactions and thus frees us from bondage to them. To read a poem like *Troilus* is to be made aware that our private experience, our imagination and the world are always dangerously at odds.

II. THE CHAUCERIAN NARRATOR

But to say only this is to remain too coolly objective in our view of Chaucer's art. It is true that, like Dante, he is concerned with freeing our minds from the prejudices of the 'foolish natural man'. But for Dante, we saw, this was itself something he too had had to struggle to achieve. Is there not evidence of a similar struggle in Chaucer? He may be impartial and ironic, playing off experience against authority and authority against experience, but, as we saw, his work is littered with unfinished fragments. Even *Troilus* seems to be caught in its own contradictions, and the rough ways of the Wife of Bath with her husband's book find an uncomfortable echo in the ending of that poem, when Chaucer, addressing his book, prays to God that 'non myswrite the,/Ne the mysmetre for defaute of tongue . . .'. Books too are subject to decay, and when they cease to be understood then what is there left of their author? The startlingly unmedieval quality of this lament should warn us that, if he shares with Dante a concern for truth, Chaucer's different way of manifesting this concern may be the result of more than a difference of temperament. To be caught between experience and authority, able to trust neither, may have far-reaching and sometimes fatal consequences for the creation of fictions. It is time to look at the springs of Chaucer's narrative art.

The Book of the Duchess is Chaucer's first major poem; it is also, as far as we know, his only extended *public* poem, being an elegy on the death of Blanche, the first wife of Chaucer's patron, John of Gaunt. This fact is in itself surprising when we consider

---

way trains must not stand on the rails in such-and-such a way. The proposition, the picture, the model are – in the negative sense – like a solid body restricting the freedom of movement of others; in the positive sense, like the space bounded by solid substance, in which there is room for a body.' (14. 11. 1914.) Cf. *Tractatus*, 4.463.

the quantity of public poems produced by later court poets such
as Skelton and Dunbar, and it is one more indication of the
strangely non-medieval quality of this fourteenth-century poet.
But what is even more surprising is that an author of Chaucer's
calibre should make such a hash of the poem – not as a poem, but
as a formal, public elegy. Clearly there must be very strong forces
at work playing against the professionalism and expertise of a
poet who was already, after all, in his late twenties or early
thirties.[1]

The formal elegy that lies at the centre of *The Book of the
Duchess* is placed in a rather elaborate setting. The poet begins
by drawing a picture of himself as an insomniac, a man who can
sleep neither by day nor by night and is consequently

> as yt were, a mased thyng,
> Alway in poynt to falle a-doun,
> For sorwful ymagynacioun
> Ys alway hooly in my mynde. (*BD* 12–15)

He is, however, a great reader of books, and it is in one of
these, which tells the story of Ceyx and Alcyon, that he finds
a possible remedy for insomnia. Reading in the tale how the
god of sleep was propitiated, he decides to offer to Morpheus

> Yif he wol make me slepe a lyte,
> Of down of pure dowves white
> I will yive hym a fether-bed,
> Rayed with gold, and ryght wel cled
> In fyn blak satyn doutremer. . . . (*BD* 249–53)

As with Chauntecleer he has hardly spoken when
> sodeynly, I nyste how,   [do not know how]
> Such a lust anoon me took
> To slepe, that ryght upon my book
> Y fil aslepe. . . . (*BD* 272–5)

He now dreams that it is morning and that he wakes up in a
beautiful ·room. It is spring, and the sound of a hunt preparing
to set out comes in through the window. He gets up and joins the
hunt, but after a while he strays from the main body and, round-

---

[1] Since Blanche died in 1369 and Chaucer was born around 1340 he
must have been about thirty.

ing a corner, comes upon a knight dressed all in black, groaning
and lamenting:

> I stalked even unto hys bak,
> And there I stood as stille as ought,
> That, soth to saye, he saw me nought;
> For-why he heng hys hed adoun,
> And with a dedly sorwful soun
> He made of rym ten vers or twelve
> Of a compleynte to hymselve,
> The moste pitee, the moste rouwthe,
> That ever I herde. . . . (*BD* 458–66)

This is a lament for the woman the Black Knight has lost, and
whom he describes at great length to the poet when he finally
becomes aware of the latter's presence. The poet is interested, and
inquires more closely as to why he is lamenting. The Knight
explains that he has played chess with Fortune and lost his Queen:

> 'A, goode sir,' quod I, 'say not soo!
> Have some pitee on your nature
> That formed yow to creature.
> Remembre yow of Socrates,
> For he ne counted nat thre strees
> Of noght that Fortune koude doo.'
> 'No,' quod he, 'I kan not soo.'
> 'Why so? syr, yis parde!' quod y;
> 'Ne say noght soo, for trewely,
> Thogh ye had lost the ferses twelve,   [chess queens]
> And ye for sorwe mordred yourselve,
> Ye sholde be dampned in this cas
> By as good ryght as Medea was,
> That slough hir children for Jasoun;
> And Phyllis also for Demophoun
> Heng hirself, so weylaway! . . .
> And for Dalida died Sampson,
> That slough hymself with a piler.
> But ther is no man alyve her
> Wolde for a fers make this woo!' (*BD* 714–41)

The scene is ludicrous. The poet, a real literalist of the
imagination (witness his offer of a feather-bed to Morpheus), is

so intent on citing his examples of fortitude that he entirely fails
to see that the Black Knight is speaking metaphorically! How
absurd, he says, whoever heard of anyone making all this fuss
just for a chess queen! I could understand it for a real live person,
but to lament in this fashion for *that*! It is only very much later
in the poem that the misunderstanding is at last cleared up and the
poet grasps the fact that the Black Knight has only been speaking
metaphorically, that it is his wife, Blanche, who is dead.

We have grown so used to this kind of misunderstanding in
Chaucer that it may take us some time to see the damage it does
to the main theme of the poem. Not only does the absurdity of
the literalist poet-dreamer draw our attention away from the
object of the Black Knight's plaint, the death of Blanche, but,
more importantly, the dreamer's naïvety throws a sudden doubt
upon the lament itself. The doubt does not turn into a genuine
question, as in the case of Troilus, because it really has no place
in the poem, but certainly our first image of the Black Knight,
since it comes to us refracted through the eyes of the naïve poet,
makes us suddenly aware of the high element of posturing involved in such an action, which a straightforward presentation
would never have done. In a similar way the poet's innocent
astonishment at such lamentation being indulged in for a chess
queen draws attention to the metaphor *as metaphor*, and thus to
its artificial and willed quality. All in all, the effect of presenting
the elegy in this way, through the eyes of a narrator so naïve that
he takes everything at its face value, is to throw into relief the unnatural and rhetorical element in the lament. Because the praise
of Blanche is filtered through the mouth of the Black Knight and
the ears of the poet-narrator, attention is drawn away from the
object to the mode of presentation itself, which is seen as artificial
and to some degree both pompous and absurd. None of this would
have happened if the poem had been a straight elegy, since its
very formality would have been proof of the poet's high concern.
But Chaucer seems deliberately to mar a public poem by developing his own private interests. This suggests that these were of more
vital concern to him than such phrases as 'experiment with point
of view' or 'interest in the use of narratorial persona' would tend
to suggest. The question we have to ask ourselves is this: Why
did Chaucer feel this overriding need to draw attention to the
speaker of the elegy, instead of letting the elegy speak for itself?

Any answer to this question is clearly going to involve an examination of Chaucer's use of the first-person narrator. The whole structure of *Piers Plowman* and the *Commedia* rests, as we saw, on the assumption that each reader can substitute himself for the hero, the 'I' figure. This is the essential condition of the allegory, and it rests on the medieval analogical view of human character: the 'I' is not so much a 'rounded figure' (though we are given some details about him) as a pair of eyes and an affective system no different from our own. Like us he is lost to begin with, but if we stay with him (in him?) we too will be led to vision and understanding. In Chaucer, on the other hand, as Rosemary Woolf has pointed out, from the early dream visions right through to *The Canterbury Tales*, we find an 'I' figure who appears as naïve, well-meaning and obtuse, the joke depending on our grasping the *discrepancy* between this figure and his witty creator. 'Thus,' says Rosemary Woolf, 'this treatment of the "I" character is new in that it presupposes the poet in a way that the other characters do not.'[1] In other words, a tension is set up between the reader, the poem and the poet, which forms the basis of the irony which is the dominant mode of Chaucer's work.

But to say this is not to say enough. The use of a naïve narrator is more than a joke, it is a positive obsession with Chaucer, as we saw in the example of *The Book of the Duchess*. Instead of allowing us to identify with the 'I' figure Chaucer does everything he can to stop us doing so. He creates the picture of a man who is so naïve, so ill-at-ease in the world, so inexperienced in its ways that we cannot possibly identify with him. But he also takes great pains to draw our attention to the private and subjective nature of this man's vision and of the absurd bias of his interpretation of whatever happens to him. In the early dream visions, for example, the parallel between the book read by the poet before he goes to sleep and the dream he then has serves to stress the purely idiosyncratic, non-prophetic nature of the dream. When, in *The House of Fame*, he tells us that his dream took place on 'the tenthe day now of Decembre' he started a veritable mare's nest of scholarly speculation on the significance of the choice of that date; but the point of the phrase is surely the mock-precision, the fact that the date means a great deal to the narrator, but *only to him*.

---

[1] 'Chaucer as a Satirist in the General Prologue', *Critical Quarterly*, I (1959) 151.

Like the lament of the Nun's Priest ('And on a Friday fell all this mischance'), the precision makes us aware of the private and meaningless nature of the whole incident. Once again, if scholars had been a little less concerned over the content of Chaucer's work and paid a bit more attention to its tone, they might have saved themselves a lot of trouble.

In *Troilus* the narrator's literalness and naïvety takes the form of a determination to follow his sources as closely as possible all the time. Of course Chaucer does not follow *his* sources all that closely, and naturally he need not have chosen this particular story if he had not wanted to. Thus the narrator's insistence on the literal and historical truth of his tale is another reminder that in one sense the tale is not true at all.[1] When he comes to *The Canterbury Tales* Chaucer combines the dreamer-narrator of the early poems with the historian-narrator of *Troilus*. He creates a naïve narrator who takes part in the action, but he makes of him a mere reporter of events and stories over which he has no control, a reporter dedicated to the 'truth' of what he says, even at the risk of offending those readers with sensitive tastes, as he points out in the general prologue:

> But first I pray yow, of youre curteisye,
> That ye n'arette it nat my vileynye,
> Thogh that I pleynly speke in this mateere,
> To telle yow hir wordes and hir cheere,
> Ne thogh I speke hir wordes proprely.
> For this ye knowen al so wel as I,
> Whoso shal telle a tale after a man,
> He moot reherce as ny as evere he kan
> Everich a word, if it be in his charge,
> Al speke he never so rudeliche and large,
> Or ellis he moot telle his tale untrewe,
> Or feyne thyng, or fynde wordes newe.
> He may nat spare, althogh he were his brother;

[1] The historian-narrator's insistence on the fact that he has no control over the action, that he must tell it as it happened, since what we are dealing with is not fiction but history, also has the effect of pulling us back from Troilus's subjective vision, and is one of the reasons why the last two books make such painful reading – there is no place for histrionics here: Troilus, like Tolstoy's Ivan Ilyitch, is made to see at the last what life really is.

He moot as wel seye o word as another.
Crist spak hymself ful brode in hooly writ,
And wel ye woot no vileynye is it.
Eek Plato seith, whoso that kan hym rede,
The wordes moote be cosyn to the dede. (*CT* 1 725–42)

The narrator appeals to a higher authority, fidelity to fact, to exonerate him from charges of bawdiness. But this naïve faith in 'the facts' as being synonymous with 'the truth' reminds us once again that all facts have to be interpreted, that since not all 'the facts' can get into a book (or a painting) a choice will have to be made, and that since this is the case we are far less likely to trust someone who is not aware of this than someone who is. Our litera-list of the imagination is unlikely to prove the most reliable of narrators.

It will be recalled that as Dante entered the ninth circle of Hell he called on the Muses to help him convey the dreadful sight before him:

Ma quelle Donne aiutino il mio verso,
ch'aiutaro Anfion a chiuder Tebe,
si che dal fatto il dir non sia diverso.[1]

These words seem remarkably close to those just quoted from the general prologue, but the effect is exactly the opposite. Because we trust Dante the pilgrim we accept his statement of the diffi-culty which confronts him and of the effort involved in reproduc-ing as accurately as possible what he sees before him; indeed, we actually *make* the effort *with* him. But in Chaucer, because the poet has so carefully dissociated the narrator from himself and from us, the insistence on fact serves only as a further reminder that the whole thing is an invention of the poet's. In Chaucer the 'I' figure is the teller of the tale, the reporter of other men's tales, but he is not the hero, he does not develop an understanding of what the world is like – in fact, he understands as little about it at the end, we feel, as he did at the beginning: like the bookish dreamers of the early poems, he remains entirely closed to experience.

Chaucer's strategy is quite simple: he isolates the narrator and, by making us laugh at him, makes sure that we recognise that

---

[1] See above, p. 35

he is a pure invention of the author's. Everything that this character then says will obviously be the result of an elaboration of
this invention, and the more he insists on the truth of what he
tells the more we will remember that the 'truth' about the teller
is that the poet has made him up. It is not very difficult to see
why Chaucer does this. If his primary concern is with the truth,
as our examination of *Troilus* has demonstrated, then the first
truth to set out is that the poem is not truth but an invention of
his own. St Augustine makes this simple point clearly when, in
his *Soliloquia*, discussing the nature of artistic illusion, he says:

> For how could he whom I have mentioned [the actor Roscius]
> have been a true tragedian, had he been unwilling to be a false
> Hector, a false Andromache, a false Hercules, and innumerable
> other things? or how would a picture, for instance, be a true
> picture, unless it were a false horse? . . . Wherefore, if it avails
> some things that they be somewhat false in order that they
> may be somewhat true; why do we so greatly dread falsity, and
> seek truth as the greatest good?[1]

From the beginning of his career, as we have seen, Chaucer found
it impossible to present a story without reminding us that it came
out of the head of a particular man – or rather, out of the mouth
of a particular man – even when this kind of information went
against the tone of the rest of his poem. And as the quotation
from St Augustine shows, it is possible to find theological backing
for this point of view as much as for that of Dante or Langland.
For to forget this truth and to speak (as the expressive lyric poet
does) as though what 'I' have seen is somehow more true, more
worthy of record than what everyone else sees, is to commit the
sin of pride, the very sin through which Lucifer fell, and which
the York *Creation* play, for example, presents so vividly in Lucifer's own words:

> All the mirth that is made is marked in me!
> The beams of my brighthead are burning so bright,
> And I so seemly in sight myself now I see,
> For like a lord am I left to lend in this light.
> More fairer by far than my feres,
> In me is no point that may pair;

---

[1] Quoted in Singleton, *Commedia: Elements of Structure*, 64.

I feel me featous and fair,
My power is passing my peers.[1]

The insistence on the 'I' here reveals the poet's skill in allowing Lucifer to condemn himself. The 'I' of a Dante or a Langland is an 'I' in the process of self-discovery; they would be poor guides were they to remain in the state they are in at the beginning of those poems.

Unlike Dante and Langland, Chaucer feels himself to be essentially a story-teller, and he is keenly aware of the folly of such an activity for one who is also concerned with truth. The only way he can differentiate himself from a January or a Chauntecleer is by stressing his own self-awareness. He is like them in all save his consciousness that he is like them. Spinning stories out of his head, he takes great care to isolate the voice that narrates from the person that he is. Like St Augustine he can say: 'I have done nothing but wish to speak; if I have spoken, I have not said what I wished to say.'[2] By creating the *persona* of a dreamer, a historian, a reporter, he distinguishes himself from that part of himself which desires to tell a story, and reminds the reader too that he must not sit back and allow his own imagination to help give solidity to the tale – for the tale has no solidity, it consists only of words issuing out of the mouth of the naïve *persona*.

Scholars have recently had a field day demonstrating the way Chaucer uses his *personae* and reprimanding older critics for confusing the author and the narrator. But this, though a step in the right direction, does not really get to the heart of the problem. Indeed, it has tended to perpetuate the idea that Chaucer is intent on creating 'character', even the character of a narrator, as though his overabundant creative power could not stop itself. But the essential similarity of all the *personae*, the fact that their voice, their *tone*, is so similar from poem to poem, should alert us to the inexactitude of such a description. It is not the *persona* who is ultimately important and needs to be understood, it is the *tone* of Chaucer's narration. The creation of a narrator who is other than the author is only the most obvious way of calling attention to this tone, of reminding us of the fact that we are in

[1] *Everyman and Medieval Miracle Plays*, ed. A. C. Cawley (London, 1967) 5.

[2] *On Christian Doctrine*, trans. D. W. Robertson Jr (New York, 1958) 10–11.

the presence not of 'the truth', but of a story being narrated. The most obvious, but not the only one. The problem of the narratorial *persona* must be subsumed under the larger problem of Chaucer's *rhetoric*. When we have understood the reasons for the ways Chaucer uses language, we will have understood not only the reasons for Chaucer's curiously ragged (though abundant) output, but also the ways in which he triumphed over seemingly impossible conditions.

As an example of how Chaucer's rhetoric works let us take the Nun's Priest's Tale. We have already seen Chaucer at work here in the use made of authorities by Chauntecleer and Pertelote. Let us turn from them for a moment and look at the manner of narration itself. The teller of this story is obviously highly conscious both of himself and of his task, and determined to tell his tale in as impressive a way as possible. Having presented us with the altercation of the two main characters over the nature of dreams, he turns and addresses us directly:

> But sodeynly hym fil a sorweful cas,
> For evere the latter ende of joye is wo.
> God woot that worldly joye is soone ago;
> And if a rethour koude faire endite,
> He in a cronycle saufly myghte it write
> As for a sovereyn notabilitee.
> Now every wys man, lat him herkne me;
> This storie is also trewe, I undertake,
> As is the book of Launcelot de Lake,
> That wommen holde in ful greet reverence.
> Now wol I torne agayn to my sentence. (*CT* VII 3204–14)

But turn again to his 'sentence' is just what he seems unable to do. The story simply won't get under way. He starts to tell us about the fox lying in wait for Chauntecleer, but then the enormity of the crime about to be committed (or his own sense of how this crime should be presented) proves too much for him, and he launches into a passage of rhetorical lament:

> O false mordrour, lurkynge in thy den!
> O newe Scariot, newe Genylon,
> False dissymulour, o Greek Synon,
> That broghtest Troye al outrely to sorwe!

O Chauntecleer, acursed be that morwe
That thou into that yerd flaugh fro the bemes.
(*CT* VII 3226–31)

It is not enough to say that this is mock-heroic. What is important
is that the tone is clearly wrong. The narrator is making too much
of it. We have seen other laments in Chaucer – that of Troilus,
of the Black Knight. There the effect of bathos was achieved by
the device of having someone else looking on, or having the narrator intrude with a common-sense comment. Neither of these
devices is employed here, and yet the effect is very much the
same. But this time it is simply by overdoing it that the narrator
draws our attention to himself and away from his subject-matter.
Because the tone is too high for the content the decorum is now
seen as artifice and the *voice* of the narrator makes itself heard,
struggling with the material.

But even at this point the narrator does not get on with his
story. Instead he modulates into a long discourse on free-will and
predestination:

Thou were ful wel ywarned by thy dremes
That thilke day was perilous to thee;
But what that God forwoot moot nedes bee,
After the opinioun of certeyn clerkis.
Witnesse on hym that any parfit clerk is,
That in scole is greet altercacioun
In this mateere, and greet disputisoun,
And hath been of an hundred thousand men.
But I ne kan nat bulte it to the bren,
As kan the hooly doctour Augustyn,
Or Boece, or the Bisshop Bradwardyn,
Wheither that Goddes worthy forwityng
Streyneth me nedely for to doon a thyng,–
'Nedely' clepe I symple necessitee;
Or elles, if free choys be graunted me
To do that same thyng, or do it noght,
Though God forwoot it er that it was wroght;
Or if his wityng streyneth never a deel
But by necessitee condicioneel.
I wol nat han to do of swich mateere;
My tale is of a cok, as ye may heere. . . . (*CT* VII 3232–52)

Scholars have usually fastened on the substance of this passage and ignored the tone. But as in similar discourses elsewhere in Chaucer the important thing is not *what* is said but *how* it is said. The narrator is clearly incompetent. He cannot cope with these hard problems, yet he will keep on trying. He is totally unaware of his ineptitude, though he does seem to have a nagging feeling that he ought to get his story under way again. The shoddy bit of non-argument which he here presents is simply the reverse of the uncontrolled high rhetoric into which he soon plunges once again as the plot gathers to a climax:

> And daun Russell the fox stirte up atones,
> And by the gargat hente Chauntecleer,
> And on his bak toward the wode hym beer,
> For yet ne was ther no man that hym sewed.
>   O destinee, that mayst nat been eschewed!
> Allas, that Chauntecleer fleigh fro the bemes!
> Allas, his wyf ne roghte nat of dremes!
> And on a Friday fil al this meschaunce.
>   O Venus, that art goddesse of plesaunce. . . .
>
> (*CT* VII 3334–41)

The plaint goes on for another forty lines, with many examples, drawn from the *Aeneid* and other classical sources, to bring home to us the full horror of the situation. The effect, however, is exactly the reverse. As in the famous passage in *Don Quixote* where the narrator stops the story short with the hero in the middle of deadly combat, or those parts of *Tristram Shandy* where a digression leaves us infuriatingly in the air at some decisive stage in the action (or what we imagine to be some decisive stage), the inept rhetoric here pulls us back from participation in the *event* and into a contemplation of the *words*. The rhetoric draws attention to itself as rhetoric, just as the ponderous mention of the date ('And on a Friday fil al this mischaunce') only reveals how ludicrous it is to try and see in this barnyard incident the working of fate through dreams and the planets.

But why does Chaucer use rhetoric in this way? Is it in order to characterise the Nun's Priest? One has only to raise the question to see its absurdity, yet scholars have devoted much time and ingenuity to trying to link tale and teller in *The Canterbury Tales*. Now it is true that this works to a limited extent in some of the tales, particularly those where Chaucer devotes a considerable amount of space to the actual prologue of the tale, as with the Wife of Bath or the Pardoner. But the trouble with this kind of approach is that it brings back the error of imagining that Chaucer is primarily interested in the creation of character. The striking thing about *this* narrator, however, is how similar his tone is to that of the naïve *persona* we have already examined. The reason why the tales are told by the pilgrims on their way to Canterbury is not so that an extra dimension may be added to their characters, but so that the poet can isolate the tone, and thus remind us that what we have before us are essentially stories, told by people, not things which have 'really happened'. It does not matter who the tellers are or what they are like, so long as we are made aware of the fact that they are tellers.

If this is a correct account of the facts then we are finally in a position to say something about Chaucer's rhetoric. Payne and Jordan, in the books referred to earlier, have both argued that Chaucer uses rhetoric like any medieval poet, building in blocks of pre-existing material in the way we saw Dante doing. They are surely right to stress the fact that the nineteenth-century opposition between rhetoric and naturalness, convention and originality, is a false one, born of Romantic (and, as we will see, ultimately Renaissance) notions of what constitutes the creative process. We have already seen how Dante uses rhetoric to create a poem that will be the model of the universe. But the dualistic scheme (medieval/modern) with which Payne and Jordan operate simply won't fit the facts. To say (as they do) that because Chaucer is not like Henry James he must be like Dante is to play into the hands of the Renaissance-orientated historians of literature they wish to oppose.

We have seen Dante employing rhetoric. When he does so his personality disappears inside the language, leaving us only with the object. Like all the greatest art of the high Middle Ages, the *Commedia* is lucid, transparent, a machine for seeing. But in Chaucer things are different. Like Rabelais and Sterne, Chaucer uses rhetoric in order to reveal it as rhetoric, as nothing but rhetoric. Even when he has a simple public elegy to write he cannot refrain from drawing our attention to the tools he is using.[1] For he is caught in a particular dilemma. Unlike Dante,

[1] The Knight's Tale is a puzzle. Surely the way to read it is as the

he no longer seems to have faith in the essential meaningfulness of the universe created by God; unlike Boccaccio he is unwilling to ignore the limited and subjective basis of his private creations. He is too conscious of the fact that all language is conventional and artificial, that all fiction is the product of a human and all too fallible author. So he builds his narratives and draws our attention to the blocks out of which they are built as well as to the process of building. He cannot make a statement without reminding us that it is only one man's statement, that he could equally well have said the opposite. And in the way he brings the rhetoric to our attention I would suggest that he is at one with a great many late medieval artists – the late Gothic architects, painters, composers and poets. All seem to share a distrust of subjectivity without a corresponding confidence in the objective. Hence theirs is an art of wild decoration, of excessive rhetoric, rather than one of simple expression (a good comparison to make is between one of Taverner's settings of the Mass and Bach's St Matthew Passion). Sometimes, indeed, we feel that the decoration becomes frenzied to keep from the artist's mind the fact that it is decoration round a hollow, an emptiness, a silence. In a rather similar way we find Donne and Marvell making use of the traditions of the Middle Ages, but putting a bracket round them, as it were, reminding us of the fact that they reserve judgement as to their ultimate status.[1] We are here in a world which is not that of Dante or of Boccaccio and Leonardo, a world, as we shall see, which has much in common with that of modern fiction.

III. FICTION AND GAME IN 'THE CANTERBURY TALES'

Chaucer differs from most other late medieval artists in that his rhetorical play is genial and ironic rather than hectic and des-

---

Knight's own conception of what a story should be. It is *too* orderly, *too* patterned. The frequent recurrence of the link-phrase 'But whether by aventure or cas' gives the game away. It is not by 'cas' (Providence, necessity), but by sheer 'aventure' (chance, the narrator's desire for pattern) that the story is constructed. The Deity here is too much like Theseus, one of the few genuine authority-figures in Chaucer. Contrast what age does to *him* with what it does to January, say. No less than the paintings on the Temple walls, the tale proclaims itself as artifact.

[1] Christopher Ricks made this point in a talk which has not, so far as I know, been published.

perate. Nevertheless, as we have seen, the irony does not always imply an overall control. It is, in fact, only in his last work that he manages to overcome the apparently impossible conditions with which, as a story-teller and a devotee of the truth, he is faced, and he does this by making explicit the notion of art as game which had been implicit in his work from the very beginning.

By distinguishing himself from his narrator Chaucer, as we have seen, turned the ensuing fiction into a game between himself and the reader. He is able to introduce this notion of game more easily and effectively in *The Canterbury Tales* because here the game played with the reader coincides with another game, played within the fiction, by the pilgrims themselves. Thus the kind of relationship Chaucer establishes between himself, his poem and the reader is mirrored in the relationship established within the poem between the pilgrim story-tellers, their tales and their audience.

It is the Host who first suggests that the pilgrims play a game in order to relieve the boredom of the journey to Canterbury, and it is he who lays down the rules for this game when the company assents to his suggestion. Each pilgrim is to tell two tales on the way to the shrine and two on the way back; the teller of the best tale is to be given dinner by all the other pilgrims; and anyone who fails to abide by the decisions of the Host is to pay a forfeit. The pilgrims agree to these rules, and, with the drawing of the shortest 'cut' by the Knight on the following morning, the game is on. The ensuing tales, then, are not simply stories told to pass away the time on the road to Canterbury; they are part of a game, with rules of its own, which all the pilgrims have agreed to play. As with the game the poet and the reader have agreed to play, it takes place in the context of real life, but the participants are answerable to none of the laws which govern real life, only to those rules which they have agreed upon beforehand.

The Host, who has set himself up as arbiter, has, it soon transpires, very clear ideas as to what it is he requires of a story. His words to the Clerk sum up his attitude:

> Telle us som myrie tale, by youre fey!
> For what man that is entred in a pley,
> He nedes moot unto the pley assente.
> But precheth nat, as freres doon in Lente,

To make us for oure olde synnes wepe,
Ne that thy tale make us nat to slepe. (*CT* IV 9–14)

His first requirement is that the story must not be boring. He is willing to listen to a tale in the high or the low style, in prose or in verse, a saint's life or a fabliau, but if he considers it boring then he has no hesitation in cutting it short and asking for something better. The ultimate crime of the storyteller, in his eyes, is that of sending his audience to sleep, since to do so is to destroy the very raison d'être of the story – as he points out to the Monk, you can't very well tell a tale if there aren't any listeners.

It is partly for this reason too that the Host warns pilgrim after pilgrim not to preach. A sermon, for the Host, represents the height of boredom. But there is another reason for his objection to preaching, which is related to this but is not to be confused with it. What the Host really objects to is that the preacher has designs on his listeners. Although Harry Bailly never loses a chance to attack or ridicule preachers, he has nothing against them as such. He simply feels that they have no place in his game. For, believing as they do that what is not true must be false, they fail to understand that a game stands outside this antithesis, and hence themselves tend to disregard the rules under which a game is played.

The Parson seems to be the chief offender in this respect. In the general prologue we are given a picture of him as an ideal figure who, with the Knight, the Plowman and the Clerk, forms a contrast to all the other pilgrims by virtue of the fact that with him word and deed are one: 'first he wrought and afterwards he taught'. In all the other ecclesiastics and in most of the laymen the gap between word and deed is more or less large, and one of the functions of the irony in the general prologue is to reveal the degree of deviation. Yet this idealised picture of the Parson is contradicted on at least two separate occasions in the body of the text before the Parson tells his own tale which brings the poem to a fitting conclusion.

In the epilogue to the Man of Law's Tale the Host turns to the Parson and asks for a tale, 'By Goddes dignitee'. The Parson's only answer is to reprove him for swearing, whereupon he turns to the other pilgrims in mock surprise and warns them that 'they shal han a predicacioun', and that 'this Lollere here wil prechen

us somewhat'. At this the Shipman leaps in and swears that no
one is going to preach in this place. The Parson subsides into
silence, but the next time he and the Host clash it is he who wins
the victory. For some unknown reason Chaucer changed his
mind about the number of tales he was going to tell and in the
Parson's prologue it emerges that all the tales have been told
except his own. The Host thus turns to him:

> 'Sire preest,' quod he, 'artow a vicary?
> Or arte a person? sey sooth, by thy fey!
> Be what thou be, ne breke thou nat oure pley;
> For every man, save thou, hath toold his tale . . .
> Telle us a fable anon, for cokkes bones!' (*CT* x 22-9)

But once again the Parson rebukes him: he will take part in the
'pley', but only on his own terms:

> 'Thou getest fable noon ytoold for me;
> For Paul, that writeth unto Thymothee,
> Repreveth hem that weyven soothfastnesse,
> And tellen fables and swich wrecchednesse . . .
>
> For which I seye, if that yow list to heere .
> Moralitee and vertuous mateere,
> And thanne that ye wol yeve me audience,
> I wol ful fayn, at Cristes reverence,
> Do yow plesaunce leefful, as I kan.' (*CT* x 31-41)

The figure who emerges from these two scenes is hardly that of
the ideal ecclesiastic of the general prologue. He is a type as
familiar as the Friar or the Summoner, a medieval Puritan,
rigidly opposed to any form of swearing and to all but overtly
moral tales on the grounds that they are lies and thus conducive
to sin. He is no different, in fact, from the real-life author of the
Wycliffite sermon which condemned the playing of Corpus
Christi plays and argued that only things done 'in earnest' were
relevant to the Christian life.[1] Yet in saying this I am aware that
I raise a problem, since the Parson, at this stage in the poem, is
clearly intended to be a figure of authority, whom the reader,

---

[1] See Kolve, *The Play Called Corpus Christi*, 18. The whole of his
second chapter, 'The Corpus Christi Drama as Play and Game', is relevant
to this discussion.

like the pilgrims, is asked to respect. After all, he ends the tales, and he ends them with a sermon, designed, as he says

> To shewe yow the wey, in this viage,
> Of thilke parfit glorious pilgrymage
> That highte Jerusalem celestial. (*CT* x 49–51)

I feel though that there is a clash of interests here similar to that found in *The Book of the Duchess*: here a Dantesque scheme of movement upwards to a final goal comes into conflict with the very Chaucerian scheme of seeing the whole work as a game, mirroring the game played by the pilgrims themselves, and therefore without beginning or end in any strictly linear sense. This last scene and the Parson's actual sermon do not present us with quite such a blatant cutting off of the main themes of the rest of the work as we find in *Troilus*, because the themes of truth and falsehood, art and life, are still present. What does happen is that they are resolved in terms of the very order and hierarchy on whose validity, or at least availability to man, grave doubts had been cast by the rest of the poem.

What the Host objects to in the Parson, then, is his tendency to destroy the game by substituting his own rules (which, he insists, are the rules of God and hence govern the universe) for those agreed upon by the pilgrims. But Harry Bailly is not really as disinterested himself as he would have us believe. To begin with there is the question of the prize dinner. Whoever wins, at least part of the proceeds will go to the keeper of the Tabard, since he has undertaken to prepare the prize meal. But there is another, less obviously material advantage, which accrues to the organiser of the game: his role as referee allows him to indulge his love of mockery and sarcasm, his need to command and control, all under cover of the rules. Thus he can insult the Cook and Monk to their faces while avoiding censure by immediately reminding them to 'be nat wroth for game;/A man may saye ful sooth in game and pley'. The Parson refuses to play the game. He confuses fiction and falsehood and stands firm in his determination to preach a sermon rather than tell a tale. The Host plays the game, but he is even more at fault than the Parson since he plays it for his own ends. So long as it is he who makes the jokes he is only too eager to invoke the game as an excuse; but as soon as the joke turns on him he forgets all about the game and its rules in his blind anger at the joker. This is just what happens at the climax of the Pardoner's Tale: as the Pardoner finishes, Harry Bailly finds that for the first time the joke is on him, and he does not like it.

The Pardoner's Prologue and Tale stands at the centre of *The Canterbury Tales* and demonstrates the final twist of Chaucer's convoluting irony. Quite simply, the Pardoner tells the assembled company of pilgrims that he is going to fool them with his words, and then he goes ahead and does so. As the pilgrims drink in the conclusion of his moral tale of the three rioters who come to a bad end, and submit to its inevitable application to the present:

> Now, goode men, God foryeve yow youre trespas,
> And ware yow fro the synne of avarice!
> Myn hooly pardoun may yow alle warice,
> So that ye offre nobles or sterlynges,
> Or elles silver broches, spoones, rynges. . . . (*CT* vi 904–8)

they automatically reach into their pockets, their hearts warm with the glow of goodness, to buy themselves a pardon – only to be brought up short by the sudden realisation that the Pardoner is only going through his old routine, explained to them at some length only a short while before:

> Myne handes and my tonge goon so yerne
> That it is joye to se my bisynesse.
> Of avarice and of swich cursednesse
> Is al my prechyng, for to make hem free
> To yeven hir pens, and namely unto me.
> For myn entente is nat but for to wynne,
> And nothyng for coreccioun of synne. (*CT* vi 398–404)

The reaction of the Host when this dawns on him is violent in the extreme:

> But, by the croys which that Seint Eleyne fond,
> I wolde I hadde thy coillons in myn hond
> In stide of relikes or of seintuarie. (*CT* vi 951–3)

At this the Pardoner grows speechless with indignation and a fight seems about to ensue when the Knight intervenes, reminding Harry Bailly of what he had himself so often said to cover up for his own insults, that all that had been said had only been said 'for pley and game':

Namoore of this, for it is right ynough!
Sire Pardoner, be glad and myrie of cheere;
And ye, sire Hoost, that been to me so deere,
I prey yow that ye kisse the Pardoner.
And Pardoner, I prey thee, drawe thee neer,
And, as we diden, lat us laughe and pleye. (*CT* vi 962–7)

It would be a mistake to imagine that the Host is angry because the Pardoner has asked him for money. What arouses his indignation is the feeling that the Pardoner has fooled him. And in this he is surely right. The Pardoner is not out to make money out of these pilgrims or he would never have revealed to them so candidly his methods for doing so beforehand. What he wants to prove is the power of words, of his rhetoric, and in order to succeed he must make the pilgrims see that he has been able to fool them in spite of their previous knowledge of his methods. In that moment, between the conclusion of his tale and the outraged cry of the Host, the moment when the rhetoric wears off just enough to be recognised as such, he finds his satisfaction. And, just as the power he is allowed to exercise over others under cover of the game is more important to the Host than the money he might make out of the prize dinner, so, we may be sure, the Pardoner would not have foregone his mental triumph for all the relics in the world.

The Pardoner has not fared well at the hands of the critics. A good example of the kind of treatment he has received is to be found in a brilliant essay by R. P. Miller, 'Chaucer's Pardoner and the Scriptural Eunuch'.[1] Miller begins by analysing the Pardoner's actual tale in terms of the exegetical tradition we examined in the previous chapter. He takes as his guiding line the notion now familiar to us that there are two ways to read any text, a foolish natural way and a spiritual way, which is the way of the Christian exegetical tradition. The tale itself is a simple and traditional one, but Miller shows how, read correctly, it is rich in the themes that interested Chaucer and the Middle Ages. Three rioters see a corpse being taken to burial and, on asking who it is who has killed the man, are told that it is Death, who is devastating the countryside. At once they decide to set out and slay Death. In their search for him they meet an old man who

[1] In *Chaucer Criticism*, ed. Schoeck and Taylor (Indiana, 1960) 1
221–44.

tells them that Death is to be found up a twisting path under a tree. They follow these directives and find not a man but a treasure. Forgetting their search for Death they make plans to carry away the treasure but secretly plot to kill each other in order to have more for themselves. Inevitably all three succeed and all three die. Their literal death, one could say, is the result of a prior spiritual death, which made them constantly interpret literally what they should have interpreted spiritually: the injunction to slay death ('Death, thou shalt die'); the 'old man' whom they meet; the treasure under the tree up the crooked path, etc. The clues are thick on the ground, but the rioters fail to read them because they are foolish natural men, and their own death is the result of their failure to alter, to become spiritual. In the same way, Miller argues, the Pardoner himself, who should be a 'eunuch in God', is in fact only *physically* a eunuch, while very much the reverse in spirit. As a false eunuch masquerading as the true one he is even more to be condemned than the three rioters whose story he tells. And Miller concludes that

the Pardoner's Tale fits generally into a scheme of opposition between Charity and Cupidity in *The Canterbury Tales* as a whole. The extreme maliciousness of the Pardoner as a person sets him at the far end of the scale among the pilgrims. As a type he is even more definitely evil. He is the false eunuch who stands and points the way up the wrong road. He represents the way of cupidity, malice, impenitence, spiritual sterility – just the opposite of the way of the Parson and his spiritual brother, the Plowman. He is that Old Man as he lives and exerts his influence in the great pilgrimage of life. And, as the *vetus homo* he is to be opposed to the Christlike figure of the *novus homo*, the true guide – the 'povre Persoun of a toun'.[1]

In the way it brings together the figure of the Pardoner as he is described in the general prologue and the themes of the Pardoner's own Prologue and Tale, Miller's article is exemplary. The only thing he forgets – and it is crucial – is that the Pardoner meets the requirements of the game so much better than the Parson. St Augustine, who asked how a horse could be a true picture unless it was a false horse, knew better. For is not Miller's reading itself the result of an overliteral interpretation of the text?

[1] Ibid. 240–1.

Does he not look simply at the content and forget the tone and context in which it is delivered? For in one sense the Pardoner is the only honest pilgrim in the group. Only he plays the game to its limits while still recognising it as a game. Although at one level his Prologue and Tale are aimed at making a fool of everyone, at another level it is not aimed at anyone at all except those who refuse to recognise it as a mere tale told as part of the game, a rhetorical exercise designed to demonstrate his virtuosity. To read it as Miller does is, in a way, to read it like Harry Bailly: as a personal affront which can only be met by showing up the evil of the teller. But the tale was only told in play and the right reaction is the Knight's: to accept the joke and learn from it. There is perhaps some excuse for the Host; his reaction is the kind one makes every day to the realisation that one has been fooled. But for the *reader* of Chaucer to react in this way is to reveal a misunderstanding of the whole nature of Chaucer's art. For if the reaction of the Host is similar to that which one makes in everyday life, that of the Knight is of the kind which games try to foster and which an art like Chaucer's or Rabelais's or Sterne's tries to produce.

Miller's error lies in his belief that because Chaucer is concerned with true and false readings and interpretations, it is up to us to read his work in the 'true' way. This is certainly the way to read Dante or Langland, but then, as we have seen, their major works describe the movement *towards* the truth. In Chaucer there is never any movement, the hero never grows into understanding or enlightenment. And this suggests that his work is not so much governed by the opposition of true and false readings, as itself an exploration of the relationship between them. In other words the right and wrong ways of reading the world is the principal *theme* of his work, as of this tale.

The tale itself, as Miller rightly saw, is about the failure to distinguish the spiritual from the literal; but since it is told by the 'literal' Pardoner, does that not mean that we must *reverse* the values in the tale? Once again we see that Chaucer has removed any vantage point superior to the poem and from which we can judge its value. For the tale itself of course we have just such a vantage point, and it is pretty easy to see just where the rioters go wrong. The short sermon set into the beginning of the tale reveals its solid base in Christian exegesis:

The hooly writ take I to my witnesse
That luxurie is in wyn and dronkenesse.
   Lo, how that dronken Looth, unkyndely
Lay be his doghtres two, unwityngly. . . .

   Adam, oure fader, and his wyf also,
Fro Paradys to labour and to wo
Were dryven for that vice, it is no drede. . . . (*CT* vi 483–507)

The focus here is the same as that of a Hugh of St Victor or a
Dante. We don't have to be particularly well up in Christian
theology to know where we stand. But then we ask who speaks
these words and the answer is: the Pardoner, the man who
boasted that his only 'intent' in preaching was not to free people
from sin but to gain money for himself! The content of what he
says is unimpeachable, but set in the context of his aims it takes
on a new dimension. And it is not enough for us simply to step
back and readjust our vantage point, for now there is no solid base
from which to operate: we are tossed backwards and forwards
from the words to the speaker, and our interpretation changes
every time our position does. And we now see that the schema
literal/spiritual with which Miller operates is not really adequate.
It only works if we have some criterion for distinguishing the two;
without such a criterion we are thrown back onto a world where
nothing is literal, everything depends on interpretation, and where
no clear criterion of interpretation seems to be present.
   There had been other tales in *The Canterbury Tales* told with
a different end in view from the winning of the prize dinner: the
Miller had told a tale about a carpenter who married too young
a wife and so rode for a fall, and the carpenter-Reeve had retaliated with a story about a miller who also got his deserts. The
pilgrims were able to sit back and laugh at the knaves who fooled
others only to be fooled in turn through a lack of self-knowledge,
and the reader could laugh confidently with them. But the
Pardoner has designs on the whole company of pilgrims and so,
implicitly, upon ourselves, the readers. When we have laughed
with the Miller at John the carpenter, and with Chaucer and the
Reeve at the Miller, and with Chaucer at the Reeve, we suddenly
find, as the Host found, at the close of the Pardoner's Tale, that
the joke is on us. At this point there is only one way of escape: to

acknowledge that one was led up the garden path and learn from the game. What we learn is not a thing, a body of doctrine, but an attitude, the attitude that simultaneously accepts the need for, and denies the reality of, stories.

V. A. Kolve, writing of the Corpus Christi play cycles, has sensitively brought out the notion of play and game which pervades the genre:

> The aim of the Corpus Christi drama was to celebrate and elucidate, never, not even temporarily, to deceive. It played action in 'game' – not in 'ernest' – within a world set apart, established by convention and obeying rules of its own. A lie designed to tell the truth about reality, the drama was understood as significant play.[1]

How similar and yet how different is Chaucer's own conception of game, implicit in all his major works and explicit in *The Canterbury Tales*! He too creates 'a world set apart, established by convention and obeying rules of its own'. But his world is not one that celebrates and elucidates the structures of the universe and God's plan for mankind. Rather, it is a world which mimes our natural propensities for misinterpretation (the result mainly of our belief that the meanings we find in the world are somehow inherently there), and, by miming, relieves us of them. To read the Pardoner's Prologue and Tale as *either* sheer characterisation and entertainment *or* as the exploration of a theological truth, is equally wrong. Both look for the meaning of Chaucer in the subject-matter, but where, in Dante, form and content inevitably coincide, since his poem is a model of the universe, in Chaucer, on the contrary, the theme is their perpetual failure to coincide. Chaucer's aim is similar to Dante's or to that of the anonymous writers of the miracle plays: a redirection of the reader's or viewer's will. Like Dante, Chaucer places false interpretations within his work as guides to the truth. But where Dante could present this truth at the climax of the poem as the discovery of the meaning (and meaningfulness) of the universe, Chaucer's truth lies solely in our response to the work itself, the creative recreation in our minds of the author's rhetorical play. Chaucer forces the reader out of his man-locked set, but the other, truer world to which he introduces him exists only in the moment of

[1] Op. cit. 32.

creative encounter with the poem, the moment when we recognise the 'set' for what it is.

In a famous letter to Vettori, Machiavelli wrote:

> On the coming of evening I return to my house and enter my study; and at the door I take off the day's clothing, covered as it is with mud and dust, and put on the garments of court and palace; then, in this graver dress, I enter the antique courts of the ancients, where, received by them with affection, I feed on that food which is only mine and which I was born for.
>
> (10 Dec 1513)

When Dante met the ancients it was simply as men who had spoken the difficult truth through mastery of their art. He had no need of special clothes or of a special setting. The world was a book, written by God, and knowledge was therefore unitary and everything was ultimately reconcilable with everything else, Roman with Jewish history, Lucan and Virgil with the Bible. For Machiavelli, on the other hand, books and the world have parted company. He gets through his daily tasks, but only because they are something that has to be done; his real life begins when he changes his clothes and enters his study, takes down his books, opens them and enters their world. In Chaucer there is neither the optimism of Dante nor the Stoic serenity of Machiavelli. In his pages books and authors, paintings and frescoes and reliefs, the wisdom of the ancients, the sayings of the Fathers, the proverbs of the people, all jostle each other, struggling for a place at the front. His reading may not be wider than Dante's, but it is far more obtrusive: he makes us constantly aware of the superabundance of things in his world, and the things include books and pictures. With all these objects mimicking each other, contradicting each other, tumbling and falling over each other in their haste to emerge into the light of day, one question detaches itself. It is never explicitly raised by Chaucer, but his very silence on this point in the midst of so much sheer talk forces it on our attention: What are all these books *for*? Are they for our instruction? Our delight? We can, like the Wife of Bath, tear the pages from one book as we back our transgressions with words out of another, but after reading Chaucer we can never again be at rest with those mysterious objects. Nor is he himself at rest. The abundance of his invention seems to reflect his awareness of the irresponsibility of words, of sayings, of stories, and his desire to exorcise each and every false voice that rises within him in order to draw attention to that which cannot be spoken, since to speak is to falsify and destroy it. This unease has of course absolutely nothing to do with a change from script to print, as some crude theorists like to argue. Chaucer never dreamt of print and the tension is as evident in his work as in that of any post-Gutenberg writer. His unease stems from the clarity of his vision and the honesty of his response, and out of it he creates his narrative art.

4 Rabelais: Language and Laughter

'Tu causes, tu causes, c'est tout ce que tu sais faire.' The
parrot, in Raymond Queneau's *Zazie dans le Métro.*

Readers of Rabelais tend to fall into two categories. There are
those who see him as a great comic writer whose content must
not be taken too seriously and hardly even needs to be understood since for much of the time it is deliberate nonsense anyway;
and there are those who see him as a sort of Renaissance encyclo-
pedist in whose pages are to be found examples of nearly every
facet of the period, held together by a frivolous and often boring
series of anecdotes modelled on the worst medieval romances and
included as a sop to a mass audience greedy for such material.[1]
There seems to be no way of reconciling the comic form with the
serious content, or, to put it in terms which Rabelais himself
would have used, of reconciling the pleasurable and didactic
elements of his work.

This split in critical reaction is not confined to Rabelais. It is
to be found in the critical response to nearly every major Renaissance writer: on the one hand there is the Romantic stress on the
beauty and sensuousness of the language and imagery, and on the
other there is the more recent scholarly stress on the argument
and theme. But with Rabelais (as with Chaucer) we have rather
a different type of critical problem from that found in the response
to Milton or Spenser, for the simple reason that the whole question of critical attitude and mode of interpretation is the central
theme of his work. It is not simply that he lays himself open to
two radically different types of interpretation; it is that he is
himself concerned with the problem of the status of the work of
art and with the possibility of reconciling these two ways of look-

[1] Since this chapter was written I have read Michel Beaujour's *Le Jeu
de Rabelais* (Paris, 1969). It is a startling exception to the run of books on
Rabelais, a brilliant and scholarly endorsement of most of my own points,
essential reading it seems to me for anyone interested in Renaissance or
modern literature.

ing at his work. Nor is he content simply to discuss the problem in the course of his book, as a writer like Thomas Mann might do; his work is in itself a solution to the problem, an example of the perfect reconciliation of *delectare* and *prodesse*, *sentence* and *solas*.

The tone of the book[1] is set in the opening pages of *Gargantua*:

> And put the case that in the literal sense, you meet with purposes merry and solacious enough, and consequently very correspondent to their inscriptions, yet must not you stop there as at the melody of the charming Syrens, but endeavour to interpret that in a sublimer sense, which possibly you intended to have spoken in the jollitie of your heart. . . .
>
> (Prologue to *Gargantua*)

Have you ever seen a dog eating a marrow bone? See how carefully he guards it, how he breaks it open, with what relish he sucks out the marrow. This is how you should treat my book, says Rabelais:

> In imitation of this Dog, it becomes you to be wise, to smell, feele and have in estimation these faire goodly books, stuffed with high conceptions [*ces beaux livres de haute graisse*], which though seemingly easie in the pursuit, are in the cope and encounter somewhat difficult; and then like him you must, by a sedulous Lecture, and frequent meditation break the bone, and suck out the marrow [*sucer la substantifique moelle*]. . . .
>
> (Ibid.)

This is a restatement of a critical commonplace which goes back to Plato and the early allegorisers of Homer, which is to be found in Gnostic and Manichaean interpretations of the Bible, and which appears everywhere in the Middle Ages in the metaphors of the kernel and the nut, the fruit and the rind, the spirit and the letter. According to this point of view the work of art – or the Sacred Book – may at first sight appear to be nothing more than a frivolous and absurd story, a tale of gods making love like mortals or of a man who is really the son of God and ends up

---

[1] I treat Rabelais's book as a whole and as it appears in every modern edition, i.e. composed of five books, with *Gargantua*, written second, preceding *Pantagruel*, which was written first.

crucified like a common criminal. But, the argument runs, beneath the patently absurd surface there lies hidden a mystical doctrine or theory of the universe, put there by the author of the text and waiting to be extracted by the initiate. Now such an attitude bears a curious resemblance to that of our second school of readers of Rabelais. It is true that these do not dismiss the story or its incidents in favour of a *spiritual* truth hidden beneath the surface and to which the incidents allude allegorically; but they do concentrate their attention on what Rabelais seems to be saying about the place of women in society, or Luther, or Neoplatonism, while shrugging off the surface meaning of the episodes that make up the book. Abel Lefranc, one of the pioneers of Rabelais studies, puts this point of view very clearly when he writes: 'The real theme appears beneath the myth. This fact is so frequent, or rather so constant that it could be erected into a principle.'[1] Such a reader (and Lefranc is the spokesman of the majority of scholars who have written about Rabelais) feels that the book's meaning cannot lie simply in the absurd incidents it recounts. To find out what the book is *really about* we have to look beneath these trivial anecdotes, he claims, to the underlying truth; and the marrow-bone passage quoted above seems to sanction just such an approach.

But does it? Listening, as we always must with Rabelais (as with Chaucer), for the *tone* of the argument, we soon realise that he may not be endorsing so much as burlesquing the allegorical approach; for, he goes on, this way of reading will reveal in the book a

> doctrine of a more profound and abstruse consideration, which will disclose unto you the most glorious Sacraments, and dreadful mysteries, as well in what concerneth your Religion, as matters of the publicke State, and Life oeconomical. (Ibid.)

The book might conceivably have held a 'doctrine of a more profound and abstruse consideration', but it could not possibly conceal mysteries which concern religion, politics, and socioeconomic organisation. Attempts to tone down the magnitude of the claims and thus rid the passage of its burlesque flavour by referring the words to Renaissance usage are not convincing. Rabelais deliberately overstresses, and, in case the reader should

1 *Les Navigations de Pantagruel* (Paris, 1905) 144–5.

still be in any doubt about his attitude, in the next paragraph he comes right out into the open:

> Do you beleeve upon your conscience, that *Homer* whil'st he was a couching his *Iliads* and *Odysses*, had any thought upon those Allegories, which *Plutarch, Heraclides, Ponticus, Fristatius, Cornutus* squeesed out of him, and which *Politian* filched againe from them: if you trust it, with neither hand nor foot do you come neare to my opinion, which judgeth them to have beene as little dreamed of by *Homer*, as the Gospel-sacraments were by *Ovid* in his *Metamorphosis*, though a certaine gulligut Fryer and true bacon-picker would have undertaken to prove it, if perhaps hc had met with as very fools as himself. . . . (Ibid.)

Rabelais is not simply deriding a specific late-medieval allegorisation of Ovid, as some scholars have self-protectively argued; he is attacking a general tendency to find hidden meanings beneath the literal surface, a tendency which usually results in reading into an author what one wants to find rather than what is there.[1]

Rabelais's book abounds in burlesques and parodies of this kind of misinterpretation. *Gargantua*, for example, ends with a verse enigma to which various solutions are proposed. The correct answer turns out to be not, as Gargantua had maintained, 'the course and maintenance of divine truth', but a game of tennis! Despite this warning, scholars have been hard at work on the riddle and even come up with the answer that it deals with the development of sixteenth-century history!

The best examples of misinterpretation, however, occur in the *Tiers livre*, and an examination of this book in a little more detail will help to explain Rabelais's concern with this problem and reveal how it relates to the form and style of the work as a whole. The *Tiers Livre* is the most unified of the five books; its one subject is Panurge's search for an answer to his double question: Should he marry? and, if he does, Will he be cuckolded? The theme of the book is not, as some scholars have supposed, the 'querelle des femmes', for that acts as a mere scaffold for Rabelais's persistent themes: Is there such a thing as absolute truth?

---

[1] Rabelais, in fact, gives a full and accurate list of the early allegorisers of Homer. See Felix Buffière, *Les Mythes d'Homère et la pensée grecque* (Paris, 1956).

If so, can we mortals ever find it? Even if we can, can we ever *know* that we have found it?

Right from the start Pantagruel points out to Panurge that it is absurd to expect an answer to his double question:

> I know not (quoth *Pantagruel*) which of all my Answers to lay hold on; for your Proposals are so full of *ifs* and *buts*, that I can ground nothing on them, nor pitch upon any solid and positive Determination satisfactory to what is demanded by them. Are not you assured within your self of what you have a mind to? the chief and main point of the whole matter lieth there; all the rest is merely casual, and totally dependeth upon the fatal Disposition of the Heavens. . . . It is therefore expedient, seeing you are resolved for once to take a trial of the state of Marriage, that, with shut Eyes, bowing your Head, and kissing the Ground, you put the business to a Venture, and give it a fair hazard in recommending the success of the residue to the disposure of Almighty God. (III x)

Panurge, however, is determined to get an answer, and to this end he consults in turn the *sortes virgilianae*, his own dreams, a sybil, a dumb man, a dying poet, a mage, a theologian, a doctor, a philosopher and a fool. Each of these encounters follows the same pattern: Panurge is never given a straight reply but is instead confronted with a riddle or an image which he has to interpret; each time he interprets it to make the answer fit in with what he himself wishes. When he cannot conceivably do this, as in the case of the reply of the mage, Cornelius Agrippa, he impugns the integrity of the speaker – who would trust such a fraud and liar? But since none of these encounters yields him unequivocally the answer he wants to hear, he is always driven to try again.

A good example of the way Panurge sets about his interpretative task is provided by the episode of the dream. In his dream Panurge finds his wife sticking horns on his forehead. He interprets this to mean that he is going to have all he wants, since these are clearly the horns of plenty, and he flies into a rage when Pantagruel points out to him that the more likely explanation is that they are the horns traditionally associated with cuckoldry. Panurge is so anxious to get married and so terrified at the prospect of his wife being unfaithful to him that he clutches at anything at all that seems capable of giving him the answer that he wants, even if this entails rejecting every plausible answer that is offered to him. In his interpretation of his dream, as in the other episodes which make up this book, he acts in exactly the same way as the friar of the prologue to *Gargantua*, who distorted the true meaning (or the meaning most likely to be correct) of Ovid's *Metamorphoses* by reading them as an allegory of the Gospels.

Throughout the book Panurge's attitude is contrasted with that of Pantagruel. Pantagruel is sure that the answer to a question of this kind cannot be given, even by those, like the sybil or the mage, who profess to be in touch with the workings of the universe, since it is not something immutably decreed for all time, but something that Panurge is free either to bring about or to keep from occurring. Panurge's attitude, on the other hand, is deterministic and mechanical. He does not believe that the answer to his questions depends on his own will but rather that in some way the answer is already present. What he really wants is to be told that if he gets married he will not be cuckolded, since this has in some way been decreed by God. He would like the universe to be meaningful, *and* for its meaning to fit in with his own wishes. Such an attitude naturally leads him to foist his own desires upon an uncertain future and then to read it off as though it implied the inevitable fulfilment of those desires. But it also leads to a secret irritation, the half-conscious thought that what he asserts so loudly may not in fact be the case at all.

One of the finest ironies of the *Tiers Livre* is that so long as Panurge maintains his mechanistic view of the world and his deterministic view of fate there can be no doubt that he *will* be cuckolded and beaten by his wife. The answers which he receives are not answers about the future at all; they are answers about the present. To ask the sort of question he does is to think of the future as already determined; but to think of it in this way is to think of one's own will as bound; and to think this is to plunge into a world that is indeed deterministic. There can be no other answer to Panurge's question than that marriage and cuckoldry go together and that therefore if he gets married it becomes logically possible for him to be cuckolded. As Coleridge noted: 'The reason can only give the inevitable conclusion, the syllogistic *ergo*, from the premises provided by the understanding itself, which puts each case so as of necessity to predetermine the verdict thereon.'[1] It is only, as Pantagruel keeps pointing out, by ceasing to ask the type of question that Panurge is asking that the possibility will present itself of his marrying without incurring the consequences he so dreads.

The belief that there is *an* answer to this type of question, and that it can be obtained by employing the right techniques – techniques which can be handed from person to person like sacks of coal and do not depend upon the exercise of judgement or the possibility of error – leads, then, to a failure to grasp the likely answer and to the substitution of one's own desires for the probable truth. This interesting psychological fact is not limited to the interpretation of an enigma, a dream or a picture. It extends to the use of language itself, as is revealed by the following argument between Panurge and Pantagruel:

> You do not then believe [asks Panurge] what *Herodotus* wrote of two Children, who at the special Command and Appointment of *Psammetichus* King of *Egypt*, having been kept in a pretty Country Cottage, where they were nourished and entertained in a perpetual silence, did at last, after a certain long space of time, pronounce this word *Bec*, which in the *Phrygian* Language signifieth *Bread*. Nothing less (quoth *Pantagruel*) do I believe, than that it is a meer abusing of our Understandings to give Credit to the words of those, who say that there is any such thing as a Natural Language. All Speeches have had their primary Origin from the Arbitrary Institutions, Accords and Agreements of Nations in their respective Condescendments to what should be noted and betokened by them. An Articulate Voice (according to the Dialecticians) hath naturally no signification at all; for that the sence and meaning thereof did totally depend upon the good will and pleasure of the first Deviser and Imposer of it [*les voix (comme disent les dialecticiens), ne signifient naturellement, mais à plaisir*]. (III xix)

To believe that language is natural is to believe that words correspond directly to reality, that meaning lies buried in each

---

[1] 'On the Distinction of the Witty, the Droll, the Odd, and the Humourous', in *Coleridge's Essays and Lectures on Shakespeare and Some Other Old Poets and Dramatists* (London, 1911) 264.

word, waiting to be extracted from it; and that this meaning was put into words by the Creator of the world. To believe that language is conventional, on the other hand, is to hold that it was invented by man; that there is no necessary relation between words and what they signify but that words have acquired their meanings because of certain decisions on the part of men; and that therefore it is no use scrutinising each word in order to make it yield its secret, since words only acquire meaning by virtue of the contexts in which they are used. Pantagruel's views not only agree with those of Saussure and modern linguists on this point, but also with medieval theory. As one scholar notes:

> The philosophical or speculative grammarians (as distinct from the ordinary practical grammarians) of the fourteenth century were much concerned with the theory of signs. Their speculations on this subject (based largely on Aristotle) were chiefly devoted to linguistic signs, but not exclusively so: they involved, to some extent, a *general* theory of signs. According to this theory, most human signs – words and hunting-calls, for example, but not groans – have their origin in an act of 'impositio'. In every case, that is, there must have been someone – the 'impositor' – who first established the sign as a sign by 'imposing it on', or assigning it to, a thing (or, more correctly, a mental concept of a thing). In doing so, the wise old 'impositor' may have been 'guided by the nature of things' – that is, he may have attributed a given meaning to a given sign on the strength of some natural similarity between the sign and thing-signified (Aquinas' 'ratio similitudinis'). This is known as 'impositio secundum naturam'. Or he may have made a quite arbitrary attribution without any such similarity to guide him, in which case the signification depends on custom and consent (Aquinas' 'ratio institutionis'). This is known as 'impositio ad placitum', 'impositio iuxta arbitrium humanae voluntatis', etc.[1]

And he concludes that 'Educated opinion in the Middle Ages

[1] Burrow, *A Reading of Sir Gawain and the Green Knight*, 187. The whole of Burrow's appendix 1 is interesting from our point of view. His arguments are based on Aristotle's *De Interpretatione* and the commentaries of Boëthius and St Thomas on it, as well as Isidore of Seville's discussion of etymology in *Etymologia*, 1, xxix.

generally regarded words as arbitrary or conventional signs. On this point, as on others, Aquinas agrees with Saussure and his successors: "nec voces naturaliter significant, sed ex institutione humana".[1] Nor is it really surprising that arguments about whether signs are natural or conventional should have coincided with arguments about free-will and predestination and about the nature of the eucharist. All three arise out of the questioning of the medieval synthesis which occupied us in Chapter 2.

It is easy to see that the views of Panurge and Pantagruel on language correspond to their views on the place and function of man in the world. And just as it comes about that Panurge's belief that there is *an* answer to his questions leads him to foist his own desires on an enigmatic world, so his belief that language is natural leads him into a far more arbitrary use of language than Pantagruel, who accepts its conventional character. The logic of this is explored by Rabelais at some length when he discusses the colours of the young Gargantua's livery in the first book. Grandgousier had dressed his son in blue and white, meaning by that to signify celestial joy. But, says Rabelais to the reader, you are bound to sit up at this and tell me that white signifies faith and blue fortitude. But who says they do? The author of the *Blason des couleurs*? And who is he? What authority does he have for his assertions? It was surely wise of him not to set his name to his book, for I do not know what I admire more about it, its presumptuousness or its absurdity:

> . . . his presumption and overweening, for that he should without reason, without cause, or without any appearance of truth, have dared to prescribe by his private authority, what things should be denotated and signified by the colour: which is the custome of Tyrants, who will have their will to bear sway in stead of equity; and not of the wise and learned, who with the evidence of reason satisfie their Readers: His sottishnesse and want of spirit, in that he thought, that without any other demonstration or sufficient argument, the world would be

[1] Saussure and his successors would not of course have any truck with wise old impositors and the like in their explanations of the way language functions. Words, for them, have *uses*, not *meanings*. But in the simple opposition to the notion of meaning inhering *in* words medieval and modern views agree.

pleased to make his blockish and ridiculous impositions, the rule of their devices. (1 ix)

Not only Panurge but, as we have seen, the allegorisers of Homer and Ovid are just such people, 'tyrants' rather than 'sages'. Rabelais then goes on to give some examples of this 'natural' use of language and signs:

> In the like darknesse and mist of ignorance, are wrapped up these vainglorious Courtiers, and name-transposers, who going about in their impresa's, to signifie *esperance*, (that is, hope) have portrayed a sphere: birds pennes for peines: *Ancholie* (which is the flower columbine) for melancholy . . . a bench rotten and broken, to signifie bankrout: *non* and a *corslet* for *non dur habit* (otherwise *non durabit*, it shall not last) *un lit sanc ciel*, that is, a bed without a testerne, for *un licencié*, a graduated person . . . which are aequivocals so absurd and witlesse, so barbarous and clownish, that a foxes taile should be fastened to the neck-piece of, and a Vizard made of a Cows-heard, given to every one that henceforth should offer, after the restitution of learning, to make use of any such fopperies in *France*. (Ibid.)

With this he contrasts the hieroglyphics of the ancient Egyptians, which contained some natural similarity between the sign and the thing-signified: a house was a picture of a house, etc. This is Aquinas's 'ratio similitudinis', as the pentangle painted on Gawain's shield both signified 'trawthe' and in some way represented it. Then, having shown up the folly of taking white to signify faith and blue fortitude, Rabelais goes on to explain why they are more likely to signify celestial joy. In all countries, he argues, black signifies grief and white is the opposite of black as joy is of grief. Nor, he concludes,

> is this signification instituted by humane imposition, but by the universal consent of the world received, which Philosophers call *Jus Gentium*, the Law of Nations, or an uncontrolable right of force in all countreyes whatsoever. . . . (1 x)

There is thus a threefold distinction to be made. First there is a *natural* language, which is an impossibility; to imagine that such a thing exists is to set up a wholly *arbitrary* and private language; instead of which we should realise that language is *conventional*, which means that it is arbitrary in so far as it is not natural, but that its arbitrariness is held in check by convention, which is the agreement of men among themselves.

Panurge's attitude rests on the assumption that he can get in touch with the workings of the universe if he can only discover the right techniques or find the right people to question. Since there is a meaning *in* each word it is only a matter of uncovering that meaning and we will be able to learn the meaning of the universe and the course of future events. But, since this is a false assumption, his attempts at wresting the truth out of language and people takes on the form of mania. For only the madman (and the tyrant, who is a madman with the power to transform his fantasies into reality[1]) imagines that his wishes and the reality of the world coincide; that, indeed, is the definition of madness. And if Panurge is not certifiably insane, he is at least the victim of his unconscious impulses in a way Pantagruel never is. Trying to raise himself above his natural condition, Panurge inevitably sinks below it; trying to by-pass the discriminating mind in order to arrive directly at the truth, he is thrown back on his subjective fantasies.

Pantagruel's view of man and of language, on the other hand, depends on his acceptance of man's limitations. His attitude to life is well summed up in a passage from the prologue to the *Tiers Livre*, where it is said of Diogenes: 'If he had some Imperfection, so have you, so have we; for there is nothing (but God) that is perfect.' Only God can know the answers to Panurge's questions, and for man to pretend to be like God is for him to sink to the level of a beast. The acceptance of man's mixed condition, between the animals and the angels, is exemplified by Judge Bridoye who, for forty years, has been able to pass correct judgement by the simple expedient of throwing dice. This, however, is not done out of any belief that the dice will reveal to him the true answer if he learns to 'read' them correctly, but out of the recognition that all the paraphernalia of the law-court will never yield any absolute certainty about the rights and wrongs of a case. In such a situation he prefers to put all his trust in God, and Pantagruel[2]

[1] In this context Robbe-Grillet's fascination with mad kings is suggestive.

[2] All the texts give this speech to Epistemon; I follow George Kaiser's convincing suggestion that it must be spoken by Pantagruel. See *Praisers of Folly* (London, 1964) 169, n. 12.

explains that the heavens rewarded Bridoye because of his 'pure Simplicity and sincere Unfeignedness', and because 'in the acknowledgement of his Inabilities . . . he did . . . most humbly recommend the Direction of his Judicial Proceedings to the Upright Judge of Judges, God Almighty . . .' (III xliv).

It is in this spirit that Pantagruel himself judges the case of Baisecul and Humevesne, cutting through the incredible tangle of legal verbiage and the crazily involved speeches of the two litigants to deliver a verdict which, miraculously, manages to please them both. And it is in this spirit that Gargantua founds the Abbaye de Thélème:

> In all their rule, and strictest tie of their order, there was but this one clause to be observed.
> *Do what thou wilt.*
> Because men that are free, well-borne, well-bred, and conversant in honest companies, have naturally an instinct and spurre that prompteth them unto vertuous actions, and withdrawes them from vice, which is called *honour*. (I lvii)

This is a freedom of the will, a freedom to use the mind to make choices in accordance with the dictates of reason backed by common sense and a sound education. It is exactly the opposite of Panurge's kind of freedom, which is the imposition of private fantasy on the world and so nothing other than a form of total bondage to irrational impulses.

It follows naturally from what has been said above about the differences between Panurge and Pantagruel that Rabelais endorses the views of the latter and condemns those of the former. In fact, at the close of the episode of the Limousin scholar, he states his own position unequivocally:

> . . . we should . . . strive to shun all strange[1] and unknown termes with as much heedfulnesse and circumspection as Pilots of ships use to avoide the rocks and banks in the sea. (II vi)

This attitude to language coincides, in Rabelais, with a homely peasant strain, and results in a style far richer and more supple than anything the Humanists were ever to produce. It is a style which reminds one of a rural Villon rather than of Montaigne or

---

[1] The word is 'espaves', which is closer to 'obsolete' than to 'strange'.

Ronsard. We have to wait for four centuries and for an Irishman, Beckett, before we find again a prose style as richly evocative and simple in form as Rabelais's:

> Or laissons-les là et retournons à nostre bon Gargantua qui est à Paris, bien instant à l'estude de bonnes lettres et exercitations athleticques, et le vieux bonhomme Grandgousier, son père, qui après souper se chauffe les couilles à un beau, clair et grand feu, et, attendent graisler des chastaines, escript au foyer avec un baston bruslé d'un bout dont on escharbotte le feu, faisant à sa femme et famille de beaulx contes du temps jadis (1 xxviii)

Urquhart does his best to catch the flavour of this, but he can't quite do it:

> But let us leave them there, and return to our good *Gargantua*, who is at *Paris* very assiduous and earnest at the study of good letters, and athletical exercitations, and to the good old man *Grandgousier* his father, who after supper warmeth his ballocks by a good, clear, great fire, and, waiting upon the broyling of some chestnuts, is very serious in drawing scratches on the hearth with a stick burnt at the one end, wherewith they did stirre up the fire, telling to his wife and the rest of the family pleasant old stories and tales of former times.

But here we come to a crucial paradox. As soon as we begin to talk in this way about Rabelais's style we become aware of the curious fact that passages such as the above form only a very small portion of the entire work. The greater part of the book in fact reads much more as if it had been written by Panurge than by Pantagruel! Now this is surely extremely odd if we are right in our analysis of these two characters and of what they appear to stand for. How are we to explain it?

The answer is quite simple. It lies in Rabelais's recognition that any work of fiction, his own included, bears a closer resemblance to the fantasies of Panurge than it does to the common-sense moderation of Pantagruel. And not only Panurge. Chapter xiii of *Gargantua*, for example, provides us with an exact model of the author at work. This is the chapter in which Picrochole and his henchmen are planning the destruction of Gargantua and the conquest of his territories. But very quickly their thoughts, un-checked by any reference to reality, move from these limited objectives to grandiose schemes for the overrunning of the entire world:

> Shall we see (said *Picrochole*), *Babylon* and Mount *Sinai*? There is no need (said they) at this time; have we not hurried up and down, travelled and toyled enough, in having transfreted and past over the *Hircanian* sea, marched alongst the two *Armenias* and the three *Arabias*? By my faith (said he) we have played the fooles, and are undone: Ha, poor soules! What's the matter, said they? What shall we have (said he) to drink in these deserts? for *Julian Augustus*, with his whole Army died there for thirst, as they say. We have already (said they) given order for that. In the *Siriack* sea you have nine thousand and fourteen great ships laden with the best wines in the world: they arrived at *Port-Joppa*, there they found two and twenty-thousand Camels. . . . (I xxxiii)

No sooner are the words spoken than they are assumed to be describing an already achieved reality. Picrochole, a tyrant in fact, is also acting like a linguistic tyrant, imagining that the world will take the shape of his desires, that word and deed are one. Rabelais draws our attention to this megalomania by emphasising the apparent common sense of what is going on: Picrochole, already crossing the desert in his imagination, becomes aware of the fact that his army needs water if it is to survive. In the world of fantasy, however, this is no problem, and the courtiers at once explain to him that this has already been taken care of. In the event, however, Picrochole is utterly defeated by Gargantua only a few miles from his own palace.

Picrochole's situation here is very like that of Rabelais or any writer of fiction. For in the writing of a fiction fantasies take on the appearance of reality, worlds can be created by a few strokes of the pen. Where, however, most writers of fiction make every effort to lull the reader into a state of mind where he will forget this fact, Rabelais, like Chaucer, is troubled by this freedom, this lack of responsibility to any reality. Nor does he wish to take refuge in the idea that he has a secret truth to convey beneath these words, as the allegorisers of Homer believed that poet had. Rabelais insists, in fact, that the *events* recorded in his book follow each other no less arbitrarily than do the words; a character appears, an action gets under way or is concluded, for no other reason than because the writer has decided that this should be so. From the start Rabelais is at pains to stress the extempore and subjective nature of his work, to make it clear that he is neither, like Herodotus, reporting on events which have actually taken place, nor delivering an esoteric truth to the initiate. Immediately after the attack on allegorisers in the prologue to *Gargantua*, for instance, he points out that 'in the composing of this lordly book, I never lost nor bestowed any more, nor any other time then was appointed to serve me for taking my bodily refection, that is, whil'st I was eating and drinking'. In the last chapter of *Pantagruel* he decides suddenly to bring his chronicle to a close because 'My head aches a little, and I perceive that the Registers of my braine are somewhat jumbled and disordered with this septembral juice.' Again and again he brings before the reader the image of himself sitting at his desk, writing down the words which we are now reading, explicitly focusing on the private and subjective nature of his fiction.

The one thing he will not do is allow the reader to settle into a comfortable suspension of disbelief, into the state of mind of Picrochole and his men. He continually interrupts the action with remarks addressed directly to him:

> I doubt me, that you do not throughly beleeve the truth of this strange nativity, though you beleeve it not, I care not much: but an honest man, and of good judgement beleeveth still what is told him, and that which he findes written. (i vi)[1]

He makes a show of denying all responsibility for what he recounts: 'For my part I know nothing, and care full little for her or any other', thus interrupting the action with the jarring note of his presence. In the first two books he even adopts the humourous *persona* of a M. Alcofribas, 'Abstracteur de Quinte Essence' (a burlesque of the alchemists' pretensions of being in touch with the secrets of the universe), and takes part in the action as one of Pantagruel's men. Rabelais, however, does not seem to have taken to *personae* as readily as Chaucer, perhaps because he is more concerned with the relations between words and speakers than with those between narratives and narrators.

---

[1] Cf. Cervantes: 'You may depend upon my bare word, reader, without any further security. . . .' (Author's preface to the reader, *Don Quixote*.)

As well as stressing that what is before the reader is nothing but a book, Rabelais also keeps reminding him that the events recorded in this book are made up of the units of speech and writing we call words, and these in turn are made up of letters. They are therefore subject to such printing errors as the substitution of an *n* for an *m*, a trifling difference, physically, but one that has large consequences as far as meaning is concerned when the word is 'âme'. The title of a chapter, 'Comment Epistémon, qui avait la couppe testée . . .' forces us again to recognise the fact that we are dealing not with a direct reality, but with language, something which is both conventional and physical. The same effect is achieved when proverbial expressions are taken literally, as in the descriptions of some of Gargantua's games ('He would flay the Fox, say the Apes Paternoster . . . put the Plough before the Oxen, and claw where it did not itch . . .'); or in some of the books in the library of St Victor; or when Panurge is made to parade about with a flea in his ear to illustrate the proverbial expression for wanting to get married. This is all very much in the style of the anonymous author of the *Blason des couleurs* or of the men who exhibited a *sphère* for *espoir*, but the effect is just the opposite. As with the Picrochole incident, the blatancy of the example serves to remind us of the way in which language and fiction really work, and of the dangers inherent in an unthinking acceptance of both. As with Chaucer's play on overliteral and overallegorical interpretations, a conflict is set up between two kinds of discourse, thus forcing the reader to register the fact that different laws operate within a book and in the outside world. A particularly good example is to be found in the episode of the frozen words, discovered by Pantagruel and his friends on their voyage in search of the Oracle of the Bottle. Sounds of battle are suddenly heard, terrifying Panurge, but it turns out that these are the words and sounds of a battle fought on the spot in the previous year, but so cold is the air that the words freeze before they have time to disappear. Now, in the warmer weather, they are thawing, and thus returning to their original natures as sounds. Pantagruel and his men, however, find a few that are still frozen:

However, he threw three or four Handfulls of them on the Deck, among which I perceived some very sharp words, and some bloody words . . . we also saw some terrible words, and some others not very pleasant to the Eye. (iv lvi)

The narrator says that he 'would fain have sav'd some merry odd words, and have preserved them in Oyl, as Ice and Snow are kept, and between clean Straw', but Pantagruel won't allow it, 'saying, that 'tis a folly to hoard up what we are never like to want'. The joke here depends on our becoming conscious of the fact that when we speak of a 'terrible' word we are speaking of its meaning; by itself it looks like any other word, a series of mute signs waiting to be interpreted by a human consciousness.

But the episode has a further function. It serves to remind us of the fact that if words are made up of mute signs, these signs also do stand for a particular set of sounds, but sounds so deeply frozen that by simply looking at them it is impossible to reconstitute the voice which made them.[1] Rabelais's efforts to make the reader aware of the merely subjective nature of his work can now be seen in a different light, as the effort to release inside the reader the distinct and individual voice which, if it is to be conveyed at all to another person, has to take the form of these conventional signs. By reminding us that what we are reading is the product only of one man's imagination, and in no sense a transcript of reality, he makes us see it as the one reality it in fact is: the words spoken by one man.

The effect of this can perhaps best be seen in the one instance where we might at first sight least expect it: in the detailed descriptions of which Rabelais is so fond. Now in a description, we might feel, the speaker/writer has the least opportunity to be himself, since he is most constrained by external circumstances. But it is for this very reason that the writer who wants to insist that he is making it all up, that there is no 'external reality', will find the tension at its most acute when it comes to straight description. Here, for example, is a typical account of a battle-scene:

Suddenly hereafter he drew his brackmard or horsemans sword, wherewith he gave the keeper which held him, on the right

---

[1] Cf. Beaujour, *Le Jeu de Rabelais*, 140: 'Dans le monde du livre, le langage est objet, chose parmi les choses, mais chose susceptible de prendre vie, de pénétrer la conscience, de parler. Le livre est le lieu du gel et du dégel des paroles. Il n'est jamais le lieu ou apparaît la Nature.'

side such a sound slash, that he cut clean thorough the *jugularie* veins, and the *sphagitid* or transparent arteries of the neck, with the fore-part of the throat called the *gargareon*, even unto the two *Adenes*, which are throat-kernels; and redoubling the blow, he opened the *spinal* marrow betwixt the second and third verteber; there fell down that keeper stark dead to the ground. (i xliv)

Where we might have thought that the more precise the description the greater the sense of realism, the opposite is really the case. By focusing minutely on the details and ignoring the context, Rabelais drains the scene of any human emotion. The whole takes on a dream-like, self-contained quality, totally unrelated to any larger context of war and death. It would not really surprise us if the dead man were to rise again, as indeed Epistémon later does from a similar position.

One of the things Rabelais is doing here, as in the equally elaborate transcriptions of the sign-contest between Panurge and Thaumaste, is drawing attention to the nature of description in literature. What use is it, he asks implicitly, to describe in minute detail a series of incidents if one is incapable of giving these incidents any meaning? And what meaning can a writer give them? He can fit them into a plot, but to give them meaning would be to arrogate to himself God's power and fall into Panurge's error of imagining he was in touch with the workings of the universe. The sign-contest is not only an attack on scholastic argumentation; it is also, and more importantly, an attack on naïve induction. Rabelais sees that both logic-chopping and 'realistic' description make the mistake of tackling the details of things without asking how these details fit into a total scheme, or else imagining that such a question will resolve itself simply through the accumulation of yet more detail. The parodies of encyclopedias of useless knowledge in Cervantes and Swift perform the same function, and those readers who imagine they are merely criticising contemporary abuses are only protecting themselves from uncomfortable facts.[1]

What emerges from a scene like the fight quoted above is how

[1] See Chapter 5. An excellent discussion of the fallacy of naïve induction will be found in P. B. Medawar, *Induction and Intuition in Scientific Thought* (London, 1969).

far fictional description normally depends on a tacit agreement between author and reader as to *how much* description will do to maintain the illusion of reality. Too much, as here, or too little, as when Nabokov covers sixteen years of his hero's life in one sentence in *The Defence*, immediately shatters the illusion by calling attention to the act of description itself. What then is the author doing, writing a book? we are forced to ask; what are *we* doing reading it?[1] The more elaborate the description the more it throws into question its relation with any external reality, and the more it draws attention to itself as the product solely of the writer's will. We are made to picture him, sitting at his desk, forcing one word out after another, words whose sole significance, it now becomes obvious, is precisely this: that a man is writing them down, a man is uttering them.[2] What emerges is the writer's voice, but not saying anything unless it is simply reiterating the desire to speak. But this desire or rage to speak, to burst out of the shell of silence in which each of us is cocooned, is here allied to the knowledge that nothing I have to *say* has any authority and so will convey any meaning to another person. Yet once this is recognised and accepted by the writer, as it is here by Rabelais, he escapes from the privacy and arbitrariness in which he seems to be caught, since the *urge to speak*, as opposed to anything that is *said*, is one which is common to all men. And the reader, recognising this as well, will find a new freedom and release from his private silence in letting the author's voice surge up within him.

The enormous lists of names, the gigantic feasts, the exuberant piling up of words and phrases – which is what we first think of when we think of Rabelais – all these serve the same purpose. Language becomes a form of *action* rather than the mirror of a pre-established reality. And this in itself is a reality, since all of us desire to speak, to release the torrent of energy within us, but to release it not through animal screams and grunts but through the controlled and human form of language. Hence the place of

[1] This whole question of the nature of literary description is explored by Jean Ricardou in his *Problèmes du nouveau roman* (Paris, 1967) 91–121.

[2] In Robbe-Grillet the minute detail of the descriptions forces us to recognise that behind them lies not a writer writing but a seer seeing. The difference is a matter of tone. What is important is that in both the extremity of the 'realism' forces us to move from the description to what gave rise to it. See Chapter 12 below.

the mock-eulogies in this book. When Panurge delivers his speech in praise of debt he is not only parodying Ficino in praise of love, as the scholars inform us. We are meant to recognise that this *is* a mock-eulogy, that it does not describe the facts and that Panurge knows it. It is the same with Dindenault's praise of his sheep:

> What do you mean, Master of mine, answered the other? They are long Wool Sheep, from these did *Jason* take his *Golden Fleece*, The Gold of the House of *Burgundy* was drawn from them. Zwoons, Man, they are Oriental Sheep, Topping Sheep, Fatted Sheep, Sheep of Quality. . . . (IV vi)

These last words ('moutons de haute graisse') are exactly the ones used by Rabelais himself to describe his *book* in the prologue to *Gargantua*: 'Ces beaux livres de haute graisse'. In both places we are meant to see that the object does not correspond to the description, that the words are far in excess of the facts. The description itself becomes the true object: Dindenault really asks us to admire his rhetoric, not his sheep. But since the description of the book is part of the book, perhaps, after all, it is accurate enough, and the book really is 'de haute graisse . . .'.

Rabelais never ceases to remind us of the speaker of whatever words are uttered, and to show us that the content of the speeches is of little importance, that it is usually no more than an excuse to give vent to the pulsating energy within. Thus every word that is uttered in his book is carefully dissociated from himself – it is not said because he has *this* to say, but only because he *has to speak*. Unlike Picrochole and Dindenault and Panurge and Ulrich Gallet and all the other garrulous knaves who fill this book, Rabelais is supremely self-conscious. We feel him inserting himself into every role he parodies, drawing sustenance from it even as he pushes it just far enough to make us realise that he is fully aware of what he is doing. This is true even of the famous Humanist documents, such as the letters of the giants or the harangue (*contion*) of Jacobus de Bragmarto, which have been so earnestly pored over by scholars. In the oration of Ulrich Gallet ('There cannot arise amongst men a juster cause of grief, then when they receive hurt and damage, where they may justly expect for favour and good will; and not without cause (though without reason), have many, after they are fallen into such a calamitous accident, esteemed this indignity lesse supportable then the losse of their own lives. . . .') the slightly overinsistent Ciceronianisms draw attention to themselves and allow us to glimpse the playful artist behind the solemn ambassador. As Rabelais speaks he stands outside himself, both exercising his voice and reminding us of the fact that this is all he is doing. If he is very much like Panurge or Ulrich Gallet or Picrochole, there is one essential difference between them. It is the difference which we register when we watch a man who is not aware that he is on a tightrope stretched between two buildings and strides gaily along as if out to buy a packet of cigarettes, and when we watch a clown teeter oh so perilously on a line of chalk he has just drawn on the ground. We hold our breath in fear for the first man, but in admiration of the performance of the second. He has enlarged our sense of what it means to be a human being.

Our laughter at reading Rabelais stems from our recognition of the gap between words and things, between private fantasy and the reality of the world. To take his language by itself and talk of his wonderful comic zest is to blur the distinction between a conscious and an unconscious use of excess, between Rabelais and Panurge. To take the discussions of education and the woman question by themselves is to look for an extractable meaning hidden in the work, justifying its apparently absurd subject-matter. But if we read Rabelais as he asks to be read we will take note both of the content and of the transformation it undergoes in the process of creation. To read him in this way is to be made aware of the gap between our wishes and the world's reality, but it is also to be made aware of the validity of these wishes – for they are what lead to the creation of the book, as they are the expression of our desire to be alive.

The difference between Panurge and Pantagruel lies in the fact that the latter is aware of the fact that he is only human, a man with a man's limitations, and is thus able to some extent to overcome these limitations; while the former, imagining that he can be like God, becomes the victim of his mechanical impulses: our wishes are valid to the extent that we do not confuse them with the way the world goes (as we saw with Proust, the ultimate conflict between our wishes and the world's reality lies in the fact of death). Unaware that his vision is limited, Panurge remains forever locked in the prison of himself, while Pantagruel, recognising the natural human bondage to the 'man-locked set' is able to achieve a measure of freedom. His freedom is signalled by his ability to laugh, an ability denied to Panurge. And as laughter is the prerogative of Pantagruel so it can be that of the reader. Rabelais's book does not, like Dante's, draw us gradually into a truer, more meaningful world. Instead, setting traps for us and bombarding us with caricatures of our likely responses, it shows us ways of fulfilling our desires without falling into the trap of Panurge. It plays with us, but never in order to humiliate us as Panurge enjoys humiliating the unwary; it frees us from our private selves by teaching us how to laugh.

Rabelais begins his book by quoting Aristotle's famous dictum that what differentiates man from the animals is not his intellect but his capacity for laughter. He might perhaps, with his Franciscan training and its stress on original sin, have modified this and said that laughter is the distinctive feature not of man but of fallen man. In Heaven there is no laughter; but then there is no art in Heaven either.

5 Some Thoughts on the Rise of the Novel

> 'A sound methodology must provide an adequate theory of
> special incentive – a reason for making one observation rather
> than another, a restrictive clause that limits observation to
> something smaller than the universe of observables.'
>
> P. B. Medawar

I. MEANING AND ALLEGORY

Not long after Dante's death Boccaccio wrote an elaborate
defence of poetry directed against its literal-minded detractors,
men like Chaucer's Parson, who insisted that poetry had no place
in a Christian universe. He wrote:

> By the same token must Christian writers escape injury; for
> many even of our own tongue have been poets – nay, still
> survive – who, under cover of their compositions, have ex-
> pressed the deep and holy meaning of Christianity. One of
> many instances is our Dante. True, he wrote in his mother
> tongue, which he adapted to his artistic purpose; yet in
> the book which he called the *Commedia* he nobly described the
> threefold condition of departed souls consistently with the
> sacred teaching of theology.[1]

In other words, Dante's work may look blasphemous to the
uninitiated, but, if they could only see beneath the veil of the
fiction, they would discover the work to be perfectly in keeping
with sacred doctrine. They would see, for instance, that the work
is an allegory in which Virgil stands for Reason, Beatrice for
theology, and the story represents what the human spirit has to do
in order to find God in this life.

Boccaccio's argument, which we have already met in Rabelais's
burlesque of Frère Lubin, seemed to answer criticism so well
that the allegorical interpretation of the *Commedia* went un-
challenged until the nineteenth century, when the general revolt
against allegory as being cold and anti-poetical led to a reconsideration of Dante's poem. The Romantic critics and their

[1] *Boccaccio on Poetry*, ed. and trans. C. G. Osgood (New York, 1956) 99.

followers – notably Croce – stressed the fact that Virgil and Beatrice are presented not as allegorical personifications but as real people; it is the humanity of Dante's characters that is important, not what they signify, what they are rather than what they represent. More recently, however, many scholars have in turn reacted against this Romantic view and have reverted to Boccaccio's approach as being historically more accurate and therefore liable to do more justice to Dante. Fortunately a few scholars – notably Auerbach and Singleton – have not been blinded by literary polemics, and their work allows us to see that the whole quarrel is in reality a false one, and that it is based on a misunderstanding, already present in Boccaccio, of what allegory meant for Dante and for the Middle Ages.

In his unfinished philosophical work, the *Convivio*, Dante discusses allegory in terms very similar to those of Boccaccio. He mentions first the literal sense, which does not go beyond the letter of any fable, and then goes on to

> the sense that is hidden under the cloak of these fables, and it is a truth hidden under the beautiful lie; as when Ovid says that Orpheus tamed the wild beasts with his zither and caused the trees and the stones to come to him; which signifies that the wise man with the instrument of his voice would make cruel hearts gentle and humble, and would make those who do not live in science and art do his will; and those who have no kind of life of reason in them are as stones. (II i 2–4)

Already in a chapter of the *Vita Nuova* Dante had digressed from his description of the course of his love for Beatrice to argue that he is a poor poet who cannot reduce a personification such as the God of Love to its psychological reality; the God of Love, that is, is nothing but a personification of an abstract quality, Love. Dante's position here seems to be very similar to that of Boccaccio. But he has only made this point in order to introduce a second, which he does in the very next chapter. Here the God of Love disappears and is replaced by Beatrice. The result of this is to make us realise that Beatrice herself cannot be reduced in the same way to a psychological quality. She is not a personification but a real person. We saw in an earlier chapter that in fact Dante's whole effort is directed at making us accept her as such; it is because she is both real *and* a miracle that she is important

to him, for it is this double fact that guarantees the meaningfulness of the universe and God's divine plan. Dante, in fact, says
what he does about the God of Love precisely in order to demonstrate the irreducibility of Beatrice. Just as he contrasts the poems
in the *Vita Nuova*, which are his own, with the prose, which
records reality, so here he contrasts the personification, which is
his own poetic device, with the reality of Beatrice. In a similar
way the description of allegory in the *Convivio* shows us Dante
exploring what he feels to be the scope of a certain kind of poetry,
of fables such as that of Orpheus. But this does not mean that
Dante conceives his own work in this light. In fact, in the famous
letter to Can Grande della Scala, where he outlines his views on
the way the *Commedia* should be read, he chooses a rather
different kind of example:

> To elucidate, then, what we have to say, be it known that the
> sense of this work is not simple, but on the contrary it may be
> called polysemous, that is to say, 'of more senses than one';
> for it is one sense that we get through the letter, and another
> which we get through the thing the letter signifies; and the first
> is called literal, but the second allegorical or mystic. And this
> mode of treatment, for its better manifestation, may be con-
> sidered in this verse: 'When Israel came out of Egypt, and the
> house of Jacob from a people of strange speech, Judaea became
> his sanctification, Israel his power.' For if we inspect the letter
> alone, the departure of the children of Israel from Egypt in
> the time of Moses is presented to us; if the allegory, our
> redemption wrought by Christ; if the moral sense, the conver-
> sion of the soul from the grief and misery of sin to the state of
> grace is presented to us; if the anagogical, the departure of the
> holy soul from the slavery of this corruption to the liberty of
> eternal glory is presented to us. And although these mystic
> senses have each their special denominations, they may all in
> general be called allegorical, since they differ from the literal
> and historical.

The difference between the story of the Exodus and the fable of
Orpheus obviously lies in the way the literal narrative is read.
With the classical fable the fictive story is there only for the sake
of the allegorical meaning; once that meaning is extracted from
it it disappears. This form of allegory is in fact to be found in the

Scriptures, notably in the parables spoken by Christ. But the
Exodus is different from the parables in that it is the account of
an event which we are asked to believe really occurred. However
many meanings may emerge from it, the event itself cannot
vanish, since it was not devised for the sake of something else but
exists in its own right. Since it does this and at the same time
yields further, allegorical meanings, it points to the fact that God
caused it to happen in order to reveal these other meanings to
man. This, indeed, is how St Thomas describes it in the *Summa*:

> The author of Holy Scripture is God, in whose power it is to
> signify His meaning, not by words only (as man also can do)
> but also by things themselves. So, whereas in every other science
> things are signified by words, this science has the property that
> the things signified by the words have themselves also a signifi-
> cation. Therefore that first signification whereby words signify
> things belongs to the first sense, the historical or literal. That
> signification whereby things signified by words have them-
> selves also a signification is called the spiritual sense, which is
> based on the literal and presupposes it. (1 i 10)

The parables of Christ say one thing and mean another; so do
the events of Christ's life. But there is a difference in *kind* between
the two. For anyone can speak in parables, but only the Son of
God can die and rise again. That is why it is useful to distinguish
between the two by calling the first a form of allegory and the
second something like *figura*.[1] To try and assimilate them, to
imagine that the events recorded in the Gospels have the same
status as the speeches recorded there is tantamount to denying
the Incarnation, and to do this is of course to deny the entire
Christian view of history, since it is the Incarnation which gives a
new dimension to such historical events as the sacrifice of Isaac
and the Exodus from Egypt. Now this is exactly what the early
Gnostic interpreters of the Gospels did, since for them it was
inconceivable that God should have allowed his Son to suffer the
brutal and ugly death recorded there. As St Thomas says:

> They [the Gnostics] pretended that whatever He did as man –
> for instance, that He was born, that He ate, drank, walked,
> suffered, and was buried – was all unreal, though having some

[1] See Chapter 2 above, p. 29, n. 1.

semblance of reality. Consequently they reduced the whole mystery of the Incarnation to a work of fiction.[1]

But of course it is on the doctrine of the Incarnation, on the belief that Christ *was* born, did eat, drink, walk and suffer, that the Christian view of man and nature rests. For the Incarnation not only reveals how God works in history, but also gives to each Christian the possibility of eternal salvation from the sin of Adam which brought death into the world. To read the Scriptures figurally is to affirm that history, and our own lives, have meaning, and it is to understand God's plan for mankind and hence for each one of us. To read them as the Gnostics read them, or as we would read the fable of Orpheus or a story involving the God of Love, is to fall back into a private world where each of us translates a fable into whatever moral or mystical meaning we wish. Instead of having our minds opened to what the world is like we reduce the world to our own preconceived ideas.[2]

But of course there is a problem here. The proof that there is a problem is that no one ever seems to agree on the meaning and nature of allegory, whereas it would appear, from my exposition, to be relatively clear. The problem rests on the fact that though there is a difference in status between the events recorded in the Gospels and the words spoken by Christ, both are presented to

[1] *Summa Contra Gentiles*, iv xxix.

[2] I am heavily indebted to Singleton's numerous studies of Dante for the foregoing paragraphs. The translations from St Thomas are his. That these remarks can be extended to all the art of the Middle Ages can be seen from Proust's remarkable comments on Giotto. When Swann compares the pregnant kitchenmaid to Giotto's 'Charity' in the Arena Chapel at Padua, Marcel is led to meditate on the effect of those frescoes: 'But in later years I understood that the arresting strangeness, the special beauty of these frescoes lay in the great part played in each of them by its symbols, while the fact that they were depicted, not as symbols (for the thought symbolised was nowhere expressed), but as real things, actually felt or materially handled, added something more precise and more literal to their meaning, something more concrete and more striking to the lesson they imparted.' (1 108; 1 81,) The whole passage conveys marvellously the sense we get from medieval art that things are as they are not because this corresponds to an inner truth, but because there is an order to the world which it lies beyond any individual fully to understand. The description of the kitchen-maid which follows this is strikingly close to Rilke – Proust conveys the sense of our bodies as a world which our mind cannot grasp, though if it could it would in some sense release us into life. See Chapter 12 below.

us in words. And, as we have seen, the nature of language is such that when we are dealing with words we are never dealing with the literal, but always with something that requires interpretation. This is why the figural view of Scripture is not self-evident, why the reading of Scripture in this way depends on a prior 'rule'. That is to say that since both the story of the Exodus and the story of Orpheus come to us in the form of words, both appear to have the same status, and it is only by accepting some external criterion that we can read the first as having 'really' happened, and the second as simply being a fable. One might be tempted to say that we read the two stories differently because the Exodus has received some confirmation from archaeology as being a historical fact. But I don't think this is really the answer we are looking for. There are, after all, many things in the Bible for which we simply lack corroborative evidence, yet our reading of it does not continually alter, depending on the state of present-day scholarship. No. Although the Bible comprises a vast number of different kinds of writings, the historical books of both Old and New Testaments elicit from us a consistent response. It would take us too far afield to see how this is achieved, but, since our examples related to the Gospels in the first place, it may be as well to look briefly at them in order to see if there is anything there which directs our reading in either the Gnostic or the Christian direction.

For the Christian, we said, there is a drama to human history, and it is this drama that requires interpretation. But the chief actor in this drama also guides us towards its interpretation: 'Even as Jonah was three days and three nights in the belly of the whale, so shall the son of man be three days and three nights in the depths of the earth,' says Christ in St Matthew, and in John: 'As Moses lifted up the serpent in the wilderness, even so must the son of man be lifted up.' Christ in fact interprets his actions for us even as he voluntarily goes through with them. He deliberately plays out his life in order to guide us to the meaningfulness of the universe. *Figura* is not an invention of modern scholars, nor even of the early Church; it is the way Christ himself conceives of his own redemptive action. And in the eucharistic sacrament he gives the Church the means to re-enact that action forever. As Dom Gregory Dix has pointed out, and as I stressed in an earlier chapter, the meaning of *anamnesis* here is a recalling

or re-presenting a thing in such a way that it is regarded not so
much as being absent as being itself presently operative in its
effects. This is a meaning which the Latin *memoria* and the
English *recall* and *represent* do not bear. The early writers on the
subject, moreover, concentrate on the eucharist as a single action,
rather than upon the matter of the sacrament itself, as modern
Westerners tend to do. The idea of 'becoming what you are' is
the key to the whole eschatological teaching of the New Testament, and it is carried out in the liturgical *action*. As Dix says,
the pre-Nicene Church conceived of the eucharistic action as one
by Christ himself, 'perpetually offering through and in His Body
the Church his flesh for the life of the world'. It is 'the perpetua-
tion in time by way of anamnesis of His eternally accepted and
redeeming act'. After St Thomas, however, the old teaching on
the eucharist begins to disappear, as it is made the subject of
purely philosophical debate. We have already seen how Chaucer
can parody the debate over free-will and predestination, which
also springs up only in the later Middle Ages, and how *The
Imitation of Christ* took the eucharist mainly as the focus for
personal piety and devotion. This view is maintained by both the
Protestants and the Catholics of the Counter-Reformation, with
churchmen and philosophers on both sides endlessly arguing
about the substance of the bread and wine and no longer seemingly aware of the overall eucharistic *action*.[1] But what it is
important for us to grasp (and it is irrelevant whether or not we
are believers) is that the Gospels themselves seem to show Christ at
some pains to distinguish his actions from his words and then
to give his actions a meaning in the context of the entire course
of universal history. The Gnostic reading of the text then, which,
because both Christ's words and his actions are communicated
in words, fails to differentiate between them and sees all in terms
of an inner spiritual struggle, may quite simply be a failure to
respond to the text correctly.

The same may be true of the debates over Dante's allegory.
We have seen how in the *Vita Nuova* he distinguished between
the words written down by him as poems and the words in the
book which are transcripts of reality – words which inform us of
details of Beatrice's life and death. Were the *Vita Nuova* about
the God of Love, as the *Convivio* is about Lady Philosophy, we

[1] Dix, *The Shape of the Liturgy*, 243 ff.

would be able to reduce the allegory to a moral content and see it as the dramatisation, for poetic purposes, of a struggle going on in Dante's psyche. But since it is about Beatrice, we are made to see that it cannot be reduced to any other terms than itself, and yet that the events it records are meaningful because the universe, like any book, is meaningful. The reader is confronted with a human being, Beatrice, who is also a miracle. He cannot get away from the fact or separate the two things. If he reads the book at all he is forced to revise his way of seeing the world, since he has to acknowledge the possibility, in his life, of such a being as Beatrice.

The same is true of the *Commedia*. There are many minor allegories in that work, just as there are many parables in the Gospels. But we cannot take refuge in saying that what is important is Dante's characterisation of Virgil, Beatrice and the hundreds of other figures in the poem, or in saying that what is important is Dante's allegorical meaning. Neither of these views comes to terms with the poem. Virgil is the real historical Virgil to Dante, *and* he has a certain part to play in the *action*. He plays this part because that is the part God has assigned to him, not that which Dante has assigned to him. All that Dante has done is to transcribe and reveal a meaningful universe; instead of seeing it as made up of discrete figures and occurrences, he has revealed its shape and therefore its meaning. To say then that the story of Paolo and Franccsca is no more allegorical than a story in *Woman's Own*[1], since both are clearly capable of being interpreted in moral terms, is to miss the point completely. There is nothing inherent in the episode which renders it any different from a story in *Woman's Own*, it is true; it derives its extra dimension of meaning from its part in the total action of the poem – which means, quite simply, with Dante, from being where it is in the poem. When we first read about Paolo and Francesca, as when Dante first sees them, our emotions are those of pity rather than revulsion. Why should they be there? we ask. What cruel God has set these innocent lovers in the torments of

---

[1] As does A. D. Nuttall in *Two Concepts of Allegory* (London, 1967) 27–8. This infuriatingly brilliant book provides the best attempt I know to get rid of the distinction between *figura* and allegory. Nuttall succeeds in doing this because he conducts his arguments in terms of logic and logically there is no essential difference between the two. It is not logical coherence that is at stake, however, but the relation to 'reality'.

Hell? But as Dante climbs down through the circles of Hell and up the slopes of Purgatory, he comes to understand why they are there, and so do we. They are there not so much because God wants them to be there as because *they do themselves*. To explain Dante's theology and say: Paolo and Francesca are in Hell because that is where the laws of the system place them, they represent fleshly lust in Dante's allegory and we mustn't on any account think of them as we would of friends – to say this is just as wrong as to say: secretly Dante knew better than his system and sympathised with the lovers and we must follow him and do the same. Both these responses to the poem are wrong because they both deny the tension within the poem which is precisely what gives it its meaning. The vision from God's own point of view is hard to attain. Hard for the poet and hard for us. There is resistance all the way, though, as Virgil tells the pilgrim Dante, the nearer to God you get the easier becomes the ascent. Because Paolo and Francesca are not reducible to anything but themselves, we as readers cannot help experiencing their fate. This fate is the torment of a mixed desire: like all the people in Hell they both want to be out of their misery and also can't bear to be anywhere but where they are. They are like drug addicts who can't kick the habit. Dante would be failing us, and we would be failing ourselves as readers of the poem, if he did not present, and we did not respond to, the conflict between their will and the pattern of the universe. Dante's understanding of their plight, which is what conditions our own understanding, can only come at the very end of the journey, when he sees them as part of the total pattern. But this does not mean that he then feels their anguish less intensely, and neither should we. After all, even Christ, the Son of God, called out at the last: 'My God, My God, why hast thou forsaken me?' This the Gnostic interpreters preferred to forget. Certainly it makes life easier that way.

II. PURITANISM, ALLEGORY AND PRIVATE WORLDS

In the journal which he kept, in common with so many Puritans, and in which he recorded the daily events of his life and meditated on their meaning, John Winthrop writes of a snake which appeared during a sermon before the synod in New England, and was killed by one of the elders. And he remarks:

This being so remarkable, and nothing falling out but by divine providence, it is out of doubt, the Lord discovered somewhat of his mind in it. The serpent is the devil; the synod, the representative of the churches of Christ in New England. The devil had formerly and lately attempted their disturbance and dissolution; but their faith in the seed of the woman overcame him and crushed his head.[1]

The serpent does not act *like* the devil; he *is* the devil. We learn nothing from this about serpents, since this one is immediately translated into a symbol for the devil. The action is never allowed to emerge in its naturalistic implications, but is at once translated into allegory; and as soon as it is given a 'meaning' the concrete event evaporates.

In Dante, as we have seen, the allegory depends on the perception of an entire pattern, whereas here, as in Bunyan, it depends on the connection of isolated facts. It is easy to see why this should be so. The one important question the Calvinist must ask himself is always: 'Am I one of the elect or one of the damned?' Yet there is no one who can give him an answer to this question. Each man must decide for himself which it is. In an effort to do so the Calvinist searches day and night within his own breast, in the Scriptures, and in the world around him, for signs of his election or damnation. Every deed, every thought, every combination of black marks on white paper must have a meaning for him. But what meaning? The whole universe is at once filled with meaning and devoid of any criterion whereby this meaning can be ascertained. Nor is it just this life that is at stake here: the whole of our eternal salvation or damnation is figured in the signs, if only we could decipher them. Clearly it is only a matter of time before the individual starts trying to prove to himself that he is one of the elect. He tries to forestall the signs, to surprise the meaning by acting as though he *were* one of the elect. For to act like this may itself perhaps be a sign of election. To shut out the inner voice which might still raise doubts about the certainty of this he works harder than ever and examines himself more closely. For every action must have a motive, and this must be drawn out and studied. We can watch ourselves acting and ensure that

[1] Quoted in Charles Feidelson Jr, *Symbolism and American Literature* (Chicago, 1960) 77–8.

our motives are worthy, which will in turn prove that we are among the elect. That is the chief reason for keeping a journal: to note our actions and study our motives.

There is something irresponsible about such an attitude. What I mean by this can be brought out by comparing *The Pilgrim's Progress* with the work of Dante and Langland. Because Bunyan's book is an allegory whose theme is the search for salvation it has usually been talked about in the same terms as *Piers Plowman* and the *Commedia*. Yet the differences are enormous. Whereas in the two medieval works the 'I' figure undertakes the journey, in Bunyan he merely dreams about Christian's journey. Instead of moving slowly towards understanding (and leading the reader with him) he passively records a film which passes before his eyes. In Dante and Langland the narrator-hero goes in search of meaning; in Bunyan the meaning is there from the start. Christian does not learn how to make sense of the world, he learns how to flee from it. He is a Pilgrim from the City of Destruction to Mount Zion, and his task is to escape the World, the Flesh and the Devil. For Dante and Langland, on the other hand, the task is to escape not from the world but from a false and subjective view of the world; what they discover is not a new set of facts, but a new understanding of the nature of that false view. Thus their poems include and account for that which is to be defeated, whereas Bunyan presents us with a simple opposition: 'Christianity and the Customs of our Town of Vanity were diametrically opposite and could not be reconciled.' We are shown a world which we either accept or reject, depending on our prior allegiances and our fear of damnation. The story itself does nothing to alter these; it teaches us how to behave but tells us nothing about either the world around us or ourselves.

At the end of the first part of his book Bunyan tells us to 'part the curtain of allegory and see the husk of truth'. We are back with Boccaccio and his defence of Dante: the story is meaningful in so far as it is reducible. But this is true of the story because it is true (as the episode described by Winthrop has shown us), for the Calvinist, of the world as well. There too every incident and every object is filled with meaning. But the very ease with which meaning can be found, the lack of any kind of tension such as we noticed in Dante, gives us the feeling that there is something arbitrary about this. That is what I meant by talking of its irresponsibility: it does not account for the opposition it sets up between light and darkness, good and evil, and so on, it merely states it. And we have the feeling that the narrative follows the course it does simply because it illustrates Bunyan's own point of view; reading him, we are never readers of ourselves.

That there is a close connection between Puritanism and the rise of the novel has long been a platitude of literary history. This is usually discussed in terms of the Puritan interest in the inner life and in the writing of spiritual autobiography as a form of self-expression, but there is rarely any questioning of the nature or implication of these things. Or perhaps we could say that the *reader* is never taken into account in such discussions. But if we introduce him and ask how he is affected, some interesting facts emerge. The world of *Moll Flanders*, for example, is clearly very different from that of John Winthrop's journal; yet the relation of Winthrop to the world around him, as presented in the example of the snake quoted above, is very much like the relationship set up between the reader of Defoe and his novel. Both Winthrop and the reader close their eyes and allow their imaginations to play on what is presented to them; neither, while engaged on this, would dream of questioning the reality of what their imagination provides. Unlike our ordinary experience of life, there is nothing, we feel, that could happen to Winthrop which would make him alter his views or his way of looking at the world. And the same is true of the reader of any Defoe novel while he is immersed in it: there is nothing in the novel to falsify what the imagination creates.

It may sound like a commonplace to say that the traditional novel – which can be said to emerge with Defoe – makes its appeal to the imagination, but I mean by this something very precise. Proust, it will be remembered, compared the imagination of childhood to a magic lantern which projects its images on the wall of any room. Proust himself was at pains to distinguish his kind of novel from such a projection, and to show that it was precisely this childlike imagination which played into the hands of Habit and stopped us from understanding either ourselves or other people. Yet it is because of the extraordinary power of his own childhood imagination that he was able to recognise its true character, and one of the wonders of his book lies in his ability to communicate this power while freeing himself – and us – from it. It so happens that in those early volumes devoted to the imagination of childhood he gives us what is perhaps the most sympathetic and understanding account of what exactly happens when we read a novel like Defoe's, a novel of the imagination.

Let us look at the scene in detail. The young Marcel, urged by his grandmother to go out into the fresh air, would take his book into the garden and sit down under the chestnut tree so that he felt hidden from the eyes of anyone who might come to call on the family. Sitting thus he would feel his thoughts about the book he was reading provided a kind of net, protecting him from the external world, rendering him invisible, a zone of feelings rather than a human being:

> Upon the sort of screen, patterned with different states and impressions, which my consciousness would quietly unfold while I was reading, and which ranged from the most deeply hidden aspirations of my heart to the wholly external view of the horizon spread out before my eyes at the foot of the garden, what was from the first the most permanent and the most intimate part of me, the lever whose incessant movements controlled all the rest, was my belief in the philosophic richness and beauty of the book I was reading, and my desire to appropriate these to myself, whatever the book might be. . . . Next to this central belief, which, while I was reading, would be constantly in motion from my inner self to the outer world, towards the discovery of Truth, came the emotions aroused in me by the action in which I would be taking part, for these afternoons were crammed with more dramatic and sensational events than occur, often, in a whole lifetime. These were the events which took place in the book I was reading. It is true that the people concerned in them were not what Françoise would have called 'real people'. But none of the feelings which the joys or misfortunes of a 'real' person awaken in us can be awakened except through a mental picture of those joys or misfortunes; and the ingenuity of the first novelist lay in his understanding that, as the picture was the one essential element in the complicated structure of our emotions, so that simplification of it which consisted in the suppression, pure and simple, of 'real' people would be a decided improvement.

'Real' people, he says, remain opaque to us, and also to themselves; we perceive them only through our senses, and so can
never really understand them:

> The novelist's happy discovery was to think of substituting for
> those opaque sections, impenetrable by the human spirit, their
> equivalent in immaterial sections, things, that is, which the
> spirit can assimilate to itself. After which it matters not that
> the actions, the feelings of this new order of creatures appear to
> us in the guise of truth, since we have made them our own,
> since it is in ourselves that they are happening. . . . And once
> the novelist has brought us to that state, in which, as in all
> purely mental states, every emotion is multiplied ten-fold, into
> which his book comes to disturb us as might a dream, but a
> dream more lucid, and of a more lasting impression than those
> which come to us in sleep; why, then, for the space of an hour
> he sets free within us all the joys and sorrows of the world, a
> few of which, only, we should have to spend years of our actual
> life in getting to know, and the keenest, the most intense of
> which would never have been revealed to us because the slow
> course of their development stops our perception of them. It
> is the same in life; the heart changes, and that is our worst
> misfortune; but we learn of it only from reading or by imagina-
> tion; for in reality its alteration, like that of certain natural
> phenomena, is so gradual that, even if we are able to
> distinguish, successively, each of its different states, we are still
> spared the actual sensation of change. (1 111–14; 184–6)

Just as in childhood to utter the name of Mme de Guermantes,
of Florence, of Pisa was in some way to possess them, so the
description of scenes in the book he was reading would give him
the impression 'of their being actually part of Nature herself' –
graspable, that is, in their essence. Nowhere have the joys of
reading been better described than in this passage, and one feels
with Proust, as with Nabokov or Seferis, that he is able to retain
throughout his life this ability to read totally and purely, as most
of us can only do in childhood, allowing the book to become a
part of himself and giving himself up absolutely to it. His essays
on books and writers, like the essays on the painters he loved, all
convey the warm glow of those Sunday afternoons under the

chestnut tree when he experienced the happiest hours of his life.

But his own novel is another matter. It is not a novel about the imagination but about reality. In childhood we imagine that the world is what we feel it to be; but this is not the case, and this trust in the imagination must be outgrown. Indeed, it comes to be seen as the one real barrier between us and the truth. The novel is the record of one disillusionment after another, the progressive discovery that nowhere does the world conform to my imagination of it. And yet it is a novel which also records the triumph of the imagination. Let us try to disentangle these different strands.

One clue is to be found, in the passage just quoted, in the discussion of character in novels, and of the contrast between this and the opaqueness of 'real' people. What Proust suggests here is that when reading a novel we feel that we can trust the characters because we can trust the author. The characters are not going to do anything we do not expect; if they do something unexpected then this unexpectedness too will turn out to have its justification. Of that we can be certain; and it is from this certainty that our pleasure derives. But how different it is in real life. The rule here is that trust is wholly absent. We can never know for certain what other people feel; the one thing of which we may be sure is that they do not feel as we imagine they do, and they certainly do not feel as we do. This, after all, is the discovery that propels the narrative forward, for it is the lesson of the mother's kiss withheld, a lesson repeated in the riverside encounter with the peasant and then at regular intervals throughout the book. Other people are – other. And the more we forget this the further from us they get. To forget it is in fact the cardinal sin for Proust, that *indifférence* which would set my trivial pleasures above another's pain, which treats other people only as adjuncts of myself. Proust's novel is therefore designed to *reverse* the expectations we normally bring to a novel: it *undoes* our trust in the characters, consciously setting itself up against the impulse of the novel form. But it can only do this successfully if it allows this trust to form in the first place. Hence the size of the book, whose reading time must be a noticeable portion of our lives in order to convey the gradual alterations of reality, the actual sensation of change. He has to present us with characters who are never the same thing twice and who yet emerge finally as themselves. His novel is built to tease us out of imagination into reality.[1]

But this does not mean that it denies the imagination. On the contrary, it recognises the enormous powers of imagination, but in so doing tries to delimit its place in our lives and thus prevent us from mistaking it for reality. Like Freud, Proust realises that the imagination is narcissistic and that it finds its allies where it can, in the superego or the web of Habit, which prevents us recognising our contingency and mortality, as well as in the fancies projected by desire. But unlike Sartre, Proust does not hold the belief that the allegiance to the imaginative world of childhood is a kind of bad faith which is to some extent socially conditioned. He knows very well that the need to tell stories and to listen to them is an essential part of our make-up: we need patterns in order to live and we need to listen to the voice which weaves the pattern. Already in one of the first books ever written we are presented with the drama of the disguised Odysseus bursting into tears as he listens to the bard at the Phaeacian court recounting the story of the sack of Troy and of his own deeds and sufferings:

With this he took a chair by the side of King Alcinous, for they were already serving the portions and mixing the wine. An equerry now came in leading their beloved bard Demodocus, the people's favourite. He seated him in the centre of the company with his back against one of the high columns, and at once the thoughtful Odysseus, carving a portion from the chine of a white-tusked boar, which was so large that more than half was left, with plenty of rich fat on either side, called to a serving-man and said:

'Here, my man, take this helping to Demodocus and let him eat it, with kindly wishes from my unhappy self. No one on earth can help honouring and respecting the bards, for the Muse has taught them the art of song and she loves the minstrel fraternity.'

... When they had satisfied their thirst and hunger, Odysseus turned to the minstrel and said:

'Demodocus, I give you the highest possible praise. ... But

[1] One could say that Proust has to create *in his book* that sense of history which Dante finds in the history of the world – an excellent illustration of the way the modern writer has to 'do it all himself'.

I ask you now to change your theme and sing to us of the making of the Wooden Horse, which Epeius built with Athene's help, and which my lord Odysseus contrived to introduce one day into the citadel of Troy as an ambuscade. . . . If you can satisfy me in telling of this tale I shall be ready to acknowledge to the world how generously the god has endowed you with the heavenly gift of song.'

The bard took his cue from Odysseus and beginning with an invocation to the god unfolded his tale. He took it up at the point where the Argives after setting fire to their huts had embarked on their galleys and were sailing off, while the renowned Odysseus and his party were already sitting in the place of assembly at Troy, concealed within the Horse. . . . He went on to sing how the Achaean warriors, deserting their hollow ambuscade, poured out from the Horse to ravage Troy; how they scattered through the steep streets of the city leaving ruin in their wake; and how Odysseus, looking like Ares himself, went straight to Deiphobus' house with the gallant Menelaus. . . .

Odysseus broke down as the famous minstrel sang his lay, and his cheeks were wet with the tears that ran down from his eyes. He wept as a woman weeps when she throws her arms round the body of her beloved husband, fallen in battle before his city and his comrades. . . .[1]

What Odysseus weeps at is the image of himself transformed into a hero of legend, someone other than the person who is weeping. As Hannah Arendt says of this moment: 'What had been sheer occurrence now became "history".' And who is to say whether the Odysseus who performed those great exploits is the Odysseus sung by the bard or the Odysseus listening to the bard?

This need to transform sheer occurrence into history by verbalising it is beautifully caught by Virginia Woolf in her description of Neville in *The Waves*, when, lying at the edge of the cricket-field, he listens to his friend Bernard telling stories:

'And now,' said Neville, 'let Bernard begin. Let him burble on, telling us stories, while we lie recumbent. Let him describe

[1] *Odyssey*, book VIII, ll. 469-530 trans. E.V. Rieu (Harmondsworth, 1946).

what we have all seen so that it becomes a sequence. . . . When he talks, when he makes his foolish comparisons, a lightness comes over one. One floats too, as if one were that bubble; one is freed; I have escaped, one feels. . . . The sentence tails off feebly. Yes, the appalling moment has come when Bernard's power fails him and there is no longer any sequence and he sags and twiddles a bit of string and falls silent, gaping as if about to burst into tears. Among the tortures and devastations of life is this then – our friends are not able to finish their stories. [1]

In Virginia Woolf, as in Homer, the poignancy of the situation lies in the double focus, in our simultaneous awareness of sheer occurrence and of history. We note the triumphant metamorphosis of the one into the other and also its pathos, just as our seeing Marcel sitting under his tree and then entering with him into the purer world of the book in which he is absorbed suddenly makes us feel the enormous gap between life and books, and makes us wonder how we could ever have imagined that the one could absorb the other.

But let us be quite clear about what is involved here. It is not, as is sometimes maintained, that art imposes form on the content of reality and so distorts it, but that the act of perception or the act of consciousness itself is never a neutral one. Proust and Homer and Virginia Woolf are all aware of this, but the traditional novel appears to ignore it. As a result it implicitly assumes that the world and the world as we are made conscious of it are one. Proust and Virginia Woolf, on the other hand, by emphasising the will to form that is characteristic of consciousness, allow us to sense both history and flux, and the gap that there will always be between them. To recognise a gap is agony, but without recognition there is no chance of ever bridging it. In all three of the passages just quoted, our sense of the gap forces us out of the shell of habit and into the sudden awareness of reality. [2]

[1] *The Waves* (London, 1960) 27.

[2] Cf. Geoffrey Hartman's comments: 'We recognise here the dogmatic factor in realism: its assumption that a direct contact with life – with things themselves – is always available. Forms are therefore a betrayal of life. A necessary evil, they stand arbitrarily yet nobly between the novelist and life, to curb and kill. Does life whelm the novelist in this manner? It is doubtful that we are as directly in touch with life as we would like to

III. WORDS AS OBJECTS

The first edition of the *Vita Nuova* appeared in 1576, only a few years after the Council of Trent, where Catholics defined the strategy whereby they were going to win back the ground they had lost to their Protestant opponents over the previous half-century. That edition, as Singleton has pointed out, contained a number of interesting changes from the original manuscript. The word *beata* for Beatrice was avoided; *beatitudine* was altered to *felicita* and *salute* to *quiete*. The most important omission occurred in chapter 24, where Dante tells how he sees a lady called Giovanna coming towards him, followed by Beatrice, and he exclaims in surprise because 'her name Giovanna comes from that Giovanni [John] who preceded the true light, saying: "*Ego vox clamantis in deserto: parate viam domini.*" ' The editors clearly felt that the analogy of Beatrice with Christ, explicit here, was blasphemous, and they tried to remove all trace of it. But what their alterations really show is that they no longer understood the nature of analogy. As far as they can see Dante is saying that Beatrice *is* Christ, and if this were the case it would of course *be* blasphemous. But, as we saw, the relationship is never one of persons but of actions: what Dante is asking the reader to accept is not that Beatrice is Christ, or even that she is to him what Christ is to mankind, but that her *relationship* to him is analogous to that of Christ's relationship with mankind – and this of course can only be the case because of the sanctions of Christ's own actions. What the editors have thus done by their alterations is quite simply to stop the book making any assertions about the real world, the world in which the reader lives. They have reduced its status to that of just another story of a poet's love for a young girl.

In his book on religious art in Europe after the Council of Trent, Émile Mâle has thoroughly documented the effects of the disappearance of the notion of analogy in the field of the visual

---

be. And the modern novelist does like to be: he suffers, more than ever, under an ideal obligation to the totality of experience.' ('The Heroics of Realism', in *Beyond Formalism* (Yale, 1970).) Hartman seems to be one of the few Anglo-Saxon critics to grasp the fact that we are not naturally, as by right, in contact with reality. Unfortunately his book of essays came to my attention too late for me to make use of his many fine insights.

arts. The change was not of course confined to the Catholic
camp. In the realm of literature in particular it was even more
marked on the Protestant side. In 1578 the French Protestant
poet Guillaume du Bartas published an epic on the creation of
the world which had an enormous success, especially in England,
for the next half-century. Gabriel Harvey, the University Professor of Rhetoric at Cambridge, proclaimed that du Bartas was
'the treasurer of Humanity, and the Jeweller of Divinity for the
highness of his subject, and the majesty of his verse, nothing
inferior unto Dante . . . a right inspired and enravished Poet;
full of chosen, grave, profound, venerable, and stately matter;
even in the next Degree to the sacred and reverend style of
heavenly Divinity itself'. Ben Jonson, however, wrote that 'he
thought not Bartas a Poet but a Verser, because he wrote not
Fiction'. What Jonson meant was that this huge poem was nothing but a paraphrase of the Biblical account of creation, and
that the 'matter' is 'grave, profound and stately' for the simple
reason that it is the 'matter' of Scripture itself. The difference
between this and *Piers Plowman* or the *Commedia* is instructive.
The medieval poems are both concerned to make us see the
pattern of God in the world we live in; that is why they set their
fiction so solidly in the present. Du Bartas does not look at this
world at all. Unfortunately it is du Bartas rather than Dante who
becomes the model of the seventeenth century, leading Abraham
Cowley to write of him that the 'Eternal Word hast call'd forth
Me/Th'Apostle, to . . . teach that Truth is truest Poesie.' It is
rather as though Chaucer's Parson had supplanted Chaucer himself.

   This argument about 'truth' and 'fiction' involves more than
a debate about a specific art form. More even than a debate about
the value of art itself. What we are witnessing is the emergence
of a new way of thinking, which is replacing the old, or if not a
new way of thinking at least a new model of the mind. We saw the
beginnings of this change in Boccaccio's defence of Dante. When
allegory is reduced to moral content and the notion of analogy
falls away then it is easy to see how fiction can be taken as nothing
more than the sugaring of a hard core of moral truth. And if
this is so then not only allegory but poetry in general comes to be
taken as merely ornament, decoration, simply that which makes
palatable a truth which can be more simply expressed in logical

terms. And if poetry and truth are thus opposed to each other, so are rhetoric and logic. The mind comes to be seen as a *space* in which logic and rhetoric jostle each other for position. The more space can be filled up by logic, the closer to the truth will we be; rhetoric, on the other hand, like poetry, belongs to the field of illusion. Peter Ramus, the Renaissance educationalist whose rhetorical theory has been seen as one of the main symptoms (and causes) of this changing view of the mind, describes the process thus:

> When you have cut out from the parts of the continuous discourse the many syllogisms therein . . . take away all the amplifications, and, after making brief headings to note the arguments used, form into one syllogism the sum total of the discourse, this sum total being ordinarily self-evident, although it may be swelled to undue proportions by accumulation of ornaments.[1]

Thus Cicero's oration *Pro Milone* is found to amount to no more than on 'dialectial ratiocination' which runs: 'It is permissible to kill a criminal.' That is its meaning; everything else is 'mere ornament'. And thus Johannes Piscator sets out to produce a 'logical analysis' of every book of the Old and New Testaments, to make it clear, once and for all, what the Scriptures 'really' say. Walter J. Ong, Ramus's most exhaustive and penetrating historian, sums up thus:

> Ramus had developed the habit of regarding everything, mental and physical, as composed of little corpuscular units or 'simples'. He never seems expressly aware of this habit, but it dominates all his thinking, subconsciously, yet stubbornly and absolutely. Ramus thus tends to view all intellectual operations as a spatial grouping of a number of these corpuscles into a kind of cluster, or as a breaking down of clusters into their corpuscular units. . . . [T]he Ramist corpuscular epistemology, supposing that knowledge consists of sets of mental items, thereby implied one-for-one correspondence between terms and things.[2]

[1] Quoted in W. J. Ong, *Ramus: Method and the Decay of Dialogue* (Harvard, 1958) 191. The following quotations and examples also come from this invaluable work.
[2] Ibid. 203

This is the model which lies behind Thomas Sprat's comment on the Royal Society's aims for philosophic discourse, in his *History of the Royal Society* (1667): 'They have . . . a constant Resolution . . . to return back to the primitive purity, and shortness, when men delivered so many *things*, almost in an equal number of *words*.' Earlier, Hobbes had pointed out that 'a man that seeketh precise truth had need to remember what every name he uses stands for; and to place it accordingly'. And John Hall 'perceived that it was better to grave *things* in the mindes of children, then words'.

This atomistic view of language, though put forward as the common-sense approach, was closely allied, as we have seen, with the development of Protestant thought. It had in fact long been a belief among Protestant commentators that Adam's naming of the animals was a function of his insight into their essential natures. Milton has Adam tell Raphael in *Paradise Lost* that 'I nam'd them, as they pass'd, and understood/Thir Nature', and in a prose pamphlet he says in passing that 'Adam . . . had the wisdom given him to know all creatures, and to name them according to their properties.' Francis Bacon drew the logical consequences from this idea, arguing that 'the true end of knowledge . . . is a restitution and reinvesting (in great part) of man to the sovereignty and power (for whensoever he shall be able to call the creatures by their true names he shall again command them) which he had in his first state of creation'. To discover the language of Adam then is to rediscover the essential nature of the world. Not surprisingly, the late seventeenth century in England is the heyday of speculation on the form this language would take, Bishop Wilkins's *Essay Towards a Real Character, and a Philosophical Language* being only the most famous example, though it is interesting to note that Thomas Urquhart, Rabelais's translator, also wrote an 'Introduction to a universal language', combined, in his case, with a 'Vindication of the Honour of Scotland'. Most people, however, made do with what they already had – the English language – but in the process revealed the fallacy of the idea both that one word equals one thing, and that there can be such a thing as a universal language. George Fox, the Quaker, confided to his journal: 'I was come up to the state of Adam which he was in before he fell. The creation was opened to me, and it was showed me how all things had their names given them according to their nature and virtue.' And again: 'I saw into that which was without end, and things which cannot be uttered, and of the greatness and infiniteness of the love of God, which cannot be expressed by words.' But of course it is words that he goes on using in order to express this inexpressible, with the following results:

> And so you that are gathered in the Name of Jesus, who have bowed to the name of Jesus, whose Name is called the Power of God, and the Word, Light, Life and Truth; and for bowing to his Name, for his Name sake have you suffered all along by many powers; but the name is a strong Tower: so who is bowed to the Name, and gathered in the Name of the Lord, ye are in the strong Tower, in which is safety and peace; for being gathered in the Name of Christ Jesus, whose Name is above every Name, for all things that was made, was made by Christ, whose Name is above every Name, into His Name are you gathered; so above all other names and gatherings are you gathered, who are gathered in the Name of Jesus Christ, by whom all things were made and created; and being gathered in the Name of Jesus Christ by which salvation is brought, by the Name of Christ, and not by any other Name under Heaven, but by the Name of Jesus Christ is salvation brought, by whom all things were made. . . .[1]

There is a certain power in this exhortation, but it is the power of the speaker's conviction of beatitude rather than of his expression of it. As J. I. Cope points out, Fox is so caught up by the sound of the word 'Name' that he loses sight of the grammatical structure of what he is saying:

> The 'you' addressed does not receive the predication of action implied in the opening. Instead, Fox discovers through this audience's epithet 'gathered in the Name', not only the divinity which was in the beginning, but even that audience's participation in a time-conquering *stasis* of Christian perfection. What

[1] Quoted in J. I. Cope, *The Metaphoric Structure of Paradise Lost* (Baltimore, 1962) 39–40. I am heavily indebted to Cope for the material and argument of this paragraph.

had begun as a warning, instruction or exhortation to act becomes, through the hypnotic utterance of the divine names, a
vision of human beatification for the Children of the Light.[1]

Self-induced hypnosis has here been substituted for rational
discourse – a development already implicit in the Lutheran
revolution outlined in Chapter 2. The Calvinist belief in an inner
light could in fact only lead to the repetition of the tautology: I
believe because I believe. The Cambridge Platonist Henry More
dresses this up a little more elegantly when he writes that 'it is
sufficient to make a thing true according to the *light* of *Nature*,
that no man upon a perception of what is propounded and the
Reasons of it (if it be not clear at first sight, and need reasons to
back it) will ever stick to acknowledge for a Truth', but even he
cannot hide its implications. We are caught in a circular argument where what convinces us of the truth of our insight is our
conviction of its truth, a circularity which shines pathetically
through the reports of the many witch-trials of the time. Argument, dialectic are in fact no longer possible, for a gulf is fixed
between the inner experiences of each man and the language he
has at his disposal to convey these. This is brilliantly expressed by
another New England Puritan, Thomas Hooker, when he writes:

> There is great ods betwixt the knowledg of a Traveller, that in
> his own person hath taken a view of many Coasts . . . and by
> Experience hath been an Eye-witness . . . and another that sits
> by his fire side, and happily reads the story of these in a Book,
> or views the proportion of these in a Map. . . . The like
> difference is there in the right discerning of sin. . . . The one
> . . . knows the relation of sin as it is mapped out, and recorded;
> the other the poyson, as by experience he hath found and
> proved it.[2]

For both Proust and Dante, as we have seen, the one journey to
be undertaken in this life was that which would lead to the discovery of the correct relation between the map and the landscape,
the world as it is said to be and as I experience it. For Hooker
the relationship of the terms has changed; only experience is of

[1] Ibid. 40–1.
[2] Quoted in Feidelson, op. cit. 42.

value; and experience has no option but to remain private.

We thus have, in seventeenth-century England, the curious situation arising where the same Protestant spirit drives men to argue that 'one word equals one thing', and to express themselves in such a way that the very words, as in Fox's exhortation, become objects, things to be hurled at the listener. What is common to both groups is a distrust of speech as dialogue, a distrust which led Sprat to fear for members of the Royal Society that 'the whole Spirit and vigour of their Design, had soon been eaten out, by the luxury and redundance of *speech*'. Behind this lies the belief that we can get at 'the Truth' more readily by eliminating the fallible human mind and using a method which starts from basic principles and observable facts and leads logically and inevitably to the solution of all our problems. And behind this again lies the belief that Truth is a thing, an essence, which can be extracted from matter or language like coal from a seam. Ong sums up:

> In this economy, where everything having to do with speech tends to be in one way or another metamorphosed in terms of structure and vision, the rhetorical approach to life – the way of Isocrates and Cicero and Quintillian and Erasmus, and of the Old and New Testaments – is sealed off into a cul-de-sac. The attitude towards speech has changed. Speech is no longer a medium in which the human mind and sensibility lives. It is resented, rather, as an accretion to thought, hereupon imagined as ranging noiseless concepts or ideas in a silent field of mental space. Here the perfect rhetoric would be to have no rhetoric at all. Thought becomes a private or even an anti-social enterprise.[1]

It is in this climate of thought about language and rhetoric that the novel emerges, and it is these very assumptions which lie behind the remarks of one of the best-known historians of the new genre, Ian Watt, when he distinguishes between the language of the novel and that of earlier fiction:

> The previous stylistic tradition for fiction was not primarily concerned with the correspondence of words to things, but rather with the extrinsic beauties which could be bestowed

[1] Op. cit. 291.

upon description and action by the use of rhetoric.[1]

Watt has rightly perceived that the novel is at one with the Royal Society and the Quakers in its distrust of language; but, because he himself seems to take for granted the premises of the emergent novel, he can only repeat its banal justification for this distrust while utterly failing to grasp its true significance. Because of course, as we have seen, this view of rhetoric as a mere sugaring of the pill is a complete misunderstanding of the way language works. The tradition of rhetoric which stretches from Aristotle to the Renaissance saw logic and rhetoric not as competing but as complementary. The codification of ways of speaking which is known as rhetoric is the result of the realisation that speech has its own laws, which are not those of logic, and that a mastery of these is necessary for a mastery of expression. The poet who thinks he can do without rhetoric, as Dante noted, is not more free but less. Language does not belong to each of us naturally as a birthright, but to the community in which we grow up, and in order to handle language we must learn the rules of the community. The attack on language as a conventional system of signs which we find developing in late seventeenth-century England had already been foreseen by Rabelais, and in its extremest form it was soon to subside. But the view of language as the fitting of words to things, while it is no longer held by any respectable linguist, still seems to float in the air breathed in by the literary critic, and it comes to the fore in the kind of defence of the novel I have just quoted.[2]

What I want to isolate here is the disappearance of the notion of a person behind the fiction, addressing another person, the reader. Talk of self-conscious narrators and the like is beside the

[1] *The Rise of the Novel* (Penguin, Harmondsworth, 1963) 29. This book, which has become something of a classic in English and American universities, demonstrates perfectly how impossible it is to say anything meaningful about the novel so long as one is operating within its own categories. Unfortunately the majority of books on the novel by Anglo-Saxon critics start from the same premises with the same results.

[2] It is interesting to note that Sartre in *La Nausée* agrees in nearly every detail with Watt's analysis of the relation of the traditional novel to a Lockean/Cartesian world view, but that where Watt takes it for granted that that view is 'true', Sartre's novel is devoted to demonstrating the falseness of every one of its assumptions – religious, philosophical, political and linguistic.

point. What we have to see is that the novel, as it emerges in the early eighteenth century, rejects the notion of genre, and that genre is to art as rhetoric is to language. Just as the ancient writers selected from three possible styles, high, middle and low, and, by their use of one or the other, gave the reader information about the kind of work he was being confronted with; so they made a decision about which genre they would use – epic, pastoral, elegy, etc. – and informed readers would then know what kind of treatment to expect. The effect of these conventions is really to give the reader – and the author – the literary equivalent of Irenaeus' 'rule of truth'. They are a reminder of the fact that before we can say anything at all we must make a decision about what rules we are going to abide by, we have to delimit the area and mode of discourse and thus provide what Medawar calls 'a restrictive clause that limits observation to something smaller than the universe of observables'. It will provide too what Medawar calls 'a theory of special incentive – a reason for making one observation rather than another', as every sound methodology must do.[1] It is for this reason that poetry, unlike the novel, in the sixteenth and seventeenth centuries is not really affected by the new views of rhetoric and logic coming into fashion. Seventeenth-century poetry is always drawing attention to its origin, either by emphasising its genre, as with Milton or Dryden, or by drawing attention to the voice of the speaking poet (or his *persona*), as with Donne and the Metaphysicals.[2]

But what of the novel? The quotation from Ian Watt gives us the clue. From the start the writers of novels seem determined to pretend that their work is not *made*, but that it simply exists. In part this is the result of the legacy of the Puritan autobiography, with its implicit assumption that one can pour out the truth about oneself if one ignores all formal considerations (the low level of education among many of the Puritan autobiographers suggests that in their case there was no formal training there to ignore); and in part it is the result of the spread of the ideas of the Royal Society about a 'plain style'. The effect is to divert attention from

---

[1] *Induction and Intuition in Scientific Thought*, 41.

[2] See Chapters 11 and 12 below for a discussion of the role of genre. The Puritans of course opposed the baroque Anglican style of Donne and Andrewes, full of similes and conceits, and insisted on cultivating the 'methodical manner', together with 'plainness, perspicacity, gravity'.

the fact that a novel, like a poem, is a made thing, a book, an object. Instead, the transparent language draws as little attention to itself as possible with the result described by Ong: noiseless concepts or ideas are ranged in a silent field of mental space.

There is one point that remains to be mentioned in this connection. It has been argued that this new silent contemplation of a work which dissimulates its private and human origin is the direct result of the growth of printing. This is certainly a plausible suggestion, especially since the new view of rhetoric is so closely allied to the invention of movable type.[1] But if my argument in the previous chapters is valid then I think we can say no more than that printing was an important contributory cause, that it speeded up a crisis that was already beginning to develop. The point needs to be made because the corollary of the argument that there is a direct link between printing and the new view of rhetoric is that we have now entered an electronic age when we can get rid of printing altogether and return to the pristine purity of speech and vision. The error of this lies once again in the mechanical nature of the solution, its suggestion that a simple *fiat* or a technological innovation of some kind is going to relieve us all of our problems. But the problem is not one of print at all; it is one that is endemic to writing of any kind, even to language of any kind. As we saw with Proust and Chaucer and Rabelais, what is necessary is simply an awareness of the *double* nature of written words: they are black marks on a white page and they are the utterances of a person. Without the black marks all would be sheer occurrence, endless flux; yet to imagine that these black marks somehow hide meaning and permanence within themselves, and that we can, by isolating them, arrive at some 'meaning' which does not take into account the context in which they are presented, the voice which utters them – that is to fall into as great an error as imagining we can do without the marks at all. Both are errors which the traditional novel unwittingly condones.[2]

[1] See Ong, op. cit. 307–14.
[2] As Ong writes: '. . . we ourselves think of books as "containing" chapters and paragraphs, paragraphs as "containing" sentences, sentences as "containing" words, words as "containing" ideas, and finally ideas as "containing" truth. Here the whole mental world has gone hollow. The pre-Agricolan mind had preferred to think of books as saying something,

IV. A TALE OF A TUB

Swift wrote *A Tale of a Tub* in the last years of the seventeenth century and went on adding to it till the fifth edition came out in 1710. It can thus be situated almost exactly halfway between Erasmus and Luther on the one hand, and Proust and Joyce on the other, at that point in intellectual history when the impetus of the Renaissance and Reformation was running out, or rather turning into many of the forces which make up the modern world picture. As if sensing that the moment was ripe, Swift has created what still remains one of the sharpest analyses and indictments of the new mentality. With unerring instinct Swift recognised that the very same premises underlay what appeared to be three very different groups of phenomena: the fanatic Puritan preaching; the new science of the Royal Society; and the views of 'modern' authors and critics. *A Tale of a Tub*, in an extraordinary display of exuberant burlesque reminiscent of Rabelais, and of controlled savagery akin to Dante at his most intransigent, not only lays bare these premises but forces the reader to recognise within himself the very tendencies he prepares to condemn.

Swift's strategy is to fasten on the spatial conception of the mind and the essentialist conception of language which is common to all three groups, and by overemphasising this to show up its inherent absurdity. Thus, from the start he presents us with an image of the 'truthful' preacher and his audience:

> From this accurate Deduction it is manifest, that for obtaining Attention in Publick, there is of necessity required a *superiour Position or Place*. But, altho' this Point be generally granted, yet the Cause is little agreed in; and it seems to me, that very few Philosophers have fallen into a true, natural solution of this *Phaenomenon*. The deepest Account, and the most fairly digested of any I have yet met with, is this, That Air being a heavy Body, and therefore (according to the System of *Epicurus*) continually descending, must needs be more so, when loaden and press'd down by Words; which are also Bodies of

---

of sentences as expressing something, and of words and ideas as "containing" nothing at all but rather as signifying or making signs for something.' (Ibid. 121). See also Butor's excellent article, 'La Littérature, l'oreil et l'œil', *Répertoire*, III (Paris, 1968) 391–403.

much Weight and Gravity, as it is manifest from those deep *Impressions* they make and leave upon us; and therefore must be delivered from a due Altitude, or else they will neither carry a good Aim, nor fall down with a sufficient Force.

And I am the readier to favour this Conjecture, from a common Observation; that in the several Assemblies of these Orators, Nature it self hath instructed the Hearers, to stand with their Mouths open, and erected parallel to the Horizon, so as they may be intersected by a perpendicular Line from the Zenith to the Center of the Earth. In which Position, if the Audience be well compact, every one carries home a Share, and little or nothing is lost. (60–1)[1]

Later he presents us with a further picture of what in today's ugly jargon might be called a 'communications situation':

In this Posture he disembogues whole Tempests upon his Audience, as the Spirit from beneath gives him Utterance; which, issuing *ex adytis*, and *penetralibus*, is not performed without much Pain and Gripings. And the *Wind* in breaking forth, deals with his Face, as it does with that of the Sea; first *blackning*, then *wrinkling*, and at last, *bursting it into a Foam*. It is in this Guise, the Sacred *Aeolist* delivers his oracular *Belches* to his panting Disciples; Of whom, some are greedily gaping after the sanctified Breath; others are all the while hymning out the Praises of the *Winds*. . . . (156)

So much for inspiration and the inner light. When Swift turns to the new scientists he shows how their attempt to get rid of emotive vocabulary altogether and to present their experiments in a totally neutral, 'plain' style rebounds on themselves: 'Last Week I saw a Woman *flay'd*, and you will hardly believe, how much it altered her Person for the worse.' Here too Swift shows how language takes its revenge on those who imagine they can ignore it. Instead of a world where the inner light of either the spirit or pure rationality makes itself immediately apprehensible to the spirit or mind of the onlookers, where, that is, spirit and rationality float free of the crippling limitations of the human

---

[1] All page references are to *A Tale of a Tub*, ed. Guthkelch and Nichol Smith (Oxford, 1958).

body, we have a world which has sunk totally to the level of the physical. Reiterating a Renaissance commonplace, Swift sums it up by saying that these people, so busy gazing up at the stars, have been betrayed by their hindquarters into a ditch.

Imagination and rationality are both dirty words to Swift. Man is not a rational animal, he is only an animal capable of reason. But to be capable of it he needs to use his memory; to keep from stumbling into the ditch he must be aware of his limitations and look carefully at the ground in front of him, guided by the street-lights of tradition, and it is memory and learning which can put him in touch with tradition. In *The Battle of the Books*, which is appended to the main text, this opposition between Reason–Imagination and Memory–Tradition is aired in a dialogue between a Spider and a Bee. The Spider argues that 'This large Castle . . . is all built with my own Hands, and the Materials extracted altogether out of my own Person.' The Bee answers that she gets her honey from the flowers of the fields, that it is up to her to choose just what she wants, and that she does no harm to anyone:

> So that in short, the Question comes all to this; Whether is the nobler Being of the two, That which by a lazy Contemplation of four Inches round; by an over-weening Pride, which feeding and engendering on it self, turns all into Excrement and Venom; producing nothing at last, but Fly-bane and a Cobweb: or that, which, by an universal Range, with long Search, much Study, true Judgement, and Distinction of Things, brings home Honey and Wax. (232)

When the issue is put in these terms of course the reader does not have much difficulty in making up his mind. Swift here unmasks the consequences of the position of the new scientists, the Cartesian philosophers and the fanatic preachers: thinking to by-pass human consciousness and human reason, history and civilisation, in order to arrive directly at 'the truth', they only fall back into a private world where their imagination roams unchecked because it acknowledges no authority outside itself, and thus transforms the real world into an image of their own desires.

But stated like that the answer looks too neat, too pat. Its substance is the same as Pantagruel's reply to Panurge, but, as we

saw, Rabelais could not give that answer straight without distorting it. Here the Bee is no doubt endorsing Swift's own conscious
beliefs, but the irony of the *Tale* has cut too deep to be encapsuled
by this image. For what the *Tale* shows is Swift himself torn by
the problem of just how the individual can *relate* to Tradition, how
he can escape from the paralysing euphoria of the Imagination,
which is so frightening because it can never be proved wrong on
its own terms. The dichotomy between experience and authority,
which we traced in Chaucer and in Rabelais, seems to present
itself so sharply to Swift, and with so little chance of reconciliation between the two, that the *Tale* becomes a desperate burlesque
designed to keep madness at bay only by the frenzy of its own
activity:

> In the Proportion that Credulity is a more peaceful Possession
> of the Mind, than Curiosity, so far preferable is that Wisdom,
> which converses about the Surface, to that pretended Philo-
> sophy which enters into the Depth of Things, and then comes
> gravely back with Informations and Discoveries, that in the
> inside they are all good for nothing. (173)

This is much closer to Rilke and Thomas Mann than to Rabelais
and Sterne. In such a world happiness can only be the faculty of
being well deceived, since surfaces will perpetually be at odds
with depths, and what we see with what we know:

> The two Senses, to which all Objects first address themselves,
> are the Sight and the Touch; These never examine farther
> than the Colour, the Shape, the Size, and whatever other
> Qualities dwell, or are drawn by Art upon the Outward of
> Bodies; and then comes Reason officiously, with Tools for
> cutting, and opening, and mangling, and piercing, offering to
> demonstrate, that they are not of the same consistence quite
> thro'. (173)

This is paralysing. It has the desperate quality of Keats's very
similar self-lacerations in the letters or the two *Hyperions*. For all
the efforts of scholars to show how much Swift was a part of his
time, how much his work is dominated by the tradition of Anglican compromise, there is little here of that ultimate faith in
common sense which characterises even so radical a thinker as

Sterne. Even Nietzsche does not look with less self-deception at our position in the world. And yet. And yet. The speaker here is, after all, not Swift himself, but the Grub Street Hack, and if there is less of a gap between Swift and his *persona* than there is between Chaucer and his, the very creation of a *persona* is proof of Swift's triumph over the paralysing dichotomy. For the burlesque *is* the solution, the Hack's error and madness the gauge of Swift's sanity. A narrow ledge of sanity, it is true, and one that is only maintained by the creation of just such a work as this, but all the more impressive for that reason. Swift presents us with no solution to the dilemma he exposes; the solution is the *Tale* itself, its creation and its recreation in the mind and ears of every new reader.

The *Tale* is an encyclopedia of the follies of the seventeenth century. It was composed some twenty years before Defoe brought out *Robinson Crusoe*. And yet in an uncanny way it lays bare the premises which the novel takes over from the late seventeenth century. It is no coincidence that in form it is a burlesque of the novel, an anti-novel to end all anti-novels. Twenty years before the first novel was written. We would do well to ponder the implications of this fact.

6 Hawthorne: Allegory and Compulsion

' "In a riddle whose answer is chess, what is the only prohibited word?" I thought a moment and replied, "The word *chess*." '
Jorge Luis Borges

For a long time now Hawthorne has been seen as a uniquely American phenomenon. Students of American society have hailed him as the imaginative historian of New England Puritanism, and literary critics have reserved a special niche for him as the first great American novelist (Henry James called *The Scarlet Letter* the first great American novel, though the affinities between the two writers go deeper than any bonds of nationality). Fortunately this parochial view has begun to be modified. Americans like Charles Feidelson, while not denying the Puritan roots of Hawthorne and Melville, have argued that there is a close link between the problems raised by Puritanism and those explored by the English Romantics and the French Symbolists; Germans like Professor Lang of Tübingen have suggested that 'it may have been the shadow of Kant as much as that of Jonathan Edwards which fell across the path of Hawthorne's pilgrim's progress'; while a modern writer like Borges has published a major essay on Hawthorne along with essays on Valéry and Kafka. From our point of view what is interesting about Hawthorne is precisely the way in which what appear to be purely Puritan concerns are mixed with the problems of the Romantic poet, while what appear to be purely Romantic dilemmas are found to be inextricably connected in his work with the problems of allegory and Puritanism. It may be that an examination of Hawthorne's work will help to clarify some of the issues raised in a more general way in the previous chapter, and show the way these tend to affect works of fiction. Before we do this, however, it may be instructive to glance at the critical response to Hawthorne as it has manifested itself in the last thirty years or so, for we shall find there the seeds of many current fallacies about the nature of fiction and the methods of interpretation.

What is perhaps the most famous essay on Hawthorne was written, significantly enough, by that champion of the anti-modernists, Yvor Winters, and as always with Winters it goes straight to the heart of the problem while totally failing to understand its real nature. Winters called his essay 'Maule's Curse, or Hawthorne and the Problem of Allegory', and in his usual incisive way he launches straight into the main issue:

> Hawthorne is, then, essentially an allegorist; had he followed the advice of Poe and other well-wishers, contemporary with himself and posthumous, and thrown his allegorising out the window, it is certain that nothing essential to his genuius would have remained.[1]

Unfortunately Winters takes it for granted that we know what he means by allegory and so does not explicitly tell us. This is a pity because, as we have seen, the question of the exact nature of allegory is a crucial and bewildering one. Winters does, however, in an aside on Hawthorne's married life, give us an idea of what he understands by the term allegory, for he talks of the writer as 'one far more likely to concern himself with the theory of mankind than with the chaos, trivial, brutal, and exhausting, of actuality'. In other words, allegory is conceived as cold and abstract, completely opposed to the 'felt life' of the novelist – in fact, the familiar Romantic definition of the term. Winters then makes the point that the 'Puritan view of life was allegorical, and the allegorical vision seems to have been impressed upon the New England literary mind'. Although, he says, it disappeared in England, the original spirit of Puritanism survived in America right through to the nineteenth century and into the work of the major writers of that century, though of course diluted in several ways. Thus

> Hawthorne, by nature an allegorist, and a man with a strong moral instinct . . . found in the early history of his own people and region the perfect material for a masterpiece. By selecting sexual sin as the type of all sin, he was true alike to the exigencies of drama and of history. In the setting which he chose, allegory was realism, the idea was life itself. . . .[2]

[1] Reprinted in *Hawthorne, A Collection of Critical Essays*, ed. A. N. Kaul (New Jersey, 1966). This quotation is on pp. 11–12.
[2] Ibid. 17.

Despite its eulogistic tone, however, this passage marks the opening of Winters's detailed attack on Hawthorne. As a typical example of Hawthorne's method he selects a passage from the eighteenth chapter of *The Scarlet Letter*. Dimmesdale and Hester are sitting in the forest, planning the flight which is never to take place, and Pearl, 'the symbolic offspring of the untamed elements in human nature and hence akin to the forest which, in the Puritan mind, was ruled by Satan in person', plays apart:

> A fox, startled from his sleep by her light footstep on the leaves, looked inquisitively at Pearl, as doubting whether it were better to steal off or renew his nap on the same spot. A wolf, it is said – but here the tale has surely lapsed into the improbable – came up and smelt of Pearl's robe, and offered his savage head to be patted by her hand. The truth seems to be, however, that the mother-forest, and these wild things which it nourished, all recognised a kindred wilderness in the human child.[1]

Similarly, Winters points out,

> in *The Marble Faun*, one never learns whether Donatello had or had not the pointed ears which serve throughout the book as the physical symbol of his moral nature; the book ends with the question being put to Kenyon, who has had the opportunities to observe, and with his refusing to reply.[2]

This device, which Winters calls 'the formula of alternative possibilities', is one with which all readers of Hawthorne are familiar, and, as Winters says, it is relatively harmless if well done but can be intensely irritating when indulged in too often. But, as Winters sees, it is a symbol of something much more central to Hawthorne than a mere narrative device. For if, says Winters, we reverse the formula

> so as to make the physical representation perfectly clear, but the meaning uncertain, we have a very serious situation; and this is precisely what occurs, in some measure toward the close of *The Blithedale Romance*, and without mitigation throughout the four unfinished romances. We have in the last all of the machinery and all of the mannerisms of the allegorist, but we

---

[1] Everyman edition (London, 1938) 246–7.
[2] Loc. cit. 22.

cannot discover the substance of his communication, nor is he himself aware of it so far as we can judge. . . . Yet we have not, on the other hand, anything approaching realistic fiction, for the events are improbable or even impossible, and the characters lack all reality. The technique neither of the novelist nor of the allegorist was available to Hawthorne when he approached the conditions of his own experience: he had looked for signals in nature so long and so intently, and his ancestors before him had done so for so many generations, that, like a man hypnotized, or like a man corroded with madness, he saw them; but he no longer had any way of determining their significance, and he had small talent for rendering their physical presence with intensity.[1]

This is the substance of Winters's criticism of Hawthorne, and it is interesting to see how he moves from a critique of the writer to a critique of Puritanism itself. For, as he insists, it is not just Hawthorne who no longer has any way of determining the significance of the signals of nature, it is something which has been at the heart of the whole Puritan tradition from the start. Winters thus seems to accuse Hawthorne at one and the same time of being a Puritan and of not being enough of a Puritan. He is, moreover, aware that in making this accusation he is not only criticising Hawthorne but the later Romantics in general. For, after saying that *The Scarlet Letter* is good only as a historical novel (it describes faithfully what Puritanism was like in New England), he concludes:

Hawthorne, when he reversed his formula of alternative possibilities and sought to grope his way blindly to significance, made the choice of the later Romantics; and his groping was met wherever he moved by the smooth and impassive surface of the intense inane.[2]

At this juncture it is worth recalling an anecdote which Julian Hawthorne quotes concerning the writing of 'Rappacini's Daughter'. Hawthorne's wife asked him how the story would end, and whether Beatrice was to be a demon or an angel. "'I have no idea!" was Hawthorne's reply, spoken with some emotion.' Was Hawthorne then as confused as Winters suggests, or is there

[1] Ibid. 22–3.   [2] Ibid. 24.

perhaps some way in which *it might not matter* what Beatrice (or Donatello) was really like? Let us bear that question in mind as we turn to possible ways of answering the charges levelled by Yvor Winters.

One possible kind of answer is to say that Hawthorne is concerned not with moral but with psychological truths, that he is interested not in what people *should* think but in what they *do* think. The case for reading Hawthorne in this way is well put by F. C. Crews in a recent book on Hawthorne. In discussing 'Roger Malvin's Burial', for example, Crews begins by pointing out that

> like all of his best tales, this one is packed with symbolic suggestions that invite a moralistic reading, and the problem it explores appears to be a problem of ethics. Yet a scrupulous examination of the main character's motives reveals that Hawthorne has approached his subject on a deeper level than the ethical – that he has not asked what someone in a certain predicament *should* do, but rather how a man may become the victim of unconscious hypocrisies over which he has no ethical control at all. Indeed, the working-out of this plot is strictly dependent, not on a religious attitude of Hawthorne's, but on an amazingly rigid logic of unconscious compulsion in the protagonist.[1]

Crews insists that questions about the extent of Reuben's guilt in leaving his prospective father-in-law to die in the wilderness are irrelevant, not because Hawthorne is uncertain of his ethical system, as Winters might maintain, but because 'Hawthorne is concerned only with subjective guilt as Reuben's conscience manufactures it, independently of the moral "sinfulness" or "innocence" of his outward deeds.' And he argues that 'the Biblical allusions suggesting redemption serve the purpose . . . of placing in relief the merely pathological nature of the case in hand'.

The evidence collected by Crews seems to confirm this conclusion. The clue to almost every ambiguity in Hawthorne is to be found not in an uncertain ethic or aesthetic but in Hawthorne's overriding concern for the psychology of his heroes. Once this is

[1] This particular quotation comes from an early version of Chapter 5 of his book, first published as an article and reprinted in Kaul, op. cit. 111–22. This passage is on p. 111.

grasped all apparent inconsistencies, as well as the apparent arbitrariness of many of the plots, can be simply resolved. It is not by a strange accident aribitrarily deployed by the author to round off his tale that Reuben returns to the place where he left his future father-in-law and there shoots his own son; for 'Roger Malvin's real "burial" takes place in what Hawthorne calls "the sepulchre of [Reuben's] heart"; in that organ the dead man lives again, directing the self-accused "killer" to perform an expiation that is not simply plausible, but absolutely necessary and inevitable.'

One of the central chapters of Crews's book is entitled 'Escapism', and he deals there with 'the idealist who has determined to learn or do something that will set him apart from the mass of ignorant men'. Crews argues that this type – Young Goodman Brown, Minister Hooper, Athan Brand – is always seen as trying to escape from his own sexuality, that he is always caught in a drama of adolescence. This character is clearly linked with that of the artist, who figures so prominently in all Hawthorne's fiction, and this leads Crews on to an analysis of Hawthorne's ambivalent attitude to his own art, and to the following conclusions:

> If the artist-figure, as I believe, is threatened by the same temptations that destroy the escapist generally, we may come to understand why art-theory is subject to Hawthorne's familiar ambivalence between ideality and cynicism. Nor will we be surprised when, in the late romances, guilt for psychological self-revelation takes the form of tireless symbolic debate about the propriety of one's being an artist at all.[1]

Crews is perfectly well aware of the pitfalls of a purely reductionist Freudian analysis of any writer, and he does not indulge in any naïve interpretation of the work in terms of the man. At the end of his book, however, he does throw out something more than a suggestion about the way the themes of compulsion, sexuality and art interrelate. He writes:

> Thus, though I have no desire to rewrite Hawthorne's biography, I would remind future biographers of certain circumstances in his life that match the conclusions we have

[1] *The Sins of the Fathers* (New York, 1966) 155.

drawn from his art. Psychoanalysis invariably shows that an obsession with incest and its prevention, and indeed a general concern with sin and guilt such as Hawthorne displays, stem from an incomplete resolution of early Oedipal feelings. This failure of development, furthermore, is commonest in men who, like Hawthorne and Melville, lose their fathers at a young age and are raised by 'well-bred' women. Unresolved fantasies of filial hatred, and of punishment for that hatred, thrive in isolation from the real parent, and the very death of that parent becomes a matter of personal guilt. Can anyone doubt that Hawthorne's fiction provides an inadvertent record of precisely this guilt?[1]

Crews assembles so much evidence to support his case, his argument makes sense of so much of Hawthorne, that one hesitates to disagree with him. Yet a doubt remains. It remains because what Crews calls 'the logic of compulsion', this logic of the unconscious that drives Hawthorne's characters to their doom, is a characteristic not only of Hawthorne's art, but of that of nearly every post-Romantic writer from Poe to Robbe-Grillet. Can it be that all these have unresolved Oedipus complexes? If so, then clearly the observation is useless as a descriptive tool. But if this is not so – and the universality of the phenomenon must raise strong doubts in our minds – then it is clear that we must find another reason for this fascination with the logic of unconscious compulsion.

The figure Crews draws of Hawthorne – that of a man uncertain of the propriety of being an artist at all, passing from idealism to cynicism and back to idealism – is a common one in modern art. We have already met it in the young Marcel, and there are plenty of other examples among major writers: Kafka in his journals, the Mann of *Tonio Kröger* and *Death in Venice*, to name but two. Can the cause of their uncertainty really be a purely psychological one? Or does Winters perhaps give us a clue to another kind of explanation when he insists on the connection between Hawthorne and Puritanism?

Let us look again at the quotation from Thomas Hooker which helped forward our argument in the last chapter:

[1] Ibid 241.

> There is great ods betwixt the knowledg of a Traveller, that in his own person hath taken a view of many Coasts . . . and by Experience hath been an Eye-witness . . . and another that sits by his fireside, and happily reads the story of these in a Book, or views the proportion of these in a Map. . . . The like difference is there in the right discerning of sin. . . . The one sees the History of sin, the other the Nature of it; the one knows the relation of sin as it is mapped out, and recorded; the other the poyson, as by experience he hath found and proved it.

There is no possible communication between the traveller and the map-reader. The traveller experiences but cannot express, the map-reader understands but cannot experience. The traveller cannot become map-maker nor the map-reader traveller. In other words there is an unbridgeable gulf between individuals, each of them shut up in a private world of experience; for me to try and draw a map of my experience to help another understand it is quite futile since the conversion of experience into map results in the loss of experience. What is wanted is a language which can communicate to another and yet retain the stamp of the unique, but such a language does not exist. The traditional novelist has always chosen to ignore this problem, but some writers of fiction, as we have seen, tried to face up to it and to find a way of overcoming it. In Chaucer and Rabelais the author obtrudes between the reader and the book, reminding him that what he has in front of him is a book and not the world, a map and not the actual journey, and that this book, this map, is governed by certain rules and conventions by which he as author has agreed to abide in order to create anything at all. There is, however, another kind of solution to the problem. The author can withdraw completely and place at the centre of his book a hero whose psychological compulsion will account for the logic of the events that occur, and the shock to the reader will come when it is discovered that what we have been experiencing as reality was nothing other than what the hero's compulsive imagination took to be reality. The book's necessity will then be the necessity not of the universe but of the hero's inflamed mind, and we will have, so to speak, not a map of an experienced journey, but the experience of a journey compulsively transformed into a map.

If this is the case with Hawthorne, then his ambiguity – of

which Winters complained – and his interest in compulsive situations – for which Crews tries to account in Freudian terms – can both be seen as facets of the same thing. Hawthorne cannot tell us what Donatello is 'really' like because this 'really' is only a convenient shorthand for: 'What I, the author, have decided to make him like.' And Hawthorne is unwilling to play the part of God in this way, since he recognises that it would be the part of a wholly arbitrary God. Donatello may have faun's ears or he may not; Beatrice may be good or she may be evil. Some of the characters think one thing and some another. But to expect an answer to the question is of course absurd, since we are dealing not with events reported in a newspaper, for which we might find corroborative evidence, but with a work of fiction. If Hawthorne tells us that Beatrice is really evil or Reuben Bourne really guilty, this will have to be translated into the statement: 'I, as author, have decided to make Beatrice evil, Reuben guilty.' Hawthorne does not wish to let such arbitrary decisions govern the structure of his fiction. But does this mean then that he is simply indecisive, that he tries to solve the problem by hedging his bets, as Winters suggests? I think we can see now that it doesn't. Hawthorne's strategy (and it is one we will find again in Robbe-Grillet and in Golding, for instance) consists of two stages: in the first stage we are presented with the unfolding of events in what might be the real world; in the second we come to see that the events follow this remorseless logic not because the world is meaningful, but because they are seen through the mind of a man under a psychological compulsion. Thus Hawthorne gets his necessity and his freedom.

One can see Winters making the general criticism here that for fiction to deal only with compulsive situations is to narrow down the field of human experience in an absurd way. I am not saying that the logic of compulsion is the only way of creating an honest work of fiction, only that it is a common one. Moreover, the writer, like Hawthorne, who takes as his hero a man in a compulsive situation is in fact being far more 'realistic' than the novelist who might appear to enjoy far greater freedom. For this freedom is an appeal to the reader's imagination in that the reader imagines that he is undergoing a series of adventures and when the book is finished he puts it down with pleasure and regret – regret because now the book is finished he has to get on with his own life, which has nothing of the shape and meaningfulness he has found in the novel. But the reader of Hawthorne, since he is experiencing in his imagination what the hero is experiencing *in his*, suddenly finds, as the book comes to an end, that what he is dealing with is not imagination but reality – the reality of the hero's fevered imagination. The hero's own discovery that what he thought was reality is only the play of his (compulsive) imagination leads to the reader's discovery that what he thought was simply imagination is nothing less than reality. And this is surely what Melville had in mind when he said of Hawthorne's stories that they had a sharp point 'which stabs from behind with the thought of annihilation'. Let us look at Hawthorne's most famous work to see just how he does it.

Few novels keep their titles so firmly before the reader as does *The Scarlet Letter*. The action opens with the emergence of Hester from the prison with the letter pinned to her breast, and shortly afterwards we learn what the letter stands for: it is a 'mark of shame' that Hester has to wear upon her bosom so that she should be 'a living sermon against sin' until the day of her death. It signifies that she is an adulteress, and she is presented to us 'with the scarlet token of infamy on her breast; with the sin-born infant in her arms; with a whole people, drawn forth as to a festival, staring at the features that should have been seen only in the quiet gleam of the fireside'. But it is more than a mark of shame, since 'it was whispered by those who peered after her that the scarlet letter threw a lurid gleam along the dark passage-way of the interior' of the prison. The narrator, however, seems sceptical about the truth of this rumour, which, he suggests, is typical of the 'vulgar, who, in those dreary old times, were always contributing a grotesque horror to what interested their imaginations'. He himself seems to favour a psychological explanation, suggesting that the letter 'seared Hester's bosom so deeply, that perhaps there was more truth in the rumour than our modern incredulity is inclined to admit'. In other words, the people of Salem were right to see in the letter something more than the mere outward sign of Hester's adultery but they were wrong in imagining that it was the sign that God himself had branded her in the flesh. The truth, he suggests, is that it was she herself who had mentally branded herself.

If the letter is indeed a 'token of infamy' and that infamy has resulted in the birth of the child, then it is wholly appropriate that Pearl should be associated with the letter. Hawthorne makes it clear that the link between them is very close indeed, as when, talking of the crimson velvet tunic in which Hester dressed her, he remarks that

> it was a remarkable attribute of this garb, and indeed, of the child's whole appearance, that it irresistibly reminded the beholder of the token which Hester Prynne was doomed to wear upon her bosom. It was the scarlet letter in another form: the scarlet letter endowed with life! (124)[1]

Hester, by dressing her in this way, seems to wish to 'create an analogy between the object of her affection and the emblem of her guilt and torture', as the narrator says. But Pearl is much more than another emblem. She is wild, wilful, uncontrollable. Hester, gazing into her eyes, fancies that she beholds 'not her own miniature portrait, but another face. . . . It was as if an evil spirit possessed the child and had just then peeped forth in mockery.' And this link with the Devil little Pearl herself seems to take pleasure in affirming; she has no Heavenly Father, she says; her father is the Prince of the Air.

Of this fact the people of Salem seem to be in no doubt whatever. She is rumoured to be a 'demon offspring', and even those who do not know who she is seem able to discern this quality in her. When Hester takes her to Governor Bellingham's hall the little girl finds herself face to face with the Governor himself and the Reverend John Wilson:

> 'What have we here?' said Governor Bellingham, looking with surprise at the scarlet little figure before him. 'I profess I have never seen the like since my days of vanity, in old King James's time, when I was wont to esteem it a high favour to be admitted to a court mask! There used to be a swarm of these small apparitions in holiday time, and we called them children of the Lord of Misrule.' (132–3)

Wilson too stares at her in amazement and asks:

> 'Art thou a Christian child – ha? Dost know thy catechism? Or art thou one of those naughty elfs or fairies whom we

[1] All references are to the Everyman edition, 1938 reprint.

thought to have left behind us, with other relics of Papistry, in merry old England?' (133)

The phrase 'merry old England' gives him away. Hawthorne is exploiting the ambiguity within Puritanism itself in order to move from a world which seems to be created according to Puritan values (within which the story has so far been unfolding) to one where those values are seen as only one *possible* interpretation of reality. The nature of this ambiguity is explored by C. L. Barber in his excellent book *Shakespeare's Festive Comedy*, where he discusses the holiday festivities of 'merry old England' and draws attention to this startlingly relevant passage from the Puritan Philip Stubbes's *Anatomie of Abuses*:

> Against May, Whitsunday, or other time [Stubbes writes] all the young men and maids, old men and wives, run gadding over night to the woods, groves, hills, and mountains, where they spend all the night in pleasant pastimes. . . . And no marvel, for there is a great Lord present amongst them, as superintendent and Lord over their pastimes and sports, namely, Satan, prince of hell.

('Stubbes', remarks Barber, 'equates the traditional summer lord with Satan!') He goes on:

> But the chiefest jewel they bring home from thence is their Maypole, which they bring home with great veneration, as thus: They have twenty or forty yoke of oxen, every oxe having a sweet nose-gay of flowers placed on the tip of his horns, and these oxen draw home this Maypole (this stinking idol, rather) which is covered all over with flowers and herbs, bound round about with strings, from the top to the bottom, and sometime painted with variable colours, with two or three hundred men, women and children following it with great devotion. And thus being reared up with handkerchiefs and flags hovering on the top, they strew the ground round about, bind green boughs about it, set up summer halls, bowers and arbors hard by it. And then fall they to dance about it, like as the heathen people did at the dedication of the Idols, whereof this is a perfect pattern, or rather the thing itself. I have heard it credibly reported (and that *viva voce*) by men of great gravity and reputation, that of forty, three-score, or a hundred maids

going to the wood over night, there have scarcely the third
part of them returned home again undefiled. These be the
fruits which these cursed pastimes bring forth.

And Barber comments:

It is remarkable how pleasantly the holiday comes through in
spite of Stubbes' railing on the sidelines. Partly this appeal
comes from shrewd journalism. . . . Partly it is the result of the
fact that despite his drastic attitude he writes in the language
of Merry England and so is betrayed into phrases like 'sweet
nosegays'. And his Elizabethan eye is too much on the object
to leave out tangible details, so that, astonishingly, he describes 'this stinking idol' as 'covered all over with flowers and
herbs'.[1]

This conflict between the language used to describe a certain
incident and the moral standpoint of the describer is something
we find again in Milton's *Comus*, and here too the ambiguity of
tone that results leads us to the heart of the poem. Is Comus a
leader of festivity or is he a form of the First Tempter? Is the
forest the realm of (innocent) nature as opposed to (corrupt)
civilisation, or of nature as opposed to grace?

Interestingly enough, the forest has precisely the same
ambiguous role in *The Scarlet Letter*, but with the important
difference that here the ambiguity is deliberate and calculated.
Hawthorne moves from a point of view within Puritanism to one
outside it by way of the notion of the Lord of Misrule with whom
Pearl is associated, but it is with the description of the forest that
he establishes himself firmly in his new key. To Hester's mind, he
tells us, the forest 'imaged not amiss the moral wilderness in which
she had so long been wandering', yet it is in the forest that she
tears the letter off her breast and loosens her hair, letting it flow
naturally over her shoulders. In the forest, she tells Dimmesdale,
he would be free; for the forest belongs to a different world from
the city, one 'never subjugated by human law'. And in the forest
Pearl is at home. It is here that the passage to which Winters
took exception, about the wolf eating out of Pearl's hand, occurs.
And it is here that Hester sees her daughter as 'one of the fairies,

[1] *Shakespeare's Festive Comedy* (New York, 1963) 21–2.

whom we left behind in dear old England', a symbol no longer of evil but of nature.

The pattern of the book would now seem to be clear. Seen from a Puritan standpoint Hester is guilty of a terrible sin and Pearl is the visible and living symbol of that sin. Seen from a 'natural' perspective Hester's adultery with the man she loves is normal, perhaps even laudable, and nature's approval of her action can be seen in the fruit of that union, a child completely untainted by the false code of the Puritans and thus able to fulfil all her natural instincts. The novel would then be the description of the psychological state of guilt, the tragedy of a woman who accepts the guilt others bestow upon her even though she herself has not really done anything to incur it. Yet this explanation, however attractive to our anti-Puritan age, does not seem able to account for enough in this mysterious book. Hester may be the central character, but both she and Pearl only function in relation to the two men, Dimmesdale the father and Chillingworth the husband. It is the conflict between these two which actually provides the force that propels the story forward and brings it to its end. Moreover there is clearly a connection between the revelation of Dimmesdale and the metamorphosis of Pearl into a sentient human being, as well as between that revelation and the ending of the book. Simply to substitute an interpretation of the book in terms of Natural/Unnatural in the place of the Puritan terms of Good/Evil is clearly not enough. It fails to account for its peculiarly elusive quality, the sense that there is always a meaning over and above what is said.

A clue may be provided by an episode that occupies a central place in the structure of the book though not in that of the narrative. This is the appearance in the sky of the mysterious sign, which is 'read' in such different ways by the different characters, and whose significance is explained by the narrator in terms which should be familiar to us from similar discussions in earlier chapters:

Nothing was more common, in those days, than to interpret all meteoric appearances, and other natural phenomena that occurred with less regularity than the rise and set of sun and moon, as so many revelations from a supernatural source. . . . The belief was a favourite one with our forefathers, as betoken-

ing that their infant commonwealth was under a celestial
guardianship of peculiar intimacy and strictness. But what shall
we say, when an individual discovers a revelation, addressed to
himself alone, on the same vast sheet or record. In such a case
it could only be the symptom of a highly disordered mental
state, when a man, rendered morbidly self-contemplative by
long, intense, and secret pain, had extended his egotism over
the whole expanse of nature, until the firmament itself should
appear no more than a fitting page for his soul's history and
fate. (186-7)

It can only be for this reason, says the narrator, that Dimmesdale
'read' the sign in the sky that night as showing forth a huge
letter 'A'. To the citizens of Salem what appeared was 'a great
red letter in the sky – the letter A, which we interpret to stand for
Angel', and which they connect with the passing into heaven of
the angelic Governor Winthrop. A little later we are told that
many people regarded Hester as a Sister of Mercy, and 'refused
to interpret the scarlet A by its original signification. They said
that it meant Abel, so strong was Hester Prynne, with a woman's
strength.' It is even suggested that the letter on her breast is a
sort of nun's cross, the sign of her good work in the town among
the poor and the sick, and near the close of the book we learn of
the Indians who have come out of the forest to look around the
town and who 'fastened their snake-like eyes on Hester's bosom,
conceiving, perhaps, that the wearer of this brilliantly-embroidered
badge must needs be a personage of high dignity among her
people'. In other words the letter forms part of a conventional,
not a natural, language, and how we read it depends on what
assumptions we bring to it, what language-game we are playing.
Our earlier discovery that the Puritan view of the world in terms
of Good and Evil was only one way of looking at things, and did
not correspond to reality should have warned us that our new
description in terms of Natural/Unnatural was similarly relative.
The different interpretations of the letter confirm us in this view.
The letter is not branded by God into Hester's flesh, it is stuck
on there by the community. Hester, in other words, is only an
adulteress because she is named one by the community in which
she lives. But it would be equally wrong to say that if she is not
an adulteress then she *is* something else. Yet that is the natural

response. If she is not this then what is she? we ask. And we come back to that ambiguity of which Winters so greatly disapproved. If Pearl is not an elf-child then what is she? Why does Hawthorne stall in this way? Why won't he tell us straight out?

The really surprising thing is not the nature of the ambiguity, but the fact of it. We don't usually feel the need to ask such questions of characters in novels – as Winters correctly intuited. Novelists usually tell us what a character is 'really' like when they first introduce him, and if they keep the answer back for a while then this too is part of the plot and we wait eagerly for the answer to come. But, as Proust noted, we cannot do this kind of thing in ordinary life. We don't ever know who or what people 'really' are. Are they 'really' anything? Proust's novel suggests that the question is meaningless as such, that it is wrongly phrased. What Hawthorne's novel suggests is that to ask a question like that in the expectation of an answer, or to give an answer and imagine it to be the 'truth', is to act like Hester's Puritan accusers. We take it as perfectly natural for a novelist to tell us that X is a thief, Y an adulteress, and Z a middle-aged man whose wife has deserted him. We are so used to the convention that we don't think about it. But if we transfer the situation from the book to life we see at once what it implies. It implies that there is an essence in a person which can be labelled, defined, spelt out. But can we really say of any of our friends that they *are* this or that and imagine that this tells us what is essential to them? Can we say it of ourselves?

One of the central features of the seventeenth-century intellectual revolution which we briefly examined in the last chapter was a desire to get to the *truth* of things combined with a desire to remove the troublesome factor of *persons* from the field of inquiry. Just as language came to be seen in essentialist terms, as secreting meaning inside individual words, so people came to be seen in terms of discoverable motives revealing essences. 'There can be no power, short of Divine Mercy, to disclose whether by uttered word, or by type or emblem, the secrets that may be buried in the human heart', writes the narrator in *The Scarlet Letter*, but Chillingworth, the leech, as the old doctor is punningly called, knows nothing of divine mercy yet will not rest until he has uncovered Dimmesdale's secret. Like the new scientist forcing nature to yield up her secrets or like the Puritans creating the genre of the autobiography in their efforts to find out what it is they really are, Chillingworth sets to work on Hester's lover. But it is not really that he wants to find out what he does not know; rather he knows that Dimmesdale is the father of Hester's child but wants the man himself to confess it to him. Why? Why this need to hear the other *say* what he already knows? And why, once the other has spoken, is he free and does he die? To find the answers to these questions is finally to understand the book.

The moment Chillingworth sets eyes on the priest he seems to grasp his secret, and, although the other is unaware of it, from that moment he begins to work on him. But he sees this work as no more than a way of helping nature with her task, for, as he says to Hester:

> By thy first step awry, thou didst plant the germ of evil; but since that moment it has all been a dark necessity. Ye that have wronged me are not sinful, save in a kind of typical illusion; neither am I fiend-like, who have snatched a fiend's office from his hands. It is our fate. Let the black flower blossom as it may! (209)

Note the way Chillingworth demythologises Puritan theology: You are not objectively sinful, he says, and I am not the devil, but your sin led to your guilt and to you my role is that of the devil, even as your sense of guilt is proof enough of your real guilt. We saw earlier that it was possible to make better sense of Hawthorne in psychological than in theological terms. Now we see that Puritanism itself conceives theology in psychological terms: demythologising is a Protestant, not a Catholic pursuit. The only difference between Chillingworth's view of Hester and that of the critic who holds that she is not really sinful but only obsessed by guilt at what she has done, lies in the interpretation of the word 'really'. It would be self-evident to a Calvinist that if someone *feels* guilty then he must *be* guilty; there is, after all, no other information to go on apart from our feelings. And as for the Freudian critic, he would no doubt agree with the linking of imagining and being, though he would feel no need to bring God into it. But the main point of the passage, and the one I wish to stress here, is Chillingworth's sense of the inevitability of the whole action, given that first, decisive event. Hester, Dimmesdale and himself, he says, are only agents in an action which it lies beyond them to influence in any way. There is a dark necessity at work in all their lives, a compulsive logic which will carry them to their inevitable ends.

Chillingworth is almost right. There is a logic of compulsion at work here, but it *can* be broken, and it is. By acknowledging his guilt in public Dimmesdale escapes at last from the clutches of his enemy – as Chillingworth is the first to realise. When what had been secret, buried from the community, from the reader, and even, we feel, from Dimmesdale's own consciousness, is brought out into the light of day, is *verbalised*, Dimmesdale, for the first time since his original guilty act, is free. But this freedom, strangely, seems to go hand in hand with death, as though what had kept him alive so far was the very thing that caused his torment, his refusal to acknowledge his guilt. And this guilt, we can now see, is what drove the novel forward, gave it its necessary direction and impetus, for it to expire when what had been repressed at last comes out into the open. What is this relationship then between fiction and guilt, between Hawthorne, his characters, and the scarlet letter itself?

Pearl *is* what Dimmesdale would suppress – both literally and figuratively. She is the embodiment of the letter, the living sign of adultery. Yet she herself does not know what the letter is. 'What is the meaning of the scarlet letter?' she asks. 'Why does the Minister hold his hand continually to his breast?' It is because she *is* the letter that she cannot know what it *means*; so that, at the very end, when she comes to understand what it means, she changes her nature completely:

> Pearl kissed [Dimmesdale's] lips. A spell was broken. The great scene of grief, in which the wild infant bore a part had developed all her sympathies; and as her tears fell upon her father's cheek, they were the pledge that she would grow up amid human joy and sorrow, nor forever do battle with the world, but be a woman in it. Towards her mother too, Pearl's errand as a messenger of anguish was fulfilled. (309)

Thus there are really two deaths: the literal death of Dimmesdale and the spiritual death of the old Pearl, Pearl-as-letter. But the two are of course aspects of the same situation. Pearl is what Dimmesdale would suppress, the scarlet letter itself; but since she is there, alive, in front of him, he cannot do so and must eventually acknowledge her. When he does so, verbalising his unconscious thoughts, he is freed from his guilt, which means that he ceases to feel it. And we, the readers, understanding what has happened, also cease to experience. Meaning has been substituted for feeling. In the words of Thomas Hooker, the experience, once articulated, becomes history, becomes a map of sin, and we no longer feel its poison. Language is what frees us from the immediate present, it allows us to make sense of sheer occurrence, as the bard made sense of Odysseus' exploits. But this freedom involves a loss, symbolised here by the breaking of the spell and the death of a man.

Pearl, we have said, *is* the letter, and so not really human; her discovery of the meaning of the letter is the equivalent of Marcel's discovery of the fact that even his mother is not one with him. It turns her into an adult, free to make choices and forced to accept responsibility in the world. Dimmesdale tries to repress the letter and is forced compulsively towards his own destruction. When he has spoken he too is freed, but, because he was an adult and therefore always responsible for his decisions, that freedom is only the freedom to die in peace. As for Hester, she wears the letter on her bosom because, unlike her lover, she accepts the judgement of society while recognising its limited and conventional character. Not even the forest can hide the letter, she says, only the ocean can swallow it – meaning that only death can remove it from its place on her bosom. But, because she accepts it, she is free of Chillingworth, who can do nothing to her which she has not already done to herself. Where Chillingworth and Dimmesdale are in agreement, accepting the same standards of right and wrong, true and false, Hester accepts the naturalness of her act. For her the letter is perhaps only a sign of her involvement in man's fallen condition, and by accepting its conventional non-natural character, she is able to transform it into the mark of Abel, a nun's cross, a sign of high worth.[1]

Chillingworth is of course one of Hawthorne's many scientist-figures. His task is to drag the secret out of nature, to turn the silence of the universe into human and meaningful discourse. In other words, to turn nature into allegory. Dimmesdale is what he

[1] Compare the way Arthur, in *Sir Gawain and the Green Knight*, alters, by a public action, the symbolism of Gawain's green girdle: instead of the sign of Gawain's guilt it becomes the sign of his common humanity.

works on, but Dimmesdale resists him. Out of this resistance art is born. For art exists in the moment between the silence of nature and the verbalisation of allegory.[1] For the silence of nature could only be conveyed in a wholly natural language; a conventional language, the language of ordinary discourse, will inevitably fail to convey it. What is required then is a language which is both natural and conventional, which can both embody the experience and communicate it: the language of hieroglyphics. For the hieroglyph represents what it means, is that of which it is the sign. Unfortunately, for a language of genuine hieroglyphs to be possible the world itself would have to be absolutely meaningful. All that the writer who is concerned with truth can do, therefore, is to articulate the conditions for a hieroglyphic language, and this is what Hawthorne does in *The Scarlet Letter*.

The artist is both Chillingworth and Dimmesdale. Like the former, he wants to force nature to speak, but success in his enterprise is synonymous with failure, since meaning, as we have seen, destroys being. At the same time, like the latter, he will feel guilt at a primal fault but will not confess it; and, confessing it, will no longer feel the necessity to write. But what is the artist's primal fault? It is his decision to write, and to write this rather than that, his choice of one theme and one beginning, which rule out all the others. His initial action is unnatural, it is the cutting up of a seamless whole for the purposes of exploration. Like adultery, it is an unnatural action, the memory of which he wishes to suppress, but the fruit of which is there, like Pearl, in front of him. And once he acknowledges it there is nothing more to write, for the novel was built out of the suppression of its own origins: unlike Pearl it is made up of words, and therefore can articulate the conflict and reveal the forces that led to its own composition.

Hawthorne, we can now see, is not primarily interested in either theology or abnormal psychology. He is interested in trying to convey the experience of the journey by means of a map of the journey, and he does this by dramatising the relations between them, between journey and map, world and book. Hawthorne is not like Dimmesdale or Chillingworth, or even like Pearl. His *book* is like Pearl, a living, irreducible symbol, but he himself is like Hester, who accepts her guilt because she recognises that all human beings are guilty – guilty, that is, of betraying 'life' to

[1] See Jean Ricardou, *Problèmes du nouveau roman*, 112–21.

'meaning' in order to make sense of experience. That is a condition of being human, and that is what Pearl herself experiences at the last.[1]

Hawthorne's book steers between the silence of Dimmesdale and the knowledge of Chillingworth, as does Pearl herself, but, accepting its original sin – that of existing at all, a book in the world – it wears its title as Hester does her badge. It can do this ultimately, only because it gains its full meaning by referring away from itself to its maker, its final significance lying in that implied relationship. For *The Scarlet Letter*, we must remember, is more than the story of Hester and her badge; it is also the story, related in the preface, of how Hawthorne himself came to settle on this subject. In the traditional novel a preface in which the author describes how he came to find the MS. which forms the main body of the work serves merely to give a spurious authenticity to what follows. In this book, however, what is found is not a MS. but the letter itself – a physical object. Hawthorne insists that the few sheets of writing that went with it only served as the basis for his imaginative reconstruction of a possible occurrence. In the preface we see him among a group of men who are described in great detail, as though Hawthorne wished to show us what he could have done had he wanted to write a novel of this kind. But he does not want to because the very freedom which he has here, and in which a Dickens or a Hardy revels, is, for Hawthorne, synonymous with irresponsibility. Language used in a non-compulsive way is a sign of man's freedom from the immediate, but this freedom to Hawthorne is meaningless unless it is set against a prior bondage. So now we see him discovering the letter, pondering on its significance, submitting himself to its reality. The letter is in a room, the room is in a building (the Custom-House), but there is nothing *in* the letter: it just is. And yet:

> My eyes fastened themselves upon the old scarlet letter, and would not be turned aside. Certainly there was some deep meaning in it most worthy of interpretation, and which, as it

[1] Lévi-Strauss recounts that 'the Jesuit missionary Sanchez Larador has described the passionate seriousness with which the natives devoted whole days to letting themselves be painted. He who is not painted, they said, is "dumb".' (*Structural Anthropology*, trans. Jacobson and Schoepf (London, 1969) 257.)

were, streamed forth from the mystic symbol, subtly communicating itself to my sensibilities, but evading the analysis
of my mind. (42)

The book which grows from this meditation, then, is Hawthorne's
scarlet letter, living, like Pearl, and evading the deadly probing
of those who, like Chillingworth, would pluck out its secret. But
it can only do this because, like Hester Prynne, it recognises that
the letter is not a natural sign whose meaning must be unearthed.
Yet it is more than the first letter of the alphabet. . . . Out of this
contradiction Hawthorne creates his novel, which mimes his own
attempt to understand and, in doing so, allows being and saying
to co-exist, turns letter into hieroglyph.

After reading *The Scarlet Letter* it might be possible to rewrite
Crews's formula about the Biblical allusions serving to place in
relief the pathological nature of the case in hand, and say that
the Biblical *and* the pathological allusions serve the purpose of
placing in relief the general and universal nature of the case in
hand. To see it in this way is to understand why it affects one
with a feeling of release rather than of compulsion. Hawthorne
is here not the victim but the master of his own impulses, since
he uses them to explore the conflict in every human being between experience and understanding. For the writer the problem
is of course more acute, but the experience of Proust has shown
us that this need only mean that the writer is a person who has
recognised the problem and cannot rest until he has explored
its implications – which effectively means never. In the end Hawthorne's novel is neither about Puritanism nor about the pathology
of guilt, but about what it means to be a human being.

Yet it cannot be denied that if *The Scarlet Letter* affects one
eventually with a feeling of release, this cannot be said for all
Hawthorne's work. There is a frequent blurring of focus, a lack
of self-criticism, a ponderousness not alleviated by his attempts at
humour, all of which makes one applaud the felicity of Winters's
remark about the 'smooth and impassive surface of the intense
inane'. However interesting they are – and they always are that
– the bulk of his works are admirably summed up by that phrase.
But why should this be so? Dickens, George Eliot and Hardy
have all written some pretty bad novels, but these always contain

many of the virtues one finds in their best work. Why should there be such a gap between the good and the bad in Hawthorne? Crews gives one possible answer when he writes:

> Without pretending to offer a simple psychological yardstick of value, perhaps we may suggest that fiction profits both from contact with unconscious material and from the participation of consciousness in that contact. Hawthorne is truly himself only within a certain range of half-perception in which curiosity and anxiety can strike an equilibrium. . . . Here, perhaps, is where a psychological aesthetic may join hands with an aesthetic of plausibility. All readers can agree that Hawthorne fails when, for whatever reason, he is forced into inconsistent characterisation, embarrassed apology and digression, and incomplete plotting. What happens to his fiction after 1850 is, in the simplest terms, a lapse of illusion. In our view the immediate cause of this lapse is a dissociation of unconscious conflict from its never sturdy tie to outward reality. When heightened obsession calls forth heightened efforts at repression, no room remains for created characters to exist freely.

On the other hand, says Crews,

> it [is] significant that Hawthorne's acknowledged masterpiece, *The Scarlet Letter*, not only treats unconscious compulsion more directly than his other romances, but also keeps his specific filial obsessions better concealed from view.[1]

The formulation is very suggestive, but, in the light of our reading of *The Scarlet Letter*, it surely needs to be rephrased. That novel is a success not because it keeps any obsession 'better concealed from view', but because it is only here that Hawthorne found in the world outside him a perfect objective correlative for what he was striving to articulate. It is fascinating to see him hunting for this in one short story after another, groping for that basic element which would release his creative energy and allow him to set off on his explorations. It is fascinating too to ponder on what he eventually did find: not a plot but a letter.

Hawthorne, there is no doubt about it, is only successful when he succeeds in finding the right objective correlative. *This* is

[1] Crews, op. cit 268.

where a psychological aesthetic may join hands with an aesthetic of plausibility – where the latter releases the former as the author released the meanings inherent in the letter. And this is true not just of Hawthorne but of nearly every post-Romantic writer. We have only to think of the gulf that separates Virginia Woolf's *To the Lighthouse* from *The Years*, Golding's *The Inheritors* from *Free Fall*, Claude Simon's *La Route des Flandres* from *Le Palace*; or to recall the ineptitude and banality of the recently published fragments of *The Waste Land* which Eliot omitted from the final version,[1] fragments which often differ only in minute details from some of what he retained but which seem to belong to a different world of poetry – we have only to think of this to realise how narrow is the line between success and failure in modern art. In the first works all is sharp and clear, cutting deep to the heart of the mystery; in the second everything is untidy and chaotic, the tone uncertain and the result most frequently boring.

It is strange that modern fiction, which dissociates itself from the more easy-going novel of tradition by virtue of its greater rigour in the face of truth, by its resolute refusal of the arbitrary, should be so dependent on a primary arbitrary act: the choice of situation. But we have seen the reasons for this and it has its parallels in the other arts. Where, as in much of Hawthorne, or in writers like Roussel and Pieyre de Mandiargues, there is a failure or a refusal to find in the world outside an adequate objective correlative, the resulting work, though fascinating in its implications, does only too often present us with the smooth and impassive surface of the intense inane. But where, as in *The Scarlet Letter*, the right objective correlative is found – after much searching, since these things are never there for the taking – then the miracle occurs and meaning turns into being, letter into hieroglyph.

[1] *The Times Literary Supplement*, 7 Nov. 1968.

7 Modernism and Romanticism

'To see something new we must make something new.'
                                          Lichtenberg

The problem I want to deal with in this chapter can be formulated quite simply: the years between 1885 and 1914 saw the birth of the modern movement in the arts. What are the specific features of that movement and how are we to account for its emergence?

Two points need to be made before we start. First of all we must be clear that in one sense our inquiry is absurd. There is no physical entity called 'modernism' which we can extract from the variety of individual works of art and hold up for inspection. Every modern artist of any worth has achieved what he has precisely because he has found his own individual voice and because this voice is distinct from those around him. Yet it cannot be denied that something *did* happen to art, to all the arts, some time around the turn of the century, and that Proust, Joyce, Picasso, Klee, Schoenberg and Stravinsky, for all their manifest differences, do have something in common.

The second point is more in the nature of a reminder of a historical fact which, if rightly interpreted, should serve as a guide and a warning throughout this investigation. Although the First World War effectively marks the break between the world of the nineteenth century and our own, both in the minds of those who lived through it and for those of us who only read about it in the history books, the modern revolution in the arts did not take place during the war, or immediately after it, as one might have expected, but a decade or so *before* it. This should make us wary of too facile an identification of art with the culture and the society out of which it springs.

The modern movement in the arts cannot be understood in isolation. It must be seen as a reaction to the decadent Romanticism which was prevalent in Europe at the turn of the century.

Some of the apologists of modernism, such as T. E. Hulme, tried to argue that the movement was nothing other than a wholesale rejection of Romanticism and all that that stood for, and a return to a new classicism. Looking back at those pre-war decades from our vantage point in the mid-century, however, we can now see that the situation was a good deal more complex than Hulme suggests; that it was more a question of redefining Romanticism, of stressing some of those aspects of it which the nineteenth century had neglected and discarding some of those it had most strongly emphasised, rather than rejecting it outright. If we are to understand what the founders of modern art were doing it will be necessary to try and grasp the premises and implications of Romanticism itself.

Romanticism was first and foremost a movement of liberation[1] – liberation from religious tradition, from political absolutism, from a hierarchical social system and from a universe conceived on the model of the exact sciences. Reason and scientific laws, the Romantics felt, might allow man to control his environment, but they formed a sieve through which the living breathing individual slipped, leaving behind only the dead matter of generality. What man had in common with other men, what this landscape had in common with other landscapes, was the least important thing about them. What was important was the uniqueness of men and the uniqueness of each object in the world around us, be it a leaf, a sparrow or a mountain range. There were moments, they felt, when man is far from the distractions of the city and of society, and when the reasoning, conceptualising mind is still, when life seems suddenly to reveal itself in all its mystery and terror. In such moments man felt himself restored to his true self, able to grasp the meaning of life and of his own existence. It is to experience and express such moments, both in our lives and in our art, that we should perpetually strive, for these are the moments when we throw off the shackles of generality and are restored to our unique selves.

The function of art thus becomes that of exploring those areas

[1] Historians like to point out that Romanticism meant very different things in England and on the Continent. This is true, but then it meant very different things to Goethe and Rousseau, to Hugo and Baudelaire – and very different things to Wordsworth and Keats. I think it is worth trying to discover what, if any, were the common elements.

of the mind and of the universe which lie beyond the confines of rational thought and of ordinary consciousness, and the hero of Romantic art becomes none other than the artist himself, who is both the explorer of this unknown realm and the priestly mediator between it and his audience. Something of this is suggested by August Wilhelm Schlegel, who was probably responsible for the introduction of the word 'Romantic' as a description of the age, when, in his lectures on dramatic art and literature of 1808–9, he made the following comparison:

> Ancient poetry and art is a rhythmical *nomos*, a harmonious promulgation of the eternal legislation of a beautifully ordered world mirroring the eternal Ideas of things. Romantic poetry, on the other hand, is the expression of a secret longing for the chaos . . . which lies hidden in the very womb of orderly creation. . . . [Greek art] is simpler, cleaner, more like nature in the independent perfection of its separate works; [Romantic art], in spite of its fragmentary appearance, is nearer to the mystery of the universe.[1]

Schlegel, it is true, is not here talking only of the nineteenth-century; he is contrasting the whole 'modern' or Christian era with the classical age of Greece and Rome. But his stress on the transcending impulse of Romanticism, on the aspiration towards the mystery of the universe, is taken up by Baudelaire several decades later when, in a discussion of the 'Salon' of 1846, he writes: 'Romanticism means modern art – that is to say, intimateness, spirituality, colour, aspiration towards the infinite, expressed by every means known to art.' And yet already here a curious contradiction begins to emerge, a contradiction which lies at the heart of the whole Romantic endeavour, and whose nature was to determine its future course. Two quotations, the first from Rousseau and the second from Schleiermacher, will bring it out into the open. In his *Rêveries du promeneur solitaire* Rousseau tells how he came to after a minor accident to find himself lying in the middle of the countryside:

> Night was falling. I perceived the sky, a few stars, and a little verdure. This first sensation was a wonderful moment; I could still only feel myself through it. In that instant I was born to

[1] Quoted by René Welleck in *A History of Modern Criticism*, II (London, 1955) 59.

life, and it seemed to me that I filled with my frail existence
all the objects I perceived. Entirely within the present, I
remembered nothing; I had no distinct notion of my individuality, not the least idea of what had just happened to me; I
knew neither who nor where I was: I felt neither hurt, nor
fear, nor anxiety.[1]

And Schleiermacher, in his *Speeches on Religion*:

I am lying in the bosom of the infinite universe, I am at this
moment its soul, because I feel all its force and its infinite life
as my own. It is at this moment my own body, because I pene-
trate all its limbs as if they were my own, and its innermost
nerves move like my own. . . . Try out of love for the universe
to give up your own life. Strive already here to destroy your
own individuality and to live in the One and in the All . . .
fused with the Universe. . . .[2]

Romanticism had begun as a movement of rebellion against the
arbitrary authorities of the eighteenth century and its abstract
laws, a rebellion undertaken in the name of the freedom of the
individual. But this freedom, which of course involves the suppression of the tyrannical intellect, in fact turns out to be
synonymous with the loss of individuality. 'In that instant I was
born to life', writes Rousseau. The world around him soaks into
his body, he becomes one with it and in so doing gains a sense of
his own uniqueness, while Schleiermacher too feels the universe as
if it were his own body. But this feeling is also one of the loss of
self – 'I did not know who I was', 'Strive already here to destroy
your own individuality . . .'. The paradox is there: the ultimate
freedom, according to the Romantic logic, can only be death.

Where consciousness itself is felt to be an imprisoning factor,
keeping man from his true self, freedom must lie in the transcending of consciousness. Yet the only time we escape from it for more
than a brief moment is in sleep, or under the influence of alcohol
or drugs, or else in madness. And the only total escape is death.
Hence the key place accorded by Romanticism to dreams, to
various forms of addiction, to madness, and to the death-wish.

[1] *Œuvres complètes*, ed. Michel Launay (Paris, 1967) 1 507
[2] I give the translation of J. L. Talmon in his *Romanticism and Revolution* (London, 1960) 160. For the full text, see Schleiermacher, *On Religion*,
trans. Oman (New York, 1958).

And in all these cases the result is, of course, ambiguous. The freedom from consciousness and from the bonds of society may result in deeper insight, but it results also in rendering the individual more vulnerable, more prone to destruction from outside as well as from within. Hence the general tone of Romantic art and literature is one of melancholy gloom, for there seems to be no way of resolving the paradox.

This tension between freedom and annihilation is even easier to discern in the forms of art than in its contents. The task of the poet, as the Romantics saw it, was to communicate those moments of visionary intensity which he experienced, moments in which the meaning and value of life seemed to emerge. But the poet's only means of expression is language, and language belongs by definition to the realm of consciousness and social intercourse. For language, as Plato had already noted, only exists at a certain degree of abstraction and universality; it takes for granted that there is some sort of social agreement among the users of a language. But if you feel that what is important is the uniqueness of this tree or that man or this experience – then how are words going to help you to convey this uniqueness? This of course has always been one of the problems of art, but with the Romantics it comes right into the foreground of their consciousness. The Romantic poet finds himself struggling to express by means of language precisely that which it lies beyond the power of language to express. He becomes a man desperately striving to escape from his own shadow.

Only one poet in the nineteenth century was fully aware of the implications of the Romantic endeavour and was also prepared to accept and overcome them. In Rimbaud's famous letter to Paul Demeny of 15 May 1871 we can see that he had fully understood the problem and had decided on a radical solution:

Thus the poet is truly a stealer of fire.

He is the spokesman of humanity, even of the animals; he will have to make men feel, touch, hear his creations. If what he brings back from *down there* has form, he will bring forth form; if it is formless, he will bring forth formlessness. A language has to be found – for that matter, every word being an idea, the time of the universal language will come! One has to be an academician – deader than a fossil – to compile a dictionary in any language. Weak-minded men, starting by *thinking about* the first letter of the alphabet, would soon be overtaken by madness!

This [new] language will be of the soul, for the soul, summing up everything, smells, sounds, colours; thought latching on to thought and pulling. The poet would define the quantity of the unknown awakening in the universal soul in his time: he would produce more than the formulation of his thought, the measurement *of his march towards Progress*! An enormity who has become normal, absorbed by everyone, he would really be *a multiplier of progress*!

The failure of this ideal can be traced through the poems themselves, and it forms the explicit subject-matter of *Une Saison en enfer*. And, indeed, how could Rimbaud succeed? What he desires is not communication but communion, the direct and total contact of one person with another through a language so charged that it will act without needing to pass by way of the interpreting mind at all; in other words, a language that is not conventional but natural. But, as we have seen, such a wish can never be more than a Utopian dream, since to give words the meanings I want them to have regardless of their dictionary definitions is tantamount to abolishing language altogether. When Rimbaud recognised this, with admirable logic he gave up writing altogether.

But just because he was so ready to push the premises of Romanticism to their ultimate conclusion, Rimbaud remains one of the key figures of the nineteenth century, marking forever one of the two poles within which modern art is to move. His contemporaries, both in England and in France (Mallarmé excepted), chose a somewhat less arduous and therefore less interesting path. They tried to solve the problem by making their verse approximate as closely as possible to their conception of music, since music seemed to them to be the ideal artistic language, with none of the disadvantages of speech. To this end they made their verse as mellifluous as possible, stressing its incantatory qualities, smoothing out all harshness of diction, minimising its referential content, and rigidly excluding all forms of wit and humour for fear these would break their fragile spell. The result was aptly described by Eliot in his essay on Swinburne:

Language in a healthy state presents the object, is so close to the object that the two are identified. They are identified in the verse of Swinburne solely because the object has ceased to exist, because the meaning is merely the hallucination of meaning, because language, uprooted, has adapted itself to an independent life of atmospheric nourishment.[1]

As with Rimbaud, the normal function of language is denied and words take on an independent meaning. But here the meaning is not just independent of general usage, it is no longer under the poet's control at all. The result is not revelation but empty cliché, not the articulation of what lies beyond the confines of consciousness and rationality but simple reflex, the verbal equivalent of the canine dribble:

Before the beginning of years
    There came to the making of man
Time with a gift of tears;
    Grief with a glass that ran. . . .

Or:

O prêtresse élevant sous le laurieur verdâtre
Une eau d'antique pleurs dans le creux de tes mains,
Tes yeux sacrés feront resplendir mes chemins,
Tes mains couronneront de cedre un jeune prêtre. . . .

For language, as we have seen, has a way of getting its own back on those who try to step over it in this manner. Just as the Romantic dreamer found that he escaped from the bonds of the intellect only at the cost of his sanity or his life, so the Romantic poet, trying to escape from the bonds of language, found himself its prisoner, uttering platitudes in the voice of a prophet.[2]

---

[1] 'Swinburne as Poet', in *The Sacred Wood* (repr. London, 1960) 149. As so often with Eliot, the secret referent here is Dante, in whom Eliot feels that word and idea *are* one, that the word *is* close to the object. Eliot seems to have operated throughout his life with a threefold distinction as far as the use of language is concerned: as Dante (and Lancelot Andrewes) uses it; as Donne uses it; and as Swinburne uses it. He develops from Donne in the early poems towards Dante in the *Quartets*; Yeats develops from Swinburne in the early poems to Dante in his maturity, missing out Donne.

[2] Of course this is being grossly unfair to a multitude of poets, especially in the first half of the century. Nevertheless the tendency is there, and the

But if the poets dreamt of living in a world freed from the stifling restrictions of language, and looked with envy at the composers, these, had the poets but known it, were in the same plight as themselves. For if language is not natural, if, that is, words are not inherently expressive, as Rimbaud had imagined, then the same is true of the language of music. Although E. T. A. Hoffmann wrote enthusiastically about the inherent qualities of the chord of A flat minor, the truth of the matter is that music is nearly as conventional a form of expression as speech. We find it difficult to grasp music which is distant from us in space or time (Indian or Japanese music, or Gregorian chant, for instance), to know when it is being 'cheerful', when 'sad'. Musical instruments too have different and highly specialised functions in other societies, and so are associated with different things; it is only through frequent hearings, through a familiarisation with its language that we can come to appreciate Indian music or the music of Bali. The composer, no less than the poet, works in a language which is largely the product of convention, and according to rules to which he voluntarily submits in order to create a meaningful work. Thus, when the initial heroic impetus of Romanticism starts to peter out, we find a development in music parallel to that which we traced in poetry: a slackening of formal control, a loosening of harmonic texture, and the emergence of a soulful, cliché-ridden style which strives to lull the listener into a state of trance while the music struggles to express the world of the infinite which Baudelaire had urged the artist to seek with every means at his disposal. Naturally enough the piano, instrument of the half-echo, the suggestive, the indefinite, becomes the favourite of composer and public alike. And in music, as in poetry, the attempt to express *everything*, the totality of experience, unfettered by the rules and limitations of conventions and consciousness, leads to self-destruction. More than any of the other arts, Romantic music is imbued with the melancholy which stems from the knowledge that to achieve its goal is to expire.

Wagner's operas, as all his contemporaries realised, form the apotheosis of Romantic art. These vast music-dramas seemed to

---

struggle. Nerval is a good example, Keats a better one. See John Jones, *John Keats's Dream of Truth* (London, 1969), and Geoffrey Hartman, *The Unmediated Vision* (Yale, 1954) and *Beyond Formalism* for more generous views of Romanticism than those expressed here.

them to be the perfect answer to Baudelaire's plea for a work of art that would make use of all the resources of all the arts, lifting the spectator into the realm of the infinite, into the very heart of the mystery of the universe. We are fortunate in possessing a critique of Wagner by one of the few men who really understood the implications of Romanticism because he was so much of a Romantic himself – Friedrich Nietzsche. Nietzsche's analysis of the 'decadent' style sums up many of the points we have already noted:

> What is common to both Wagner and 'the others' consists in this: the decline of all organising power; the abuse of traditional means, without the capacity or the aim that would justify this. The counterfeit imitation of grand forms . . . excessive vitality in small details; passion at all costs; refinement as an expression of impoverished life, ever more nerves in the place of muscle.[1]

This is extraordinarily perceptive. Nietzsche has put his finger on one of the main characteristics of expressionism: the richness of sensual detail, of the feel of things, allied to the poverty of overall form. And how could it be otherwise, once the dichotomy expressed by Thomas Hooker is accepted? We are left with either meaningless sensation (the traveller) or knowledge devoid of feeling (the historian, map-maker). Thus it becomes easy to trace even a historical connection between Luther, the Puritans, the German Romantics, the German expressionists, and a film-maker like Bergman. This has little to do with innate German or northern characteristics or geography and a great deal to do with cultural tradition.

But Nietzsche is not content with a simple catalogue of Wagner's characteristics; he wants to understand what lies behind them and to try and account for Wagner's enormous popularity. He sees first of all that for Wagner music is only a means to an end: 'As a matter of fact, his whole life long, he did nothing but repeat one proposition: that his music did not mean music alone! But something more! Something immeasurably more! . . . "*Not music alone*" – *no* musician would speak in this way.' And he explains what this 'more' is: 'Wagner pondered over nothing so

[1] *The Case of Wagner*, trans. A. M. Ludovici, *The Complete Works of Friedrich Nietzsche*, viii (Edinburgh, 1911) 44.

deeply as over salvation: his opera is the opera of salvation.' And this, thinks Nietzsche, is the source of Wagner's power and popularity: what he offered was nothing less than the hope of personal salvation to a Europe – and especially a Germany – bewildered by the rapid social and technological changes of the previous half-century. 'How intimately related must Wagner be to the entire decadence of Europe for her not to have felt that he was decadent,' he writes in the same essay. And again: 'People actually kiss that which plunges them more quickly into the abyss.' We remember that Schlegel had already talked about a 'secret longing for the chaos . . . which lies hidden in the very womb of orderly creation', and that this longing was nothing other than the Romantic desire for an absolute freedom. Nietzsche's suggestion that with Wagner this longing spills out of the realm of art into that of politics allows us to glimpse the connection between decadent Romanticism and mass hysteria. The cataclysmic events of the first half of the present century would have occasioned him little surprise.

What Nietzsche particularly objects to in Wagner is precisely the fact that by trying to turn his music into a religion he debases both music and religion; by trying to turn the entire world into a music-drama, drawing the audience up into the music until they shed their dull everyday lives and enter the heart of the mystery, he dangerously distorts both the life of everyday and the true nature of art. By blurring the outlines between life and art he turns art into a tool and life into an aesthetic phenomenon – that is, into something which is to be judged entirely by aesthetic criteria and where the rules of morality therefore no longer apply.

Only one other thinker in the nineteenth century had seen as clearly as Nietzsche where the assumptions of Romanticism were leading, and that was Kierkegaard. In *Either/Or*, written in 1843, he set out to analyse what he calls the aesthetic attitude to life, and from then on the category of the aesthetic or the 'interesting' occupied a key place in his writing. He noted that the point about a work of art is that we are not in any way committed to it. We can pick up a book and put it down again, turn from one picture to another in a gallery. We are surrounded by a growing number of works of art and we can move among them at will, sampling here or there according to our whim. Art makes no claims on us, and surely an attitude of disinterested contemplation is the correct one when we face a work of art. It so happens, however, that people carry this attitude over into their lives. A man will take up with one woman, for instance, because she 'interests' him, and when she begins to bore him he will turn to another. The philanderer, Don Juan, is the archetype of the aesthetic attitude to life, an attitude which depends on a complete surrender to the moment, the immediate, the sensual, and which for that reason is wholly amoral. That is why music is the most perfect medium for the aesthetic mode, and why, Kierkegaard argues, Mozart's *Don Giovanni* is the greatest work in that mode. But when we transfer this attitude from art to life its immediate implication is that no choices are binding. The person who lives in the category of the aesthetic never thinks in terms of 'either/or', but always of 'and/and'. Yet life, Kierkegaard argues, does not consist of a series of aesthetic moments. Choices are essential in life, and a genuine choice implies a genuine renunciation. That man is a creature who must make choices is evinced by his awareness of *time*. The aesthetic category does not know the meaning of time,[1] but man is a creature of time, as can be seen from the fact that no absolute repetition is possible in life although it is perfectly possible in art. Repetition in life always implies change and difference, and so always forces us to recognise the fact that we do not exist in the category of the aesthetic.[2]

The extension of the term 'aesthetic' to imply an attitude to life as well as to works of art allows Kierkegaard to show how much the European bourgeoisie of the nineteenth century had in common with the Romantic artists, just as Nietzsche had noted the close links between Wagner's art and the mentality of his patrons. But Kierkegaard was able to extend his insight into a critique of the prevalent philosophy of the time, Hegelianism. For Hegel, as he saw, was the supreme philosopher of aestheticism. He it was who had undertaken to show that all history should be contemplated as a work of art, the product of one great Mind, moving inevitably forward towards the completion of its pattern.

[1] This shows how much Kierkegaard's category of the aesthetic has in common with Freud's Unconscious and Pleasure-principle, and how clearly Romanticism can be seen as the attempt to make the Pleasure-principle supreme. See the two essays on 'The Unconscious' and 'Negation', in *Freud's Collected Papers*, IV and V respectively.

[2] See his brilliant little book entitled *Repetition* (1843).

But this view of history, though tempting, is also subtly distorting, as Kierkegaard noted. Luther or Cromwell or Napoleon, when confronted with a choice between one action and another, did not have the benefit of Hegel's vision of the totality of history to guide them. For them the future was open, their choice fraught with consequences they could not foretell. It is only by virtue of hindsight that a pattern emerges, and each of us lives life forwards rather than backwards. Hegel sees history as akin to the plot of some great novel, sees it, in fact, as an aesthetic object, to be contemplated and understood; whereas in fact history – and our own life – can almost be defined by the fact that it is *not* a book.[1]

Kierkegaard's attacks on Hegel and on the 'aestheticism' of the society in which he lived were of course made in the name of his own particular brand of Christianity. But he felt that it was essential that he make them, if only to reveal to his readers the impossibility of his task. For how is he to convey the difference between life lived according to the religious or the ethical category and life lived according to the aesthetic category, when all he has at his command is his pen, an instrument good only for the creation of aesthetic objects? How can he bring home to each reader the uniqueness of his life and the irreversibility of his choices through the generalising medium of language and of philosophical discourse? The answer is of course that he can't, except by the roundabout way of drawing the reader's attention to the problem in the first place. That is why reading Kierkegaard and Nietzsche is such an uncomfortable activity, for they introduce us not to some foreign realm of experience, but to ourselves.

Kierkegaard's problems, and some of his solutions, are the problems and solutions of modernism. For even as Wagnerism swept through Europe and Nietzsche sank into his final madness, the reaction to Romantic decadence had begun. This did not take the form of a movement in the sense that, say, surrealism, was a movement, with polemical manifestos and self-appointed leaders and spokesmen; it was not even a movement of men who thought

[1] Cf. Sartre's critique of naïve fiction discussed in Chapter 5 above. The influence of Kierkegaard on Sartre cannot be underestimated, though for obvious reasons he has played it down. Interesting in this respect is his early nativity play, *Bariona*, an English translation of which has appeared in *Adam International Review*, xxxv (1970), and which shows such close affinities with Auden's *For the Time Being*, another work heavily influenced by Kierkegaard.

alike on such general topics as human freedom and the role of the artist in society, as Romanticism had been in its early stages. Proust and Joyce met once and did not take to each other; Schoenberg loathed Stravinsky; Eliot was more interested in Donne than in Mallarmé or Mann; Kafka ignored and was ignored by all the rest. Yet it is easy for us today to see that all these men were united by one common attitude, albeit a negative one: they all insisted on the *limitations* of art. More than that, they all stressed, in their art itself, that what they were creating were artifacts and not to be confused with life: that painting was first of all a series of brushstrokes on a flat canvas; music certain notes played by certain combinations of instruments; poetry the grouping of words on a page.

The Romantics had regarded art as simply a means to a transcendental end, and they therefore tended to see all art as more or less interchangeable – it didn't matter what train you caught since they all arrived at the same destination. The insistence on the part of the moderns that their work was art and not something else, their stress on the particular *medium* in which they were working, was not meant to be a denial of the importance of art. On the contrary, it was a reassertion of art's vital function. Art, they argued, was not a means of piercing the sensible veil of the universe, of getting at the 'unknown', as Rimbaud and others had claimed, for there was nothing *beyond* the world we see all around us. The whole mystery is there, in front of our eyes – only most of us are too blind or lazy to see it. What most of us tend to do in the face of the world, of ourselves, of works of art even, is to neutralise what is there in front of us by referring it to something we already know. Thus we are forever shut up inside our preconceived ideas, reacting only to that which makes no demands on us to see. As Giacometti wittily remarked:

Where do we find the greatest number of people? In front of the *Sacre de Napoléon*. Why do people look in particular at this painting? Because they imagine themselves to be present at the scene, participating in it. They become 'little Napoleons.' At the same time the spectacle becomes the equivalent of the reading of a novel.[1]

[1] Quoted in G. Charbonnier, *Le Monologue du peintre* (Paris, 1959) 173.

In other words, it becomes an excuse for daydreaming. The modern artist, on the other hand, holds that the work of art is meaningful precisely because it reveals to us the 'otherness' of the world – it shocks us out of our natural sloth and the force of habit, and makes us see for the first time what we had looked at a hundred times but never seen. Art is not the key to the universe, as the Romantics had believed; it is merely a pair of spectacles. Valéry, echoing Proust's Elstir, points out:

> In general we guess or anticipate more than we see, and the impressions that strike the eye are signs for us rather than *singular presences*, prior to all the patterns, the short cuts, the immediate substitutions, which a primary education has instilled in us.
>
> Just as the thinker tries to defend himself against *words* and those ready-made expressions which protect people against any feeling of shock and thus make possible everyday practical activities, so the artist may, through the study of objects with a unique form [a lump of coal which is like no other, a handkerchief thrown anyhow onto a table, and so on], try to rediscover his own uniqueness.[1]

Art, then, does not feed us information and it does not provide us with a passport to some higher realm of existence. What it does is to open our eyes by removing the film of habit which we normally carry around with us. The work of art does this by shocking us into awareness through its insistence on itself as an object in its own right, an irreducible *singular presence*. The cubist picture, for instance, teases the eye as we follow shape after shape on the canvas, always on the verge of understanding it, yet never quite allowed to do so. For understanding would mean fitting the picture into our preconceived world, in other words denying its uniqueness. And because we cannot step back and say: 'Ah yes, a mandolin, a glass of wine, a table . . .', we go on looking at the canvas and in time learn to accept its own reality instead of reducing it to our unthinking notion of what a mandolin or a glass of wine looks like. Thus Braque can say: 'The painting is finished when the idea has disappeared', and Valéry, elsewhere in the essay on Degas: 'To look means to forget the names of the

[1] 'Degas, Danse, Dessin', in *Œuvres*, ed. Jean Hytier (Pléide, Paris, 1960) II 1195.

things one is seeing.' Proust's whole novel, of course, can be seen as the attempt to substitute the object for the name, to render the uniqueness of existence by relentlessly destroying all the names by which we explain it to ourselves.

An art of this kind makes the spectator work. It does not, like Wagnerian opera, claim to hand him the key to salvation, or, like the 'Sacre de Napoléon', allow him simply to indulge his daydreams. What it claims to do is to *recreate* within the willing listener or spectator the liberating experience of the artist himself as he makes the object. When Picasso said of his famous sculpture of the bull's head made out of the seat and handlebars of a bicycle that the whole point would be lost if the viewer, through excessive familiarity with it, were to see *only* a bull's head, he neatly illustrated this aspect of modern art. What is important is not the finished product, but the process. Picasso wants us to be aware of the fact that what is in front of us is not a bull's head but a man-made object. The product is not there to be contemplated for its own sake but to make the viewer re-enact the creative discovery for himself. What is important is to see the bull's head in the handlebars, and handlebars in every bull's head. It is the play of wit which turns a universe we had taken for granted into a source of infinite possibilities, and therefore wakes us up to the miraculous nature of everything that *is*. The object – the head/handlebars – is necessary, for wit is always the result of the transformation of what is given, never the creation of something totally new; but Picasso is not interested in bicycles or bulls as such, he does not want us to say: 'Now I understand what a bull is really like,' but, if anything: 'Now I understand that a bull is.' We must not rest with the object, but with the object-as-created-by-wit. In much the same way *A la Recherche du temps perdu* does not so much tell *a* story as create within the reader the possibility of telling the story Marcel is about to set down as the work ends. In this way the artist's acceptance of limitation, his open acknowledgement of the medium in which he is working, leads to the creation of an art that strikes more directly at the life of the reader or viewer than any art since the Middle Ages.

The modern revolution in the arts was a reaction to decadent Romanticism, but this reaction, we can now see, entailed a break with four centuries of the Western artistic tradition. Shifts in taste and in the forms of expression had of course occurred at regular intervals throughout these four centuries, but they were adjustments and alterations of emphasis within a fixed framework. Romanticism, by trying to give full and unfettered expression to the individual, burst this framework and so made it possible for the moderns to step out of the wreckage and discover that the frame only enclosed a small fraction of the universe. Or perhaps a more accurate way of describing the change would be to say that what the artists of the previous four centuries had taken for *the* universe was now seen to be nothing else than the universe as seen through the spectacles of Renaissance norms. It is not by chance that the birth of the modern coincides with the discovery or rediscovery of Japanese graphics, Balinese music, African sculpture, Romanesque painting and the poetry of the troubadours. This is not simply a widening of the cultural horizons; it is the discovery of the *relativity* of artistic norms. Perspective and harmony, far from being a datum of experience, are suddenly seen to be as much the product of convention as the sonnet form, though, unlike the latter, they were clearly the product of certain metaphysical assumptions which began to emerge in the West in the years between 1350 and 1700.

All art, since the Renaissance, had been based on the twin concepts of expression and imitation. In some of the previous chapters I tried to suggest why the two should always go hand in hand and why they should have emerged as the primary criteria of art at a time when medieval notions of analogy were no longer acceptable. The Romantics, by stressing expression at the expense of imitation, helped to bring the hidden assumptions of both out into the open. Baudelaire, writing about the 'Salon' of 1846, quotes at some length from Hoffmann's *Kreisleriana*. The passage is central not only to Baudelaire's own aesthetic, but to that of Romanticism in general:

It is not only in dreams, or in that mild delirium which precedes sleep, but it is even awakened when I hear music – that perception of an analogy and an intimate connexion between colours, sounds and perfumes. It seems to me that all these things were created by one and the same ray of light, and that their combination must result in a wonderful concert of harmony. The smell of red and brown marigolds above all produces a magical effect on my being. It makes me fall into a deep reverie, in which I seem to hear the solemn, deep tones of the oboe in the distance.[1]

The implicit belief behind this passage is that individual sights, sounds, smells and tastes touch each one of us in the same way and are themselves interchangeable. There is an analogy here, but it is not between two sets of events, two orders of reality, but between the different senses. And this correspondence can find an echo in each one of us because the senses speak a natural language. The poet has simply to reach down into himself and express what he feels and it will immediately enter the soul of the reader. We have seen how this mistaken view of the poetic process[2] led to the breakdown of art into a series of utterances so private that they no longer made sense, or turned into the banal expression not of vision but of cliché. This failure made it clear to the moderns that art is not the expression of inner feeling but the creation of a structure that will allow us to understand what it means to perceive, and will thus, in a sense, give us back the world. Already at the start of the Romantic movement, as though to spite the historian of ideas with his clear notions of historical change and development, Lichtenberg had written: 'To see something new we must make something new.' And this explains the insistence on the part of the moderns on the impersonality of the poet, that distinction between the man and the artist which forms the basis of the work of Proust, Valéry, Rilke and Eliot. For the artist, *qua* man, is no different from other men; the only difference lies in the fact that he is a craftsman, a man who makes objects which will refract reality in a way the tired eyes of habit never do. Thus St. Beuve's biographical method is not only useless as a critical tool, but misleading, since the artist has, if anything, a less interesting life than other men, since so much of it is given up to the making of artifacts. Robbe-Grillet expresses the extreme position with wit and elegance: 'The artist is a man with nothing to say.'

[1] *Art in Paris 1845–1862: Salons and Other Exhibitions Reviewed by Charles Baudelaire*, trans. and ed. Jonathan Mayne (London, 1965) 51.

[2] As often happens, Baudelaire's aesthetics were at odds with his practice – in the late prose poems at least there is a strong sense of struggle between 'life' and 'poetry' and a questioning of naïve Romanticism.

The Romantic artist claimed in some way to be a magician. Words and sounds, he implied, hid within themselves certain magical properties over which he alone had power. Through this power he could confer salvation on the rest of mankind; the reader or listener (I am thinking of Rimbaud and Wagner, different though they are in so many respects) had simply to submit to the words or sounds in order to shed the pains and frustrations of his daily life and to emerge into a free world where there was no conflict between desire and fulfilment, imagination and reality. The consequences of this view were quickly seen by Nietzsche, and the modern reaction to this notion of art as magic was to stress the idea of art as game. The work of art, said the moderns, does not offer permanent salvation to anyone. Its function is to increase the reader's powers of imagination, to make him see the world again cleansed of its stiff and stubborn manlocked set. This requires active participation rather than passive submission, and a willingness to play according to the rules laid down by the artist. At the same time the modern rediscovery of the hieratic and stylised arts of other periods went hand in hand with the rehabilitation of forms of art which had not been considered serious enough to form part of the mainstream of post-Renaissance art in Europe: the puppet play, the shadow-play, children's games, street games and ballads were all used by Jarry, Stravinsky, Picasso and Eliot, and all helped them to forge their own individual styles. In these archaic and popular forms of art there is no pretence at illusion. Art is a game and its creation involves making something that will be of pleasure to others.

This is a very different view of art from that held by the Romantics. But it is not perhaps all that far removed from art as it was known from the time of Homer down to the Renaissance. The acceptance by artist and audience of the rules of genre and rhetoric shows that there was always an implicit awareness of the fact that for art to be true it must not pretend to be other than it is, a made thing, an object put together according to the rules of tradition and convention in order to satisfy. It is in fact only with the painting and the fiction which emerged from the Renaissance revolution in thought that the extraordinary belief grew up that art could do without rules altogether, that it could simply imitate external reality and tell the whole truth starting not from axioms but from observable facts.

But we have seen that the imitation of the external world, however detailed, does not really answer the questions: Why this bit of the world rather than that? Why should the artist paint *this* subject, include *this* detail, why should the novelist tell *this* story, recount *this* incident? Is it enough to say: Because he feels like it? Will he feel like it tomorrow? If there is no answer to these questions then the freedom of the artist to do what he likes is a meaningless freedom. The hero of Kafka's last novel, standing in the snow outside the inn, recognises the force of this paradox only too well:

> It seemed to K. as if at last those people had broken off all relations with him, and as if now in reality he were freer than he had ever been, and at liberty to wait here in this place usually forbidden to him as long as he desired, and had won a freedom such as hardly anybody else had ever succeeded in winning, and as if nobody would dare to touch him or drive him away, or even speak to him; but – this conviction was at least equally strong – as if at the same time there was nothing more senseless, nothing more hopeless, than this freedom, this waiting, this inviolability.[1]

The problem had already haunted the Romantics and we find it everywhere in their poetry. But so long as they held to an expressive theory of art they could never resolve it. We see them trying to blur the outlines of their fictions, their music, their painting, until the artifact almost merges with the surrounding world – but of course it never does completely or it would cease to be an artifact, and until it does so they are bound to remain unsatisfied. In music they try to slow down the forward thrust of their art so that it ceases to unfold in time according to the premises laid down at the start and spreads instead like a sluggish river in marshy country. This is particularly evident in the work of Bruckner and Mahler, but again, it is not till the entire nature of the medium is reconsidered that they can escape the inner contradictions of their art. Schönberg undertakes such a reconsideration, introducing a new, non-linear principle of composition to

---

[1] *The Castle*, trans. Willa and Edwin Muir (Penguin, Harmondsworth, 1957) 105.

replace the subjective and time-bound principles of the sonata
form, and in Webern we find the tradition reaching its logical
conclusion, since in a three-minute work he can present us with
the means of generating a hundred Mahler symphonies (just as
a five-page work by Borges is capable of generating a hundred
three-decker novels). In painting the decisive break comes with
Cézanne, and his phrase 'Je pars neutre' is the key to this aspect
of modernism. What he means by this is that in his painting he
wishes to eliminate the personal slant in the choice of both
subject-matter and treatment, and to seek instead to discover the
general laws of light and space present in the scene before him –
as in every other. Thus it is not so much that the artist refines
himself out of existence as that he tries to establish the laws of
perception and of the process of art itself. In a similar way Wittgenstein was to argue that he wished to develop not a new *area*
of philosophical inquiry, but an investigation of the nature of that
inquiry. This has led to the charge that his work is concerned
with trivialities, since it is not concerned with 'life', a charge
familiar enough to the ears of modern artists who are accused of
wilfully shutting their eyes to the world by writing books on the
writing of books and painting pictures whose subject-matter is
the painting of pictures. Proust, whose design is similar to
Cézanne's, comes back to this point again and again in *Le Temps
Retrouvé*: he is not interested in imitating a flat reality, in writing one more book which tells one more story; what he wants to
do is to draw out the laws inherent in love, in speech, in
perception, in art. And, thinking perhaps of a Cézanne, and
comparing it to one of those society portraits so popular at the
time, he writes:

> If, in the realm of painting, one portrait makes manifest
> certain truths concerning volume, light, movement, does that
> mean that it is necessarily inferior to another completely
> different portrait of the same person, in which a thousand
> details omitted in the first are minutely transcribed, from which
> second portrait one would conclude that the model was
> ravishingly beautiful while from the first one would have
> thought him or her ugly, a fact which may be of documentary,
> even of historical importance, but is not necessarily an artistic
> truth? (*TR* 29; III 719)

It might be thought that such an art, an art of total potentiality, of laws rather than subject-matter, would result in a dry abstraction. Many modern works certainly display this characteristic, though different people would have different works in mind as they made that statement. There is of course no legislation for art or for criticism, and membership of a school, whether it be Imagist or Nouveau Roman, does not confer automatic value. We are not really concerned with the countless imitations of the great modern masters, imitations no better or worse than those of the great classics. What is important is that such an art need be neither solemn nor cold. On the contrary, there has never been an art more joyous, or one that brings joy back to our response to older art, than that of Stravinsky, Picasso and Eliot. For the interest of these artists in the tradition is of course bound up with their search for laws rather than new subject-matter. Stravinsky has called *Pulcinella* 'the epiphany through which the whole of my late work became possible. It was a backward look, of course – the first of many love affairs in that direction – but it was a look in the mirror, too.' Such a love affair was Picasso's with Velasquez when, by producing dozens of imitations of 'Las Meninas', he made us see that picture anew by revealing the necessity of its particular being. Had 'Las Meninas' not been reworked by him we would have taken it for granted and thus in a sense failed to see it. By showing us all the things it *might* have been Picasso as it were freed it from the realm of the 'given' and revealed to us how all its elements were both chosen *and* necessary. And in a precisely similar way the greatest modern art, concentrating as it does on laws rather than on subject-matter, paradoxically gives us back the world we had lost through force of habit. Picasso, in conversation with his friend the photographer George Brassai, sums up the spirit of modernism as I have tried to sketch it in this chapter:

I always aim at the resemblance. An artist should observe nature but never confuse it with painting. It is only translatable into painting by signs. . . . But such signs are not invented. To arrive at the sign you have to concentrate hard on the resemblance. To me surreality is nothing and never has been anything but this profound resemblance, something deeper than the forms and colours in which objects present themselves.

With this in mind we can, in the next three chapters, explore the
relation of form to content in the work of three major novelists,
remembering that they belong to no 'movement' and that what is
important is the uniqueness of each man's vision and of his
solutions to the problems of art and of life.

8 *Lolita*: Parody and the Pursuit of Beauty

To comment in print on the work of Vladimir Nabokov one must be either very foolish or very daring. For Nabokov has never made a secret of his contempt for critics; in preface and postscript, in interviews with the papers, on radio and on television, he has poured scorn on all those who would try to 'place' him in relation to his contemporaries, who would examine his 'themes' or decipher the 'messages' his novels contain. In the preface to his son's translation of *Invitation to a Beheading* he tells us that critics have found in his work the influence of Cervantes, Kafka, Tolstoyevsky and many others. He himself denies it. The only influence he will admit is that of the French writer Pierre Delalande, whom he has invented. And in his essay 'On a Book Entitled *Lolita*' he asserts that critics who have not read his earlier novels – the best of which, he claims,[1] have not been translated from their original Russian – are in no position to pass judgement upon him. He has, moreover, no message, nothing to communicate, and writes 'with no other purpose than to get rid' of a book – to get it out of his system.

In the face of this onslaught there seems little for the sympathetic critic to do except praise the author's mastery of invective and self-protective irony and turn to more amenable writers. And such an attitude would seem to find justification in the novels themselves, and in Nabokov's way there of destroying the pretensions of all those he hates and despises: the Goodmans and Paduks and all the shallow and pretentious bores who throng his pages, talking of Freud or Marx, Ball Zac or Doll's Toy. Yet it is just such passages as these which should make the critic pause in his understandable desire to escape as quickly and silently as possible. For is there not more in Nabokov's personal attitude than

---

[1] That essay was written in 1956. Since then a good deal of the early work has been translated, but there are still one or two novels behind which the author can hide from non-Russian-reading critics.

a simple dislike of the critical profession as such? The theme of the critic as buffoon, of the academic mind run mad, of the moral perversion involved in explaining human beings in terms of heredity or environment and books in terms of mechanism or organism – these themes are so central to Nabokov's work that it is impossible not to see his attitude towards his own critics as an extension into real life of the preoccupations of his novels. Indeed by an irony which cannot have failed to appeal to him, the patterns of misinterpretation established in his novels have been faithfully reproduced in the critical reception accorded to these novels. Perhaps if we look at *Lolita* as, among other things, a model of the relationship between the writer and his book and the reader and the writer, we may come closer to grasping its real nature. As Nabokov knows – it is one of the reasons for his profound melancholy – it is the critic's prerogative always to have the last word.

All the tragic events recorded in the 'Memoir of Humbert Humbert' spring from his desire for certain kinds of girl-children. It is therefore necessary, if we are to understand the meaning of these events, to make sure that we understand the nature of the desires. In his foreword to the Memoir, John Ray Jr, Ph.D., gives one interpretation, when he explains that 'had our demented diarist gone, in the fatal summer of 1947, to a competent psychopathologist, there would have been no disaster'. Ray, that is to say, sees Humbert's craving for nymphets as an abnormal condition, but one susceptible to psychiatric treatment. The events narrated in the Memoir he regards as 'a general lesson . . . "Lolita" should make all of us – parents, social workers, educators – apply ourselves with still greater vigilance and vision to the task of bringing up a better generation in a safer world'.

These are noble sentiments, and such an interpretation of the tragic tale of Humbert Humbert is clearly in keeping with the character of a man who has just been awarded the Poling Prize for 'a modest work ("Do the Senses Make Sense?") wherein certain morbid states and perversions had been discussed'. But it is not Humbert's interpretation, and even the most cursory reading of the Memoir should be enough to convince us that it is grossly inadequate. Humbert, it is true, does for a while believe that his love for nymphets may be the result of his unconsummated passion for little Annabel in the Kingdom by the Sea; but what he recognises all along, and what is made clear beyond all possible doubt by his ironic attempt to relive that youthful experience with Lolita and the Pacific as substitutes for Annabel and the Mediterranean, is that an explanation in psychological terms can never account for the nature of his case. For even if that unconsummated youthful passion did change him from a child like other children into a man different from other men, who is to say that it is not he who is normal and the others abnormal? What Humbert challenges is not the method but the assumptions of the psychiatrist:

> I am ready to believe that the sensations I derived from natural fornication were much the same as those known to normal big males consorting with their normal big mates in that routine rhythm which shakes the world. The trouble was that those gentlemen had not, and I *had*, caught glimpses of an incomparably more poignant bliss. (20)[1]

What that bliss was he explains later:

> Indeed, it may well be that the very attraction immaturity has for me lies not so much in the limpidity of pure young forbidden fairy-child beauty as in the security of a situation where infinite perfections fill the gap between the little given and the great promised – the great rose-grey never-to-be-had. (257)

It is not that Humbert does not have the same desires as other men. He has those, but he has additional ones too. And these are not of the body but of the spirit: he longs for unattainable beauty – for that which is beautiful *just because* it is unattainable. In an earlier novel of Nabokov's, *Laughter in the Dark*, we find the hero, Albinus, in a somewhat similar situation. Although he is quite handsome he has never been able to satisfy his very strong sexual desires. He has had a few affairs, but they have not given him what he really craves for:

> Alongside of these feeble romances there had been hundreds of girls of whom he had dreamed but whom he had never got to know; they had just slid past him, leaving for a day or two that

[1] All references are to the English edition published by Weidenfeld & Nicolson, London, 1959.

hopeless sense of loss which makes beauty what it is: a distant
lone tree against golden heavens; ripples of light on the inner
curve of a bridge; a thing quite impossible to capture.[1]

Humbert's desires, like those of Albinus, are much closer to those
of the poet than of the sexual maniac. And it is in fact as a poet
that he sees himself. 'We poets never kill', he says at one point,
and 'we poets' is one of his favourite expressions in the early
sections of the Memoir. In one passage he explicitly makes the
distinction between poet and maniac, for of his night in The
Enchanted Hunters with the not-so-drugged Lolita he says:

> If I dwell at some length on the tremors and gropings of that
> distant night, it is because I insist upon proving that I am not,
> and never was, and never could have been, a brutal scoundrel.
> The gentle and dreamy regions through which I crept were the
> patrimonies of poets – *not* crime's prowling-ground. Had I
> reached my goal, my ecstasy would have been all softness, a
> case of internal combustion of which she would hardly have
> felt the heat, even if she were wide awake. (130)

But what gives *Lolita* a depth lacking in the earlier novels is the
fact that Humbert *does* reach his goal, and that his ecstasy proves
to be far more than a case of internal combustion. As soon as he
has made love to Lolita for the first time he recognises his terrible
error: by possessing Lolita, who was desirable precisely because
she appeared to be unpossessable, Humbert seems to have destroyed everything in himself which had hitherto set him above the
'normal big males'. He is quite clear, as he recounts the story,
where the watershed of his fortunes lies. Having locked the
drugged Lolita into the hotel bedroom he goes downstairs to give
her time to go soundly to sleep:

> In a few minutes . . . I would let myself into that '342' and
> find my nymphet, my beauty and bride, imprisoned in her
> crystal sleep. Jurors! If my happiness could have talked, it
> would have filled that genteel hotel with a deafening roar. And
> my only regret today is that I did not quietly deposit key '342'
> at the office, and leave the town, the country, the continent, the
> hemisphere – indeed, the globe – that very same night. (122)

---

[1] *Laughter in the Dark* (London, 1961) 11.

From the moment they make love, despite all Humbert's attempts
to rationalise away the feeling by telling himself that he was not
even her first lover, he is caught in a web of guilt and remorse.
He cannot understand the reason for this since he has only
followed his desires, the desires of a poet: 'I have but followed
nature. I am nature's faithful hound. Why then this horror that
I cannot shake off?' He feels that by making love to Lolita he
has destroyed not only something *in* her, but that somehow he
has destroyed *her*: 'More and more uncomfortable did Humbert
feel. It was something quite special, that feeling: an oppressive,
hideous constraint, as if I were sitting with the small ghost of
somebody I had just killed.' From that moment too any love
Lolita may still have had for the handsome lodger disappears and
they remain bound together only by fear on her side and lust on
his. In this way they set out on their aimless journey through the
circles of hell-America, a parody of that parody of the love of
parents and children which is incest, each of them forced into a
role that is not his, he into deliberately superficial witticisms, she
into her magazines and her tough talk. Now that he has at last
attained the goal for which his mind and body had striven for so
long he finds himself in a realm where values have ceased to
exist, and where the mind turns against the body and the body
against the mind.

And when eventually, inevitably, Lolita escapes, his artificial
world collapses and he arrives at the heart of his spiral of hell.
But – and this is the miracle – out of this descent there emerges a
quality which the earlier Humbert, with all his talk of poets and
beauty, had most conspicuously lacked: the quality of love:

Somewhere beyond Bill's shack an afterwork radio had begun
singing of folly and fate, and there she was with her ruined
looks and her adult, rope-veined narrow hands and her goose-
flesh white arms, and her shallow ears, and her unkempt
armpits, there she was (my Lolita!), hopelessly worn at seven-
teen, with that baby, dreaming already in her of becoming a
big shot and retiring around 2020 A.D. – and I looked and
looked at her, and knew as clearly as I know I am to die, that
I loved her more than anything I had ever seen or imagined
on earth, or hoped for anywhere else. . . . What I used to pam-
per among the tangled vines of my heart, *mon grand pêché*

radieux, had dwindled to its essence: sterile and selfish vice, all *that* I cancelled and cursed. You may jeer at me, and threaten to clear the court, but until I am gagged and half-throttled, I will shout my poor truth. I insist the world know how much I loved my Lolita, *this* Lolita, pale and polluted, and big with another's child, but still grey-eyed, still sooty-lashed, still auburn and almond, still Carmencita, still mine. . . .
(270–1)

It is this new love which makes it possible for the Memoir to be written. The early Humbert, despite his frequent references to 'we poets', had not written one line of literature. It is only with the replacing of lust by love that he becomes a poet in deed as well as in name.

But what is this change if not the recognition that he cannot possess Lolita, that she is a human being with a destiny of her own and not merely the object of his desires? At the very end, when he has lost her for ever, Humbert goes to a Catholic priest to try what he calls 'an old-fashioned Popish cure' for the remorse that is tormenting him. But naturally the cure fails; he has deprived another human being of her childhood, of the possibility of freedom, and he finds it impossible to believe that this sin can ever be wiped out. So, having failed, he sees 'nothing for the treatment of my misery but the melancholy and very local palliative of articulate art'. The descent into hell to which he was led by his attempt to possess the unpossessable is only made bearable, in the end, by the transformation of that hell into art and the partial redemption of the girl he had destroyed in his pursuit of beauty by the conferring upon her of the immortality of art:

And do not pity C[lare] Q[uilty]. One had to choose between him and HH, and one wanted HH to exist at least a couple of months longer, so as to have him make you live in the minds of later generations. I am thinking of aurochs and angels, the secret of durable pigments, prophetic sonnets, the refuge of art. And this is the only immortality you and I may share, my Lolita. (300)

In the course of his exposition of the theory of nymphets Humbert makes the following curious statement: 'Humbert was perfectly capable of intercourse with Eve, but it was Lilith he longed for.' Now Lilith was the first wife of Adam who was dispossessed by

Eve, according to Rabbinic mythology, and she is linked, in folk-lore and legend, with the snake and the vampire. In case it may be thought that Humbert is here indulging in a scholarly antithesis without realising the implications of what he is saying, he refers a short while later to Lolita as 'the body of some immortal demon disguised as a female child' – it is only the villains in Nabokov who use language without realising its full implications. Humbert knows exactly what he is saying about the nature of nymphets in general and Lolita in particular: she is none other than that amoral, ever-desirable female who leads those who pursue her to destruction. It should occasion no surprise that Humbert, who regards himself as a poet and his pursuit of nymphets as essen-tially a poetic endeavour, who is fond of literary allusions and who, it will be recalled, is the author of a learned paper on Keats, should link Lolita in his mind with the Belle Dame Sans Merci, the Lamia, who figures so prominently in Romantic mythology as a symbol for that which lies beyond reason and language and which the poet seeks to capture, even at the risk of his life, and always in vain.[1]

Margot, the vulgar little cinema usherette in *Laughter in the Dark*, who leads Albinus to his destruction, is similarly presented in terms which link her to this conception. We have already seen the close resemblance between the desires of Albinus and of Hum-bert, and the two books have many other parallels. What lends *Lolita* a depth quite foreign to the flat grotesquerie of the earlier work is that Lolita herself is not only a Lamia but also a little American girl whose mother is dead and who now has nowhere else to go except into a home for orphans or into the arms of her monstrous stepfather. Margot is herself without any feeling, a young woman out to get what she can and not unversed in the ways of doing so. How different it is with Lolita! It is her help-lessness that makes Humbert's lust so terrible for both of them. Neither her nymphet charms nor his violent desires really belong to them. It is as though their bodies had been taken over by

[1] John Jones in *John Keats's Dream of Truth*, has some pertinent things to say about Keats's use of the Lamia figure. Keats's failure to make of her both a credible being *and* a symbol finds its parallel in the work of the other Romantics. In this sense *Lolita*, like *Herzog*, is a critique of Roman-ticism: it shows what happens when the Romantic imagination is placed in the real world.

powerful alien forces, leaving their true selves helpless onlookers in a ghastly tragedy being played out with those bodies. It is because Lolita is more than a Lamia that the story is tragic rather than grotesque. It is because she is a human being who can be pathetic as well as vicious that Humbert's lust can ultimately turn to love. When this happens her story can be written, her nymphet charms immortalised.

Beside Humbert's sudden surges of tenderness, his constant ability to put himself in her place, Lolita's total lack of imagination is horrifying. She is quite unable to imagine his state of mind, and thinks of him only as a dirty old man. But she is not wholly to blame. The weight of Humbert's hatred and sarcasm falls not on her but on the country which has nurtured her, and especially on its system of education.

America enters the novel in the person of Mrs Haze, with her *ne montrez pas vos zhambes*, her interminable questionnaires, and her pathetic attempts to behave as she imagines a lady should behave. Towards her Humbert feels only a slight awe and a good deal of pity. Not so the camp where Lolita is sent to live the healthy outdoor life and where she loses her flower to hideous red-haired Charlie-boy. Lolita explains how 'we loved the sings round the fire . . . where every girl merged her own spirit of happiness with the voice of the group', and we recall Paduk, the dictator in *Bend Sinister*, with his injunctions to his subjects to merge their individual egos in the virile oneness of the state. Such a merging can only lead to the destruction of a man's freedom and imagination. Imagination is what enables a man to put himself in the place of others and lack of it can only lead to cruelty and brutality, when people are no longer treated as human beings but as objects. After their first love-making Humbert comments:

> Suffice it to say that not a trace of modesty did I perceive in this beautiful hardly-formed young girl whom modern co-education, juvenile mores, the campfire racket and so forth had utterly and hopelessly depraved. She saw the stark act merely as part of a youngster's furtive world, unknown to adults. . . . My life was handled by little Lo in an energetic, matter-of-fact manner as if it were an insensate gadget unconnected with me. (132)

Although the tone here and throughout the novel is gentler than in *Bend Sinister*, the offence is the same: through a total lack of imagination man has been reduced to a gadget, love to a form of gymnastics, and beauty to a saleable commodity.

But for Nabokov, as for Swift or Chaucer, give a fool enough rope and he is sure to hang himself. Nabokov's satire is at its most biting in the long set speeches he gives to the materialist perverters of the imagination. The pompous bonhomie of the foolish and the corrupt arouse his especial hatred, and he lets such people damn themselves by making them reveal, beneath the common-sense façade, the folly and bestiality of their unvoiced assumptions. *Bend Sinister* is full of people who try to fool themselves and others into substituting the beast for the man under cover of professed reasonableness and high motives. But language, which for Nabokov, as for the writers of the Renaissance, is the clearest evidence of man's unique place in the universe, always takes its revenge on such hypocrisy. In *Lolita* the best example of this is perhaps to be found in the wonderful speech delivered by the Principal of Beardsley College to poor Humbert:

> We are not so much concerned, Mr Humbird, with having our
> students become bookworms or be able to reel off all the capitals
> of Europe which nobody knows anyway. . . . What we are
> concerned with is the adjustment of the child to group life. . . .
> To put it briefly, while adopting certain teaching techniques,
> we are more interested in communication than in composition.
> That is, with due respect to Shakespeare and others, we want
> our girls to *communicate* freely with the live world around
> them rather than plunge into musty old books. We are still
> groping perhaps, but we grope intelligently, like a gynecologist
> feeling a tumour. We think, Dr Humburg, in organismal and
> organisational terms. . . . What do we mean by education?
> In the old days it was in the main a verbal phenomenon. . . .
> [But] we live not only in a world of thoughts, but also in a
> world of things. Words without experience are meaningless.
> (173-4)

The utter moral and intellectual confusion of a person who believes communication to be the most important thing and yet would do without words reminds one of Swift's Grub Street Hack and of Swift's indictment, in *A Tale of a Tub*, of both the scientist who would make one word equal one thing and the religious enthusiast who would raise words to the status of objects. As we have seen, what both try to do is to by-pass the free and conscious mind which translates language into meaning, and they thus reduce man to either a simple mechanism or a simple organism. There is no need to analyse the Principal's speech to discover the kind of education her pupils are really going to get.

In each of Nabokov's novels there is one person who stands out as even more grotesque and terrifying than the brutal subhuman and unimaginative creatures who oppose the hero. The horror induced by this character stems from the fact that he has so many of the characteristics of the hero and yet these are so perverted as to present us with a hideous parody of everything for which the hero stands. The clearest portrait of the type is once again to be found in *Laughter in the Dark*. Axel Rex, once a brilliant faker of Old Masters, now a successful caricaturist, has all the characteristics of the artist except one: he lacks the capacity to love. Love is essentially disinterested but Axel Rex sees all art as reducible to a trick played by the artist upon the world for the furthering of his own ends:

> It amused him immensely to see life made to look silly, as it slid helplessly into caricature. . . . The art of caricature, as Rex understood it, was . . . based . . . on the contrast between cruelty on one side and credulity on the other. And if, in real life, Rex looked on without stirring a finger while a blind beggar, his stick tapping happily, was about to sit down on a freshly painted bench, he was only deriving inspiration for his next little picture.[1]

Art has here been diverted from its true function, which is to give pleasure by making available to the realm of consciousness more of the world than we can normally grasp, and has been used for a purely selfish purpose, to humiliate and hurt. The disinterestedness which is the basis of art has been replaced by a deliberate mingling of art and life to provide amusement for the artist at the expense of another human being. There is an imagination at work here but it is a parody of the natural function of the imagination and springs not from love but from envy and

[1] Op cit. 102–3.

hatred. In *Bend Sinister* the different forms that this perversion can take are almost clinically examined and contrasted to the attitude of the hero; in *Invitation to a Beheading* it is the executioner, M. Pierre, who embodies the type; and it is probable that if *Pale Fire* leaves one vaguely dissatisfied, despite its brilliance, this is because the equivalent figure there is of course Kinbote, the editor of the poem, who has now moved from a position as the foil of the hero into the very centre of the picture. An experiment with such a scheme was obviously to be expected of Nabokov sooner or later (in some of the early books it is not so much that the villain is the protagonist as that all the characters are infinitely dislikeable), but it is difficult not to feel that he was making things too hard for himself by denying himself any outlet for the sympathy and understanding that are as much a part of his vision as the bitterness and satire.

Clare Quilty is the anti-hero of *Lolita*, the parody of Humbert. With his collection of erotica and his arty plays, his hobbies (as *Who's Who in the Limelight* informs us) of fast cars and pets, he is a worthy member of that grotesque company. Humbert himself, at the height of his despair, when he has lost Lolita and is driving back over a thousand miles of American highway to find a clue to her kidnapper, half-grasps the part played by Quilty in the tragedy, though he remains ignorant of his identity:

> The clues he left did not establish his identity but they reflected his personality, or at least a certain homogeneous and striking personality; his genre, his type of humour . . . the tone of his brain, had affinities with my own. He mimed and mocked me. . . . His main trait was his passion for tantalization. . . . With infinite skill, he swayed and staggered, and regained an impossible balance, always leaving me with the sportive hope – if I may use such a term in speaking of betrayal, fury, desolation, horror and hate – that he might give himself away next time. He never did. (243–4)

Quilty, it will be recalled, had abducted Lolita from the hospital where Humbert had been forced to leave her, by posing as her uncle. It is doubtful whether the nurse realises the horrible irony of her statement when, after refusing for a long time to reveal to Humbert the identity of the kidnapper, she finally whispers, her eyes on the hundred-dollar note he has put into her hand: 'He is your brother.'

Lacking the power to love, Quilty can escape unhurt from the relationship that destroys Humbert. For him Lolita, like all human beings, is an object to be used for his own amusement and thrown away if she won't play the games he devises for her. But, despite this, and by a final irony, he remains the one man Lolita ever really loves. Neither her education nor her imagination allow her to distinguish between the truly perverted and nature's faithful hounds. Or rather, she does distinguish, but wrongly, seeing in Humbert only a dirty old man and in Quilty a genius whose superior qualities render necessary a slightly eccentric way of life.

Humbert's story ends in prison. Here, alone, consumed by guilt and remorse, he is forced to sit idly and await his trial for the murder of Clare Quilty. In such a situation the only thing that can keep him from going mad is to write down the story of his passion. After the frenzied activity of the last few months he finds himself shut up in a tiny room with nothing to do but play with words. 'Oh my Lolita,' he cries, 'I have only words to play with!' No wonder then that he plays with them with such controlled frenzy, such fiendish concentration. Words are now all he has left and only by playing with words can he keep the spectre of madness at bay. So that behind the dazzling barrage of wit lies the sad and disillusioned Humbert, the man who had once seen himself as infinitely superior to other men, a poet of poets. Occasionally the mask drops and he allows us to catch a glimpse of this: 'Oh let me be mawkish for the nonce! I am so tired of being cynical.' But before the reader can extend his sympathy, the mask is on again and the hectic play with language once more under way.

The story of Humbert Humbert and Lolita comes to us refracted through Humbert's baroque prose. Never does Humbert allow the reader to forget the fact that what he has in front of him are words and that these words are being manipulated by one man: himself. In order to keep this fact constantly before the reader he continually interrupts his narrative to address him: 'Your Honour', 'Winged Gentlemen of the Jury', '*touché*, reader'. He slips in an aside: 'You can count on a murderer for a fancy prose style'; he writes down a sentence and then takes it back: 'Then I pulled out my automatic – I mean that is the kind of fool thing the reader might suppose I did'; he warns an imaginary secretary not to correct a mistake he has made transcribing something into the Memoir and orders the printer to 'repeat till the page is full'. Everywhere he burlesques the conventional novelist who, with the connivance of the reader, blurs the distinction between art and reality, words and events: 'But now I am convinced that prude and prurient Miss East –; or, to explode her incognito, Miss Finton Lebone. . . .' He may be a murderer, and he may be in prison, but he knows the power even mere words can exert and he uses it to the full.

The most notable instance of this kind of play with the reader occurs not in any single episode but in the way he keeps Quilty's identity hidden till the very end of the book. Even when Lolita divulges it to him he carefully withholds it from the reader:

> She said really it was useless, she would never tell, but on the other hand, after all – 'Do you really want to know who it was? Well, it was –'
>
> And softly, confidentially, arching her thin eyebrows and puckering her parched lips, she emitted, a little mockingly, somewhat fastidiously, not untenderly, in a kind of muted whistle, the name that the astute reader has guessed long ago.
>
> Waterproof. Why did a flash from Hourglass Lake cross my consciousness? I, too, had known it, without knowing it, all along. There was no shock, no surprise. Quietly the fusion took place, and everything fell into order, into the pattern of branches that I have woven throughout this memoir with the express purpose of having the ripe fruit fall at the right moment; yes with the express and perverse purpose of render- ing – she was talking but I sat melting in my golden peace – of rendering that golden and monstrous peace through the satis- faction of logical recognition, which my most inimical reader should experience now. (265)

Humbert appears to be playing with the reader exactly as Clare Quilty had played with Humbert himself, leading him on, tantalising him with the knowledge that the answer lies just round the corner, and taking a perverse delight in his power to withhold this answer for as long as he pleases. But there is an important difference between them. Clare Quilty was dealing with Humbert's life, his game was played out in the arena of actuality, whereas Humbert's game is played out only with the reader's imagination. So long as he persists in confusing the two the reader will indeed feel cheated and frustrated, but if he recognises the difference he will see that such devices not only help but are the necessary condition for the fulfilling of Humbert's task. For Humbert does have a task: 'I am not concerned with so-called sex at all,' he says, as he cuts short the narrative of his seduction by Lolita. 'A great endeavour lures me on: to fix once and for all the perilous magic of nymphets.' Unlike Axel Rex and Clare Quilty, his motives are not selfish, he does not use art for his own ends or his own private pleasures, he uses it to try to render once and for all that magic and ineffable beauty which he had once dreamt of possessing but now only wishes to articulate.

For if Humbert's story can be said to end in prison, from another point of view we can see that it is only in prison that it begins. It is only there that he writes down the Memoir that is to be the sole testimony to his strange and tragic passion. Nor is it the simple retelling of something that is over and done with, the artistic imitation of a reality that has ended. Rather, it is itself the culmination of Humbert's lifelong quest, a quest of which his life with Lolita was only the penultimate episode. Humbert's desire for nymphets, we saw, was never that of the sex maniac. It was the manifestation of a longing for unpossessable beauty, for that which is beautiful just because it cannot be possessed. As such it was closer to the desire of a poet. Yet this simple faith in himself as somehow above ordinary mortals, because more imaginative, more sensitive than they, was shattered when he did in fact finally possess Lolita and found, instead of the fulfilment of his desire, the despair of mingled guilt, lust and futility. With Lolita's escape and subsequent marriage, Humbert's lust is replaced by love, which means that though he still longs for her more than for anything in the world, he recognises her right to choose her own life. It is as if, no longer having any hold on her, Humbert himself had been released from an atrocious burden. And it is this new love which Humbert carries with him into prison, and which allows him, once there, to set about the task of capturing Lolita's mysterious beauty not through carnal possession but through language. Thus if, from one point of view, Humbert is forced into writing the Memoir by the fear of impending madness and the impossibility of ever possessing Lolita in the flesh, if, that is, the Memoir is simply a poor substitute for the living girl, from another point of view the shift from life to art is the logical outcome of his discovery that he had somehow gone wrong in his previous attempts at capturing the elusive beauty of nymphets. It is not a poor substitute, but the true and only way of capturing Lolita and fulfilling his poetic longings. Thus the Memoir, like Proust's novel, spirals in upon itself, being at once the history of how it came to be written and the climax of that history, at once the quest and the goal. For the goal is the quest transmuted into language.

Let us look again at what Humbert himself recognised as the decisive moment in his life, a moment where, if things had gone differently, there would have been no tragedy for Humbert and no Memoir for us to read:

> In a few minutes . . . I would let myself into that '342' and find my nymphet, my beauty and bride, imprisoned in her crystal sleep. Jurors! If my happiness could have talked, it would have filled that genteel hotel with a deafening roar. And my only regret today is that I did not quietly deposit key '342' at the office, and leave the town, the country, the continent, the hemisphere – indeed, the globe – that very same night. (122)

Because he doesn't, because he decides to stay, Humbert destroys Lolita *and* eventually writes the Memoir that captures her charms for ever. What is the explanation of this paradox? Why does Humbert need to leave 'the gentle and dreamy regions' which are the patrimonies of poets, and enter 'crime's prowling-ground' before he can indeed become a poet? We can see that before that decisive event Humbert's life was all potentiality; that every girl he longed for held out the promise of indescribable bliss precisely because she was out of reach, because the only boundaries of that bliss were those of the imagination and the imagination knows no boundaries. But once he has made love to Lolita he has crossed a threshold, made a choice, and he is constrained by an external reality in the form of Lolita herself. Thus we could say that before that event he was like the poet whose boundless imagination creates a thousand masterpieces, but who, because he will not submit to the discipline of language, because he will not accept the fact that language and subject-matter restrict and falsify, never writes anything at all. On the other hand we can see that people like Clare Quilty, or Axel Rex in *Laughter in the Dark*, will make use of reality for their own subjective ends, arbitrarily using life for the purposes of their private whims. In a sense they are like the novelist, whose irresponsibility lies in the fact that he manipulates people and events in a completely arbitrary way in order to create his fictions. Nabokov brilliantly conveys this at the end of *Laughter in the Dark* when the blind Albinus is made to rely wholly on Rex and Margot for information about the house in which he is living, just as the reader is made to depend on the whims of the novelist.

Quilty and Rex remain unaffected by people and events because they are completely lacking in feeling, which means feeling what another person is suffering. And it is because Humbert feels so strongly the pain he is causing Lolita that his entanglement with her is so tragic. Once that night at The Enchanted Hunters has been gone through he realises that there is no turning back; it all becomes a dark necessity, as Hawthorne would have said. But again *Laughter in the Dark* provides an instructive contrast. Margot, the vulgar little cinema attendant with whom Albinus falls in love, and Lolita are both, as we saw, identified with the Lamia/Belle Dame Sans Merci figure. Both Albinus and Humbert, once their decisive choice has been made, are like the Romantic poet, longing for the chaos which will engulf him but which will give meaning to a life which before had seemed purely arbitrary and meaninglessly free. *Laughter in the Dark* follows the Romantic pattern closely: Albinus is wrenched out of his comfortable bourgeois existence by his passion; Margot, quite without scruple, drains Albinus of his money and slowly reduces him to utter dependence on herself and her lover Axel Rex, helped by the accident in which Albinus loses his sight. Inevitably, the novel ends with his death. The first paragraph, in six succinct phrases, presents us with the Romantic pattern, which the rest of the novel simply fills out. But in *Lolita* things are not so simple. Because Lolita is seen by Humbert to be a little girl as well as Lilith, a human being forced to suffer his lust as well as a creature of myth, there is, in the later work, the possibility of tragedy and the possibility of love. Or perhaps we could say that Humbert Humbert is able to respond to Lolita as a human being other than the creature of his desires because he is a richer, more imaginative being than Albinus. Since the story comes to us through Humbert's own words the two cannot be disentangled.

The imaginative equivalent of the physical destruction of Lycius in Keats's *Lamia* is the surrender of the mind to unconscious impulses. But this, as we saw in the last chapter, leads not to art but to silence or to a loss of control which expresses itself in cliché. Both Humbert and Albinus take the Romantic plunge, but where this leads quickly and inevitably to Albinus's death, Humbert changes profoundly on the way. If, as we said, the decisive event is the one that takes place in room '342' of The Enchanted Hunters, there is another crucial change, less easy to chart, which transforms Humbert's lust into love, his desire to possess Lolita carnally into the desire to immortalise her in art. His recognition of his error in this respect, like Marcel's similar error with regard to Albertine, is what allows him to write the Memoir that he does; for it is a recognition of the fact that the world is not amenable to my desires, that the longings of my imagination will always be at odds with the will of other people. When he realises this, Humbert steps forever outside the world of Clare Quilty and Axel Rex, and is able at last to achieve his lifelong aim of capturing the elusive beauty of nymphets. And because he realises this Lolita comes to us as more than a Romantic myth, but more too than one more fictional heroine. One could say that the traditional novel tries to make us forget that what we are reading is only a book: transparent words give the illusion of reality; while the Romantic poem tries to deny reality and turn the world into pure imagination. Humbert's Memoir moves and mediates between the two, and the point at which the two meet is in Lolita herself. For her and for the book which conveys her to us there can be only one language: the language of parody.

In the place of Romantic daydream or the novelist's commonsense, Humbert accepts the language that is given him and proceeds to undermine it from within. What he does is to use his *situation* as a means of creating the language he needs. His situation – that of a grown man, the legal father of Lolita, and yet her lover against her own wishes – is a parody of the conventional notions of love between the sexes and of the love of parents and children. These conventional notions are embedded in our language and cultural traditions. Humbert thus takes this

language and this culture as his field for a monumental exercise
in parody and burlesque. Just as he is caught by a dark necessity
as soon as he makes love to Lolita for the first time, so the writer
is caught by the logic of language once he has set pen to paper.
He can either ignore this, as does the traditional novelist, or
chafe against it, as does the Romantic poet. Humbert does neither
He accepts it and then parodies his situation. He establishes himself not outside language and culture, as the Romantic hero
would try to do, but, so to speak, in their interstices, and from
there proceeds to reveal to us the conventional and contingent
quality of what we unthinkingly take to be both natural and
necessary. And at every turn the language and culture play into
his hands: the Mann Act is deplored as 'lending itself to a dreadful pun, the revenge of the God of semantics against tight-zippered
philistines'; the harmless title of a popular book, *Know Your Own
Daughter*, becomes a cynical comment on society when confronted by Humbert and his Lolita; the shops are found to sell
pumps of crushed kid – for crushed kids, notes Humbert – and
pyjamas in popular butcher-boy style – for Humbert the popular
butcher. And the well-known, quasi-mythical love of Dante for
Beatrice, and of Petrarch for Laura, takes on equivocal colouring
when ironically brought up in defence of Humbert's vice.

The movement, however, is two-way. Just as Humbert makes
of America a magic land by frequently taking literally the exalted
claims of the advertisements he meets *en route*, so the evocations
of Poe and Ronsard, Horace and Catullus, place the work within
an elegiac frame which perfectly sets off the theme of a lost Eden.
Yet the reader is never allowed to bask in these elegiac echoes.
Ovid's *noctis equi* become nightmares and the sentences twist
and turn in mid-air, straighten out abruptly and finish where we
least expect them to:

> Ah, gentle drivers gliding through summer's black nights, what
> frolics, what twists of lust, you might see from your impeccable
> highways if Kumfy Kabins were suddenly drained of their
> pigments and became transparent as boxes of glass! (116)

The constant two-way movement between the tone of culture, of
the entire Western heritage, and the present horror of Humbert's
situation forces us to experience the past as actuality and the
present itself as part of that Western tradition. The clichés of

habit by which we view what is past and what is in books as one
thing and what we experience daily as another are constantly
being shattered by Humbert's extraordinary style. Parody reveals
the gap between world and book, past and present, tradition and
experience, the private and the public, the desires of men and
the nature of the world. To be subjected to this style is less like
reading a story than like having a prism pressed to one's eyes and
suddenly seeing everything glow with a new life.

Just as Humbert had come to love Lolita only when he
accepted the fact that she was not his to do what he liked with,
so it is only when he accepts the fact that words are all he has
to play with and that we cannot each of us forge a new language
but must take words as they are, with all their unwanted and
irrelevant associations – it is only then that he can succeed in
his poetic attempt. For the true poet has power over words only
in so far as he realises that it is only over words that he has power,
that this power is only that of bringing them together in new
ways, never of creating new meanings. To accept this is the first
step to the moulding of a language which can bring into the
consciousness, articulate and communicate, the mysterious beauty
of that which lies perpetually out of reach. It is the way of creative
parody, which Valéry understood so well when he wrote that 'a
literary *langue mandarine* is derived from popular speech, from
which it takes the words, figures, and "turns" most suitable for
the effects the artist seeks' and invents contrasts, juxtapositions,
contractions or substitutions 'which excite the mind to produce
more vivid imitations than those sufficient for understanding
ordinary language'.

Humbert's story, then, can only be seen through Humbert's
words, the baroque language capturing Lolita as could no other
medium. But Humbert himself is of course only made up out of
the words of Nabokov. Humbert's burlesque of the traditional
novelist in the 'Miss East' episode is mirrored in Nabokov's insistence that the whole Memoir is a fiction, through the device of
the parody preface, with its information about the destinies of
the 'real' people beyond the 'true' story, 'for the benefit of old-
fashioned readers'. Humbert's situation mirrors that of his creator,
Nabokov, who also has only words to play with and the violent
urges of a poet to articulate. When Nabokov said that his novel

was about his love affair with the English language he spoke more literally than his critics realised. The novel is about his love affair with language, but since there are many languages it is necessary to make a choice. A language not his native one was forced on Nabokov by tragic circumstances; but since no language is ever 'our own' perhaps the circumstances were in one way fortunate.

For the reader to ask what the novel is 'about', for him to try and extract its 'theme' or 'message' is for him to be guilty of Humbert's initial error: to try and possess carnally what can only be apprehended imaginatively. The novel does not reveal its secret once and for all; the imaginative effort must be renewed each time it is reread. Ultimately the theme is the imaginative effort itself, that progress towards inevitable failure and loss which is the pattern of success. In the end Humbert does fail. The beauty is not there for us to behold. Lolita has once again slipped through his hands. In the actuality of the fiction he is about to die and all that is left of his story is a pile of paper: art is only a *local* palliative, it will not save anybody's life. He has had his vision, made his effort, and now it is the turn of life, of the ordinary, of that which is silent and without meaning. Despite Humbert's disclaimer, he was *not* one of nature's faithful hounds, his initial act was not natural, no matter how much he desired it. Just as Nabokov's first act, his choice of subject-matter and of how and when to start, was not natural. And for this unnatural act life will have its revenge. As Kafka wrote in another context: 'I perhaps am the stronger and more skilful of the two; he, however, has more endurance.' When the novel comes to an end there is nothing *there* for us to hold. The palliative of art works only while Humbert is actually writing, or the reader actually reading. But the miracle of art lies in the fact that we can reread this novel as often as we like.

9   *Herzog*: Freedom and Wit

There's a lot of movement in Saul Bellow's *Herzog*, but the only action is a botched action: Herzog's failure to carry out his plan and kill his former wife Madeleine and her lover Valentine Gersbach. Anguished Herzog rushes from New York to the peace of Vineyard Haven and his friend Libbie but he's no sooner there than he decides to fly back to the capital. He spends the day in his apartment and the night with his current mistress; but the next day he's off again, to Chicago this time and his murderous mission. Instead of murder, however, he is involved in a minor traffic accident and hauled off to the police station for illegal possession of firearms. Bailed out by his brother, he ends up where we have first found him, in his vast decaying house in the middle of the Berkshires. It is not, however, all this flurry of meaningless activity that gives the book its sense of continuous turmoil. That comes from the ceaseless inner activity which grips Herzog and of which the external movement is merely a symptom. The greater part of the novel is taken up with Herzog by himself, writing compulsive letters to his friends, his enemies, the newspapers, politicians, 'and at last to the dead, his own obscure dead and finally the famous dead'. Sometimes the letters are only scribbled on odd bits of paper and promptly forgotten; most of the time they never get put onto paper at all. But though they seem to burst out of him wildly, spontaneously, and often peter out after no more than a sentence and nearly always before the end, a clear and consistent position does emerge from them, a position whose defining characteristic is that it cannot be reduced to any purely abstract statement, but which relates at almost every point to Herzog's own troubled life. To understand the novel we need to understand what this position is.

Like that of Swift in *A Tale of a Tub*, it can be expressed diagrammatically as the rejection of two false extremes. These Herzog calls 'crisis ethics' and 'potato love' respectively. Like

Swift too, Herzog goes behind the labels that people and movements give themselves and brings out the essential similarity
between many apparently disparate phenomena. And like Swift
he believes that extremes meet and that crisis ethics and potato
love are only facets of one attitude to both man and history.
What meaning then do the terms have for him?

'Dear Doctor Professor Heidegger', writes Herzog, 'I should
like to know what you mean by the expression "the fall into the
quotidian." When did this fall occur? Where were we standing
when it happened?' The question is of course, rhetorical, but the
ploy is the same as Swift's: by making concrete what his
opponents keep at the level of metaphor he shocks us into an
awareness of the implications of their position. He himself
answers his questions later on, when he writes:

> Very tired of the modern form of historicism which sees in this
> civilization the defeat of the best hopes of Western religion and
> thought, what Heidegger calls the second Fall of Man into
> the quotidian or ordinary. No philosopher knows what the
> ordinary is, has not fallen into it deeply enough. (106)[1]

Nor is it simply German existentialism which is dominated by
this idea. Herzog sees in it a Christian, and especially a Protestant
view of history, one which regards 'the present moment always
as some crisis, some fall from classical greatness, some corruption
or evil to be saved from'. This idea has taken hold of modern
man because it seems to be a way of saving him from himself and
his daily responsibilities:

> Everybody was in the act. 'History' gave everyone a free ride.
> The very Himmelsteins, who had never even read a book of
> metaphysics, were touting the Void as if it were so much salable
> real estate. This little demon was impregnated with modern
> ideas, and one in particular excited his terrible little heart: you
> must sacrifice your poor, squawking, niggardly individuality –
> which may be nothing anyway (from an analytic view point)
> but a persistent infantile megalomania, or (from a Marxian
> point of view) a stinking little bourgeois property – to historical
> necessity. And to truth. (93)

[1] All references are to the edition published by Weidenfeld & Nicolson,
London, 1964.

And what is truth? 'Truth is true only as it brings down more disgrace and dreariness upon human beings, so that if it shows anything except evil it is illusion, and not truth.' Facts are what's nasty, the rest is just idealism. The only way to get away from facts then is through ecstasy, through achieving an 'inspired condition':

> This is thought to be attainable only in the negative and is so pursued in philosophy and literature as well as in sexual experience, or with the aid of narcotics, or in 'philosophical', 'gratuitous' crime and similar paths of horror. (It never seems to occur to such 'criminals' that to behave with decency to another human being might also be 'gratuitous'.) (164)

But all this, Herzog argues, all this talk of crisis and inspiration, is only a projection into history of private fantasies; they are ideas put out by intellectuals who long for the death of the intellect, something that will free them from the burden of daily living:

> Civilized individuals hate and resent the civilization that makes their lives possible. What they love is an imaginary human situation invented by their own genius and which they believe is the only true and the only human reality. (304)

We must get it out of our heads that this is a doomed time; such talk is merely irresponsible, and is likely to lead to a loss of nerve which will bring about just such a doom:

> Are all the traditions used up, the beliefs done for, the consciousness of the masses not yet ready for the next development? Is this the full crisis of dissolution? Has the filthy moment come when moral feeling dies, conscience disintegrates, and respect for liberty, law, public decency, all the rest, collapses in cowardice, decadence, blood? Old Proudhon's visions of darkness and evil can't be passed over. But we mustn't forget how quickly the visions of genius become the canned goods of the intellectuals. The canned sauerkraut of Spengler's 'Prussian Socialism', the commonplaces of the Wasteland outlook, the cheap mental stimulants of Alienation, the cant and rant of pipsqueaks about Inauthenticity and Forlornness. I can't accept this foolish dreariness. We are talking about the whole life of

mankind. The subject is too great, too deep for such weakness, cowardice. . . . A merely aesthetic critique of modern history! After the wars and mass killings! (74-5)

It is time, argues Herzog, covering sheet after sheet with his desperate letters, it is time we stopped talking about human nature being this or that or the other thing. Total explanations are a delusion, the desire to see everything in terms of simple antitheses a sign of paranoia.

But is it possible to see life in any other way? Herzog discovers that the people who talk most about the 'hard facts' of life are really the most sentimental, the believers in what he calls, talking of Eisenhower, 'potato love': 'The general won because he expressed low-grade universal potato love.' But this too is a delusion, a form of self-pity, the wish to get rid of one's responsibilities by merging with the mass, the universal. Yet this merging is what Rousseau preached, and its appeal is enormous. Herzog is under no delusion about the power of words and ideas: 'He took seriously Heinrich Heine's belief that the words of Rousseau had turned into the bloody machinery of Robespierre, that Kant and Fichte were deadlier than armies.'

What is common to both the believers in crisis ethics and the believers in potato love is the notion that the world can be changed by a *fiat*, that if we will it hard enough we will find that our wishes and the reality of the world will coincide. It springs from the desperate need to shed the responsibility we are born with, a need which finds its ironic epigraph in what Tante Taube tells Herzog about making love with her first husband: 'Kaplitzky-alehoshalom took care on everything. I didn't even looked.' And yet the Romantics — for Herzog is in no doubt that if this is a Christian, and in particular a Protestant, movement, then it is with Romanticism that it gained its full momentum — the Romantics cannot so easily be refuted. For what model have we got to put in the place of the one they offer us? Herzog sympathises with T. E. Hulme's rejection of Romanticism, but he cannot agree with his solution of the problem:

He wanted things to be clear, dry, spare, pure, cool, and hard. With this I think we can all sympathize. I too am repelled by the 'dampness', as he called it, and the swarming of Romantic feelings. I see what a villain Rousseau was, and how degener-

ate. . . . But I do not see what we can answer when he says:
'Je sens mon coeur et je connais les hommes.' Bottled religion,
on conservative principles – does that intend to deprive the
heart of such powers – do you think? Hulme's followers made
sterility their truth, confessing their impotence. This was their
passion. (129)

The men Herzog admires are not the conservatives, who want to
preserve at all costs, for he sees that this too is a falsification of
the reality of the world in the interests of a private wish. No. It is
men like Montaigne and Pascal, politicians like Adlai Stevenson
and Martin Luther King, who do not shy away from the complexity and uniqueness of every situation by opting for a single
clear-cut solution, but on the contrary try to face and understand
and control, knowing that their work will take a long time, that
it will require patience above all things, and that it will constantly
be undermined by extremists. They accept man as he is, try to
keep close to the ins and outs of his thoughts and feelings. They
accept a personal responsibility for history, a responsibility, notes
Herzog, rooted in both Testaments. And they are always beaten
by the idealists.

It is by such idealists, all talking the same language of 'truth'
and 'hard facts', but all driven on only by the need to fulfil their
private desires, that Herzog is surrounded. These people derive
their power from the fact that for them life is simple. They know
the score. And they know Herzog better than he knows himself.
There is the psychiatrist, Dr Edvig; Sandor Himmelstein, the
lawyer – 'I know this isn't easy for you to hear, but I better say
it. Guys at our time of life must face facts. . . . I know about
suffering – we're on the same identical network.' Above all, of
course, there are Madeleine, Herzog's former wife, and her lover
Gersbach, his former friend. 'She brought ideology into my life,'
Herzog recognises, at the end of the book. 'Something to do with
catastrophe.' For she and Gersbach never have enough of talking
about Truth, though neither is very interested in the details of
daily life. When Herzog, unable to contain himself any longer,
corrects Gersbach's dreadful Yiddish, the latter brushes this aside
and goes on with his man-to-man talk:

'*Fe-be*, who cares. Maybe it's not so much your reputation as
your egotism. You could be a real *mensch*. You've got it in you.

But you're effing it up with all this egotistical shit. It's a big deal – such a valuable person dying for love. Grief. It's a lot of bull!' (61)

And Herzog, looking at the man, with his game leg and fiery hair, is forced to admit:

Dealing with Valentine was like dealing with a king. He had a thick grip. . . . He *was* a king, an emotional king, and the depth of his heart was his kingdom. He appropriated all the emotions about him, as if by divine or spiritual right. . . . He was a big man, too big for anything but the truth. (61)

What is important for Valentine Gersbach is the *intensity* of an experience, not its content. This intensity, this physical glow which seems to guarantee the genuineness of his emotion, goes into everything he does, whether it's talking about Buber on television or advising Herzog about the nature of life. And the same is true of Madeleine:

Before Soloviev, she had talked of no one but Joseph de Maistre. And before de Maistre – Herzog made up the list – the French Revolution, Eleanor of Aquitaine, Schliemann's excavations at Troy, extrasensory perception, then tarot cards, then Christian Science, before that, Mirabeau; or was it mystery novels (Josephine Tey), or science fiction (Isaac Asimov)? The intensity was always high. (72–3)

Excessive rationality, the inability to bear criticism, to accept ambiguity, the desire to assert oneself continuously – all these are paranoic traits, Herzog is convinced, and all can be found in Madeleine. How can he leave his children in the charge of people like her and Gersbach?

Yet are they unique? The whole of Western society seems to have aquired these traits, and Herzog, in the course of his wild letters, finds their roots in such things as the notion of outward composure in Calvinist societies, where each man, fearful of damnation, has to *behave* as one of the elect in order to convince himself that he *is* one; in the fear of an increasingly mechanised world; in Rousseauistic notions of pity. There is no lack of evidence for the historically minded. But it is also there in the present, facing him, and Herzog doesn't know how to fight it.

Even his current mistress, Ramona, beautiful, exciting Ramona, whom Herzog likes so much, is convinced that she understands Herzog's *real* needs better than he does himself:

> To listen to Ramona, it was all very simple. She said she understood his needs better than he, and she might well be right. . . . She told Herzog that he was a better man than he knew – a deep man, beautiful (he could not help wincing when she said this), but sad, unable to take what his heart really desired, a man tempted by God, longing for grace, but escaping headlong from his salvation. . . . What he had to learn from her – while there was time; while he was still virile, his powers substantially intact – was how to renew the spirit through the flesh (a precious vessel in which the spirit rested). (184–5)

The difficulty with such arguments is that Herzog is perfectly well aware that they might all be true. Because he does not know what he *really* is, he cannot counter such assertions with any of his own, only with vague unease at such a formulation of the problem. Nor is it only Ramona who could be right. All of them – Madeleine, Gersbach, Edvig, Himmelstein – they might be right too, he might indeed be all that they say he is. Who is to say if they are wrong? Certainly not Herzog. And yet deep down inside him there remains the stubborn conviction that they *are* in some obscure way wrong, every one of them, including Ramona. The book, which charts his partial recovery from a mental breakdown, also shows his growing awareness of the nature of his own inarticulate attitudes and beliefs. He may not have the answers to the confident assertions of those who surround him, but that is perhaps a kind of strength, even if it makes him more vulnerable to their initial attacks. For one thing, he recognises very well the propensity within himself to fall for this kind of argument:

> It's about time I stopped laboring with this curse – I think, I figure things out. I see exactly what I should avoid. Then, all of a sudden, I'm in bed with that very thing, and making love to it. As with Madeleine. She seems to have filled a special need. (333–4)

But even as he says this he knows he will labour under the curse all his life, that there will always be moments when he cries out

INTELLECTUAL AND EMOTIONAL ALIGNMENTS IN HERZOG

| Crisis Ethics

Dissolution of
the self in universal
TRUTH | Acceptance of
responsibility
for oneself | Potato Love

Dissolution of
the self in universal
LOVE |
|---|---|---|
| Calvin
Kant
Fichte
Nietzsche
Spengler
Heidegger | Montaigne
Pascal | Rousseau |
| Calvinism
Marxism
Freudianism
Existentialism
Russian mysticism
 (Soloviev, Berdyaev,
 etc.) | | |
| Faust | | |
| Black Muslims

Tina Zokóly | Adlai Stevenson
Martin Luther King | Eisenhower |
| Madeleine
Gersbach
Dr Edvig
Sandor Himmelstein
Shapiro
George Hoberly | Herzog
Asphalter | Gersbach
Sandor Himmelstein
Mother Herzog
Tante Taube |

under his breath, as he does earlier to Ramona: 'Marry me! Be
my wife! End my troubles!' – only to be immediately 'staggered
by his rashness, his weakness, and by the characteristic nature of
such an outburst, for he saw how very neurotic and typical it
was'. Knowing this, though, he is determined not to be a victim,
not to indulge in bitter self-criticism. He is what he is – why
always be looking for a motive? His duty is to live. To be sane and
to live and to look after his children.

His self-awareness does not stop with the recognition of his own general desire to give up, be safe, not have to make decisions. He realises too that just at this time he is in the grip of a particular violence, that these letters, this way of talking are not the actions of a normal man. And, recognising it, he can take steps to fight it, can even see that his own failure all along the line might not mean that his opponents are right but simply that he was confused and inadequate to the task. What he must avoid at all costs is imposing his own pattern on reality, trying to get at the essence of people and slotting them into pigeon-holes in his mind. For man is always more complex than any of the models we create to explain him, be they Freudian, Jungian, Marxian, Thomist, or anything else. It may be, Herzog comes to see, that he cannot counter the image of himself that other people have, as being essentially this or that, simply because he has no essence, because he is not reducible in this way. The episode of Lucas Asphalter and his monkey is an essential element in this self-discovery. Asphalter, Herzog's old friend with whom he goes to stay when he returns to Chicago with the object of killing Gersbach, recounts how, after the death of his pet monkey, he felt he had no more to live for, and, on the advice of a psychoanalyst, tried to follow the prescriptions of the Hungarian analyst Tina Zokóly. These consist in such spiritual exercises as imagining your own death: you pretend you are already dead and try to conjure up the coffin and attendant paraphernalia. Asphalter, however, finds that with him this doesn't work. His mind keeps shifting from the scene of his death to the image of his enormously fat old aunt being carried down a ladder from one of the top windows of the building in which she lived when it caught fire, or to that of the whores who used to play baseball in the street outside the flophouse where they work. Asphalter recounts his failure to his friend in despair, but Herzog interrupts him excitedly:

'Don't feel so bad, Luke. Now listen to me. Maybe I can tell you something about this. At least I can tell you how I see it. A man may say, "From now on I'm going to speak the truth." But the truth hears him and runs away and hides before he's even done speaking. There is something funny about the human condition, and civilised intelligence makes fun of its own ideas. This Tina Zokóly has got to be kidding, too.'

'I don't think so.'

'Then it's the old *memento mori*, the monk's skull on the table, brought up to date. And what good is that? It all goes back to those German existentialists who tell you how good dread is for you, how it saves you from distraction and gives you your freedom and makes you authentic. God is no more. But Death is. That's their story. And we live in a hedonistic world in which happiness is set up on a mechanical model. All you have to do is open your fly and grasp happiness. And so these other theorists introduce the tension of guilt and dread as a corrective. But human life is far subtler than any of its models, even these ingenious German models. Do we need to study *theories* of fear and anguish? This Tina Zokóly is a non-sensical woman. She tells you to practice overkill on yourself, and your intelligence answers her with wit.' (271)

Wit is the element that won't be captured, the individual response of a man trying hard to lose his individuality. It is grotesque, but reminds him that man is always something else, over and above any description of him that we can give. It is consciousness of this that leads Herzog at last to say (in his mind) to Madeleine and Gersbach: 'Excuse me, therefore, sir and madam, but I reject your definitions of me.'

But it is this too that stops Herzog from murdering Gersbach. As he looks through his own bathroom window and watches the man bathing his little daughter he is forced to realise that Gersbach is decent after all, perhaps even kind, according to his lights. Herzog, aware how much his condemnation of his former wife and her lover may be the result of his own uncontrollable emotions, understands in that brief moment that he could never kill. Especially not this man. Killing him is one more role into which he has tried to slip – a role and not himself. Leave the roles to the movies, creators of myths. He steps down from the window and goes his way. Something, however, must happen. All that pent-up emotion has to find an outlet. Typically, what happens is both farcical and banal, another victory of reality over any of its models. Herzog, taking out his little daughter for a drive the next day, is involved in an absurd car accident. No one is seriously hurt, but he is shaken by it, and especially by the confrontation at the police station with the furious Madeleine. How could he act like this, and show himself in this light to his daughter? Can she ever forgive him?

And yet the accident finally brings him down to earth 'from his strange spiralling flight of the last few days'. He can no longer run away from himself, he is, at last, up against the wall. Because, for all his talk of the ordinariness of life being the important thing and how one must be what one is and ask no questions, the whirlwind activity of those last few days did represent a flight from himself, from reality. Exactly like George Hoberly, Ramona's discarded lover, who tries to reawaken her sympathies by acts of deliberate self-destruction, Herzog has attempted to force from life an answer to the question: What am I? What am I really? The accident and its aftermath serves to free him from this compulsion. In a sense he bangs into reality. Not hard, but hard enough to remind him of what might have happened – like the blow the Green Knight delivers to Gawain, 'nikking his neck'. Herzog sees now how difficult it is to eradicate the notion of crisis from our minds, how we all unconsciously long for some one event that will change things irrevocably and tell us how from then on we are to lead our lives.

But now, back in his crumbling house in the heart of the countryside, he realises that 'I have wanted to be cared for. I devoutly hoped Emerich would find me sick. But I have no intention of doing that – I am responsible, responsible to reason. . . . Responsible to the children.' And, realising this, he finds a kind of peace:

> Why must I be such a throb-hearted character? . . . But I am. I am, and you can't teach old dogs. Myself is thus and so, and will continue thus and so. And why fight it? My balance comes from instability. Not organisation, or courage, as with other people. It's tough, but that's how it is. On these terms I, too – even I! – apprehend certain things. Perhaps the only way I'm able to do it. Must play the instrument I've got. (330)

Now at last he can answer Rousseau. True, the only kind of knowledge we can have is what the heart feels, and yet 'My face too blind, my mind too limited, my instincts too narrow.' We must not generalise from our own heart, just learn to be content with it. And so, at the end, 'I am pretty well satisfied to be, to be just as it is willed, and for as long as I may remain in occupancy.'

Thus the letters come to an end. Herzog has no more messages for anyone. And the novel too ends, leaving him there in his decaying mansion, waiting for Ramona – another mistake? – to arrive. The letters were a symptom of his illness, but it is they which helped him through it. Like Hamlet he deliberately exaggerated his condition, 'as if by staggering he could recover his balance . . . or by admitting a bit of madness could recover his senses'. The others, Madeleine, Gersbach, Sandor Himmelstein, George Hoberly, are the really sick ones, because they do not know they are sick, imagine they are well: 'It's possible to see that a man like Hoberly by falling apart intends to bear witness to the failure of individual existence. He proves it *can't work*.' Their madness lies in imagining that they are sane, reasonable, *animal rationalis* instead of only *animal rationis capax*. This is the other side to their insistence on Truth and their desperate desire to label, define, organise, their inability to live with paradox or ambiguity – with wit. Herzog, recognising the infinite complexity of the human psyche, will not judge someone like Madeleine's mother Tennie:

> Tennie took off her elaborate glasses, now making no effort to disguise her weeping. Her face, her nose reddened, and her eyes, shaped to make what seemed to Moses a crooked appeal, darkened blindly with tears. There was a measure of hypocrisy and calculation in Tennie's method, but behind this, again, was real feeling for her daughter and her husband; and behind this real feeling there was something still more meaningful and somber. Herzog was all too well aware of the layers upon layers of reality – loathesomeness, arrogance, deceit, and then – God help us all – truth, as well. (109)

Nor, in the end, will he judge Madeleine either. Judgement had best be left to God. He's got enough to do making sense of his own life to try and make sense of those of other people too. Because Herzog is so aware of the infinite regress of consciousness, he remains far saner than all the people who surround him, with their constant search for the one essential truth, the one revealing motive.

Yet if his weakness is his strength, his strength is also his weakness. If he is open to details, careful not to force the multitude of facts into a private mould, the very profusion of these facts, details, overwhelms him. He looks at everything as if he was seeing it for the first time, but the very sharpness of his perceptions is a sign of his instability: 'A rat chewed into a package of bread, leaving the shape of its body in the layer of slices. Herzog ate the other half of the loaf spread with jam. He could share with rats too.' The childhood memories, the physical details he notes in everything, all threaten to submerge him – 'at first there was no pattern to the notes he made'. It is all very well saying 'foo' to all categories, but if one has responsibilities there is an urgent need to organise one's life. Herzog's follies and errors come as much from his unwillingness or inability to categorise as from his wish to force matters to a head. Reading Geraldine Portnoy's letter, in which she tells him how Gersbach is treating his children, he finds the handwriting keeps getting in the way of the meaning. He can see so many sides to every question that in the end he is inhibited from acting at all. He is aware that all reasoning is rationalised instinct, that Shapiro dribbling at the mouth as Madeleine serves up the food is as much a part of the picture as Shapiro's apocalyptic ideas. As Nietzsche saw, we can never sever the system from the man, we must always ask: 'Why does *this* man advocate *this* system?' But it might be better for him to be a little less aware of such things. It is as though he is too close to the world to be able to make sense of it. Others are too far but he is too close.

This being so it is easy to see that the book, while charting his recovery from breakdown, simultaneously describes the final failure of his intellectual ambitions. It is clear by the end that Herzog will never write the sequel to his book on Romanticism and Christianity. The material is there, he's been lugging it around for years, but the will to put it together seems to be absent. No amount of letters is going to make up for that. Herzog knows – and it hurts him to acknowledge it – that to imagine he will write that book is to indulge in a Utopian dream.

But the reason for this failure is surely clear to us, if not to him. Were he to write the book he would himself be guilty of just the thing that he condemns in others: he would be setting up a model, albeit a highly sophisticated one, and saying: *this* is what man is like, this is what history *is*, this, ultimately, is what man is. As with the young Marcel and his literary ambitions, it is more than a failure of the will which keeps him from his task. It is the unconscious recognition that to give shape to the feelings of the heart is to falsify the experience, that intellectual history, no matter how subtle, must always leave out more than it puts in. No volume in the history of ideas can do justice to Herzog's insight into the infinite regress of human self-awareness. If, as soon as I say: 'This is what I am', a part of me immediately dissociates itself from the definition, then what is required is a form that will convey the living person behind every speech and every gesture. What is required, in other words, is not history, but fiction, for only fiction can present the speaker as well as the words he speaks, can register the afterthought as well as the thought, and the afterthought to the afterthought, and the unspoken commentary on that. Thus Saul Bellow's *Herzog* emerges as the work which Herzog, the fictional hero of that book, found it impossible to write.

All Herzog is able to do is battle with his demons and let the future look after itself. But Bellow, through his fiction, has been able to articulate the variety and richness of the world without being overwhelmed by it and without on the other hand imposing upon it the rigid categorisation of the traditional novelist who only includes as much of the world as is necessary for his plot. Bellow has in fact succeeded in constructing a work which is an attack on the structuring activity of the mind; in conveying a sense of the infinite mystery of human beings in a book which is a critique of the traditional link between motive and action; in keeping close to the twists and turns of a man's thoughts and feelings without either putting him in a straitjacket of theory or allowing the book to fall apart in chaos. He has done all this because his book is not called *Saul Bellow* but *Herzog*.

The name Moses Elkanah Herzog is to be found in James Joyce's own novel, *Ulysses*. By making use of it Bellow makes it clear from the start that he is writing fiction, not fact, much as Defoe, by using ordinary English names, tried to persuade his readers that he was writing fact and not fiction. But what is fact? Who am I? Who is Bellow? What is certain is that while writing *Herzog* he is Herzog and yet not Herzog, since he is always clear that he is the creator of Herzog. In his most recent novel Bellow writes ironically of Marx's vision of the proletarian revolution needing no historical models and comments on the colourful variety of present-day Americans: 'They sought originality. They were obviously derivative. . . . Better . . . to accept the inevitability of imitation and then to imitate good things. The ancients had this right. Greatness without models? Inconceivable. One could not be the thing itself – Reality. One must be satisfied with the symbols.' Thus, had he written directly about himself, he would have fallen into the trap of either sentiment or prophecy, have been either a Gersbach or a Shapiro. Writing fiction, he frees himself from the dead weight of his own personality. 'That suffering hero' Herzog writes of himself, and, having written it, knows that he is more than that since he has just formulated the description. And Bellow, formulating the formulator, creates himself as he writes. Creates us too if we follow Herzog and do not try to reduce the novel, as Madeleine and the others tried to reduce him, to a single meaning, an essence. A piece of fiction is like a man: to ask what it means and expect an answer is to destroy it. But, unlike a man, it has the power to stay alive forever. Or as long, at least, as there are people to read it.

10 Golding: The Hidden Source

'Art is partly communication, but only partly. The rest is discovery. I have always been a creature of discovery.' Thus Samuel Mountjoy, the hero of *Free Fall*, and the statement, like so many in that novel, could apply to Golding himself. In reading his novels one has the same sense of exploration as one has reading the great revolutionaries of the century: Proust, Joyce, Virginia Woolf. There is the same feeling of immediate relevance, the same sense of the irreducibility of the work. It takes less than a page to know that here we are reading the work of a master who uses the medium instead of being used by it, and who stretches it a little further with each new attempt. And yet, if one pauses to think about it, this is a rather surprising impression to gain from Golding's works, for how can a writer only one of whose five main novels is set within present-day civilisation give us this sense of relevance? And how can Golding, who never talks about his art and whose books seem more like boys' adventure stories or science fiction, be said to share the concerns of a Proust or a Joyce? A rereading of the novels may supply answers to these questions. As with the other writers we have looked at, it will be necessary to move through what have become critical commonplaces (few writers have been more talked about in their lifetime to less effect), into an awareness of how the novels mime their own creation by the author and their recreation by the reader.

If any criticism can be levelled at Golding's work it is that it is too schematic. This is particularly true of his first novel, *Lord of the Flies*. Golding's avowed intent was to demonstrate the false premises of a book like *Coral Island*, that Victorian boys' classic. Thus he strands his children on a desert island just as Ballantyne does, and then shows us how they would *really* behave. It is a demonstration in laboratory conditions, so to speak, of the forms taken by human behaviour once the restraints of civilisation have been removed.

Three boys surround the hero, Ralph. The first is Piggy, an adult in a child's body, whose implicit belief in the triumph of reason and common sense would have endeared him to Ballantyne – he shares, in fact, all the basic beliefs of the author of *Coral Island*. Next there is Jack, the living refutation of these beliefs. He is not interested in what is reasonable (the need to make every effort to ensure that they are rescued), but only in gaining control of the little band of children. It is in him that the reversion to the primitive is most clearly shown. There are three stages to this. First comes the painting of the face into a mask, for 'the mask was a thing on its own, behind which Jack hid, liberated from shame and self-consciousness'. Once the mask has been painted on, a person sheds his social personality and can allow his instincts free play without any feeling that he will be called to account for what he does; it allows him to split his actions off from the individual person, Jack, with the unique set of names and the unique history. It is the first liberation from civilisation and its restraints. The second is the killing of the sow and the breaking once and for all of the taboo on bloodshed. Once that is done any form of 'inhuman' behaviour becomes possible, and the third step, the killing of Piggy and Simon, becomes not only natural but inevitable.

Piggy is powerless against Jack because he fails to understand him. He never doubts that reason will triumph over the irrational. But this smugness and assurance is reason's greatest enemy, for it blinds us to the realities of the situation and prevents us from taking the appropriate steps to fight the forces of unreason. The third important figure surrounding the hero is Simon. He is as powerless as Piggy but for exactly the opposite reason. He seems to be the only one of the boys who really understands what is happening to them. He is the only one to see what horrors are going to follow from each small act, for he is the only one who seems to be aware of the demonic element in human nature. This awareness, in some mysterious way, seems to free him from having to submit to it. The Beast, he realises, is not something outside man, to be placated by human and animal sacrifice. It is something inside each of us, which needs to be recognised and mastered. This is what he tries to explain to the other boys, but they only hoot him down with jeers and laughter. And this is what Golding makes abundantly clear in the central scene of the

book, the confrontation between Simon and the boar's head, the
Lord of the Flies, which, in his semi-conscious state, Simon hears
addressing him in the prim tones of a sarcastic schoolmaster:

> 'Fancy thinking the Beast was something you could hurt and
> kill!' said the head. For a moment or two the forest and all
> the other dimly appreciated places echoed with the parody of
> laughter. 'You knew, didn't you? I'm part of you? Close, close,
> close! I'm the reason why it's no go? Why things are what
> they are?' (137)[1]

Yet Simon seems to be able to understand the nature of the Beast
only at the cost of not being able to communicate that understanding to the others. In the later portions of the book he ceases
even to try, as though he felt that he too was destined to be killed
by the Beast and that there was nothing he could do about it. He
accepts his death almost as though it were the *condition* of his
knowledge: that one can only know the secret of the Beast if one
is very close to being destroyed by it, desires it even. That is why
Simon, who fully understands, and Piggy, who does not understand at all, both have to die, the one accepting, the other
disbelieving to the end, while the hero Ralph, with that mixture
of innocence, luck, honesty, courage and intuition which marks
him out as a natural leader, survives till rescue arrives and the
world of civilisation once more swallows up the boys.

It is not too much to say that Simon is a kind of saint. His goodness seems to be bound up with his insight into the nature of man,
his awareness that the Beast is inside all of us. Golding's next
book, *The Inheritors*, sets out to show how man first externalised
the Beast, and why. This time he takes as his starting point a
passage from another and better-known Victorian, H. G. Wells:
the description, in Wells's *Outline of History*, of Neanderthal
men as 'gorilla-like monsters, with cunning brains, shambling
gait, hairy bodies, strong teeth, and possibly cannibalistic
tendencies'.

The novel sets out to show not just *that* Wells is wrong, but also
why he should be wrong in just this way. The Neanderthalers,
as Golding presents them, are supremely innocent and gentle

---

[1] All references are to the paperback editions of Golding's novels: *Lord
of the Flies* and *Free Fall* in Penguin Books, the rest in Faber paperbacks.

creatures. They don't kill and are mainly vegetarian. When they do tear up a doe whose blood has already been drained by a wildcat they feel that 'this is very bad. Oa brought the doe out of her belly' – as she brought them and the entire creation. They have no consciousness and cannot think, but they can 'share images'. Man's 'primitiveness', his irrational desire for blood and death, Golding seems to be saying, is not a *given*; it seems to be something that appears at a certain point in history, that is con-comitant with civilisation and that can be understood only in terms of it. In this book man is seen from the outside. Men are the 'inheritors', and for ten and a half of the twelve chapters of the book they are only seen from the point of view of the Neanderthalers. And very strange they appear from that angle.

The book opens with the small clan of ape-men crossing a stream. They are terrified of water, as we know gorillas to be, and find to their surprise that the log which usually acts as a bridge for them has disappeared. In jumping across the oldest member of the clan falls in and it is from the fever he catches as a result of this wetting that he eventually dies. The log, we later discover, has been taken by the 'new men', the 'inheritors', for their own use, so that their arrival on the scene is indirectly responsible for the death of the old creature. By the end of the book they will have been the cause of the deaths of all except two members of the clan, one of whom, a youngster, they will have taken prisoner. Yet there are no open battles between the two groups, since the new men are terrified of the Neanderthalers and the latter simply curious of them and quite unable to realise the danger of contact with them. Yet they are also compulsively drawn to them, and instead of escaping, as they could have done after the initial shock of the encounter, they hover in the trees and bushes near by, trying to see and understand what is going on, frightening the new men more and more, and making their own eventual annihilation inevitable. The book gives a wonderful sense of the lack of awareness of any of the characters of what it is that has really taken place. For the Neanderthalers the new men are simply 'the other', the unimaginable, that which is not them. For the new men the Neanderthalers are devils lurking in the forests, come to destroy them, to be placated by animal and even human sacrifices. Only we, the decendants of the new men, reading this book many thousands of years later, can realise the crucial significance of those shadowy events. Without them we would not be reading this book. We would not *be*.

Man, as we see him from the Neanderthal point of view, is a weak and oddly shaped creature, but he is bound to triumph because he can do two things which the Neanderthalers, for all their speed and strength, cannot do: he can use his hands to fashion tools and he can plan for a future when these tools may have to be used. The two are indissolubly linked, and it is clear that they act on one another to produce yet more careful planning and better and better tools. The gap that divides the new men from the old is a small but vital one, yet it is one that contact between the two peoples could easily bridge. We see this happening when Lok, the Neanderthal protagonist, watches the new men from his hiding place in a tree and discovers what it means to think:

> Lok discovered 'Like'. He had used likeness all his life without being aware of it. Fungi on a tree were ears, the word was the same but acquired a distinction by circumstances that could never apply to the sensitive things on the side of his head. Now, in a convulsion of the understanding Lok found himself using likeness as a tool as surely as ever he had used a stone to hack at sticks or meat. Likeness could grasp the white-faced hunters with a hand, could put them into the world where they were thinkable and not a random and unrelated irruption.
>
> He was picturing the hunters who went out with bent sticks in skill and malice.
>
> 'The people are like a famished wolf in the hollow of a tree.'
> (194–5)

It is this convulsion of the understanding which is at the basis of man's civilisation, for it is this that allows man to connect the random, to relate cause and effect, and thus to begin that mastery of the environment which has led to the world we know today. It is this that ensures that the new men, the inheritors, will turn into the men of Antiquity, of the Middle Ages, of the Renaissance – into H. G. Wells himself at last. But of course there is another side to this, one not noted by Wells but clearly seen by Nietzsche and Freud: If I can plan ahead then I can also desire what I do not at present have; I can envy what another man has and I have not; I can imagine and desire the embrace of another man's wife. Greed, envy and lust are the inevitable concomitants of civilisation. Moreover, they bring with them the nostalgia for a time when they did not exist, when there was no need to fear, to plan, to calculate, to think – in short, no consciousness, with its weary burden of choice, and its awareness of the fact that I have infinite possibilities but only one lifetime in which to make use of them. But what this time of innocence was like we cannot know, for knowing means thinking and thinking is exactly what led to the disappearance of the state of innocence. As Samuel Mountjoy is to put it in *Free Fall*:

> If I imagine heaven metaphorically dazzled into colours, the pure white light spread out in a cascade richer than a peacock's tail, then I see that one of the colours lay over me. I was innocent of guilt, unconscious of innocence; happy, therefore, and unconscious of happiness. Perhaps the full sheaf of colours is never to be experienced by the human being since if he experiences these colours they must lie in the past or in someone else. Perhaps consciousness and the guilt which is unhappiness go together. (60)

Consciousness and guilt go together, for guilt is the result of that initial repression which led to consciousness – or which is perhaps the definition of consciousness. For I must deny the claims of the immediate, I must be able to stand back from the pressure of the present, in order to make use of 'like', in order to draw analogies, to think. As Freud suggested in a brilliant late essay,[1] negation, language, thought and civilisation all go together.

It is the extraordinary achievement of *The Inheritors* that it manages to convey to us precisely what Sammy Mountjoy felt could never be experienced and expressed by any human being: what it feels like to exist in a state of innocence. Yet the book, like all Golding's novels except *Free Fall*, starts at a point from which there can be no return: the disappearance of the log-bridge is the silent witness of the arrival of the new men. After that it is only a matter of time before all the Neanderthalers are destroyed. Though neither side recognises this fact, we, the readers, are slowly made to realise that the intrusion of 'the other' will mean the disappearance of 'the people' and all they stand for. But

---

[1] 'Negation', *Collected Papers*, v.

Golding does not leave it at that. Having shown us the clash from the point of view of the Neanderthalers for almost eleven chapters, he suddenly switches viewpoint, so that we are abruptly made to see the world he has created from the position we would normally have occupied all along – that of the neutral, *human* spectator. The effect is horrific. For Lok, whose anguish and bafflement we have until then been feeling as our own, is suddenly seen from the outside, as 'the red creature', glimpsed scurrying away into the darkness, carrying with him his bewilderment and loneliness. And now, although we are inside the minds of the new men, we can understand more than they ever could. Above all, we can understand why they are as they are. And we discover too their fear – fear of the forest, of the darkness, of the 'devils' hiding they know not where – and their desperate desire to get as far away from the spot as they can. As they sail away, with a captured baby 'devil' (the last Neanderthaler) in the boat with them, one of them breaks the silence:

'They live in the darkness under the trees.'
Holding the ivory firmly in his hands, feeling the onset of sleep, Tuami looked at the line of darkness. It was far away and there was plenty of water in between. He peered forward past the sail to see what lay at the other end of the lake, but it was so long, and there was such a flashing from the water that he could not see if the line of darkness had an ending. (233)

The line of darkness has no ending. For to be aware of the light as light is to be aware of the darkness as its opposite. To be born a new man is to inherit a consciousness, and that consciousness will always be aware, dimly, of the darkness from which it springs, of the darkness beyond. But, being thus aware of it, man turns it into an enemy, into that which is evil, as the new men turn the forest and its innocent and harmless inhabitants into a place of terror haunted by devils. And as, many centuries later, H. G. Wells turned the gentle Neanderthalers into horrifying monsters: 'We know very little of the appearance of the Neanderthal man, but this seems to suggest . . . gorilla-like monsters . . . cunning brains . . . possibly cannibalistic tendencies.' Once again Golding has revealed to us not just the underside of civilisation, but the negatives upon which civilisation itself is built. Having experienced what Lok has experienced we can now see more clearly both the necessary triumph of the new men and its inevitable cost.

Golding's next novel takes yet another classic of rational liberalism as its starting point, though this time it is a slightly older one – none other, in fact, than *Robinson Crusoe*. His intention here is to isolate one of the new men, the 'inheritors', and thus to explore what man is like – not what he thinks he is like, but what, stripped of the protective clothing of civilisation, he really is.
 What then is man?

> I will tell you what a man is. He goes on four legs till Necessity bends the front end upright and makes a hybrid of him. The finger-prints of those hands are about his spine and just above the rump for proof if you want it. He is a freak, an ejected foetus robbed of his natural development, thrown out in the world with a naked covering of parchment, with too little room for his teeth and a soft bulging skull like a bubble. (190)

But before we arrive at this insight we have to go a long way. The novel, *Pincher Martin*, describes one man's struggle to retain his identity in the face of an alien nature. He is alone on a rock in the middle of the Atlantic, waiting to be rescued. It is vital for him to keep himself healthy and sane till rescue arrives, and the first thing he has to do if he is to achieve this is to humanise his rock, to 'tame' it and thus turn it into something he can control and understand. So he names its parts: Oxford Circus, Piccadilly, Leicester Square. To name is to master. Men give names to nature and make patterns which they superimpose on nature, whether it is simply by moving two stones so that they come into line with a third or building a city. This is culture, civilisation: the separation of oneself from nature. It is vital too that he retain his identity, so he makes a mirror out of silver paper in which he can see himself reflected. He makes marks on the ground to keep track of the days. With an animal will to survive allied to a civilised intelligence which tells him how to control his environment Pincher Martin seems truly to be a latter-day Robinson for whom nothing is impossible.
 But things are not so easy for him as they were for his illustrious predecessor. To maintain one's identity in his circumstances is as

hard as it was for Ralph to remain alive in *Lord of the Flies*. Even sleep is dangerous, for

> Sleep is a relaxation of the conscious guard, the sorter. Sleep is when all the unsorted stuff comes flying out as from a dustbin upset in a high wind. In sleep time was divorced from the straight line. . . . Or sleep was a consenting to die, to go into complete unconsciousness, the personality defeated, acknowledging too frankly what is implicit in mortality that we are temporary structures patched up and unable to stand the pace without a daily respite. . . . (91)

But why is Pincher Martin so afraid of sleep? Why does he not dare to relax even for an instant the vigil over his own personality? We have already seen the answer given by Golding's two earlier novels: human identity is a fragile thing and the forces of darkness constantly tug at it, seeking to destroy it. To imagine that one can retain absolute control over our own identity is both foolish (Piggy) and dangerous (the new men). In *Pincher Martin* the theme is made even more explicit in the conversations the hero recalls between himself and his friend Nathaniel. Standing awkwardly in his Oxford rooms, Nathaniel had said: 'Take us as we are now and heaven would be sheer negation. Without form and void. You see? A sort of black lightning destroying everything that we call life.' And again: 'You could say that I know it is important for you personally to understand about heaven – about dying – because in only a few years—'

And here he is, Pincher Martin, who has always gone out and got what he wanted in life, a few years later, fighting to stay alive on a rock in the middle of the Atlantic. And this time it does not seem to be a fight that he can win. Not because his body betrays him, but because his mind does. Even madness, that last refuge of the proud self, as both Richard II and Lear half-recognised, that last bit of play-acting which allows us to keep the facts from ourselves – even that is seen by Pincher Martin for what it is, as he is slowly forced to face himself. In the end comes the recognition of what he really is. But what is his end? The last sentence of the book tells us that all we have previously experienced with the hero, the struggle to reach the rock, the rock itself, the fight for survival, all this is a mirage, conjured up by the drowning man's desperate imagination. Pincher Martin drowned without even having time to take off his sea-boots. All the rest was the projection of his desperate desire to stay alive, to retain his identity.

Now we can begin to see why he feared sleep so much, why it was vital that his defences should not come down, even for a moment. For the defences are the bulwarks of the lie that even in this extremity his desire to cling to his identity at all costs has conjured up. The fear of sleep is the fear that if his will goes passive his mind will recognise the terrible similarity between the shape of the island on which he is stranded and one of his own teeth, encountered by his roving tongue. For so long as the connection between island and tooth is kept from his brain he will not have to face the fact that the island is something that he has *invented*.

Take us as we are now, Nathaniel had told Martin, and heaven would be sheer negation, everything, that is, which the self is not. But what is this self to which we cling so desperately that each night's sleep seems to be some sort of death, a temporary negation? This 'self' is not something to which we find the beasts clinging, it is not something which had much meaning for Lok or the old creature, Mal, who curled himself up and lay down peaceably, prepared to return to his mother, the earth, the Oa. This 'self' is a product of civilisation just as civilisation is built upon its emergence. It is because of it that man names things and imposes patterns on nature, builds towns and fights wars, trying vainly to perpetuate himself, to deny that he is a 'temporary structure'. 'Pincher' Martin, christened Christopher, the Christ-bearer, whose vision of life is that of each man getting what he wants for himself, and whose last act is a murder attempted out of a mixture of envy and hatred, this man, like all men, must discover that he belongs to the world. He must witness the dissolution of this self before the black lightning until he is reduced to the consciousness only of a desperate pair of claws, clinging now to nothing but themselves. And even that has eventually to give way to the black lightning, which wears them away 'in a compassion that was timeless and without mercy'.

How long does Pincher Martin take to die? A second? An hour? A few hours? The question is without meaning, since dying is a negation of time as we know it, the dissolution of the self which has created time. Golding does more than tell a story of shipwreck and adventure. He does more than show us how one man dies or even how all men die. He shows us the perpetual state of man *in this life*, much as Dante would have done had he placed Pincher Martin in one of the circles of the Inferno. We do not learn how Pincher Martin dies after one week of struggling to remain alive, or after two minutes, but how he dies in every instant of his life. He is a man who tries to live as a true 'inheritor', totally in control of himself and in command of the world and other people. But this can only be done at the price of repressing the knowledge that man owes God a death, that he is not a proud conqueror but an ejected foetus robbed of its natural development. If a moment in time had to be found for it, then we could say that the death of Pincher Martin occurred when, like Lok, he discovered 'like'.

If the creation of the self is bound up with the discovery of consciousness then we can never really understand what led to the creation of the self, for understanding is a product of selfhood. Golding's first three novels are all fictions which embody this fact without trying to state it explicitly. All three present us with an action, taken at a point from which there is no turning back and from which the end follows more or less inevitably. That action could in every case be seen as the gradual destruction of what we are first presented with by 'the other': where, at the very start, there appeared to be nothing but what was present, by the end there is nothing but 'other'. At that point the book ends, for 'the other' is always silent. In his next novel, *Free Fall*, however, Golding tries to articulate the 'other'. The novel deals with Sammy Mountjoy's attempt to understand when and where it was that he stopped being innocent and became guilty, stopped being free and became the conditioned puppet he now feels himself to be. Where did the fall occur? He calls up scene after scene from his past, but none seems to yield the clear answer for which he is looking. Was there no fall then? But why does he now feel so trapped?

For trapped he definitely does feel. 'I am shut in a bone box,' he says, trying to describe his efforts at communicating to the reader, 'and trying to fasten myself on white paper. The rivets join us together, and yet for all the passion we share nothing but our sense of division.' But this he can't stand: 'I want fusion and identity – I want to understand and be understood.' It is this need that drives him to force what he thinks is love on the apparently entirely self-contained Beatrice. 'Beatrice,' he asks her, 'what is it like to be you?' But that is a question which cannot be answered, and Sammy's reward for trying to get an answer to it is to be left wondering whether it was he who pushed Beatrice over the border into madness.

Free Fall is an unpleasant novel to read. It is stifling, restricting, but it also manages to be boring. All the Golding themes are there, but somehow it doesn't work. It is possible, of course, that an author more used to working with the novel of ideas, a Mann or a Hesse, might have been able to do something with it, but Golding is not such a writer. His strength lies in the violent force of his imagination and in the way he is able to make concrete his imaginative perceptions in specific fictions. But it is as if in *Free Fall* he had forgotten the lessons of his earlier novels, had forgotten why Simon cannot explain what he feels, why Lok cannot both be Lok and use the language of the 'new men'. Here Golding is himself trapped in the fluid consciousness of his hero (it is no coincidence that this is the only first-person novel he has written), free to roam where he wants in Sammy's past, but always trapped inside the prison of Sammy's consciousness. Trying to articulate 'the other', instead of demonstrating its presence, he flounders in a sea of clichés and is drowned. Nor is it enough to say that what he is giving us is a man similarly caught in the toils of his own subjectivity. *The Inheritors* and *Pincher Martin* were really able to do this because they were able to give us a double vision: we were shown the new men and Pincher Martin both from within and from without, and thus given a far stronger sense of their own imprisonment in the 'bone box'.

Fortunately Golding (unlike Sartre and Camus) was able to pull back from this desire to explain, to remember that art is more discovery than communication, and to confound those critics who said that he had written himself out. His next novel, *The Spire*, is his richest and most perfect creation to date, displaying the same sure touch as *The Inheritors* in its presentation of a vanished world through which to explore the meaning of our present lives.

The Spire is set in the Middle Ages. Jocelin, the Dean of a cathedral church, has had a vision during his prayers. An angel

at his back called on him to build a spire on his church and thus
make it the highest in the country. Against every opposition by
his subordinates he determines to turn the vision into actuality
and have the spire built, to the greater glory of God. But the
foundations of the church are practically non-existent, since it is
built on marshland, and it seems to be the height of folly to persist in his plans. Yet Jocelin drives the workmen on and on, slowly
the spire rises, till in the end it is completed and the giant
capstone set upon it. But the strain of what amounts to willing
the spire into being against the evidence not just of the masons,
but of his own senses, proves too much for Jocelin, and he
collapses and dies. As for the spire, we are not told if it succeeded
in staying up, though the implication is that it did, bent, but
'rushing upward to some point at the sky's end, and with a silent
cry'.

In fact, as with the problem of how long it takes for Pincher
Martin to die, the question of whether the spire stands or falls is
entirely irrelevant. The story, as with Golding's first novels, deals
with a single obsessional act, taken from a point at which there is
no turning back, and rushing forward to its inevitable conclusion.
The spire, Jocelin feels, is the visible sign of prayer. But the question which he ignores at first, but which slowly pushes its way
into his consciousness is this: Did his own vision really come from
God, or is it only the product of his own pride or desire – or even
of his uncomfortable kneeling posture and the sickness which is
already affecting his spine? We see him move from complete
confidence in the God-given quality of the vision to doubt and
the eventual certainty that he has made a terrible mistake – and
then, in a final twist, to a questioning of even this certainty.
But by then it is his body which has cracked under the
strain and there is nothing left for him but the annihilation of
death.

What causes Jocelin to doubt the source of his vision? Partly,
of course, the sheer physical massiveness of the spire and its effect
on the rest of the church, so wonderfully conveyed by Golding –
the churning of the earth when the foundations are uncovered,
the eerie singing of the pillars as they take the growing strain, the
gradual desertion of the workmen as the spire rises higher and
higher into the air, the absurdity of the whole enterprise when
measured by the scientific standards of what is likely to stand up

and what isn't. But this Jocelin could have withstood. As he says early on to the master-builder, Roger Mason: 'You'll see how I shall thrust you upwards by my will. It's God's will in this business.' What breaks his confidence is the gradual discovery that good and evil are inextricably mixed in the entire operation. At first the actualising of his vision seems to be nothing but good, truly God's will. But as it rises the spire seems to change into some pagan deity, demanding more and more sacrifices to keep it from turning against its makers. Jocelin's first awareness of this comes when he finds himself recognising the attraction Goody Pangall and Roger Mason feel for each other, and assenting to it, because he knows that now he need have no fear that the master-builder will give up the job: 'She will keep him here.' This reaction of his torments him, but surely nothing can be evil if it results in the building of the spire? Then Pangall is killed by the builders, and Jocelin unconsciously assents to it; he sees what is happening but shuts the sight out of his mind. He does not want to know what lies in the foundations at the foot of the tower. He feels that 'There was a watershed in circumstances', though what lies on the other side of that watershed he cannot remember, and what the watershed itself consists of he represses as persistently as Pincher Martin repressed the knowledge that his island was only his own tooth.

To get away from thoughts of this kind Jocelin climbs to the top of the growing spire. But the thoughts are inside him, and he cannot get away from them. He has started something that he is now powerless to stop. He becomes aware of the attraction Goody Pangall has – has always had, he now realises – for him. Is there lust then mingled in this as well? The phallic nature of the spire cannot escape him, especially when one of the workmen picks up the model and sticks it obscenely between his legs. Can it be *this* which lay behind the call to build? Not God but his own repressed lust? Like the boys on the island, like the new men and Pincher Martin, he now tries to project his guilt outwards: 'It must be witchcraft; otherwise how could she come so flatly between me and heaven?' But he knows inside himself the weakness of that theory. And so the spire grows to its full four hundred feet and the master-builder refuses to go on and the stones of the church shriek beneath its weight. There is an official investigation sent to look into the whole business, and Jocelin, now no longer in control of his mind, is quietly relieved of his office. His back, suspect for so long, gives way, and he becomes a cripple.

He can no longer keep from himself the fact that his determination to build the spire has resulted in two deaths, perhaps many more. And if after all it was not God but some private whim masquerading as the voice of God, the angel, then what is to keep the spire up on foundations obviously incapable of maintaining it? If it is only Jocelin himself who is responsible for the spire, if God does not come into it at all, but only a man's pride, his lust, his desire for glory, perhaps his physical disabilities, then how can the thing possibly stand up? As the truth is finally allowed to enter his consciousness, Jocelin realises that it is only *his* willpower that has raised the spire up, and only his will-power that is holding it there. The weight of that thought is too much for him. With his back shattered he crawls through the filthy lanes of the town to confront the master-mason, who has long ago fled from the site but even so is himself a broken man, broken by the terror of working at that height, with his knowledge of what weight has to be supported by what foundations. In the Star Inn they confront each other, and for the first time Jocelin speaks the truth – to himself and to another:

> 'Once you said I was the devil himself. It isn't true. I'm a fool. Also I think – I'm a building with a vast cellarage where the rats live; and there's some kind of blight on my hands. I injure everyone I touch, particularly those I love.' (210–11)

And, rhetorically, he asks: 'What holds it up, Roger? I? The nail? Does she, or do you? Or is it poor Pangall, crouched beneath the crossways, with a sliver of mistletoe between his ribs?'

Yet this is not quite the end, and the end, when it comes, brings with it at least the suggestion that the truth he has so painfully come to accept may perhaps not be the truth after all. As he lies dying he sees through the window the spire and, mingled with it, a tangle of red hair, the hair of Goody Pangall, but also an image of the heavens: 'That's all, he thought, that's the explanation, if I had time.' And the words come to him suddenly: 'There is no innocent work. God knows where God may be.' And, by his bedside, in the moment of his dying, the little priest, Father Adam, whom Jocelin had despised for so long (but who is he now to despise anyone?), the little priest suddenly cries: 'I believe, Jocelin, I believe!'

A priest has found his faith in the ruins of another man's. And perhaps this is the explanation. There is no innocent work, yet God only knows where God may be. Perhaps after all it was only one final trick of Jocelin's pride to imagine that it was he alone who was responsible for the spire, that God was not at work in it at all. Perhaps even those deaths were, if not necessary, at least part of a pattern, if we could only see it. Perhaps the saving of Father Adam's soul is what the whole episode has been about. We cannot know. We have no right to judge these things, to apportion praise or blame, to imagine that we are anything more than pieces of a larger pattern. All that we can say is that Jocelin did wrong, that he suffered for it, and that the spire was built.

Golding is not interested in playing with language or teasing the reader in the way that Rabelais and Nabokov are. The texture of his novels is, in fact, a good deal less interesting than that of many of the authors we have so far dealt with. Instead, his books have an extraordinary hardness, a steel-like quality which makes one feel that every superfluous flourish has been removed in order to make them move more cleanly towards their inevitable destinations. This has left me with something of a problem: since the overall shape of a Golding novel is what is interesting about it I have felt it important to deal with all the major novels; but since they are, in one sense, very simple novels, I have not wanted to spend too much time on any single one, and the total impression so far may have been of a series of jottings rather than the kind of working through that I have attempted with the novels of Rabelais, Proust, Nabokov and Bellow. So far much of what I have said has been said in one form or another by a good many commentators on Golding. My only excuse is that without this what I now want to say would not have made much sense, and it is here that Golding's essential quality lies.

As we have seen, what Golding wants to do is to show us the whole man, man as he is rather than as he sees himself. Man's 'fall' into consciousness is also his 'rise' into civilisation; consciousness and civilisation buttress one another up. But if this is so how can the writer, whose tool is language, itself a product of the 'fall', get behind it and show us the ways in which man is a creature of the 'fall'?

The simple answer is of course that Golding doesn't try to do this directly, except in *Free Fall*. But this does not mean that he simply ignores the problem. What he does is to lead us up to the point of understanding and leave us there. He shows us the false-ness both of Piggy's rationalistic position and of Jack's primitivis-tic one, and, having done so, puts us in a position to understand what Simon experiences but cannot express. No character in the novels can ever articulate this experience, as Sammy Mountjoy discovers (he is the only one to try), for every attempt to do so merely pushes the mystery further back. In *The Inheritors* we rest easily inside Lok's sensibility till the last pages show him to us as we would normally see him: an unalterably alien creature, loping away into the forest. The sudden shift of perspective here reveals to us that we are both Lok (who is what he cannot under-stand) and the 'new men' (who hanker after what they know they are not). In that moment the skin of habit is torn away from us and we remain poised between the two, both inside man and outside him. In *Pincher Martin* the same effect is achieved but in reverse, so to speak: we suddenly move out of Pincher Martin's consciousness (our normal consciousness) and recognise that the world he has been living in (the world we as readers have been living in) is not the real world but only the projection of his imagination. At this moment we are delivered from the seduc-tions of our own imagination and made aware of the limitations it imposes on our vision. In this way Golding uses the nature of fiction itself as a prime element in his own fictions. Most interesting from this point of view are *Pincher Martin* and *The Spire*, though much of what I have to say about this aspect of them applies equally well to *Lord of the Flies* and *The Inheritors*.

Pincher Martin is characterised by his own greed and selfish-ness. The novel is, as we saw, about the self's last efforts to control the world in which it exists. This it can only do by suppressing the truth – that he is dying, is going to disappear, while the world goes on as it always has – and creating a false world in which he is triumphant. The only trouble with this is that such a world is *his* world and not *the* world, which means that there will always be the nagging feeling that he is deceiving himself in imagining that it is the real world. But Pincher Martin's situation is in many ways similar to that of the novelist. The novelist also creates a world out of his own head and tries to believe in its reality in order to complete his story. And the reader, in a parallel movement, recreates the world of the novelist, and basks in it, free, for a few hours, of the pressures and uncertainties of actuality. Any novelist and any reader, but here, quite simply, this novelist and this reader, for what Pincher Martin imagines and projects as reality is what Golding has imagined and created, and what the reader lives as reality while he is engrossed in the book.

But the book is about the disintegration of the will and the imagination of the hero before the silent but all-powerful 'other', the black lightning of reality. Pincher Martin, clinging with every instinct at his command to his unique self, makes himself believe that there is an island in the middle of the Atlantic, providentially there to help him remain alive. But as the novel progresses the features of the island begin to remind us of something else, though at first we are simply puzzled. Suddenly we – and Pincher Martin – know: it reminds us of the tooth inside his mouth. The discovery brings with it the shiver Mallarmé described when he talked of the 'démon de l'analogie', for the analogy is indeed demonic, forcing us to realise, as it does, that we have been inhabiting not a real world but the projection of the hero's desperate imagination. In this way the act of reading becomes the subject of the novel, and the final twist shocks the reader into the recognition of what novels normally pass over in silence: the difference between our imagination and the world.

One of the results of the fall, Golding suggests, is the creation of individual character. Indeed, the fall can be seen as man's sudden consciousness of himself as unique and distinct from other men; and the fall is perpetuated because once this discovery has been made man is at pains to protect and nurse this unique self till all its desires are fulfilled, including the most basic desire of all, the desire to be immortal, to retain our consciousness of ourselves for ever and ever. Animals lack this desire because they lack a sense of self, and so do the Neanderthalers, accepting, as they do, the need to return to the Mother Earth from which they were born. It is, we could say, a human aberration, and it is one which civilisation fosters and which fosters civilisation. It is also one upon which the novel depends and which it tacitly reinforces. Not for nothing is *Robinson Crusoe* the first novel, and not for nothing is it linked with a newly acquisitive society. Golding's novel, by standing *Robinson Crusoe* on its head, does more than hit out at a certain view of man or show up the inadequacies of the traditional novel. By making us experience with Pincher Martin and then revealing the basis of that experience it turns us into accomplices and forces us to recognise what we normally try to deny: that we are more than the self of which we are conscious.

In *The Spire* the fiction is even closer to miming its own origins and creation. As the spire rises, foot by foot, pushed up by Jocelin's will, so the novel moves forward page by page, the product of nothing but the writer's will. And the rat in the cellarage, the body sacrificed and hidden at the foot of the tower – is that not one with Golding's own guilt at the suppressed knowledge that what he is making has no justification apart from the appeasement of his own desire to write? And we, the readers, are made to experience the making of the spire, of *The Spire*, as stone is laid on stone and paragraph follows paragraph, till we grow dizzy from the height and our knees turn to water at the secret feeling that perhaps it is only we who hold up this edifice. Again the act of reading, as of writing, is made the subject of the fiction, and, by being recognised as a specific activity, a form of violence done to the world instead of being simply equated with the world, both its true nature and that of the world is revealed. For the world is that 'other' which encroaches slowly on the mind of the protagonist, the pull of gravity in its simplest form, but also the stone and the wood and the wind which form the physical reality of the construction.[1]

But a strange thing happens at the climax of this book. The dying man sees the spire, which had for so long threatened to fall,

[1] The perfect blending of theme and subject-matter, what we might call Golding's perfect choice of objective correlative, is shown by one particular incident. Jocelin climbs to the top of the growing tower and, looking down on the little town, he is able to see over the walls into a courtyard where a woman is adulterating milk with water. In a very literal sense Jocelin is here in God's position, able to see what men try to keep hidden. But because it is a position which he has not attained, like Dante, through suffering and humiliation, it is a parody of God's position, lacking the element of understanding and forgiveness. Similarly it is a warning to the reader of the errors of imagining that he can judge from any solid position, raised above the flux and stress of the action. Cf. my comments on the words of the Curé about the steeple of Saint-Hilaire in Proust, above, p. 23.

still standing, still there, outside his window. Unlike Pincher Martin's island it does not vanish with the recognition of its dubious and guilty origin. For, after all, who is to say what that origin is? And is every work to be equated with or reduced to its origins? There is no innocent work, it is true, but then God knows where God may be. Origin is never synonymous with the completed work. Any object, whether it is made of stones or words, no longer belongs solely to the man who made it or first dreamt of it. It has become public property since it is made out of public things: words, wood, stones. As Jocelin notes, surprised at the disparity between the graceful model and the massiveness of the real spire: 'The world of stuff was a new thing.' Whatever its origins the spire now has a place in the world, it can be seen by all men, it is outside and beyond the man who conceived it and willed it into being. It is right that he should acknowledge his guilt, that he should recognise the hidden source of his own desires, and right perhaps that the object should destroy him for his presumption. But now it is free of him and of all men, as Father Adam seems suddenly to understand.

To make something – a building, a book – is to launch out into the unknown, it is to place one's faith in something which is other than oneself. Much will happen between the conception and the achievement, and once work has begun matters are no longer entirely in our hands. When the thing is done it will stand up by itself, free of the man who built it. Yet it is in the process of making that we will discover what we knew and didn't know, both our own guilt and the freedom that comes from an acknowledgement and articulation of that guilt. *The Spire* is not only about process, the process of building, of making; it is itself process, and each rereading is a re-enactment of that process. (That is why it is of no importance if the spire goes on standing after the end of the book or not.) But it is also a book, an object, which, though it carries the name of William Golding on the title-page, belongs now to the public world of literature. Let us accept it with gratitude, as Father Adam accepted that other product of mingled innocence and guilt, Jocelin's spire, but let us remember that such acceptance is never passive, that it requires an effort of the imagination. Such an effort this book can teach us to make.

11 Surfaces and Structures

> 'In this work more than any other it is rewarding to keep on
> looking at questions, which one considers solved, from another
> quarter, as if they were unsolved.'
>
> Wittgenstein

Old myths die hard, for the simple reason that they are rooted in human psychology. We persist in seeing things in a certain way because such seeing corresponds to a need, and no matter how often we are proved wrong we will revert whenever we can to our old habits. It may therefore be useful at this stage to show certain kinds of interpretation or misinterpretation in action, much as Chaucer and Rabelais, Swift and Nabokov do in their fictions, though our examples will not be fiction. In this way we may be able to see more clearly the nature of the temptations offered by outworn myths and to discover some of the pitfalls that lie in wait for the interpreter who would reject them outright. An excellent test case lies to hand in a literary dispute which recently broke out in France and which has not yet subsided.

In 1965 Professor Raymond Picard of the Sorbonne, a notable Racine scholar, published a little book entitled *Nouvelle Critique ou nouvelle imposture*, which was a sharp attack on the premises and methods of the Nouvelle Critique, based on a detailed examination of a collection of essays on Racine by Roland Barthes, one of its leading exponents. This sparked off a virulent controversy between the supporters of the Old and the New, which would have delighted Swift, but which may surprise the present-day English reader by the bitterness of its tone and the variety of non-literary issues which it appeared to raise in the minds of both parties. There was, one sensed, a strong feeling on both sides that to succumb to the arguments of the opposition would be to betray not simply the cause of art, but that of freedom, even of civilisation itself. Memories of the controversies surrounding *Scrutiny* in its heyday, or of the tired exchanges of our Snows and Leavises are misleading; the real parallels are with the reactions of men like Wyndham Lewis and Julien Benda to the avant-garde movements of the first third of the century.

Though the present controversy in France, in its initial stages at least, centred on the criticism of Racine, it is in effect only another round in the fight modernism has waged with its enemies for close on a hundred years. Picard of course would deny that his critique of the 'new criticism' implied any condemnation of Mallarmé, Valéry or Proust. On the contrary, it is often in their name that he castigates his opponents. Nevertheless, as we shall see, it is the nature of modernity that is at issue, and this accounts both for the violence of the tone and for the total lack of any middle ground on which the two parties can agree.

The debate, as we might by now expect, centred on the seemingly simple and harmless question: How does one read a book? In the course of the controversy a number of answers have been given and a number of presuppositions laid bare, which should help us to see more clearly the nature of modernism in general and of the modern novel in particular. In order, however, to avoid the danger of unwittingly accepting the premisses of either side, it will be useful to enter the area of argument from the vantage point of an earlier writer. I have chosen to begin with Proust, since we have already grown familiar with his mode of thought and expression, but Mallarmé or Valéry would have served our purpose equally well.

In one of the few flashes of light which brighten the gloom of Albertine's imprisonment and act as heralds, in the lost world of carnal desire, of the triumphant coda of *A la Recherche du temps perdu*, Marcel, listening to Albertine playing some of Vinteuil's music on the pianola, starts to meditate on the nature of art and on its relation to the artist and to truth:

> This music seemed to me to be something truer than all the books that I knew. Sometimes I thought that this was due to the fact that what we feel in life, not being felt in the form of ideas, its literary (that is to say an intellectual) translation in giving an account of it, explains it, analyses it, but does not recompose it as does music, in which the sounds seem to assume the inflexion of the thing itself, to reproduce that interior and extreme point of our sensation which is the part that gives us that peculiar exhilaration which we recapture from time to time and which when we say: 'What a fine day! What glorious sunshine!' we do not in the least communicate to our neigh-

bour, in whom the same sun and the same weather arouse
wholly different vibrations. (x 232–3; III 374–5)

Marcel is of course recalling the incident of his childhood when
the sun, shining in the water, filled him with such joy that all he
could do was shout: 'Zut! zut! zut!', but which, when he tried
to communicate it to a passing peasant by calling out happily:
'What a fine day!' evoked nothing but an angry grunt. This made
him realise that what we convey in normal discourse are generali-
ties, never our unique sensations. Language itself, of course, only
functions as a system of communication because there is a
conventional agreement about what signs stand for, but for this
very reason our feelings, once translated into words, fail to convey
the sense we wanted. 'What a fine day!' does not give another
person any idea of what I really feel about the day. Not only that:
it does not even give me any idea of what I feel. We are no nearer
to knowing what we feel than other people are to knowing this;
the gap between what we feel and what we think we feel when
we put it into words is as wide as that between what we feel and
what another person thinks we feel. We are, in fact, two people,
one who has the experience of the sunlight on water, and one
who expresses this in such terms as 'What a lovely day!' Most
people are not aware of this dualism, since the initial sensation
is so quickly smothered by the habitual response, but Marcel of
course is different, and the encounter with the peasant forces
home to him the extent to which we are shut up in our own
worlds and the part which habit plays in keeping us there,
unaware that we are letting our real life slip away by converting
it into cliché. His life, from then on, is spent trying to draw these
vague sensations of joy into his consciousness, to articulate and
therefore master them without destroying their unique quality.
Music, of course, can resolve this problem, since it can recompose
sensation in a communicable and permanent form. As Swann had
already noted on first becoming aware of the Vinteuil sonata,
music has the capacity to reveal to us 'quelle richesse, quelle
varieté, cache a notre insu cette grande nuit impénetré et décour-
ageante de notre âme que nous prenons pour du vide et pour du
néant'. That is why Marcel can go on to compare his sensation
on hearing Albertine play with that caused by the sudden influx
of involuntary memory on tasting again the *petite madeleine,* and

by the sudden view of the three spires at Martinville. In all three cases the deadening and generalising force of habit, which reveals itself in the clichés of language, seems suddenly and mysteriously to drop away and he feels a surge of joy allied to a renewed sense of sheer physical existence such as one only normally feels at the moment of awakening. Listening to a great work of music makes us aware of ourselves, of the dark worlds hidden from our consciousness, because music embodies and conveys the uniqueness of another. And Marcel concludes:

> This unknown quality of a unique world which no other composer had ever made us see, perhaps it is in this, I said to Albertine, that the most authentic proof of genius consists, even more than in the content of the work itself. 'Even in literature?' Albertine enquired. 'Even in literature.' (x 234; III 376)

Albertine's is a sensible question. If it is not the content of a work of art that is important but the way in which it gives form to ineffable feelings, inchoate sensations, an individual's uniqueness, then music appears to be in a specially privileged position. But Marcel is not content to answer Albertine's question in the affirmative by pointing to a poem of Mallarmé's, say, or to some other work of literature which consciously strives to arrive at the contentless status of music. He goes on to explain to her that what he has said about music applies even to the most content-laden form of literature, the novel, and even to its apotheosis, the late nineteenth-century novel itself. In Hardy, for instance, he points out, more important than the plot, or the sentiments expressed by the characters, is that 'stone-mason's geometry' which crops up again and again in his writing. In the end all of Hardy's diverse fictions can be laid one upon the other 'comme les maisons verticalement entassées en hauteur sur le sol pierreux de l'ile'. For the diversity is only apparent: in reality they are all one, expressing one unique being, forming one gigantic novel. And in Dostoevsky, he asks, is it not the mysterious women, whose facial expressions change so suddenly from serenity to a terrible insolence and who are always the same woman, whether she be called Nastasia or Grouchenka; is it not the houses, the rooms (so minutely described and yet always the same room), which form the core of the vision, rather than the Gothic plots or the reactionary ideology?

> That novel and terrible beauty of a house, that novel beauty blended with a woman's face, that is the unique thing which Dostoevsky has given to the world, and the comparisons that literary critics may make, between him and Gogol, or between him and Paul de Kock, are of no interest, being external to this secret beauty. (x 237–8; III 379)

Even in a novel by Hardy or Dostoevsky the complications of the plot are only incidental, only a strategy, so to speak, whereby the unique world of these writers can take on form and permanence. That is why we can say that all novelists, even the most prolific, have really only written one book, which in the case of Dostoevsky could be called *Crime and Punishment*, in the case of Flaubert *L'Education Sentimentale*. Some authors have recognised this fact about their own output and have retrospectively given one single title to a large number of superficially diverse works: *La Comédie Humaine*, *La Légende des siècles*. That they did this *after* the event and not before proves that they were not consciously following out a programme but that their novels and poems took on a certain shape of their own accord, as though complying with some secret law which the writer could recognise once it had emerged into the light of day, but could not consciously control or direct.

Genuine art, then, Proust argues, even when it appears to be purely naturalistic fiction, always contains references to that secret world which is the artist's alone and which is normally inaccessible to his or another's consciousness. But to call this world 'inner' or 'unconscious' is to invite confusion, for it implies that there is already something there below the consciousness, which the author simply needs to bring to the surface and hand over to the reader. But, as we have seen, this is not the case. There is only a formless, wordless feeling, which attaches itself to certain images, stones, rooms, faces, and slowly grows into the author's consciousness as he presses on with the problem of writing his novels. This feeling does not attach itself to the overt content of a novel, and it can never be discovered by an analysis of the content, but only by a response to what Proust calls style. This 'style' may be the recurrence of certain images, as in Hardy or Dostoevsky, but it may also manifest itself in the peculiar choice of verbal tense in which the narration is conducted, as Proust noted it in

Flaubert. And to grasp an author's distinctive 'style' it is never enough to read only one book by him. Proust insists that two are an absolute minimum, and we can see why. For it is only because of the repetition of certain elements that we can begin to sense the *constants* that underlie the changing fictions. These constants are what Proust elsewhere calls an author's 'secret signature', the keys to his private universe. In Proust himself they are easy to discover, since his own novel records his search for just these constants, for a way of making accessible to his consciousness and embodying for others his own unique world. That is why Proust wrote only one novel, and why that novel is both the record of a search and itself a process of exploration. But in other authors it is we who have to do the work ourselves, listening to the works as Proust told the poet to stand in front of a tree, looking both outwards at it and inwards into himself, trying to distinguish the secret signatures from the external elements of plot and characterisation, with nothing to guide us but our own sensitivity. It is not very difficult to see the problems which such a procedure is likely to set for the critic, and the charges of arbitrariness and misinterpretation to which he can lay himself open. As we shall see, it is around this problem of the critic's response to an author's 'secret signature' that most of the Picard/Barthes controversy will circle.

Having completed his short lecture on the nature of nineteenth-century fiction, Marcel starts to meditate on Albertine herself, his mistress and his prisoner. Is she not also a work of art, a precious object, hoarded by him as Swann had hoarded his Old Masters? The comparison is no sooner made, however, than Marcel realises how little it applies:

But no, Albertine was in no way to me a work of art. I knew what it meant to desire a woman in an artistic fashion, I had known Swann. For my own part, moreover, I was, no matter who the woman might be, incapable of doing so, having no sort of power of detached observation. . . . The pleasure and the pain that I derived from Albertine never took, in order to reach me, the line of taste and intellect; indeed, to tell the truth, when I began to regard Albertine as an angel musician glazed with a marvelous patina whom I congratulated myself upon possessing, it was not long before I found her uninteresting;

> I soon became bored in her company, but these moments were of brief duration . . . we love only what we do not possess, and very soon I returned to the conclusion that I did not possess Albertine. (x 245; III 384–5)

But the contrast between art and woman is misleading. The view of art presented here is not Proust's but Swann's, and it is in relation to his inability to write that Marcel later repeats that he lacks the powers of observation and description. His realisation of the fact that such powers may be of use to the Goncourts but have no place in the kind of art he is about to write, is only an acknowledgement that there is no essential difference between what he looks for (and fails to find) in women, and what he looks for (and succeeds in finding) in art. His approach to Albertine is in fact like his approach to Hardy or Dostoevsky: he seeks their uniqueness, their essence, and to find it he listens patiently for the laws of their being to emerge from the details of plot or conversation or gesture. So that what we have in the quotation is not the contrast between an attitude to art and an attitude to love, but simply two radically opposed views of art and life. The first, Swann's, sees *beauty* as the necessary condition, and must have a prior set of values against which to match the work of art or the woman. It guards the object as a precious possession, to be taken out and contemplated occasionally, or proudly shown to others, and then put away again. The second has *truth* as its condition, and it strives to enter into the otherness of the object, while knowing all the time that it can never fully do so. There is, however, a difference between the woman and the work of art, a difference that will eventually lead Marcel out of his despair over the loss of Albertine to joy in the creation of the work which is to be *A la Recherche du temps perdu*. To hold a woman prisoner is to rob her of her mystery, to destroy the otherness which is what we love in her; yet, as other, she remains eternally elusive. Not so the work of art. It can be made prisoner in the sense that it is put down on paper and hence accessible whenever we desire it; yet it retains its freedom because the work only exists through its specific 'style', which we cannot simply extract from it before throwing away the work. It always requires an imaginative effort on our part if we are to understand it; more than that, it requires that we *re-create* it within ourselves. Thus it is both prisoner and free.

There are important differences between the art that Marcel is going to create and the art that Hardy and Dostoevsky have created, but we will ignore these for the moment and press on with the implications of Marcel's discovery. These are clearly momentous. For if what he says is true then there are clearly two ways in which criticism can fail to come to terms with a work of art. It can first of all remain satisfied with an analysis of the content of art – the psychology of the characters, the moral choices involved in their actions, etc. Or it can ignore the surface and look underneath for the author's 'true' meaning which is to be extracted from the work. But in this case the 'inner' meaning is also seen in terms of content, seen, that is, as a 'thing' to be dug out and removed. Barthes describes this approach in these terms:

> The second [fallacy] consists in interpreting the symbol scientifically by stating on the one hand that the work is open to interpretation (thus accepting its symbolic nature) while on the other hand performing this interpretation by means of literal and unambiguous terms which tie down the infinite metaphor of the work and thus capture its 'truth'. Of this type are the scientifically orientated symbolic critics (sociological or psychological). In both cases it is the arbitrary disparity between the language of the work and of the critic which denies the symbol, since to reduce the symbol is as excessive as to see nothing but the letter.[1]

Both errors result from the belief that there is a prior content which is embodied in the work of art and which it is the job of the critic to extract and present to the public. The two errors are complementary and, as we have had ample occasion to see in the course of this book, both make nonsense of art.

But if the work is seen not as a direct imitation of either an external or an internal reality, but rather as an action or process, a construction and an exploration, which embodies a truth which would otherwise remain ineffable (my unique response to sunlight in water, say), then our whole view of the nature and function of criticism changes. If art is not a means of beautifying nature or of sugaring the pill of moral or metaphysical truth, but an essential and central element in our lives, our sole means of bridging the gap between our senses and our intellect, then

[1] *Critique et vérité* (Paris, 1966) 73.

criticism becomes the study not of the content of art (which is arbitrary and ephemeral), but of the forms which art can take. In this way it ceases to be a parasite on art and becomes a legitimate and important subject of investigation. As Barthes says:

> We possess a history but not a science of literature because, no doubt, we have not been able to recognise clearly the nature of the literary *object*, which is a written object. From the moment that one admits that the work is made with writing (and draws the consequences from that admission), then a *certain* science of literature becomes possible. . . . This cannot be a science of content (which only the strictest historical science can grasp), but a science of the *conditions* of content, that is, a science of forms. Its sphere will be the variations of meaning engendered and *engenderable* by works of art: it will not interpret symbols, but only their polyvalence. In brief, its object will no longer be the 'sens plein' of a work, but on the contrary, the 'sens vide' which makes all meanings possible.[1]

The terms 'sens plein' and 'sens vide' are borrowed by Barthes from structural linguistics, and it is this which provides him with a model for his new science of criticism. The reason for this is that linguistics finds itself seemingly in the same relation to language as criticism does to art:

> Confronted with the impossibility of mastering all the phrases of a language, the linguist decides to set up a *hypothetical model of description*, whereby he can explain how the infinite phrases which make up a language are engendered.[2]

English readers, however, will immediately note the similarity between Barthes's approach and that of Northrop Frye, a similarity all the more striking in that neither appears to have heard of the other. Frye too starts from the position that literature is more than 'simply the name given to the aggregate of existing literary works', since art is a form of displacement of a primary impulse or desire rather than an imitation of the external world. Thus, like Barthes, he feels that it is possible to draw up a grammar of the *forms* of literature, although he takes music, not linguistics, as his model:

[1] Ibid. 56–7.　　[2] Ibid. 57.

In this book we are attempting to outline a few of the grammatical rudiments of literary expression, and the elements of it that correspond to such musical elements as tonality, simple and compound rhythm, canonical imitation and the like. The aim is to give a rational account of some of the structural principles of Western literature in the context of its Classical and Christian heritage. We are suggesting that the resources of verbal expression are limited, if that is the word, by the literary equivalents of rhythm and key, though that does not mean, any more than it means in music, that its resources are artistically exhaustible.[1]

Frye's point of departure, however, is not musical theory but the poetry of William Blake, but this merely emphasises the fact that despite their scientific vocabulary and abstruse references to Russian formalism, structural linguistics and structural anthropology, the French 'new critics' have developed their ideas in response to what is essentially a literary and cultural situation. Like Frye, they are only seeking to draw the full consequences for the study of literature from the discoveries of the Romantics and the revolutionary moderns.

One way of describing the nature of the modernist revolution is to say that in the last hundred years art has come to full consciousness of itself. This is what Frye means when he says that symbolism 'succeeded in isolating the hypothetical germ of literature'. Art has come to see itself no longer simply as a 'donnée', but as the result of deliberate choice. And if art is neither simple expression nor simple imitation, what is it? And how can its making be justified? Since Baudelaire the best French criticism has been concerned with these questions and these alone. For clearly the analysis and evaluation of specific works cannot be carried out with an easy conscience if these questions remain unresolved – once they have entered our consciousness. But these questions, of how art can be justified, are precisely the ones that art itself has asked and attempted to answer. Hence the curious feeling generated by so much French criticism that it is simply another form of literature, no different in kind from what it purports to discuss. Yet the situation is perfectly understandable.

---

[1] *Anatomy of Criticism* (Princeton, 1957) 133.

After all, *Contre Sainte-Beuve* was a decisive step on the road from *Jean Santeuil* to *A la Recherche*. It does, however, lead to a number of very real difficulties.

One of the most interesting of the post-war French critics, Maurice Blanchot,[1] has devoted most of his work to a study of these difficulties, and he is really a much better example of the criticism generated by modernism than either Barthes or any of the other critics cited by Picard in *Nouvelle Critique ou nouvelle imposture*. Blanchot is concerned with the ways in which the 'private signatures' of modern writers have been filtered through the public language; with the special nature of what he calls 'l'éspace littéraire', the space that both is and is not in this world, and which literature creates for itself; with the ways in which the discoveries of Mallarmé and Cézanne have radically altered our attitudes to art; and with all the other questions that follow in the wake of these. A good example of his method is his little essay on writers' journals, where he argues:

> To write every day under the guarantee of that day and to recall it to ourselves is an easy way to escape from silence, as from that which is extreme in any speech. Each day gives us something to say. Each day jotted down is a day preserved. Thus the act has a double advantage, since it allows one to live twice over: one keeps oneself from forgetting and from the despair of having nothing to say.[2]

Anglo-Saxon criticism does not start as far back from the work as this. It takes the work for granted in precisely the way Blanchot is unwilling to do. Brought up in the school of Proust and Kafka, he recognises the bad faith of the diary, and in analysing it he implicitly condemns those countless novels which are in effect nothing else but fictionalised diaries. Like Barthes, he starts with the question all the great modern writers have struggled with: Why write at all? (What justification can there be for my act?) And the works he admires most are naturally those which have been written out of the fullest awareness of the

[1] His early novel, *Aminadab*, greatly impressed Sartre, who was led by it to make some interesting remarks on Kafka. See '*Aminadab* ou du fantastique considéré comme un langage', in *Situations*, 1 (Paris, 1947).

[2] 'Le Journal intime et le récit', in *Le Livre à venir* (Paris, 1959) 226.

implications of such a question, like Beckett's *L'Innomable*, of which he writes:

> Perhaps we are not here in the presence of a book; perhaps, though, we are in the presence of much more than a book: the pure approach to that movement from which all books emerge, that original point where no doubt the work loses itself, and which always ruins the work. . . . The Unnameable is condemned to exhaust infinity.[1]

For who is it who speaks in that work? Beckett? The name is on the title-page, but that is only a convenient convention. The whole of Beckett's effort, culminating in this work perhaps, is directed towards freeing that voice from the shackles of his own personality, Samuel Beckett, an Irishman living in Paris. This is what Blanchot is driving at. His criticism is criticism from the inside, criticism which is aware of the fact that Beckett's real subject-matter is not the garrulousness or impotence of old men or any nonsense about the failure of communication, but an act, a process, the process of freeing that voice which is inside him and yet not him. Since such freedom is unattainable, his work is truly interminable.

Clearly Blanchot's is not traditional literary criticism, as it is practised in the academies and in the market-places of the civilised world. But what is traditional literary criticism to do when faced with a Mallarmé, a Beckett, a Robbe-Grillet? Their work itself is a radical questioning of the premises of all previous literature and hence of the criticism based upon it. For Raymond Picard of the Sorbonne, however, there is simply no problem. The explanation of a work of art, he says, should surely be sought inside it, not outside. This is an admirable sentiment, but what *is* the inside? What at first sounds like plain common sense may turn out to be based on a set of assumptions which are themselves in just as much need of justification as those of Barthes or Blanchot. And it may be that Picard's common-sense approach distorts and falsifies the nature of the work of literature just as much as any other bias. A good example of the way this can happen is to be found in a comment on Proust, not by Picard himself, but by Jean-François Revel, the general editor of the series (significantly

[1] 'Ou maintenant? Qui maintenant?', ibid. 260

entitled 'Libertés') in which the attack on the Nouvelle Critique appeared. Proust, Revel says,

> may have this or that theory at the back of his mind, but he always expresses more than his theories in the narrative itself. And, in fact, the reader always forgets Proust's theories and remembers only the events, the scenes, the characters, and the concrete emotions.[1]

In other words *A la Recherche du temps perdu* is a good yarn with plenty of fine characters and moving scenes, but, unfortunately, rather a lot of dull theorising about life and art in it too. Luckily, however, we can forget the theories and concentrate on the characters and events. One does not need to read far into Proust to see the total ineptitude of such a comment.

The trouble is that the opponents of the Nouvelle Critique operate with an oversimplified scheme of what literature and literary creation actually are. They seem to believe that what is not conscious must be there in the subconscious (I deliberately avoid the Freudian term *un*conscious, with its dynamic implications, and use the purely spatial concept which best renders the thought of Picard and Revel on this matter); that what does not deal with the external world must deal with the author's psyche; that if the 'new critics' are not concerned with the surface content of the work they must be concerned with some sort of hidden content lying underneath the overt subject-matter. Thus Picard winds up his attack by saying that the 'new criticism', by relegating the overt content to a secondary place, does away with the work altogether, and he asks rhetorically: 'How could it be otherwise, since the work is considered in large part as though it were the product of the unconscious?' Finally, with a pompous irony which Barthes is surely justified in comparing to that of Proust's Norpois, he concludes:

> I myself, who love literature, have made up my mind – at least in the present state of our knowledge – to remain satisfied with the conscious meaning. I will be told that this is to limit myself to appearances. But the appearance is the reality even in literature, as it is in painting. To look at a painting only for

[1] *Pourquoi les philosophes?* (Paris, 1957) 99.

the canvas on which the picture is painted is to condemn one-self to see nothing of the painting.[1]

This is the heart of Picard's attack, and it illustrates clearly the source of his misunderstanding. Taking a common-sense view, as he calls it, he argues thus: *either* you see this as a portrait of X *or* you see it as a mere daubs on a canvas behind which it is necessary to go in order to discover the plain surface beneath. But, Barthes would surely answer, I am interested neither in X nor in the canvas, but only in the painting – neither in the subject-matter of the story nor in the writer's subconscious, but only in what the writer has made of his subject, his distinctive 'style'. Thus we see that it is Picard himself who is always reducing art to something else, since his insistence on the primacy of the subject-matter is really the denial of any legitimate sphere for art, a denial of that 'éspace littéraire' on which Barthes and Blanchot so rightly insist and whose topography they see it as their task to try and map.[2]

It should be clear now that Picard confuses the issue by bring-ing the wrong kinds of assumption to bear upon it. Yet it must be admitted that he is not without provocation, and that if the issue is so confused that is largely the fault of Barthes and his fellow-critics, who so overstate their case as to lay themselves open to almost every conceivable objection.

Barthes, as we have seen, rightly insists on the irreducible nature of the work of art: it is 'open' in the sense that we cannot

[1] *Nouvelle critique ou nouvelle imposture* (Paris, 1965) 126–7.

[2] Cf. Proust's discussion of the function of the portrait painter, quoted above, p. 198. It is interesting that the problem of the viewer's attitude to a painting should have arisen again, in recent criticism of Frye. Frye has argued that what he is trying to do is 'stand back' from literature in order to see its total shape instead of individual details. To W. K. Wimsatt this suggests only a blurring of what is unique to each work: 'Who really wants to see a painting that way?' he asks. 'Perhaps a pure neo-Kantian "formalist" in art criticism – a Clive Bell or a Roger Fry. Scarcely a critic who has literary interests in the verbal art of literature.' (*Northrop Frye in Modern Criticism*, ed. Murray Krieger (New York, 1966) 91. The real criticism to be levelled at Frye is not that he is inattentive to detail – he isn't – but that to stand back from a work leads to the annihilation of the element of reading time, of unfolding, which is vital to our experience of literature. See Geoffrey Hartman's essay in the same volume, where this point is well made, and below, Chapter 12.

paraphrase or translate it into discursive terms, but must understand it on its own terms. That is clear enough, a commonplace of symbolist and modernist aesthetics. But Barthes now takes a further step by saying that since the work is irreducible, it is open to *any* interpretation the reader may wish to impose on it:

> A work is 'eternal' not because it imposes a single meaning on different men, but because it suggests different meanings to a single man, speaking the same symbolic language in all ages: the work proposes, man disposes. Every reader who is prepared to resist being intimidated by the letter knows this; does he not sense that he is coming into contact with what lies *beyond* the text, as though the primary language of the work gave rise to other words in him, teaching him a new tongue? That is what we call dreaming.[1]

But to say this is to play right into Picard's hands. For Barthes is giving up precisely the quality of otherness which Proust saw as the real mark of a work of art, and reducing it to a simple mechanism designed to trigger off whatever emotions and memories the reader brings with him. Instead of Marcel, with his patient groping for the author's 'secret signature', we have Swann, treating art no longer as a means of exploring himself and the world but as a form of daydream. Barthes has in fact fallen into the Rimbaudian fallacy of imagining that because a dictionary will not exhaust the meaning of a word in a poem that word can mean anything we want it to. Proust, as we have seen, meant something very different from this when he said that every reader was the reader of himself.[2]

---

[1] Op. cit. 51–2.

[2] John Bayley makes some pertinent comments on the implications of this: 'The idea of the film *L'Immortelle* . . . is that nothing happens except what the viewer wishes to think happens. Fiction thus abdicates its seat, for the only really boring stories are those which we can always tell ourselves, and the only essential paradigm of fiction (. . .) is that it is made up by someone else.' .'Against a New Formalism', in *Word in the Desert*, ed. Cox and Dyson (London, 1968).) Bayley is surely correct in pointing out the fallacy of the *theory* of autonomous art. But he is quite wrong in his belief that the theory fits the facts of a work by Robbe-Grillet, say – though that does not mean that Robbe-Grillet really belongs to Bayley's category of the 'imitative' artist. As we will see in the next chapter, the claim of autonomy is only the prelude to a more vital involvement.

Barthes does not stop here, however. He goes on:

Literature is the exploration of the name: Proust created a complete world out of these sounds: *Guermantes*. At bottom, the writer has always held the belief that signs are not arbitrary and that the name is natural to the thing: writers are of the school of Cratylus, not Hermogenes.[1]

He could hardly have picked a worse example. For if poets and novelists always start with the belief in a natural language, they soon learn – as did Proust and Rimbaud, though with vastly different consequences – that such a belief, if pushed to its logical conclusion, can only lead to silence. In fact one of Proust's major themes is precisely this, that in childhood we do believe that signs are not arbitrary and that therefore direct communication is possible, but that part of a writer's apprenticeship consists in learning the error of this belief. Ironically, Proust shows us that the *only* stable thing about the Guermantes is their name, and it is out of his meditation on the *disjunction* between the name and the person or place that he learns the true function of literature. In this exploration Proust is only playing his personal variation on one of the main themes of modern art, the demarcation of the gap between the word and the thing, the work and the world, with the dangers involved in confusing the two.[2]

Barthes is not even content to rest with this reference to the *Cratylus*. He insists that 'the writer and the critic come together in the same difficult condition, in the face of the same object: language'. And that: 'The book is a world. The critic experiences before the book the same linguistic conditions as does the writer before the world.' This is to exchange Rimbaud for Mallarmé at his most idealistic, to substitute for the belief in a natural language the belief in a book which is the totality of the world. But writer and critic do *not* face the same object. The world and the book are entirely different, since the latter is an artificial, man-made object, the result of multiple choices on the part of its author.

[1] Op. cit. 52.
[2] Since this was written I am pleased to have found a French critic to confirm my views. See the brilliant analysis of Proust's attitude to language by Gérard Genette in *Figures*, ii (Paris, 1969) 223–94, and in his article 'Métonymie chez Proust ou la naissance du récit', in *Poétique*, 2 (1970) 156–73.

Once again we find Barthes reverting to an undiluted Romantic idealism from which Proust and Valéry had been at pains to extract both art and aesthetics (though to put it like that suggests that they had a programme, which of course they hadn't). Barthes continues:

> Classical criticism is based on the naïve belief that the subject is a 'plein' and the relations between subject and language are those of a content to an expression. The recourse to a symbolic language leads, it seems to me, to quite the opposite conclusion: the subject is not an individual plenitude which we may or may not evacuate in the language . . . but, on the contrary, a 'vide' around which the writer weaves a speech that is infinitely transformed . . . in such a way that all writing *which does not lie* points not to attributes within the subject, but to the absence of subject.[1]

Once again Barthes has taken a respectable theory too far. Just as there can never be a wholly natural language, so there can never be a wholly 'empty' work – as even Mallarmé was forced to recognise, and as Barthes himself certainly seems to do in *Le Degré zéro de l'écriture*, where he analyses so well the subterfuges employed by art to negate both subject-matter and the pressures of an alien language.

Nor is this all. Barthes not only insists on a radical division between ordinary discourse and literary discourse; in the end literary discourse becomes synonymous with language itself, so that every statement, whether critical or part of a work of art, is seen to have the same attributes:

> Writing *declares*, and it is in this that it is writing. How could criticism possibly be interrogative, optative, or dubitative, without bad faith, since it is writing, and that to write is precisely to encounter the apophantic risk, the ineluctable alternative of the true/false?[2]

Though this sounds a good deal worse in English than it does in French, the translation is still a fair indication, unfortunately, of Barthes's style and mode of thought, and what he says here is of course the logical outcome of his intransigent position. But, be-

[1] Op. cit. 70.   [2] Ibid. 78.

lieving in such a hypothesis, has he any right to enter into argument with Picard or anyone else? He has in fact no option but to retire, like Rimbaud or the Wittgenstein of the *Tractatus*, into total silence.

Barthes's excesses do nothing, however, to justify Picard's common-sense approach. The question we must ask is whether these excesses are an inherent part of the kind of criticism Barthes or Blanchot practise, or whether they are a personal aberration. It is easy to feel that Barthes is wrong when he becomes extreme, less easy to see how to correct him without falling into the trap of a Picardian type of criticism. For there is no doubt that we face a real methodological problem here: once we leave the safe shores of description and comment on a work's overt content, how are we to guide ourselves in the sea of subjective interpretation? This is a familiar dilemma; in fact most of the authors discussed in these pages have made their art out of the attempt to resolve just this problem. But the critic, we said, *pace* Barthes, faces not the world but a book, or a series of books. Does this make his problem any easier, or any different?

Let us take a brief example of Barthian criticism and see whether an analysis of it can help us. In his first book, *Le Degré zéro de l'écriture*, Barthes describes Camus's *L'Étranger* as 'la façon d'exister d'un silence'. This must I suppose be translated in some such fashion as 'the mode of existence of a silence', or 'the way of existing of a silence'. Neither way does this seem to make much sense. What can Barthes mean by the phrase? Surely, Picard will say, the novel is about a crime and a trial. Or perhaps about a certain type of man. There is nothing whatever in it about silence. Meursault, it is true, is somewhat taciturn, but that cannot be what the phrase is referring to. And how, anyway, can a silence be said to exist? Why should a writer bother with silence, since he presumably writes because he wants to say something? And how on earth does a critic read a novel for him to come up with this kind of statement?

We, however, should be a little more in tune with Barthes than this by now. He has been arguing in his book that since language is the medium of the writer he is forced to use a tool which is heavy with social and political associations, with the weight of tradition, and which therefore inevitably takes on meanings which the writer not only may not desire, but of which he is probably not even aware. What he 'says' is therefore only to a very limited extent what *he* says, and it is to a great extent what the language says. The writer of fiction, moreover, through such things as his quasi-automatic choice of narrative tense, the *passé simple*, unconsciously provides reassurance for his readers (and for himself) since he presents them with a world which is both familiar and close, and yet infinitely far, since it is past, concluded, done with: 'The finality common to both the Novel and narrated History, is the alienation of events: the *passé simple* is society's act of possession of its past and of what is possible to it.' Thus however much a writer tries to be true to his experience, *l'écriture*, the act of writing, which is monologue not dialogue, implies that his work will always be a distortion and falsification of experience, the result of what one might almost call the will to embalm. Barthes is here only drawing out the consequences of what Sartre had said about the way life gets falsified in the telling in *La Nausée*. In his comment on *L'Étranger*, too, he is also clearly referring to the peculiar style of that work, so brilliantly analysed by Sartre in an early essay. It is a style which, by making use of the *passé composé* rather than the *passé simple*, succeeds in conveying a sense of complete neutrality, breaking up the narrative into tiny discrete units which seem to exist independently, and giving the whole work the sense of floating free of author and reader, of consciousness itself. All this is suggested by that little phrase of Barthes's and anyone who has noted how Camus struggled in his journals to get the opening sentence right and how, once he had hit on the right tense and tone, the whole novel seemed more or less to write itself, must feel that there is a great deal of truth in it.

But it remains a puzzling phrase. Barthes is clearly not limiting himself to talking about the style of *L'Étranger*. Or rather, what he says about its mode of presentation seems to take in all the other aspects of the book. Picard might well admit that he's got a point about the style, but still feel puzzled that he should say that this *is* what *L'Étranger* is about. The phrase is puzzling because it is clearly different *in kind* from some such judgement as the following: 'Meursault really loves his mother more than his accusers could ever love theirs, despite their condemnation of him for not loving her at all.' This sort of statement can be defended by looking at the way Meursault's character is presented in the book. We may note the opening paragraph, for instance, with its contrast between Meursault's own way of thinking about his mother – 'Aujourd'hui maman est morte' – with the impersonal telegram he receives: 'Mère décédée. Enterrement demain. Sentiments distingués.' We may note the way in which Camus builds up sympathy for Meursault by showing that his accusers are simply taking for granted the clichés of social behaviour – such as that one must cry at one's mother's funeral or tell the girl one enjoys sleeping with that one loves her – while Meursault, out of respect for the truth and for other people, is unwilling ever to use words whose connotations he doesn't understand, like 'love' or 'duty'.[1] In all these ways we could defend a remark like the above and feel that we were saying something about the novel. But Barthes's phrase cannot be treated in this way. Like Blanchot's remark about Beckett's *L'Innomable*, it seems to act as a directive rather than an observation. It tells us that the 'real' meaning of the novel lies not in anything it describes but in its relation to the author: it is 'a way of making silence exist' or a way of seeing to it that silence exists, just as Beckett's work is 'the pure *approach* to the movement from which all books come'.

One is tempted to say, I think, that the statement: 'Meursault really loves his mother, etc.' is a statement of *fact* whereas Barthes's cryptic comment is really saying something like: 'Look at it my way and you'll see that the work makes more sense.' But that is not quite the answer. After all, as we have had ample occasion to note, no series of words is ever entirely unambiguous. Since language is not literal but conventional, all statements require interpretation, and unless there is some way of verifying them there is always the possibility of being wrong. And of course there is no way of verifying the kind of psychological criticism of Meursault which I have used as an example, since he is a fictional creation. It would in fact be quite possible for someone else to 'read' the character in a very different way. He could say that Meursault was really a vicious and heartless man who was quite rightly condemned to death for the brutal murder of an Arab who had done him no harm. It would be impossible to prove that this view of Meursault was wrong and the one I first put forward was

[1] Meursault in fact carries out perfectly the recommendations made by Wittgenstein at the close of the *Tractatus*. See Chapter 12 below.

right, though one or other interpretation might appear to correspond better with all the other elements in the novel and with
what we know of Camus's own intentions at the time. All criticism, in fact, is to some extent a directive, with the critic simply
asking the reader to 'look at it my way'.

There is no doubt though that Barthes's comment on *L'Étranger*
has a very different ring about it from any of the above statements. Are we dealing perhaps with a difference between attitudes
to the work's meaning and to its significance? An example of the
latter would be Blake's famous remark about Milton in *Paradise
Lost* being of the devil's party without knowing it, which is a
fascinating comment on the poem but not the same thing as an
analysis of its meaning.[1] But though this is a plausible suggestion,
we quickly see that it doesn't fit the facts. Barthes is not evalu-
ating the work in relation to some completely different set of
criteria from the ones Camus was using; his comment seems to
draw meaning out of the text and to make us see it as a unity
rather than as something in conflict with itself. A real parallel to
Blake's comment would be this sort of thing: 'Despite Camus's
known sympathies, the colonialist mentality was something too
deeply embedded in him to be shaken off, and this emerges in
L'Étranger, which is really a novel in support of colonialism.'
This remark clearly springs from the critic's own political beliefs,
and it uses the novel in support of a general indictment of Camus.
But Barthes, we can see, has no position from which he operates,
in this sense. He would agree wholeheartedly with Frye's remark
that 'One's "definite position" is one's weakness, the source of
one's liability to error and prejudice, and to gain adherents to a
definite position is only to multiply one's weakness like an infec-
tion.'

What then (for the last time) are we to make of the phrase: 'la
façon d'exister d'un silence'? It suggests first of all that the surface, the 'story', must not simply be looked at as the repository
of psychological and metaphysical truths. But it suggests too that
the 'story' is a vital element, since without it the silence would
not exist. Is there anything in the novel itself, apart from the style,
which reinforces such a point of view? I think there is. The clue
lies in what was said earlier about there being at least two ways of
'reading' Meursault's character. Now the really interesting fact

[1] See the discussion in Hirsch, *Validity in Interpretation*, 139 ff.

about the novel is that we are shown there that *both* ways of seeing Meursault are possible. And this suggests that perhaps Camus is not so much asking us to adjudicate between rival possibilities as drawing our attention to what it is that gives rise to diverse interpretations. In other words it is not asked of us that we make up our minds but that we grasp why people make up *their* minds in certain ways. In a similar way the question: 'Did Meursault really intend to kill the Arab?' is not so much one to which the novel provides an answer but one to whose implications the novel alerts us. For what does the question mean? What *is* intention? What is the relation between motive and deed, word and action? It is not asked of us that we take sides – Meursault has clearly killed the Arab, but on the other hand there is not the simple correlation between motive and deed that the prosecution try to make out – but that we understand what is at issue.

Camus, as Sartre noted, presents us in this novel first with life 'as it is lived' and then with life 'as it is told'. When Marie cries, during the trial: 'It didn't happen like that at all', we find ourselves in an unusual position as readers of fiction, since we are in a position both to agree with her and to recognise that nothing that can happen will alter the attitude of the law. For it is not the case, as it might be in a thriller, that the whole thing happened in 'quite a different way', and that, if there is sufficient corroboration for Marie, her account of the events will be seen to be the true one. The two accounts are not symmetrical, for that of the prosecution only differs from 'reality' by virtue of the fact that it is a retelling, and that in the retelling life gets subtly altered. As soon as we start to tell a story we make connections where before there were none, and in this case the connections link Meursault very directly with the death of another man. In the eyes of the law therefore he is guilty.

But how does Camus manage to present us with life 'as it happens' in the first part of the novel? Only through the creation of a man, Meursault, whose own life has no pattern, who never connects, thinks back, plans or pieces together. Meursault tells his story in the *passé composé* and not the *passé simple* because his life *is* a set of discrete moments, each one lived entirely for itself and none linked to any other. At his trial, therefore, he cannot defend himself, because he is not aware that he has done anything wrong, since doing wrong implies a degree of self-awareness:

'L'innocent', Camus wrote in his journals, 'est celui qui n'explique pas.' Meursault is innocent because for him there is nothing to explain. And yet, clearly, he has killed the Arab. For, as Camus also said: 'Nous sommes tous un peu coupables.' No man is wholly innocent because to be human means to be involved with others, means, therefore, taking part in a social game in which it is impossible not to have bad faith. Meursault tries to resist this bad faith, which is inherent in language, refusing to say 'I love you' to Marie simply because she expects him to, since he does not know what he feels or if what he feels corresponds to the word 'love'. And by refusing to accept the conventions of society Meursault shows them up as the hollow things they are. Yet his murder of the Arab does involve him, against his will, in the world of men. He had refused to say 'I love you' to Marie because he could see no link between the word and his feeling; there is as little relation between his feeling and the dead Arab, yet it is he who has killed him. And it is perhaps to expiate the arbitrary and unnecessary death of the Arab that Meursault seeks for himself, at the end, a death that is wholly willed and necessary.

We may feel that at the close of the book Camus himself breaks his own precept, that, trying to *explain* that Meursault is innocent, he himself becomes guilty, guilty of explaining. But this very weakness of the book should bring home to us even more clearly the relation between Camus's own endeavour and that of Meursault. Barthes's comment, cryptic at first glance, can now be seen as not only different in kind from that of the psychological critic, but also better in that it seems to be called for by the book itself. Criticism of the story in and for itself fails to make the connection between the style (Camus's and Meursault's) and the murder, and thus fails to reveal the necessity of the book. Barthes, on the other hand, because he is aware of writing itself as something problematic, and is aware too of the relations between the forms of the traditional novel and the structure of society, is in a position to show us the kind of choice available to Camus and the necessity for the choices he has in fact made.

When we have said all this, however, the problem still remains. Barthes's criticism may work with *L'Étranger* but there is something about it that will go on disturbing the common-sense reader. We feel that we cannot argue with him as we might with a psychological critic, that he asks us to accept his premises and we then either do, and agree with him, or don't, and feel him slipping away from us. When we say that the 'real' theme of Butor's *La Modification* is not whether or not a man will leave his wife, but the modification of consciousness itself; that the 'real' theme of *Le Voyeur* is not whether or not Mathieu killed the girl but the destruction of the anecdote by means of objects; that the 'real' theme of Keats's 'Hyperion' is not the defeat of the Titans but the poet's attempt to grasp the nature of the imagination – when we say these things we seem to be leaving the solid ground of facts and people and talking a language which appears at first sight to have nothing to do with literature at all. By what criteria do we make these judgements? What sort of evidence do we require to change our minds? And are we not in danger of foisting our own private concerns upon these works and then proudly announcing that they form the 'real' or 'essential' themes?

Such questions would clearly not worry Barthes. After all, if literature gives us the licence to daydream then anything would seem to be allowed. (Picard would surely agree with him in this description of his own activity although he would attach a rather different value to the notion of daydream.) But there is no doubt that there is a genuine problem of method here, and it is one that is not confined to literature or even to art. It is no coincidence that Picard's critique of Barthes should have been published in a series whose general editor, Revel, has himself written a number of polemical works attacking the major culture-heroes of present-day France: Sartre, Lévi-Strauss, Merleau-Ponty, etc. These polemics are all delivered, interestingly enough, in the name of an eighteenth-century scepticism and empiricism that will have a familiar ring to English ears. Hume and Diderot are constantly invoked, and it is always their common-sense debunking of the pretensions of enthusiasts that is stressed. *Nouvelle Critique ou nouvelle imposture* even carries this epigraph from Beaumarchais:

In this way have all the absurdities of the world gained a footing, thrust to the front by audacity ... adopted by idleness, confirmed by repetition, fortified by enthusiasm; but reduced to nothingness by the first thinker to take the trouble to examine them.

Picard and Revel clearly see themselves as the upholders of Enlightenment in the face of a horde of enthusiasts, whose anti-rationalism is likely to have disastrous consequences not just for literature or philosophy or anthropology, but for civilisation as a whole. And they are of course right to see in Barthes and Lévi-Strauss the descendants of the Romantics, and to discern in their guiding ideas some of the elements which, in another context, might easily lead to dangerous totalitarian ideologies. For there is no fundamental difference between Hegel's attempt to uncover the structure of history beneath individual historical events, Freud's attempt to reveal the structure of repression and desire beneath the individual incidents which make up the history of a person, and Barthes's attempts to reveal the structure of a novel beneath the individual incidents that make up the plot. In all three cases the basic premise is a rejection of the notion of a transcendental cause, standing outside the subject examined and directing its course, *combined with* an affirmation of the unity and meaningfulness of the subject. Thus in all three we have the idea of a secret history or of a secret signature, discoverable only in the concrete events and yet not to be identified with them, but which, once found, will make sense of what would otherwise remain a series of disparate elements only fortuitously connected. And in all three cases the rejection of transcendentalism implies the rejection of all external criteria and causes the positivist to throw up his hands in despair and say: 'But what do I have to *do* to show this man – Hegel or Freud or Barthes – that *in this case* he is wrong?'

Yet, as Barthes is quick to point out, the Enlightenment attitude is no more *natural* than his own. There is all the difference in the world between wishing that there were objective criteria to use in such cases, and imagining that common sense provides them. For the Enlightenment attitude itself stands in as much need of justification (and is just as incapable of providing it) as his own. It too can be seen to be the product of a specific society and specific ideologies. To take as one's criteria the norms of objec-tivity, taste and clarity, Barthes argues, is to plead covertly for a return to a rigidly hierarchical universe where such norms *appear* to be inherent in nature. But such a turning back is no longer possible. The French Revolution and Romanticism put paid once and for all to the idea of total objectivity (we have seen in Chapter

2 how Luther struck the first blow). As Bellow's Herzog noted with sadness, we cannot get round Rousseau's statement that 'Je sens mon cœur et je connais les hommes.' For better or worse we live in a world where value is no longer absolute, and where our only criterion remains the fallible and self-deceiving heart.

All this is commonplace. It has been endlessly repeated from the time of Nietzsche onwards. The important point to grasp here is that any genuine debate between Picard and Barthes can clearly be seen to be out of the question, because they are not really arguing for different views of the same problem. Where Picard takes the work of literature for granted and feels that criticism should devote itself to an elucidation of what is in front of it, Barthes feels that this taking for granted is *already* a choice of attitude, since he wants to cast doubt on the whole concept of literature. And there is nothing Picard can reply to this. The Enlightenment may provide a good stick with which to beat the aberrations of Romanticism, but it remains a stick and not a solution. Nor is the problem removed by pointing to a factual error here, a failure of observation there, on the part of a Hegel, a Freud, a Lévi-Strauss, a Barthes. To imagine that this destroys the theoretical premise on which they are building is to misunderstand completely the nature of the problems involved, and thus, in the end, to do a greater disservice to the cause of rationality and common sense. For Piggy, we must not forget, was Jack's first victim.

What neither Picard nor Revel seems to realise is that to accuse a person of being subjective in his judgements or interpretations does not necessarily mean that what he says bears no relation whatever to external reality. Barthes, it is true, frequently seems to think in the same absolutist way, but the Proustian example should save us from that mistake. There is a wide spectrum between total subjectivity and total objectivity. A related error occurs when, Barthes having claimed in his book on Racine to be trying to write 'une sorte d'anthropologie racinienne', to be trying to describe *homo racinianus*, Picard laughingly calls this a purely abstract concept and insists that there are only individual Racinian heroes. But Barthes is not, like an eighteenth-century painter, trying to establish a composite portrait of the *ideal* Racinian hero, with the nose of Thesée, the chin of Britannicus and the eyes of Bajazet; rather, like Henry Moore or Giacometti, he is trying to cut down through the soft flesh to the essential bone structure underneath. Such an undertaking, it is true, calls for the kind of sympathy with individual artists which Proust had in abundance, but which a more abstract and theoretically inclined critic like Barthes sometimes seems to lack. Nevertheless, to ignore the very real problems with which he is struggling and condemn his theories at large is not common sense but bigotry.

If Barthes, then, is the victim of a Romantic idealism, Picard is certainly the victim of a rationalist positivism; they match each other perfectly and neither can make any sense of the other. Yet much can be learnt from their quarrel.

First of all it brings to our attention the presence of a real problem of method raised by the Romantic rejection of transcendental authority, and shows us the implications of this for literary criticism. But is this an issue which affects *all* literature or only post-Romantic literature? This is a question that is clearly of vital importance, yet it is one which has not been touched on by either party, and for obvious reasons. The controversy between Barthes and Picard was sparked off by the latter's slashing review of the former's book on Racine, and since then Racine has figured prominently in the argument of both sides. It does not seem to have occurred to either that the critical problems presented by modern writers might be rather different from those presented by Racine, mainly because both of them wish to make their claims as absolute as possible: common sense and public opinion on the one hand, the irreducibility of the word, the symbol, on the other. Proust, for one, was more modest, or more sensitive. In his examples it is significant that he chose only nineteenth-century authors, explicitly stating elsewhere that it was a characteristic of the nineteenth century to produce only incomplete works of art, works, that is, which need to be seen in the context of the author's whole output rather than in that of a specific genre or by themselves. In saying what he did about Hardy and Dostoevsky, then, he was making a historical point as well as a theoretical one: this kind of approach for *this* kind of book. And surely Proust is right, just as Picard is right when he argues that to understand Racine properly we must learn how certain key words which he uses were employed in his day and must master the laws of the different genres in which he worked. For it is a characteristic of Romanticism that a rejection of genre goes hand in hand with an attempt on the part of poets to free words of their everyday associations and mould them to their own private uses. Thus, when an eighteenth-century poet uses the word 'wit' for example, we need to make a historical effort of the imagination and learn the different connotations of the word in his day, whereas when Wordsworth uses the word 'power' or Keats the word 'beauty' it will not help us to discover how Byron or Shelley or the *Edinburgh Review* use them; what we need to do is to find out how Wordsworth and Keats use the words in the rest of their work. And the same is true of genre, whose public dimension requires us to look outwards from the poem to the tradition before moving back into the poem, and which really ceases to operate with Romantic poetry. Thus the kind of approach that is called for by Wordsworth or Hopkins or Dostoevsky or Proust or Beckett is clearly very different from that called for by Racine or Milton. Before we can learn to listen to the 'private signatures' of the latter we need to master a whole world of public discourse, and this we can only do with the help of scholars who have devoted themselves to the period and the subject. In England and America the errors of the 'new criticism' – a very different affair from the French – have today made most people aware of this simple fact, but in France, where academic criticism has remained in the mould of nineteenth-century scholarship, the perils are clearly not so evident. It is unfortunate, though, that the debate should have centred on Racine, since it has allowed Picard to score some easy points and appeared to justify his general condemnation of Barthes's position.

It has also had the effect of leaving the historical problem out of account altogether, and presenting the debate in purely general and theoretical terms. But clearly the historical problem is a central one. For if there is a difference between kinds of literature, some of which would seem to be more amenable to the Nouvelle Critique than others, then our earlier comparison of the work of art with the history of mankind or the history of an individual person breaks down. For it suggests that certain kinds of art at least are created in a highly conscious and public way, and that we cannot therefore ignore this public dimension in our search for 'secret signatures'. Hardy and Dostoevsky, yes, but what of Spenser or Ronsard? We simply cannot treat art as we would history or a psychological case-history. Freud was aware of this, and even in a reductive work like his 'Leonardo' essay he makes it clear that the working out of the painter's fantasies in a public medium altered their nature.

And this brings us to the second point. A great deal of Barthes's confusion seems to arise from the fact that although he has a clear conception of a literary language, he has none of the literary work. Now it is easy to see that Picard's insistence on 'simply looking at what the work says' is open to all sorts of objections. No work ever 'says' anything by itself, and already in the sixteenth century men were becoming aware of the fact that it is easy to talk of a literal reading of the Bible but rather less easy to put this into practice. Since all reading is a matter of interpretation we need certain criteria for reading any work, but where to find these is the question. Once again Proust showed a certain sound-ness of judgement in both taking the author as his unit and sticking to nineteenth-century examples. But Barthes, at any rate in his later writing, seems to jettison the notion of both author and work. For him there is only literary language, and the work of art is seen only as a field of possibilities. But, as we have seen in the course of this book, modern art is vitally concerned to show that it is *art* and not reality, and to draw attention to itself as an artifact. If we have said that the critic standing before the work of art is in a totally different position from the artist standing before the world, our claim has rested on the modern works them-selves, which continually call upon us to recognise the difference. In this, as we have seen, modern art has affinities with the more formal art of the past. But what exactly do these affinities consist in? How does modern art relate to pre-Romantic art? How does it relate to nineteenth-century art? Above all, what is the relation-ship between the writer and his work, and between the work and the world? For Picard all art can be discussed in the same terms, in terms of surfaces, plots, 'what the work says'. For him the relationship between the writer and his work is a direct one: the writer says what he wants to say and the reader's task is to under-stand what this is. For Barthes too all art can be discussed in the same terms, in terms of 'empty' structures clearly visible through the 'fullness', the content. For him there is no relationship at all between the writer and his work, and the work makes no claim on the reader. Both views fail to account for the characteristic note of modern art, which is the sense of tension that exists between the subject and its annihilation, the work's freedom and its bondage, the artist's words and his despair of words. It is with this tension that my concluding chapter will be concerned.

12 The World and the Book

'Yet the absence of imagination had
Itself to be imagined.'
                    Wallace Stevens

It is sometimes said by literary people that the novel is dead. What they mean by this is that the form has run itself into the ground or is somehow no longer relevant to the present age. This of course is nonsense. The novel is the most natural form of literature that exists. Unlike the epic, which was the product of a closed group and required long training and a complete immersion in the traditions of the group for its effective production and assimilation, the novel asks for only a minimal literacy and an abundance of solitude and leisure. Since modern society seems likely to go on providing its members with all three requirements for as long as it is possible to foresee, no one need be unduly concerned about the decease of the novel. It will be there to comfort the lonely and fill in the empty hours of us all for a long time to come.

The novel is the most natural literary form because in a sense it has no form; it is the nearest thing to a conversation, whether between friends or acquaintances. Provided it keeps within the very flexible limits of verisimilitude, it is entirely free to do what it pleases, to move in any direction it wants. The novelist can invent at will, bringing characters together in the most unlikely coincidences, killing off the unwanted and revealing new complications in the plot whenever the tension appears to be flagging. As Leonardo said of the painter, the novelist is truly a God, with a God's powers and a God's freedom. If he exercises these with skill the reader will feel satisfied: his spare time will have been effectively used up and he can return refreshed to the labours of his daily life. As one would expect, the detective story is the most popular form of fiction, for it reveals the quintessence of fiction.

For some writers, however, this freedom has been a source not of pleasure but of irritation and anxiety. For if I can really say *anything* (provided I account for it in some vaguely plausible

way) then what is the point of my saying anything? Why should
I spend time and energy shut up in a room by myself, making up
a story, if all the time I could just as well be making up a hundred
totally different stories, or if I could at any moment alter the
direction of the one I am engaged upon? It may of course be
that I do this in order to earn my living, but then what I write
will only acquire significance through the pleasures it allows me
to indulge in my spare time. If, however, writing is a need, something which fills up my spare time and for which I am prepared
to give up other pleasures, then the problem of justification becomes all the more pressing. And the reader of course is in a
similar position, asking perhaps why he should continue with *this*
particular book when the story it tells could just as well be told
completely differently, or could even be replaced by another
story altogether. Normally we shut such questions out of our
consciousness, but the need to find answers to them was what led
Proust to hesitate so long over the subject of his novel, and led
to the perpetual self-doubts of Kafka. Indeed, modern art could
be said to spring out of the artist's struggle to come to terms with
these questions.

By and large they do not seem to have worried nineteenth-
century novelists. For this reason their works often strike us as
being akin to the characters who fill the pages of Proust's novel:
supremely voluble, they are nevertheless blind to the sources of
their own volubility. It is left to Marcel to discern these sources –
in a Charlus, a Mme Verdurin, a Hardy, a Dostoevsky – listening
patiently, but with every sense on the alert, for the secret signatures which will gradually work their way free of the torrent of
words and gestures. Proust's novel, in fact, shows us just how
natural the traditional novel is as a form of literature. It is the
literature of the normal man, who, however much he may
occasionally revolt from the values of his society, is never in any
doubt that value exists, and that it can be found. And when the
normal man, alone in his room in the early hours of the morning,
begins to have doubts about such things, he must also begin to
have doubts about the novel. Where, he will ask, is the meaning
of my life? Does my life have a meaning? What must I do to give
my life necessity, to get off that patch of ice on which I seem to
be slithering towards my death faster than I can understand.

Such questions are destructive not just of normal life but of any form of life. They are the first signs of rebellion against the veiy fact of consciousness, and they lead logically towards madness and death. In art such a rebellion naturally takes the form of a revolt against the restrictions of language, which comes to be seen as a screen keeping reality at bay. But (and this is the Romantic dilemma) to destroy language is to give oneself up to silence, another form of death. Thus there would appear to be no middle ground between the life of habit and normality, which cannot really be considered living at all, and the life of truth and necessity, which turns out to mean not life but death. No middle ground, we could say, exists between the nineteenth-century realist novel and the poetry of extreme Romanticism.

Mann's *Death in Venice* is the classic description of the conflict. It shows the metamorphosis of a 'traditional novelist' into a Romantic poet, of a normal man into a neurotic, and it ends in the silence of self-destruction. But what is often forgotten is that Mann is not Aschenbach. He is not completely distinct from him (or he would in fact be like the Aschenbach of the opening pages, with his classicist's ability to create character and plot to suit some prior ideal), but he cannot be completely identified with him either. The reason is that Mann is, whereas Aschenbach isn't, able to write the story of Aschenbach's final descent into silence and death. For Mann himself *the end is not silence but the articulation of silence*. In this he is at one with Proust and Kafka, Nabokov and Golding and Robbe-Grillet: in the course of each of their works we are made to move from the content of the fiction to the maker of the book, and to recognise that the final meaning of the work is one which it is itself powerless to say, and this is *that it has been made*.

But we must be careful that we understand the precise meaning of this. We are not talking here of the biographical import of a work of art, the relation of a work to a specific person, Thomas Mann, Kafka, Proust. That is fairly obvious. On the other hand, does not this act of calling attention to itself as a made object seem characteristic of most older forms of art? Is it not precisely the function of genre and convention in *The Aeneid* or 'Lycidas' or Pope's *Essay on Man* to warn the reader of the rules according to which the work is composed and to direct him as to how he should respond? Genre and convention free the writer from the whims of his private impulses and allow him to draw on the funds of a long tradition even if he inverts or distorts the tradition in the process. But if this is the case then we may be tempted to argue that it is not modern literature which is in any way unusual, but nineteenth-century literature, which moves towards the two poles of extreme objectivity (Zola) and extreme subjectivity (Rimbaud), in both cases attempting to deny or ignore the fact that art is not primarily imitation but the making of things. Modern literature would then be seen as reverting to an older and truer view of the aims and possibilities of art.

Such, at any rate, would seem to be the view of Northrop Frye, who, more than anyone else, has helped to bring us back to an understanding of the role of literary convention and tradition. 'Sixty years ago,' writes Frye, 'Bernard Shaw stressed the social significance of the themes of Ibsen's plays and his own. Today Mr Eliot calls our attention to the Alcestis archetype in *The Cocktail Party*, to the Ion archetype in *The Confidential Clerk*. The former is of the age of Manet and Degas; the latter of the age of Braque and Graham Sutherland.' And again, in the same vein:

> The age that has produced the hell of Rimbaud and the angels of Rilke, Kafka's castle and James' ivory tower, the spirals of Yeats and the hermaphrodites of Proust, the intricate dying-god symbolism attached to Christ in Eliot and the exhaustive treatment of Old Testament myths in Mann's study of Joseph, is once again a great mythopoeic age.[1]

Although Frye is undoubtedly right to stress this aspect of modernism and to insist on the difference between it and the naturalism of the nineteenth century, I think we instinctively feel that there is something wrong with his formulation. Of course the moderns do make use of what Frye calls myths, but their attitude to them seems radically different from those of earlier writers. Blake and Shelley employ myth differently from Spenser or Milton, and it might be argued that Eliot and Mann and Proust and Kafka simply perform further variations on the same basic themes. But this would not really get to the root of the matter. Modern writers seem to be drawn to myth more by a sense of its alienness than its naturalness; and they seem less concerned to create or exploit myth than to understand its nature and the ways it relates to themselves. The reasons for this should have

[1] *Fearful Symmetry* (Princeton, 1958) 423.

been clear to Frye, whose own work, as he admits, springs from the same source as does modernism itself. Nonetheless, his failure to see is itself of particular interest.

Like the French structuralists, Frye is aware of the fact that the implicit belief in literature as the imitation of life is the product of certain nineteenth-century attitudes. Our distrust of convention, he says, is part of 'the tendency, marked from Romantic times on, to think of the individual as ideally prior to society'. But to think in this way is to confuse the discursive writer and the poet. The former has a message to convey, but 'the poet, who writes creatively rather than deliberately, is not the father of his poem; he is at best a midwife, or, more accurately, the womb of Mother Nature herself: her privates he, so to speak'. The true father 'or shaping spirit of the poem is the form of the poem itself, and this form is a manifestation of the universal spirit of poetry'. What creates poetry is not the wish to reproduce a portion of the visible world, but *desire*, which is 'an impulse towards expression, which would have remained amorphous if the poem had not liberated it by providing the form of its expression'. Literature can thus be classified according to how directly desire expresses itself. At one pole is the undiluted desire of myth, Frye argues, and at the other the extreme verisimilitude of a Zola novel. Literature moves between these two poles according to the principle of displacement or accommodation:

> In myth we see the structural principles of literature isolated; in realism we see the *same* structural principles (not similar ones) fitting into a context of plausibility. . . . The presence of a mythical structure in realistic fiction, however, poses certain technical problems for making it plausible, and the devices used in solving these problems may be given the general name of *displacement*.[1]

Anatomy of Criticism thus sets out to sketch 'a few of the grammatical rudiments of literary expression', that is, to provide what one might call a generative grammar of literary expression according to the laws of displacement.

This notion of displacement is of course central to Freud's work, its classic formulation occurring as early as the *Three Essays on Sexuality* of 1905. But it is also, as we have seen, central to

[1] *Anatomy of Criticism*, 136.

Proust. Marcel's discovery of the laws governing his own life, as we saw, led him to observe bitterly that 'just because we are furiously pursuing a dream in a succession of individuals, our loves for people cannot fail to be more or less of an aberration'. We never love people for themselves, Freud and Proust argue, but only as resting places for that dream which we spend our lives secretly trying to recapture. But to note the parallels between this view and Frye's is immediately to see the differences. Both Proust and Freud recognise the ambiguity of displacement and its terrifying implications. For them it is the final proof of each man's isolation, since it implies that I can never see the world as other than I wish it to be. Once we have recognised the laws of displacement, moreover, we can no longer live and love with the same innocence, the same ease. We know that this woman or that country only seem to satisfy us because they seem to incarnate that for which we have always longed and often suspected we had found. For Frye, on the other hand, displacement is a simple matter of fact. He notes its presence but fails to see its implications. He does not see that once displacement is recognised it becomes impossible for the writer (as for the man) to ignore it. He cannot go on adding yet more items to the tradition, just as he cannot simply fall in love with yet one more woman. Where Frye is perfectly happy to reiterate Shelley's remark that all literature is 'that one great poem, which all poets, like the co-operating thoughts of one great mind, have built up since the beginning of the world', a writer like Kafka or Eliot feels himself forced to ask: 'But how do *I* relate to this great poem?' Sainte-Beuve may have been wrong to try and relate a man's work directly to his life, but it would be equally wrong to imagine that there is *no* relation between the two. For, quite simply, if everything I write belongs to the 'one great mind' then what is the point of my writing at all? And if all desire is transmuted into one public form or another, then how can I express what *I* have uniquely felt and seen?

Two possibilities seem to be open to the writer: either he can go on adding yet more items to the body of literature and ignore the problem altogether; or he can give up writing altogether. The modern writer does neither. Instead, he makes his art out of the exploration of the relation between his unique life and the body of literature, his book and the world. In a wonderful parable

Borges has summed up many of the essential features of this relationship. It is called 'Borges and I':

> The other one, the one called Borges, is the one things happen to. I walk through the streets of Buenos Aires and stop for a moment, perhaps mechanically now, to look at the arch of an entrance hall and the grillwork on the gate; I know of Borges from the mail and see his name on a list of professors or in a biographical dictionary. . . . It would be an exaggeration to say that ours is a hostile relationship; I live, let myself go on living, so that Borges may contrive his literature, and this literature justifies me. It is no effort for me to confess that he has achieved some valid pages, but those pages cannot save me, perhaps because what is good belongs to no-one, not even to him, but rather to the language and to tradition. Besides, I am destined to perish, definitively, and only some instant of myself can survive in him. Little by little I am giving over everything to him, though I am quite aware of his perverse custom of falsifying and magnifying things. . . . I shall remain in Borges, not in myself (if it is true that I am someone), but I recognise myself less in his books than in many others or in the laborious strumming of a guitar. Years ago I tried to free myself from him and went from the mythologies of the suburbs to the games with time and infinity, but these games belong to Borges now and I shall have to imagine other things. Thus my life is a flight and I lose everything and everything belongs to oblivion, or to him.
> I do not know which of us has written this page.[1]

Although this is even more condensed than most of Borges's work, its theme is the same. 'Borges and I' is not an aside, a meditation on his art: it *is* that art. But an art of a special kind, of course, one that deals not with an invented anecdote, but with the relation between all anecdotes and that desire which is the impulse behind them, between that desire and the person in whom it finds itself, and who in this case happens to be Argentinian, an ex-librarian, and a lover of books. It is typical of this kind of writing that the last sentence sets us off again, rereading the entire parable, and that at the end of this second reading the last sentence will once again set us off for a third time; for the subject of the page is the writing of the page.

[1] In *Labyrinths*, trans. *J. E. Irby* (New Directions, New York, 1964).

The notion of displacement which Frye uses is based on the distinction between possibility and actuality. This distinction has of course been at the heart of modern developments not just in the arts but in a whole range of disciplines from linguistics to logic. Saussure's famous distinction between *langue* and *parole* is nothing other than the application of this distinction to language. Interestingly enough, Roland Barthes's radical critique of literature, *Le Degré zéro de l'écriture*, is based on the discovery that writers do not usually recognise the ways in which their *paroles* (their choices out of the pool of possibilities which is the *langue*) are conditioned by their social context, and by the forms they have decided to employ: the novel, narrative history, etc. In his later work, however, Barthes seems to take it for granted that all literature moves inevitably towards a mode of total possibility – a *langue* without *paroles*. This was certainly Mallarmé's ideal, but it is one that is incapable of fulfilment. Thus Barthes's insights, which, like Frye's, are the direct outcome of his response to modernism, betray modernism in exactly the same way. For both fail to take into account the tension that exists in each writer between the awareness of possibility and the necessity of choice, and which is resolved in the exploration, through art itself, of the dialectic between *langue* and *parole*, desire and reality.

This dialectic is the theme as well as the substance of Borges's parable. But it must not be understood only as a struggle between the writer and the tradition. It is also a struggle between the writer and the reader. By insisting that his book is a book and not the world, the author recognises that *reading* is itself an activity, and he makes of it, in fact, the subject-matter of his work. A splendid example of this is to be found in Beckett's early short story 'Dante and the Lobster'. It opens with the hero, Belacqua, struggling through the opening canto of the *Paradiso*:

It was morning and Belacqua was stuck in the first of the canti in the moon. He was so bogged that he could move neither backward nor forward. Blissful Beatrice was there, Dante also, and she explained the spots on the moon to him. She showed him in the first place where he was at fault, then she put up her own explanation. She had it from God, therefore he could rely on its being accurate in every particular. All he had to do was to follow her step by step. Part one, the refutation, was plain sailing. She made her point clearly, she said what she had to say without fuss or loss of time. But part two, the demonstration, was so dense that Belacqua could not make head or tail of it. The disproof, the reproof, that was patent. But then came the proof, a rapid shorthand of the real facts, and Belacqua was bogged indeed. Bored also, impatient to get on to Picarda. . . .

The passage is typical of Beckett in its off-handedness, the sense of someone going through the motions of paraphrase because it has to be done, the mixture of preciousness and colloquialism. But what is interesting here is that it *is* a paraphrase. Beckett presents us with a picture of his hero (whose Dantesque name adds to the complication) trying to read a book, the *Commedia*. Belacqua is bogged down in his reading. But he is also bogged down in the first circle of Paradise, with Dante, listening, like him, to Beatrice. Beckett shifts the levels brilliantly, so that at moments we are within the great poem, at others with the struggling Belacqua. Even the pronouns play into his hands. 'She showed him in the first place where he was at fault, then she put up her own explanation' refers to Dante, but a little later the 'he' turns into Belacqua. And this is perfect because Belacqua reading is at moments Dante and then at others, faltering, returns to an awareness of himself:

Still he pored over the enigma, he would not concede himself conquered, he would understand at least the meanings of the words, the order in which they were spoken and the nature of the satisfaction that they conferred on the misinformed poet, so that when they were ended he was refreshed and could raise his heavy head, intending to return thanks and make formal retractation of his old opinion.

He was still running his brain against this impenetrable passage when he heard midday strike. At once he switched his mind off its task. He scooped his fingers under the book and shovelled it back till it lay wholly on his palms. The Divine Comedy face upward on the lectern of his palms. Thus disposed he raised it under his nose and there he slammed it shut. He held it aloft for a time, squinting at it angrily, pressing the boards inwards with the heels of his hands. Then he laid it aside.

For the body needs to be fed, and midday means the preparation
of his lunch. But that is not the end of the matter. The climax of
the story is the boiling of the lobster alive. Belacqua has brought
it home for his aunt, and he stands horrified in the kitchen: he
had no idea one boiled the creatures while they still lived:

> 'You make a fuss' she said angrily 'and upset me and then
> lash into it for your dinner.'
>   She lifted the lobster clear of the table. It had about thirty
> seconds to live.
>   Well, thought Belacqua, it's a quick death, God help us all.
> It is not.

What does it feel, to be a lobster boiled alive? The aunt does not
think about it, but Belacqua does. Beckett is no moralist like
Proust, but it is clear that here too the primal sin is indifference,
a failure of the imagination. What is interesting is the way he tries
to get the reader to experience too, first by presenting him with
the scene of a book being read, and the failure of the book to
hold the attention for even a second after the midday clock has
rung. And, implicitly, it makes us see how little hold *this* book
really has on us. The last three words then come at us, outside
Belacqua's own consciousness, and therefore outside ours, truly
as a sort of necessity, the voice of reality, shocking us into experiencing the creature's agony.[1]
    In this struggle between the writer and the reader it is not
Saussure, but the later Wittgenstein who comes to mind. Wittgenstein saw his task not as the defining of new language games, nor
as that of playing new games with the old rules, but rather as the
unmasking of what we had all along taken for 'reality' as only
one of a number of games. Of course the model of a game should
not make us think that he is talking about some light-hearted bit
of foolery; Wittgenstein, like his compatriot Schoenberg, was
constitutionally incapable of lightheartedness. Rather he is concerned, like Borges or Proust or Beckett, with freeing us from the

---

[1] For the greater part of his work Beckett has preferred to allow the
human voice to roam unchecked and thus reveal its solipsism, its inability
to stand outside the world of man as that last sentence does. But in his
most recent work he has taken up the Godlike position again – see
especially *Imagination Dead Imagine*.

compulsions imposed by habit and the failure of the imagination.
He gives an image of our normal situation:

> We have got on to slippery ice where there is no friction and so
> in a certain sense the conditions are ideal, but also, just because
> of that, we are unable to walk. We want to walk: so we need
> *friction*. Back to the rough ground![1]

He is talking here of doing philosophy, but the similarity with
Kafka's language is significant. The task as he sees it is not an
academic one. It involves a reorientation of one's whole being,
and this is no simple matter, for: 'A picture held us captive. And
we could not get outside it, for it lay in our language and language seemed to repeat it to us inexorably.' The way to free
ourselves of this is to see that the picture is *only* a picture, not
reality. So his task becomes that of making us recognise this fact,
and the way to do this is to show us why and how we have been
bewitched: 'One thinks one is tracing the outline of the thing's
nature over and over again, and one is merely tracing round the
frame through which we look at it.' But this does not of course
mean that we can simply wrench off the frame and look at the
world 'as it really is'. Neither for Wittgenstein nor for any of the
moderns does the answer lie in this kind of neo-Platonism. Rather
it is that the reality must be seen as the fact that we are condemned
to see through frames. And recognition of this brings with it a
kind of freedom, for it stops us from falling into the trap of thinking that meaning inheres in words, objects or events. This task,
however, is not one that can be done once and for all, for our
natural *tendency* is to think in this way. Thus the philosopher
must keep on going over the ground again and again.

But even this formulation of the matter does not quite do
justice to it. When, at the end of Golding's *The Inheritors* or
Pincher Martin, we are pulled suddenly out of the consciousness
of Lok or of Martin we are not meant to slip into the consciousness of the 'new men' or of the discoverers of the dead sailor. We
are left swinging between the two consciousnesses, suddenly aware
of the fact that neither is the 'reality', that both are only
'pictures', 'games', ways of looking at the world. And these
examples reveal how unwilling we are to give up the single view-

[1] *Philosophical Investigations*, trans. G. E. M. Anscombe (Oxford, 1963)
46.

point, how painful it is for us to acknowledge that 'our universe' is not *the* universe. As *Pincher Martin* makes clear, to do so is in a sense to give up one's very self. St Augustine, as Wittgenstein must have known, had a name for it; he called the desire to cling to the single vision pride, or *amor sui*, and he regarded it as the primal sin and its extirpation as the primary requisite of conversion to Christianity. For pride, or the love of self, is the belief that the world and my wishes are one, a belief which springs first of all, as Freud saw, from my unwillingness to admit that one day I too must die. And Freud saw it as his task to try and educate man, or the ego, into accepting this fact, against the combined pressures of the unconscious or the id and the superego. He had no illusions, moreover, as to how difficult this task would be, since he knew that reason itself would use all its cunning to protect itself from recognition of this fact. And this is why it is so easy to misunderstand both Freud and Wittgenstein: we prefer to discuss their contributions to knowledge instead of recognising that what they are asking of us is a reorientation of our entire being.

To give up the belief that we are immortal is indeed hard. It requires nothing less than an imaginative earthquake. Hence Golding's sudden *volte-faces*, hence the deception of the reader which is a prime strategy of Nabokov, of Robbe-Grillet, of Borges. First they lull us into taking the 'picture' for 'reality', strengthening our habitual tendencies, and then suddenly our attention is focused on the spectacles through which we are looking, and we are made to see that what we had taken for 'reality' was only the imposition of the frame. But for this to work we must first of all have been really taken in, and what better way of taking in the reader than through the medium of the novel, which is almost not a medium at all, almost like life itself. For the premises upon which the novel is based are not the formal ones of literature but rather the premises upon which most of us base our lives. Thus it is only through the medium of the novel that we can be made to recognise the figure in the mirror as ourselves, for we have not had time to prepare our defences against such a confrontation. And that is why it would be wrong to read a Golding or a Borges story as simply a game played with the reader in order to sharpen his wit. This is still to protect ourselves from these works, to deny the enormous power of naturalistic fiction, a power so well described by Proust when he recalled the passions evoked by the books of childhood.[1] It is for this reason that the modern novel is an anti-novel. Not because it sets itself up in direct opposition to the novel, but because it enlists the help of the novel to lull the reader into a false sense of security and then, by pointing to its own premises, pitches him into reality. But devotees of the novel need have no fear of its demise; as Eliot noted, human kind cannot bear very much reality.

The modern novel draws attention to the rules which govern its own creation in order to force the reader into recognising that it is not the world. Pre-Romantic literature also calls attention to itself, to its genre and to the conventions with which it is working, so as to establish itself as an artifact. But the feeling we get from a work like *The Aeneid* or 'Lycidas' is that the author is confident that he is both writing about and in a world which makes sense, which is itself constructed according to rules capable of being apprehended by the human mind. In Dante in particular these rules are seen as corresponding directly to the laws which govern the creation of his own work because the universe, if properly understood, can itself be seen as a book. Dante can eventually stand outside our world and look down upon it because the world is conceived of as being created by a God who stands outside all space and time and yet who can be known to the senses of man through Christ's mediation. A study of Dante and of the art of the Middle Ages, then, provides us with more than simply an enlarged perspective on recent development in the arts; it provides us, rather, with a model of what the novel *can never be*.

Dante's universe is built on a series of analogies: between the physical and spiritual worlds; between secular and sacred history; between the history of the universe and that of each man; between the natural cycle and the Christian year; between the

---

[1] Michel Beaujour, in his study of Rabelais, points out how the narrative of the birth and childhood of Pantagruel and Gargantua gives new power to the subversive elements of his book, a power quite lacking in the 'praises of folly' and satires of Erasmus and Brandt, because these are immediately recognised as belonging to a specific genre and the reader is therefore immunised against them almost before he starts. In Rabelais, however, we automatically identify with the giants and therefore find ourselves involved whether we like it or not. (*Le Jeux de Rabelais*, 29.)

days of the week and the ages of man. Underpinning all these is
the analogy of God and man, man made in God's image and
able, through Christ's mediation, to recover that image though it
might have been distorted and blurred by the Fall. In modern
literature analogy has become demonic – 'le démon de l'analogie',
Mallarmé called it. For to discover correspondences in the world
around us does not lead to the sensation that we are inhabiting
a meaningful universe; on the contrary, it leads to the feeling that
what we had taken to be 'the world' is only the projection of our
private compulsions: *analogy* becomes a sign of *dementia*. The
device which French writers have called 'mise-en-abîme' and
related to certain baroque effects – the sudden transformation,
say, of Pincher Martin's island into a tooth inside his own head,
the transformation of a painted landscape into a real one and its
further metamorphosis into a jumble of lines on the ceiling of a
room in Robbe-Grillet's *Dans le Labyrinthe* – this is really demonic analogy. We become aware of it with a shock of
recognition, suddenly realising what we had dimly sensed all
along, that what we had taken to be infinitely open and 'out
there' was in reality a bounded world bearing the shape only of
our imagination. In that moment we are pulled back into the
compulsive mind of the hero (Robbe-Grillet, Golding), or into the
playful mind of the author (Proust, Nabokov), but, since we had
established ourselves imaginatively in the 'real' world first presented to us, the effect is really to pull us back inside our own
minds, to make us recognise the boundary of *our* world. In Dante
the discovery of analogy serves to make us realise that the universe
is meaningful, no longer a series of discrete objects or events such
as the foolish natural man observes, but parts of a well-bound
volume, no longer isolated notes but a tune. The *trompe-l'œil*
effects of modern art, on the other hand, the playful inver-
sions of the novel form and the parody of language and convention in modern fiction, have the opposite effect, making us realise
with a shock that we are dealing not with the world but
with one more object in the world, one made by a human
being.

The effect of demonic analogy is to rob events of their solidity.
Proust draws the fullest consequences from this, revealing how
the play of constants and variables affects life as well as art, but
we get similar effects in other works as well. In *Pincher Martin*,

for example, the transformation of the island into the tooth does not simply shock us by its implications for the narrative – that the island is only a figment of the hero's imagination and that therefore he is in the process of drowning without any hope of being saved. It also makes us aware of the fact that if an island can be changed into a tooth then neither of them has any special status, and the tooth could, by a further metamorphosis, change into something else with a similar structure (Robbe-Grillet is fond of multiple metamorphoses of this kind). We are in a world of infinite correspondences, but this time without any stable objective reality underpinning them all. The effect is to rob the content of the work of all its solidity and to turn the book into a field of play for form.

This point is one that is continually being stressed by the French structuralist critics, but in a most misleading way. There has always been structure in works of art, they say, but what is special about modern art is that whereas the structure previously would refer back to God or Society or some other fixed point of departure, now the structure is purely immanent and the elements therefore infinitely permutable. This is perhaps a good way of describing the difference between structural linguistics or structural anthropology and their causally orientated predecessors, but it is misleading when applied to works of art. In fact it is precisely here that art parts company with linguistics, anthropology, psychoanalysis and the rest. For the point about a work of modern art is that it insists on its own status as an artifact and that it cannot therefore be treated like a piece of language or an aspect of society. This distinction is so important and so often overlooked that it may be as well to examine it a little more closely.

John Bayley, in a recent article, has some shrewd things to say about the fallacy of a structural approach of this kind. In the process, however, he also reveals his own failure to grasp what is at issue, a failure typical of Anglo-Saxon criticism in general, but one which may help us to see what is really at issue here. He begins by contrasting an artist like Tolstoy, 'whose intention is solely to communicate', with what he calls the 'dumb' artist: 'The dumb artist is concerned with what he conceives as an independent and autonomous product', he 'considers his work as an aesthetic object' pure and simple. Having set up this opposition between the two kinds of artist, Bayley comments:

By externalising itself, by 'annihilating its subject', the contemporary work can only nestle down in the most passive, least participatory part of the reader's consciousness. And here – according to Robbe-Grillet and other theorists – is where it should be. When Robbe-Grillet says that he has rediscovered in himself 'the entire arsenal of the popular imagination', this seems to mean, in practice, that he is interested in techniques for touching off the daydreams of his readers and making them scurry round and round their tiny familiar cages. . . . Fiction thus abdicates its seat, for the only really boring stories are those which we can always tell ourselves, and the only essential paradigm of fiction (. . .) is that it is made up by someone else.[1]

Bayley is surely justified in attacking certain kinds of talk *about* literature as 'formalist'. Barthes and Robbe-Grillet do indeed often give the impression in their criticism that the work of art is a pure object, a 'field' of possibilities waiting to be activated by the reader. But Bayley also chooses to forget a number of important things. First of all, even if 'the only really boring stories are those which we can always tell ourselves', it is also true that it is hypothetically possible for each of us to tell ourselves all the stories that could ever be imagined. Moreover, even if an artist's intention is 'solely to communicate' such communication is not so straightforward a procedure as Bayley seems to imagine. No writer can really say what he wants to say because no writer ever possesses language as his own. We have seen how Rimbaud, attempting to create a purely personal language, a natural language of the senses, had to acknowledge defeat and retreat into silence. This and the previous point are really facets of the same problem. Frye can draw up a generative grammar of literature, Barthes can assimilate literature to structuralism, precisely because no writer can ever fully communicate, even to himself. Or, to put it in terms which we have already used, 'reality' is not our natural habitat, something we are close to all the time but which the forms of art destroy. Reality has to be worked for, habit and the wiles of the imagination have to be overcome before it can even be glimpsed.[2]

[1] 'Against a New Formalism', in *Word in the Desert*, ed. Cox and Dyson, 68.

[2] See p. 139, n. 2, and Chapter 7 *passim*.

Bayley's main error, however, lies in his believing that such talk about literature, even when it comes from a practising artist like Robbe-Grillet, really corresponds to the *effect* of the works themselves. What both Bayley and the formalist critics he attacks fail to take into account when they deal with the work of Robbe-Grillet or Pinget or Simon is the sense of shock administered to the reader when the work reveals itself as a 'pure object'. 'Mise-en-abîme' and demonic analogy do indeed make us see the work as work and not as 'the real world', but we should not rest there. The final meaning of a Robbe-Grillet novel (or, as we have seen, of a Nabokov or a Golding or a Bellow novel) resides in the effect which this discovery has upon us, an effect far greater than that which a novel by George Eliot or Tolstoy could have, since it is shock administered to that most precious part of ourselves, our pride or inherent narcissism.

To understand just what happens to the reader at such a moment it is necessary to tackle the most puzzling paradox of modern literature, the paradox of solipsism and communion. Solipsism is at the heart of modern literature. People who do not read this literature often accuse it of being 'depressing', with the implication that they would therefore rather have nothing to do with it. Simple-minded supporters of modern literature usually retaliate by saying that it may be depressing, but that this is because of its honesty in the face of the facts and its unflinching determination to describe the human condition (whatever that means). But anyone who has read Proust or Rilke or Eliot must surely have felt that the extraordinary thing about these writers is the quality of joy and the sense of the richness of life which they present, and this despite the fact that they do undoubtedly deal with despair, deprivation and isolation to a degree unparalleled in any previous literature. How are we to explain this?

I argued earlier that we instinctively feel that the formulations of Northrop Frye are wrong when applied to modern literature because myth and tradition are not so much used by modern authors as questioned and examined, and I suggested that one of the characteristic features of modernism was just this play on the relations between the unique self and the world of literature, between the individual talent and tradition. But discussion of this relation in terms of Wittgensteinian language-games and the freeing of the reader from the bondage of habit and what St

Augustine called pride did not perhaps get to the heart of the problem. It did not explain, for instance, the encyclopedic tendency of modern literature, its exhaustive exploration of every facet of a situation or of the tradition. It is time we looked at this a little more closely.

For Borges and Eliot, as for Frye, the imagination of man can enter any world, invent any stories, participate in any event. The difference between the two artists and the theorist is that for the former this is a faculty of the imagination alone, whereas the latter blurs all distinctions between imagination and reality.[1] Borges's stories constantly evoke the Shelleyan ideal of poetry, only to bring hero (and reader) up sharply at the end with the fact that he has a body as well as an imagination, and that though he can participate imaginatively in any aspect of human experience, it is also necessary that he should die and disappear from the face of the earth for ever: 'Besides, I am destined to perish, definitively, and only some instant of myself can survive in [Borges].' Borges's idealism brings him very close to Frye, but there is always in his work the further twist, the final dissociation of imagination and reality, the world I can imagine and the one in which I must live and die. It is as though the idealist discovery of the power of the imagination only brought home more sharply the distinction between imagination and reality, as if the mind's ability to roam unchecked over the entire field of the possible gave an edge to the writer's sense of the unique and the actual. Eliot's early fascination with Bradley stems from the same source. His early poems are miniature encyclopedias of idealism, with the mind of the protagonist ranging over the whole of past tradition only to come up, ultimately, against the sense of his own solitariness and isolation. The ironic apotheosis of the Shelleyan ideal is surely the poor Sybil, suspended in her cage and forced to go on living eternally in her decaying body, registering the events of the universe upon her retina but incapable of accomplishing a single action, even that of suicide.

In Eliot, Kafka and Borges literature is made out of dialogue

[1] This is not an oversight, any more than it would be an oversight in Blake. Like Blake, Frye seems to be firmly convinced of the *ultimate* triumph of imagination. I suppose I simply have to say that Proust and Freud and Eliot seem to me to be more honest in the face of reality than Blake.

with the tradition, but tradition is seen as a crushing, alien force, which keeps man from coming to terms with his own unique existence. Unless, of course, he can in some way internalise it, make it his own. But how can he do this? To imagine he can do so, to think he is already and at every moment at one with tradition, to take the past for granted, in other words, is to be robbed by it of his present. Yet without tradition the present is devoid of meaning or value. Kafka's heroes, caught in this dilemma, seek desperately for an impossible reconciliation of two elements of whose separation other people are scarcely even aware. Both Eliot and Kafka wrench fragments of the past and lay them alongside the present not, like Pope, in order to let the one comment ironically on the other, but with the desperation born of the knowledge that we can never really come to terms with either the past or with anything that lies outside the locked tower of our selves. The fragmentation of the past into Fisher Kings, broken towers, Thermopylae, Agamemnon's murder, the Hunter Gracchus, Prometheus on his rock, Bucephalus and all the rest – all this presses home on the reader not the richness of tradition but the impossibility of making any sense of it. For to make sense of it we would need to stand outside it, outside the world itself, and who can do that? Instead of, as with Dante and Milton, giving us a sense of belonging to a tradition which is meaningful because the whole universe is meaningful, this fragmentation brings home to us the alienness of history and of the world, the impossibility of getting past the frontal bone of our own skull, as Kafka puts it. The bits and pieces hang there in the void, fragments shored against our ruin, or else echo in our ears with meaningless insistence, while all we can say, with Gerontion, is: 'I was not there.'

Habit and pride make us take it for granted that the tradition justifies us and has a meaning. Kafka and Eliot and Proust and Borges plant dynamite in the stronghold of habit. They present us with the tradition as we habitually conceive it and then break it up and shower us with its fragments. Theirs is perhaps a true mythopoeic age, but if so then they have lost the key to myth. But for just this reason they rage against it, coming back again and again in a desperate effort to make sense of it, even if it is only to understand why they can make no sense of it. Frye, like Sidney and Blake and Shelley, feels confident that myth, if properly understood, can give us back our golden world. But Kafka and Eliot know that myths, the forms taken by the imagination, are only forms taken by the imagination. How is one to get past them, to get to the reality, how, quite simply, to give sense to what *I* feel?

The past cannot simply be suppressed: we know too much. We cannot innocently rely either on an ordered tradition or on subjective inspiration. Kafka too has a parable on the subject; it is called 'The Truth about Don Quixote':

> Without making any boast of it Sancho Panza succeeded in the course of years, by devouring a great number of romances of chivalry and adventure in the evening and night hours, in so diverting from him his demon, whom he later called Don Quixote, that his demon thereupon set out in perfect freedom on the maddest exploits, which, however, for the lack of a preordained object, which should have been Sancho Panza himself, harmed nobody. A free man, Sancho Panza philosophically followed Don Quixote on his crusades, perhaps out of a sense of responsibility, and had of them a great and edifying entertainment to the end of his days.[1]

In the same way Kafka frees himself from his own demon: not by suppressing him or ignoring him and letting him roam free, but by understanding him and following him responsibly. Responsibility in this case means awareness of the way in which each impulse towards the telling of a story leads to a series of choices from language and the tradition which are irresponsible in that they are arbitrary. He does not simply decide upon a genre and a form as would a pre-Romantic artist, nor does he simply follow his inner promptings, as would a nineteenth-century artist, novelist or poet; instead he gives his inner promptings rope, but draws attention to what he is doing so that the reader grows conscious of the relation of what is written both to the public world of literature and to the unspoken and unspeakable form of desire itself.

But this is not all. The writer follows his demon, the imagination, into the world of total possibility; but the more freedom he gives his demon the more clearly he comes to recognise his own solipsism. For the world, as Wittgenstein remarks in the *Tractatus*, remains independent of my will, and 'Even if all that we wish for

[1] In *Parables and Paradoxes* (Shocken Books, New York, 1961).

were to happen, still this would only be a favour granted by fate, so to speak: for there is no logical connexion between the will and the world, which would guarantee it.' The more Gerontion remembers and the further afield Don Quixote roams, the more their powerlessness to alter anything in the world is brought home to us. The more we struggle to understand the world around us, the harder we look at it and at the past, the greater grows our sense of our own isolation. As Wittgenstein again points out, and as the commentators on Robbe-Grillet would do well to bear in mind, a complete realism is indistinguishable from a complete solipsism, since I am not an object in the world but the limits of my world.. A total description of my world would therefore be a complete description of myself – but I cannot step out of that self: 'Here I am, an old man in a dry month, being read to by a boy, waiting for rain.'

The rain never falls in 'Gerontion', or in the novels of Robbe-Grillet. But for the reader the rain comes. How does this happen? When, Meursault-like, Wittgenstein remarks in the *Tractatus* that 'the limits of my language mean the limits of my world', and that 'What we cannot speak about we must pass over in silence', we must remember the statement he makes at the end of the preface to that work:

> I therefore believe myself to have found, on all essential points, the final solution of the problems. And if I am not mistaken in this belief, then the second thing in which the value of this work consists is that it shows how little is achieved when these problems are solved.

It would be wrong to take this as a mere gesture. Wittgenstein draws the net of solipsism tight around us so that we may recognise the limits of our world. But, recognising them, we are able to sense what lies beyond them, for, as he says, to draw a boundary round anything is to suggest something beyond that boundary. In a similar way Eliot and Kafka and Proust and Robbe-Grillet draw the line in tight around their protagonists, giving us a sense, from the inside, of the limits of their world, and thus revealing what cannot be spoken: the existence of the world beyond these limits. 'It is the mystery of negation', Wittgenstein wrote in the *Notebooks* of 1914–16: 'This is not how things are, and yet we can say *how* things are *not*.' By pulling the net of solipsism in tight around us, Wittgenstein makes us aware, in the *Tractatus*, of that which is not inside the net: 'I can construct the infinite space outside only by using the picture to bound the space', he writes in the *Notebooks*, and what he gives us in the *Tractatus* is not so much a ladder which must be thrown down once we have hoisted ourselves up, as a picture whose *negative* is what the world is, since the positive reveals the boundaries of what the world is not. Similarly Golding, in *Pincher Martin*, gives us a true picture of what a man is by showing us all that a man is not and then negating that.

This may explain then, why modern literature, which repeatedly depicts an extreme solipsism, affects us not with a sense of constriction but of release. For though the subject-matter is death and loss and degradation and the self enclosed in its private world, the act of following through and articulating these things brings with it a powerful sense of joy and release. The encyclopedia of fragments which makes up 'Gerontion' or Robbe-Grillet's *Le Voyeur* allows us to experience the limits of our world and so to sense what lies beyond, the absolutely other, distinct from me and my desires. And this momentary and silent experience, as Proust knew, is worth all the deep thoughts and beautiful phrases that have ever been penned.

The modern works I have been talking about must indeed be seen as objects, but objects of a very special kind. Not things of beauty to be taken out occasionally and admired, but *negatives*, pictures of how things are not. At the end of such a work we realise that if the world of the hero is only his world, then what we had taken to be that world is only a book. The real world is that which the book is not, but since I cannot step outside my world this negative is all that can be expressed. To imagine, like the traditional novelist, that one's work is an image of the real world, to imagine that one can communicate directly to the reader what it is that one uniquely feels, that is to fall into the real solipsism, which is, to paraphrase Kierkegaard on despair, not to know that one is in a state of solipsism. The modern novelist, seeing, like Wittgenstein that his first task is to wake man to this difficult insight, constructs a book which is the negative of reality and which always asks of us that we move from it to its silent referent.

The labyrinth is the dwelling place of demonic analogy. From the cunning passages, contrived corridors and issues of 'Gerontion', through the mazes of Kafka, Proust, Beckett, Borges and Robbe-Grillet, the labyrinth has been the favourite image of modern literature.[1] In place of Dante's ordered journey we find ourselves involved with heroes who wander without map or compass along paths which are endless for the simple reason that we would not recognise the end even if we came to it. Dante emerges from his long climb and can look back, standing on solid ground, over the winding uphill way, with its little figures of men and women dotted about at various stages of their own ascent. But there is no emergence for the heroes of modern fiction from the labyrinths of reflecting mirrors and demonic analogy. At the end they are no nearer the exit than they were at the beginning. All they have done is to move through all the arteries of the labyrinth. Yet this, if they but knew it, is both the exit and the answer. What Proust discovered at the end of his long wanderings was that the twists and turns led not to another, truer world, as he had once idealistically imagined, but that these very twists and turns formed the pattern of his life, a pattern the comprehension of which would provide him with an answer to all his questions. By following the endless paths (as Kafka's Sancho followed Don Quixote), he comes at last to the realisation that this *activity* is itself the meaning for which he had been searching for so long. Then at last he understands that his perseverance has led him not to the discovery of a new world, but to the apprehension of the most alien yet nearest land of all: his own body.

For the labyrinth along which he has travelled is in effect his own body, since he is not an object in the world but the limits of his world. But it is also the book he has written, for the travelling did not come first and the writing after; rather, the writing *was* the travelling. And what is true of Proust is also true of Kafka and Golding and Robbe-Grillet. Having made his work, the author is now both the book and outside the book. Outside not in any space-occupying place, as St Augustine would say, for our world, unlike Dante's, provides no such area, but outside by virtue of the fact that he *made* the book. And the reader too can stand out there, with him, because, experiencing the limits of his own world, he too is momentarily freed of his imprisonment within it. But

[1] The demonic analogy of labyrinth/intestines is one Freud was surely correct in drawing to our attention.

let us be clear as to what is involved. It is only so long as the book is being read, so long, that is, as the human imagination is travelling along the arteries of the labyrinth, that we are aware of the boundaries, and therefore of what lies beyond them. When that activity ceases we fall back into our old habits, and enter once more that real labyrinth, which is so deadly just because we are unaware of it as such. Closed, the book becomes an object among many in the room. Open, and read, it draws the reader into tracing the contours of his own labyrinth and allows him to experience himself not as an object in the world but as the limits of his world. And, mysteriously, to recognise this is to be freed of these limits and to experience a joy as great as that which floods through us when, looking at long last, with Dante, into the eyes of God, we sense the entire universe bound up into one volume and understand what it is to be a man.

A CRITIC'S POSTSCRIPT

Language is not plenitude, nor is it an emptiness waiting to be filled. Only when we pause to examine it does it seem to us to be the sign of an absence for which we need to search; while we use it we do not worry about it and it works as well as it needs to. But language in a piece of literature is frozen language. It belongs in a book, with a beginning and an end, and therefore surely a meaning. But how is this meaning to be discovered? And where does it come from? Who, in other words, is the author of a work of literature? The man whose name appears on the cover? But by what authority does this author determine the meaning of what he writes, since he is after all only deploying a language which belongs to his culture and not personally to him?[1]

The old authors were aware of these problems. They accepted the fact that an author is not the source of meaning but rather an organiser of pre-existent material. As a result they were able to delimit the boundaries of interpretation. It is, for example, the genre quite as much as John Milton which is responsible for 'Lycidas', and if we are to understand that poem fully we need to know more than the meanings of the words on the page or the

[1] I owe this formulation of the problem to Jeremy Lane's as yet unpublished essay 'Authenticity and Error'.

private life of the poet; we do not, however, have to know every-thing. The authors of what we have called the traditional novel, like most post-Romantic poets, have been unwilling to accept such a situation. Each of them writes as though he was the first and the last, as though, in fact, the language was his own. In the course of this book we have seen some of the results of such an attitude. Here I merely want to draw attention to a curious corollary. This is that we read with pleasure what a man whose personal qualities we admire (an Auden or a Thomas Mann) has to say about traditional fiction, but feel bored or cheated when Professor X or Dr Y ventures into this territory; whereas we often get more out of the latter's work on Spenser or Milton than we ever would from the comments of an Auden or a Mann. For the scholar can reveal to us the laws according to which Spenser or Milton were writing, provide us with a context in which to under-stand their conventions, and thus generally illuminate their work. Whereas, commenting on Hardy or Dostoevsky, he is reduced to his own subjective impressions or to the repetition in his own words of what the novelist has already said. The result is a terrible feeling of *redundancy*. On the other hand we read Auden or Mann on a novelist as we would read them on the notebooks of Hopkins or the letters of Van Gogh: to find out what the en-counter has touched off.

With the modern novel, however, neither scholarship nor profundity and experience are required. For the modern novel, aware as it is that language is not and never can be plenitude, reveals itself as process and not as meaning. The critic's task is to point out the logic of its necessity and thus account for all its elements. Such criticism is itself under the law of necessity, since there is clearly only one correct way of accounting for all the elements. It can only spiral down in one direction, towards the silence of the work's relationship with its maker. Criticism of the traditional novel, on the other hand, can go on for ever, since it really consists of chatter (there is of course nothing wrong with chatter as such; there can be few more pleasurable experiences than listening to an Auden or a Mann). Such chatter, I am afraid, has not been entirely absent from the general chapters of this book; there, where I had to rely on my own subjective ideas and beliefs, I am aware that I have frequently gone on for too long or else stopped before I had made my meaning clear. Too often I was conscious of my voice, shrill or pompous as the case might be, but indubitably there, holding the stage. Perhaps those chapters can best be seen, like these very words, as one more example of the capers of that poor buffoon, the critic. In the other chapters, however, those dealing with specific works or authors, I hope that my voice has been muted in the service of my subject. Having read those chapters the reader of this book will, I hope, be in a position to embark on the essential task without my voice ringing in his ears: *now* the experience of reading, (for which silence is essential) can begin.

Index